HARVARD SEMITIC SERIES
VOLUME XII

MARRIAGE LAWS IN THE BIBLE AND THE TALMUD

MARRIAGE LAWS IN THE BIBLE AND THE TALMUD

BY

LOUIS M. EPSTEIN, L.H.D., D.D.

CAMBRIDGE, MASSACHUSETTS
HARVARD UNIVERSITY PRESS
1942

Reprinted with the permission of
The President and Fellows of Harvard College

JOHNSON REPRINT CORPORATION
111 Fifth Avenue, New York, N.Y. 10003

JOHNSON REPRINT COMPANY LTD.
Berkeley Square House, London, W. 1

First reprinting, 1968, Johnson Reprint Corporation

Printed in the United States of America

לאשתי האהובה חנה מנוחה

האוהב את אשתו כגופו
והמכבדה יותר מגופו...
עליו הכתוב אומר:
וידעת כי שלום אהלך.

יבמות ס״ב:

PREFACE

OF ALL human relations, paradoxically enough, the marriage relation is at once the most private and the most public. On the one hand, society recognizes the inviolable privacy of the home and affords it certain measures of protection against outside interference; but on the other, it takes unto itself the right to interfere in that privacy by setting up rigid laws restricting the individuals in choosing their mates for the establishment of a home. And that society of which we think in this connection is not only the contemporary group, but all generations of ancestry seem to rise from their graves to tell brides and grooms what they may do and what they may not.

Nowhere as in the law of marriage can one find a standard of action that so faithfully preserves the traditions of all past ages, and nowhere as in marriage does group conscience so dominate the individual. This is certainly true of the marriage laws of the Jewish people. Deflections from some of the fundamental laws of Judaism are not rare among Jews today, but very rare is the case of the Jew who dares defy Jewish marriage law. The cohesiveness of the Jewish people around its marriage law is best illustrated by the historic fact that while almost any degree of heterodoxy was tolerated by Judaism, the moment a group subscribed to a doctrine which taught a fundamental deviation from the accepted law of marriage, it was doomed to the status of a "sect" and was gradually eliminated from Jewish group life. That potency and validity of the Jewish marriage law have ever been a lure to me in the study of the subject and, it is hoped, will be of distinct interest to the reader.

In this work, I have attempted to present a comprehensive survey of Jewish law on the subject of marriage as it has developed historically from the beginning of our records to the present day. Various monographs on sections of the subject have been written by Jewish and non-Jewish scholars; they have proven very valuable in the more extensive study here undertaken. But in the main, the material contained in this work comes directly from primary sources, biblical, apocryphal, and rabbinic writings.

Many technical legal terms in the original have no exact English equivalent, and by this circumstance I have been compelled often to employ the original terminology of the rabbis of the Talmud. Hardly could adequate English substitutes be found for such terms as ḥaliẓah, ḥalalah, ʻissah, mamzer, zikah, or zonah. Every such term has been defined and sufficiently explained when it first appears and in its proper context. In the employment of English legal terminology, I have been careful not to violate technical definitions of legal terms; but where a term has a certain technical meaning and a somewhat different popular connotation, I have used the term in its popular sense, keeping in mind the reader without technical legal training.

I am indebted to a small group of young friends for kindly assistance given to me in the preparation of this work. They are Rabbi Abraham Burstein of New York, Professor Bernard S. Gould of the Massachusetts Institute of Technology, and Doctor Albert M. Freiberg of the Harvard University School of Business Administration. I offer them my sincere gratitude for their helpfulness.

I have often discussed both subject matter and form of presentation of this work with my friend, Professor Harry A. Wolfson of Harvard University. His interest was stimulating, his suggestions were always constructive, his assistance in many practical ways was very valuable. For all these things I gratefully record my appreciation.

Louis M. Epstein

Brookline, Massachusetts

CONTENTS

CHAPTER I: POLYGAMY

CHAPTER II: CONCUBINAGE

CHAPTER III: LEVIRATE

CHAPTER IV: INTERMARRIAGE

CHAPTER V: INCEST

CHAPTER VI: OTHER MARRIAGE PROHIBITIONS

MARRIAGE LAWS IN THE BIBLE AND THE TALMUD

CHAPTER I

POLYGAMY

I

THAT there is a tradition of polygamy among the Jews no one can deny. But there is room for speculation whether this tradition is native with the Hebrews or was acquired during their history as a result of foreign influences. There are no records of the native origins of Hebrew life, for they go back to the very dawn of human history. But the biblical records, it is claimed, lend themselves to two interpretations. According to one interpretation, the Hebrew family was essentially monogamous and it was only due to foreign influence that polygamy was tolerated as a deviation from the standard. According to another interpretation, polygamy was the norm and standard of Hebrew family life but certain internal cultural developments operated toward the ideal of monogamy.

Those who maintain that monogamy was the native Hebrew tradition point to a series of biblical evidences in support of their view.[1] The story of creation in the Bible argues for a native Jewish ideal of monogamy, for God created only one wife for Adam, and the Bible sets forth that act as an example for all times, that "man shall leave his father and his mother and cleave unto his wife and they shall become one flesh." The early generations lived in monogamy. Lamech is the only exception – with implied apologies by the biblical author – which helps prove the rule of monogamy. Abraham lived in what may be called "legal monogamy," his other consorts being concubines. Isaac was strictly monogamous. Jacob intended to have a monogamous marriage, but through the deception of Laban was forced into bigamy. His

[1] Leopold Loew, *Gesammelte Schriften*, Szegedin, 1889–1900, III, pp. 33 f.

sons, so far as records go, lived in monogamy.[2] The monogamous marriages of Moses and Aaron and Eleazar and the repeated references in the Law and the Prophets to the monogamous marriage as the ideal,[3] though some belong to a later date, indicate that in the Jewish conscience there lingered their native predilection for monogamy. All that may be said is that polygamy gradually infiltrated Hebrew life from foreign sources, Canaanitish or Egyptian; that two forces brought about its acceptance in Judea, the frequent wars which yielded many female captives, and the ambition of tribal chieftains to display their pomp and power by means of large harems and numerous offspring. Yet polygamy was never more than the exception in Judea; monogamy was the rule. The law acknowledged the fact of polygamy,[4] but never made peace with it morally.[5]

As against this view, those who maintain that polygamy was the native Hebrew tradition muster a series of biblical evidences to prove their contention. The frequency of polygamous marriage among the leading personalities of the Bible, without explicit protest, denotes the absence of any tradition against it. Those of whom polygamy is recorded are Lamech, Abraham, Nahor, Esau, Jacob, Simeon, Gideon, Elkanah, Saul, David, Solomon, Rehoboam, Jehoash, Abiah, Manasseh, and Sheharaim.[6] The Law assumes polygamy as not uncommon and not unworthy. It teaches that one wife shall not be neglected for the other[7] and that the children of one shall

[2] A second wife is ascribed to Simeon (Gen. 46.10), but it remains doubtful whether he had both wives together.

[3] Isa. 50.1; Jer. 2.2; Ezek. 16.8; Prov. 12.4; 18.22; 19.14; 31.10–31; Ps. 128.3. Significant also is the word *lizeror* in Lev. 18.18, which means "to be a rival," also the covenant that Jacob made with Laban not to take other wives (Gen. 31.50), as well as the frequent reference in the Law to the wife, in the singular.

[4] Ex. 21.10; Deut. 21.15. These two cases, however, cannot be taken as definitely implying an acceptance by the law of polygamy. The first case speaks of one wife and one concubine, which is still "legal" monogamy. The word *senu'ah* in the second case may not mean "the hated one" but the "divorced one" and refers to successive marriages. See Epstein, *The Jewish Marriage Contract* (JMC), p. 198 note 19 and pp. 201–202.

[5] See Loew, o.c., pp. 39–41.

[6] Gen. 4.19; 16.3; 22.24; 28.9; 29.23 f; 46.10; Judg. 8.30; I Sam. 1.2; II Sam. 3.2 ff; 5.13; 12.8; I Kings 11.3; I Chron. 7.14; 8.9; II Chron. 11.21; 13.21; 24.3.

[7] Ex. 21.9.

not be given preference over those of another.[8] It rules also that two sisters may not be the wives of one husband,[9] implying that two strangers may. How widespread the practice was among the masses of Jews during the biblical period can be seen from the report of the Chronicler that polygamy was general in a branch of the tribe of Issachar.[10] Mathematical proof for the prevalence of polygamy may be found in the census reported in Numbers of the military strength of the Israelites in the wilderness. Male members of the people above the age of twenty numberd 603,550. It is fair to assume that the male population below twenty, if added to this number, would make a total of about a million. We will assume an equal number of females, making a total population of two millions. For this population only 22,273 first-born males are recorded and probably an equal number of first-born females. This gives us 45 children to every first-born. So large a family is impossible except under conditions of polygamy.[11]

All evidences of monogamy in the Bible, according to this view, represent a superimposed morality on a polygamous foundation. The monogamous tendency grew with the progress of Hebrew history under the influence of law-giver and preacher. The law-giver, finding polygamy at the root of Hebrew life did not or could not eradicate it by outright prohibition, but sought to eliminate it gradually by such laws as the required purification after contact with a woman,[12] or the command to treat all wives alike,[13] or the prohibition against castration.[14] The preacher taught monogamy by the

[8] Deut. 21.15. See note 4 above.

[9] Lev. 18.18.

[10] I Chron. 7.4.

[11] This proof is offered by Michaelis, *Mosaisches Recht,* II, pp. 163 f., based on Num. 2.32 and 3.43. Its weakness lies in the fact that even in polygamous marriages forty-five children for the average family is too many; also in the fact that the first-born in respect to holiness (except in the matter of inheritance) is the first-born of the mother, who "unloosens the womb" (3.12), and polygamy does not answer the difficulty. The answer to our difficulty may lie in the fact that only those first-born after the Exodus were consecrated, for it was in the Exodus event that the consecration of the first-born was proclaimed.

[12] Lev. 15.18.

[13] Ex. 21.8–11.

[14] Deut. 23.2; see also Lev. 22.24.

story of creation, by the censure he offered Solomon for his plural marriages,[15] by prophetic utterances in favor of monogamy,[16] and by subtle apologies for the polygamy of some prominent biblical personalities.[17]

In this controversy, it seems to us that the evidences advanced in support of the theory of polygamy are more compelling than those offered to prove monogamy. A polygamous society also permits monogamous families, while a monogamous rule generally excludes polygamy altogether. Polygamous records in some biblical families, therefore, do offer refutation of the theory of monogamy, but instances of monogamy in no way refute the theory of polygamy. Furthermore, records of monogamy in the early generations cannot be taken too seriously, because the Bible tries only to trace genealogy, in which heads of families count but younger descendants and inferior wives are omitted from the record as irrelevant to the genealogical table. The story of creation is no proof of monogamy, if we recognize the principle of "biological economy." That is to say, even if polygamy was accepted by the author of the story, he still would find it unnecessary to have God create more than one male and one female, since one pair would be sufficient for the perpetuation of the species. The same motive applies to survival of the human family in pairs at the time of the flood. In fact, even beasts were admitted into the ark in pairs, and surely it was not meant for them to be monogamous. Nor does "the wife," in the singular, so generally used in the Bible, imply a consciousness of monogamy, for the Bible speaks also of a man's ox or slave in the singular.

Though we find the view of those who maintain that polygamy is rooted in native Hebrew life more plausible and more acceptable to us, we do not go the whole distance with them in their arguments. We do not claim a *native* Hebrew tradition of polygamy. Questions of native origins in a group as old as the Hebrews cannot be solved. The records, which are the only sources of reliable information, do

[15] Deut. 17.17; I Kings 11.3.
[16] See note 3 above.
[17] Loew, o.c., pp. 33–35; Michaelis, o.c., pp. 163 f.

not go back to origins. Whatever one may say as to whether polygamy was native or acquired can at best be speculative and conjectural. The extent to which we do go with this view is that polygamy was an established institution in Hebrew society from time immemorial. In this conclusion we are supported by the accumulated opinion of scholarship. We do not know native Hebrew predilections to account for polygamy, but we do know forces in Hebrew history, some inner and some outer, some economic and some cultural, that sufficiently account for its existence from the beginning of their records. We may then turn our attention to those forces and historic incidents which shaped their policy of polygamy.

The Bible generally assumes a patronymic family organization among the early Hebrews. Marriage represents acquisition, ownership. That form of marriage is called *ba'al* marriage, where husband is owner of his wife in the same sense as he owns his slaves. Polygamy is the logical corollary of *ba'al* marriage, for as one may own many slaves so he may espouse many wives. Even the Babylonian law which restricted polygamy does not challenge the logic of polygamy inherent in *ba'al* marriage. Babylonian restrictions are based upon a concept that just as there is a single male head in the household, the patriarch, so should there be a single female head, the matriarch. It is the special dignity of the matron that stands in the way of full, free polygamy in Babylonia. We find no such concept among the early Hebrews, except in Abraham's family under Babylonian influence, and therefore we have a right to assume that to the extent to which *ba'al* marriage predominated polygamy was considered proper and permissible.

But we find traces in the Bible also of a metronymic family structure, and sometimes of marriages that have a combination of patronymic and metronymic elements. These types of family organization, however, do not exclude polygamy. Under a metronymic rule it is not likely that two women of different tribes would have one husband in common, but it is quite likely that two sisters might take one husband. The ownership idea would there be reversed. The two sisters having common ownership in various chattels of the family would look upon their common husband also as their common possession. It is not impossible that the marriage of Jacob to Rachel and Leah, though it has *ba'al* elements, was that kind of a metronymic polygamous union; and possibly Lamech's two wives, Ada and Zilla, were also sisters, whose marriage was of the same pattern. Where patronymic and metronymic elements mix within the same social group, it was also possible for a man to have both, a metronymic wife and a patronymic one. This possibility is implied in the records of Gideon's [18] and Jephthah's [19] families.

From the family organization of the early Hebrews and its effect upon polygamy, we go over to a survey of the other sociological elements in their history so far as they helped to mould their family life. The course of their history presents migrations, economic changes, cultural influences from without and cultural progress from within. All these contributed in a measure toward the formulation of the Hebrew attitude to polygamy.

Abraham emerges from Ur of the Chaldees with a family constructed on the Babylonian pattern. He is patriarch and Sarah his only matriarch, as required by Babylonian law. He dare not violate the dignity of her position, and throughout her life she has no rival matron. Childless, she gives Abraham a slave-wife, fully in accordance with Babylonian law. To take concubines in addition to the slave-wife given to him by Sarah would be a violation of Babylonian restrictions,[20] and if Abraham took concubines during Sarah's lifetime, it was the first Hebrew relaxation of the restrictions of Chaldee.

In Canaan polygamy was practiced by the natives; pastoral life encouraged it; patriarchal family organization permitted it. Jealousy for the dignity of the matriarch's position in the household had no significance to the Canaanite population. Isaac and Jacob, marrying Babylonian born maidens, showed some regard for the dignity of the matriarch, as required by

[18] Judg. 8.31.
[19] Judg. 11.1.
[20] Code Hammurabi (C.H.), 144, 167.

Babylonian standards.[21] But Esau, marrying in Canaan, showed no scruples concerning unrestricted polygamy. Laban evidently knew the prevalence of polygamy in Canaan, but seeking to preserve his daughters' dignity, made Jacob swear before leaving Haran that he would take no other wives to rival them.[22]

The Canaanite influence did not wholly dispose the Hebrews to unrestricted polygamy. No polygamous marriages were contracted by any of the sons of Jacob, save perhaps Simeon.[23] Was it a matter of conscience with them or of cultural superiority to the Canaanites? Probably not. The reasons for their resistance to free polygamy were probably practical ones – the costly purchase price of wives, the plentitude of female slaves to give sexual satisfaction outside marriage, and the difficulty in maintaining peace in a household with rival wives of equal position. These obstacles did not deter the head of a large patriarchal family from taking many wives, because he found therein a lavishness of luxury and a means of attaining prestige among his neighbor chieftains. But the ordinary Hebrew accepted monogamy as the practical pattern of family life, even though his law did not forbid him polygamy.

During the sojourn of the Hebrews in Egypt, their own attitude to polygamy found corroboration in that of the Egyptians. To the Egyptians, too, polygamy was permitted by law, but the common folk did not indulge in it. If the Hebrews still retained memories from their Babylonian days that it is an insult to the matron to bring a rival into the household, that feeling was counteracted by Egyptian life as they saw it. For here was a people of culture who maintained their wives on a fairly high level of dignity and respect even when they had more than one matron. Perhaps also the institution of the harem came to the notice of the Hebrews for the first time during their Egyptian period, but it cannot be said that they adopted that institution from

[21] Jacob's polygamy, being of the metronymic type, marrying two sisters, cannot be counted as an exception to the rule of monogamy.

[22] Gen. 31.50.

[23] Gen. 46.10.

Egypt, for Egypt had no monopoly on harems; and the Jews did not adopt it until they were again settled in Canaan and came more intimately in contact with it through their immediate neighbors.[24]

A suggestion of specific influence that the Egyptians had on the Hebrews in respect to polygamy may be worth noting, with the understanding, however, that it is offered as a mere conjecture. The Egyptian priesthood was by law restricted to monogamy. The monogamy of priests in a polygamous country is highly significant. The Bible, it is true, does not prescribe monogamy for priests and the Talmud has several records of priests living in polygamy. Yet it is noteworthy that not a single case is recorded in the Bible of a priestly family living in polygamy. The Zadokites, who seem to have modelled their sectarian law on priestly tradition and discipline, prohibit it. The New Testament denies polygamy to bishops.[25] The Mishnah assumes that the high priest had only one wife,[26] and the Talmud reads into the biblical text itself the prohibition of polygamy for high priests.[27] These facts give us ground for the suspicion that perhaps older Hebrew tradition restricted the priestly tribe to monogamy.

On their return to Canaan, the Hebrews found polygamy and harems prevalent among the inhabitants. Yet the Hebrew masses were at first satisfied with their monogamy, partly because their economic condition did not permit plural marriage, and partly also perhaps because of a higher moral sense. With better times, however, even the masses indulged in polygamy, and it is so reported especially of the tribe of Issachar.[28] In that formative period, it seems, bigamy became common among the Hebrews. Noble and wealthy

[24] On polygamy in Egypt see Edward Westermarck, *The History of Human Marriage*, N. Y., 1922, (HHM), III, pp. 40–41. On its influence upon the Hebrews, see Loew, o.c., pp. 37–38.

[25] I Tim. 3.2; Tit. 1.6.

[26] M. Yoma 2a.

[27] Yoma 13a, deriving from Lev. 16.9, 11, also Yeb. 59a. According to Maimonides (Yad, Issure Bi'ah 17,13 and *Maggid* thereto) the talmudic derivation is from Lev. 21.13.

[28] I Chron. 7.5.

families had full polygamy and larger or smaller harems, but the common folk were satisfied with two wives. Bigamy is recorded of Elkanah [29] and Jehoash.[30] Bigamy is anticipated by the law which prescribed that one wife should not be neglected for "the other"; [31] also by that which demands that the father should not favor the children of one wife against those of the other; [32] and finally by the law prohibiting marrying "a woman and her sister to be rivals." [33] Bigamy is also assumed by the next law considered.

Polygamy to an excessive degree was distasteful to the Hebrews. The ruling class was too often guilty of such excess, imitating chieftains of the Canaanite tribes in the magnificence of large harems of wives and concubines. To them the Bible turns with the injunction that the ruler "shall not multiply wives." [34] The trend toward harems among the ruling class is too frequently recorded in the Scriptures. Gideon had a sufficient number of wives to give him a progeny of seventy sons.[35] Jair the Gileadite raised a family of thirty sons, exclusive of daughters.[36] Reference is made to Saul's harem, but the number of wives is not given; while David's harem counted seven or eight wives mentioned by name, a number of additional principal wives, and some ten concubines.[37] Solomon had the proverbial thousand consorts, of whom seven hundred were conjugal princesses and three hundred concubines.[38] Rehoboam had eighteen wives and sixty concubines.[39] Abiya was more moderate, for he

[29] I Sam. 1.2.

[30] II Chron. 24.3. Though a royal person, he was restricted in accordance with the standards of the common people, by his high priest guardian, as will be explained later.

[31] Ex. 21.10. Notice *aḥeret* in the singular.

[32] Deut. 21.15. The proof is not conclusive, as stated in note 4 above, for the rule of polygamy; but if polygamy is implied then its linguistic form suggests bigamy rather than polygamy.

[33] Lev. 18.18.

[34] Deut. 17.17.

[35] Judg. 8.30.

[36] Judg. 10.4. The same number of sons and an equal number of daughters were born to Ibzan from his polygamous marriages. Judg. 12.9.

[37] II Sam. 2.2; 3.2–5; 5.13; 11.27; 15.16.

[38] I Kings 11.3.

[39] II Chron. 11.21.

had only fourteen wives and an unknown number of concubines.[40]

The people felt uneasy about these sex indulgences of their rulers. They expected moderation on the part of their chieftains in all things. The king was not to have too much gold and silver, nor too lavish a stable. These were maintained at the expense of the tax-burdened people. A harem too was a breach of moderation, and it was also an expensive luxury for the king. But the harem held additional dangers. The wives or concubines were imported from foreign countries, and brought with them their idolatrous beliefs and customs. A weak king might, as was often the case, fall prey to the idolatry of his wife and mislead his people as well. This national sentiment against harems expressed itself in the deuteronomic law that the king must not multiply wives.

What constitutes a multiplication of wives we are not told. The phrase probably meant general moderation. However, from one incident in the biblical record we learn that in all likelihood "moderation" meant two wives and no more, the standard for the common people. We are told[41] that Jehoiada the high priest was left in charge of the infant king, Joash, whom he raised, crowned, and directed. As guardian, he gave his royal ward two wives. We know of no law limiting the king to two wives, but this incident is an indication of what the king would do if acting decently in the eyes of a priest. Post-biblical Judaism knows no such law either, so that Herod the Great had nine wives,[42] and rabbinic tradition permits the king eighteen wives, even twenty-four, up to forty-eight, outside of slave-wives and concubines.[43]

II

In the main stream of Judaism there is no new teaching on the subject of polygamy in the literature of the Second Commonwealth. The Jewish family during that period was very

[40] II Chron. 13.21.
[41] II Chron. 24.3.
[42] Jos., *Ant.*, XVIII,1,3.
[43] San. 21a.

like its counterpart in the biblical period. Rulers permitted themselves plural wives; bigamy was not infrequent, but the people as a rule practiced monogamy. New developments in the law of polygamy, however, can be found in the teaching of sects that arose in Judea during this period – Zadokites and Christians.

The Zadokites were a sectarian group that lived in Damascus during the first century before the common era. They taught and practiced strict monogamy. Their scriptural sources for monogamy were the biblical account of creation, where one man and only one wife were brought into being, and the monogamous pairs that were saved from the flood in Noah's ark. The deuteronomic injunction that a king shall not multiply wives meant to them that the king, like any other Israelite, might have no more than one wife. If polygamy was practiced by some of the righteous rulers of Israel, it was because they knew no better, for the Law, according to their teaching, was hidden until the days of Zadok, their sectarian saint ancestor.[44] Without going into explicit exegesis, they took the levitical law (18.18) decreeing against marrying "a woman and her sister" to mean "one woman and another," which is linguistically quite possible, and derived from it an express prohibition against polygamy.[45] The teachings of this sect, according to Professor Louis Ginzberg, falls into two stages, the first while the members of the sect resided in Judea, the second when they retired to Damascus in separation from the Jewish community. While in Judea they did not teach or practice strict monogamy, but it became a feature of their law when they established their own community in Damascus.[46] Because this teaching did not develop to its full on Palestinian soil and because it was sectarian in nature as a defiance of the teachers of the Law, it has had little or no influence on the main stream of Jewish life.

[44] Fragments of a Zadokite Sect, ed. R. H. Charles in *Apocrypha and Pseudepigrapha of the Old Testament*, London, 1913, 1.1–7.

[45] Louis Ginzberg, *Eine unbekannte jüdische Sekte*, (*Sekte*) N. Y., 1922, pp. 24–25.

[46] Ibid., pp. 374–5.

To the Christian sect that developed in Judea at the time of the fall of the Second Commonwealth, the question of polygamy raised no sectarian problem. They found the lower strata of the Jews living in monogamy; and that was satisfactory to them, because their adherents came from that social level. The moral ideal of monogamy was admittedly maintained by the teachers of the Law, and with this the Christian sect had no quarrel. Out of their own spiritual resources, the Christians added two influences in the direction of monogamy. First, the leaning of the sect toward asceticism was definite. It taught that marriage in itself was a compromise with the flesh and sinful. If marrying one wife was a sin, then marrying two was, of course, a double sin. Second, Christianity, spreading its activity into the West, Romanized itself greatly in the process of gaining converts among the heathens. The Roman influence was definitely toward monogamy. Yet with all these tendencies, early Christianity, it may be said at best, made a policy of monogamy but did not bring it down to legal teaching. The fact that the early Christians never entered into sectarian controversy on the subject of polygamy, as did the Zadokites, should prove this assertion.

It is said that the New Testament teaches monogamy in I Corinthians 7.2, which reads, "Let each man have his own wife and let each woman have her own husband." But this no more proves monogamy for the New Testament than does the verse "Therefore shall a man leave his father and his mother and shall cleave unto his wife, and they shall be one flesh" prove it for the Old. A more compelling proof is found in the Gospels of Matthew (19.9) and Mark (10.11), which declare that "Whosoever shall put away his wife. . . . and shall marry another committeth adultery." Now, if the term "adultery" is to be taken literally and in a legal sense, then the conclusion is definite that legal prohibition of polygamy is here implied, for where polygamy is permitted there can be no adultery on the part of the man save where the woman is married to another. But one has reason to believe that the term "adultery" is employed only for rhetorical effect and means no more than "sexual sin," or that it is used loosely for stylistic effect, to match the other half of the verse: "and whoso marrieth her which is put away doth commit adultery," where "adultery" is the proper technical term. An earlier passage in Matthew (5.32) is more careful in terminology. It gives the law with legal accuracy: "Whosoever shall put away his wife . . . causeth her to commit adultery, and whosoever shall marry her that is divorced committeth adultery." [47]

Even if we should assume that the apostles wished to prohibit polygamy, it is thoroughly impossible under the old patriarchal family concept to consider polygamy equal to adultery, unless we are ready to consider sex relations between a married man and a prostitute adultery on the part of the man. That was not the idea of the monogamous Romans nor of any other group in the early centuries of the common era. Whether we know how to explain the term adultery in the verse or not, it certainly cannot mean adultery in the technical legal sense, and therefore does not prove a legal prohibition against polygamy.

On the other hand, there are some New Testament passages which seem to indicate permission of polygamy. We have in mind the teaching that a bishop or deacon may not have more than one wife.[48] The natural inference would be that no such prohibition applies to a common layman.

Probably during the early centuries, the Christian teachers were fully aware that no prohibition against polygamy could be adduced from apostolic writings. Nor do we find a new legislation on the matter in the early sources of canon law, although the assumption is frequently made therein that polygamy is contrary to Christian teachings.[49] It is not surprising therefore that history records polygamous unions on

[47] Mark 10.11, "Whoever shall put away his wife and marry another committeth adultery *against her*," may have the same meaning as the passage in Matthew, for the words "against her" indicate that it is not his adultery but causing her to commit adultery that is pointed to.

[48] I Tim. 3.2, 12; Tit. 1.6. The Greek Orthodox Church interprets these passages as teaching that laymen are permitted successive marriages (in widowhood) while deacons are not permitted more than one marriage in a lifetime. See Loew, *Gesammelte Schriften*, III, p. 34 and note 3.

[49] *Corpus Juris Canonici* in the German translation by Bruno Schilling, Leipzig, 1834, of which the following sections can be cited as implying sentiment against polygamy:

Caussa XXVIII, Quaestio II, sec. 1, declares that marriage before conversion

the part of Christian dignitaries in earlier as well as in later times,[50] and often with the consent of Church and clergy. The Council of Trent in 1563 was still troubled with those insubordinate, critical minds who taught that "polygamy was permitted to Christians and was not prohibited by any divine law," and, seeking to make an end to this teaching, legislated by the full authority of the Roman Church an unequivocal prohibition of polygamy, pronouncing a ban upon those who might teach otherwise.[51] For Catholicism this law has remained binding to this day and became part of the New Canon (#1069, sec. 1); Protestants have not accepted the binding authority of canon law and find themselves without legislation on the subject of polygamy. Their attitude, therefore, is that of the early Church Fathers, that there is no apostolic prohibition against it but that it is contrary to Christian morals.

Returning to the main stream of Judaism at the beginning of Christianity, we find the teachings of the Pharisees a con-

---

remains valid thereafter, and second marriage is then not permitted because the first is still in force. (Date, 845).

Caussa XXXI, Quaestio I, sec. 8, declares a second marriage in widowhood prohibited and no priest shall participate in its ceremonies. (Date, 314).

Caussa XXXI, Quaestio I, sec. 9, second marriage (in widowhood) though permitted is immoral; nevertheless valid. (Date, 400).

Caussa XXXII, Quaestio I, sec. 2, Jerome explains that after divorcing a wife for unfaithfulness the husband cannot marry another so that he will not be tempted to make false charges against his wife in the hope of remarriage. The implication is that before he divorces his first wife he cannot marry another. (Date, 388).

Caussa XXXII, Quaestio II, sec. 11–12, Leo I rules that marriage to a man who has a concubine is not prohibited, because concubines are not wives. (Date, 443).

Caussa XXXII, Quaestio VII, sec. 10, St. Augustine says that marrying another wife after divorcing the first is not as bad a sin as polygamy. (Date, 419).

Caussa XXXII, Quaestio VII, sec. 18, Gregory III permits a man to marry a second wife if his first wife is sick or unable to have intercourse with her husband. (Date, 726).

Caussa XXXII, Quaestio VII, sec. 27, Augustine is in doubt whether a second marriage is permitted when the first wife is childless. (Date, 419).

[50] Instances are cited by Westermarck, HHM, III, pp. 50–51 and by Loew, *Gesammelte Schriften*, III, pp. 33–35. The latter cites permission granted for bigamous marriage by papal decree as late as 1804.

[51] *Corpus Juris Canonici*, ibid., Concil Trident, Sessio XXIV, Canon II.

tinuation of the biblical attitude to polygamy, and the teaching of the rabbis thereafter an extension of the pharisaic tradition. This tradition accepted polygamy as legally permissible and did not even imply a policy of monogamy as did the Church; for while the Church shifted its center to the West, where monogamy was the rule, the Synagogue continued in its oriental setting, where polygamy was native. Any resistance to polygamy in talmudic times as in biblical days was created by life itself and was not formulated into law.

Instances of polygamy in talmudic times are not rare and they are found mostly in high places. The two sons of Herod, Archelaus and Herod Antipas, contracted second marriages on top of their first.[52] The Talmud also reports a bigamous marriage for an *epitropos* to Agrippa.[53] Similar marriages are recorded for members of the priestly families, such as Alubai, Caiaphus, and Josephus.[54] Also a representative of the learned class, member of the Sanhedrin, Abba son of Rabban Simeon ben Gamaliel I, is recorded to have had two wives at the same time.[55]

More freakish forms of polygamy are reported of rabbinic personalities. R. Tarphon, both priest and tanna, betrothed unto himself three hundred maidens in order to feed them out of the priestly heave-offering.[56] Rabbi Judah the Prince sponsored twelve levirate marriages for one poor Israelite and helped to maintain that large family.[57] Of two famous amoraim, Rab and R. Naḥman, it is told in the Talmud that they had their wives at home, but contracted new marriages on their visits to new communities.[58]

Justin Martyr in the second century was correct when he hurled the accusation against the Jews that they have "four or five wives" and marry "as they wish and as many as they

[52] Jos. *Ant.* XVII,13,1.
[53] Suk. 27a.
[54] Tos. Yeb. 1,10; Yeb. 15b; Yer. Yeb. 3a. See Ginzberg, *Sekte*, p. 183, note 4; Jos. *Life*, 75. See JE, s.v. "Josephus."
[55] Yeb. 15a. Cf. Ginzberg, *Sekte*, p. 184, note 1.
[56] Tos. Ket. 5,1.
[57] Yer. Yeb. 6b.
[58] Yoma 18b; Yeb. 37b.

wish."[59] Josephus informed the Roman world long before: "It is the ancient practice among us to have many wives at the same time."[60] In theory at least, the Talmud assumes polygamy as the marriage rule without question. The co-wife (*Ẓarah*) is a prominent figure in tannaitic discussion of the levirate law.[61] Likewise multiple marriages are assumed in the *ketubah* provision of *benin dikrin* and the rabbinic discussions of priority of lien as among children of several mothers. It is reported that in Jerusalem even the hour was recorded in the marriage instrument in order to establish priority when a husband contracted two or more marriages on the same day.[62] The assumption of polygamy accounts in part or in whole for such moral injunctions as "A man shall not drink out of one cup and have an eye on the other,"[63] or "A man shall not marry one woman in one place and then marry another in another place, lest the children (unknown to one another) meet and a brother marry a sister."[64] Because of polygamy, the rabbis ridicule Pharaoh's decree to drown the male children of Israel; for so long as the females remain, the population will grow, "because one man can marry ten or a hundred women."[65] Theoretically, a man can say in his marriage formula, "Be thou betrothed unto half of me," and the law will interpret this to mean that he reserves the other half for another wife whom he expects to marry.[66] There are various views whether a man may retain a barren wife, but according to the positive opinion the law compels him to marry an additional wife in order to fulfill the duty of procreation.[67]

[59] *Dial.* 134, 141. Cf. Büchler's review of Schechter's *Sectaries* in J.Q.R., N.S., III, pp. 433 f; Krauss in J.Q.R., O.S., V, p. 130.

[60] Jos., *Ant.*, XVII,1,2, 15; *Wars*, I,24,2.

[61] Mishnah, first chapter of Yeb., etc.

[62] M. Ket. 93b.

[63] Ned. 20b.

[64] Yoma 18b. The possibility of successive marriages instead of polygamy is not excluded, but the phrasing indicates polygamy.

[65] Ex. Rab., 1,18.

[66] Ḳid. 6a.

[67] M. Yeb. 61b; M. Sotah 24a. Dr. Ben-Zion Bokser in his *Pharisaic Judaism in Transition*, N. Y., 1935, pp. 83–4, asserts on the basis of the mishnah in Soṭah that R. Eliezer was in favor of polygamy while his contestants opposed it. This does not seem entirely conclusive. The opponents of R. Eliezer

Where polygamy was more generally practiced, the wife could not offer the husband's polygamy as ground for divorce; where it was less usual, polygamy constituted a cause recognized by the courts. Raba of Babylonia, therefore, taught that a man can take as many wives as he wishes, despite his wife's objections, so long as he can support them. R. Ami of Palestine, where polygamy was less usual, ruled that if a wife objects to her husband's marrying another, she has valid ground for divorce.[68]

Just as in the biblical period we have seen that while plural marriage was permitted, excessive polygamy was resisted, so in the rabbinic period the Jewish moral sense rose against too many wives. Hillel, grandson of Rabbi Judah the Prince, is quoted as saying, "He who multiplies wives multiplies witchcraft." [69] Rab was more specific when he advised his pupil, "Marry not two wives, but if you marry two, then take a third" [70] – for he found greater chances for peace at home with three wives than with two. The Talmud actually formulated a rule to govern polygamy, a rule which somehow found its way into Mohammedanism; – a man shall not marry more than four wives, in order that he may distribute his weekly marital contacts equally among them and give each marital satisfaction once a month.[71]

---

agree to polygamy, but they insist that the polygamous marriage should be a fact and not a speculation, i.e., when polygamy is merely an anticipation of the future, the marriage of a barren wife is a distinct sin. See Tosafot, Soṭah 26a s.v. *lo* quoting Yerushalmi.

As to the propriety of marrying a barren wife or retaining her after marriage, the law seems to be clear enough that a childless man may not marry or retain her, Yeb. 61a–b, 65a; Tos. Yeb. 8,4. If he has children by another wife, it seems from a strictly legal point of view that he may marry a wife who is barren, Yeb. 61a–b, Yad, Ishut 15,7. References in the Talmud to the duty of divorcing such a wife—Yeb. 64a; Ket. 77a—must be understood as having in mind the average family, which was monogamous. Yet, a statement of R. Joshua (Ab. R. N., ch. 3; Yeb. 62b) that a man's duty to beget children never comes to an end, no matter how many he has, has raised the question in the minds of later authorities whether it is not sinful for a man to retain a childless wife even if he has another wife and children by her. See *Maggid* ad Yad, ibid.

[68] Yeb. 65a.

[69] Ab. 2,5.

[70] Pes. 113a.

[71] Yeb. 44a.

On the other hand, despite permission by the law, polygamy was quite rare in actual life among the Jews of the rabbinic period. Economic conditions curtailed it to some extent and moral aversion also came to the surface. The Midrash finds in Lamech's polygamy an indication of the degeneracy of the antedeluvian age.[72] Elkanah's polygamy is justified in the Midrash by the childlessness of Hannah.[73] Similarly, the redeemer, in the Book of Ruth, justifies his action in rejecting the right of the levirate by saying, "I cannot redeem for myself lest I mar my own inheritance." To the Midrash this means, "I cannot redeem her for myself because I have a wife, and may not take another lest there be a quarrel in my house and I will thus mar my estate." [74] A certain town Ḳushṭa (meaning "truth") fulfilled God's plan of creation perfectly; the people never told a lie, and therefore did not die until advanced in years. Every man married one wife and begot two children. And this to the rabbis was the ideal life.[75]

Evidence of how the people felt about polygamy in rabbinic times is found in a few interesting legal items. The law teaches that a judge or a witness instrumental in granting a married woman permission of the court to remarry, may not thereafter marry that woman himself, because of the suspicion that the testimony or legal opinion was inspired by personal interest. But if at the time of the trial the judge or witness had a wife, who died thereafter, he could marry the woman.[76] The suspicion that he might have an eye on the woman even though he were married looked farfetched to the rabbis. The Talmud, in passing, quotes a litigant in court who desired quick disposal of his levirate obligation: "So long as I am bound to this one (the levirate woman) people will not give me another." [77] When a son

[72] Gen. Rab. 23,3.

[73] Yalḳuṭ Shim'oni, I Sam. 1.2; Midrash Shemuel, I Sam. ibid.; Pesiḳta Rabbati, ch. 43, ed. Friedmann, p. 181b.

[74] Targum ad Ruth 4.6.

[75] San. 97a. See Ginzberg, *Sekte*, pp. 184–85.

[76] Yeb. 25b–26a.

[77] Ket. 64a.

of Rabbi Judah the Prince, on his return from the academy after twelve years' absence, found his wife barren and contemplated a second marriage, his father said this would outrage public opinion, for people would call one his wife, the other his mistress.[78] Apparently, despite the law, people disliked polygamy and protested it when it occurred.

Post-talmudic teachers accepted both the legality of and the moral revulsion to polygamy which they found in Talmud and Midrash. The degree of antagonism, however, was a matter of local policy. Very little is known about Palestinian Judaism after the Talmud, but it is fair to assume that the tradition begun with the Palestinian amora, R. Ami, continued after the close of the Talmud – that even though permitted by law, the wife may offer polygamy as ground for divorce. Babylonia during the gaonic period was dominated by the two academies of Sura and Pumbedita. The Sura school, under influence of Palestinian tradition, permitted the wife to interfere with her husband's polygamous marriages.[79] Likewise, the levirate woman might object to polygamy and demand *ḥaliẓah* instead of levirate marriage.[80] The academy at Pumbedita followed the teaching of its historic progenitor, Raba, the Babylonian amora who taught that the wife could raise no objection to her husband's polygamy; they ruled there that the wife's objections were to be treated as rebellion, meriting the penalty prescribed for the "rebellious woman." [81] They agreed, however, that a woman cannot be forced into a polygamous levirate marriage, not so much because polygamy is a valid objection as because the Pumbedita academy had a tradition of preferring ḥaliẓah to levirate marriage.[82] At the end of the gaonic period,

[78] Ket. 62b.

[79] *Sha'are Ẓedeḳ,* IV,4,60 in the name of R. Hilai (ninth century); Ginzberg, *Geonica* II, p. 152. See also *Toratan shel Rishonim,* II,46.

[80] *Sha'are Ẓedeḳ,* I,52 in the name of R. Hilai, Sura. The Sura tradition was otherwise in favor of levirate marriage as against ḥaliẓah. See B. M. Lewin, *Oẓar,* Yeb. pp. 67–78.

[81] *Sha'are Ẓedeḳ,* IV,4,30; Geonic Responsa, ed. Coronel, 66; *Halakot Gedolot,* ed. Warsaw, 1874, p. 136a; *Halakot Pesuḳot,* ed. Schlosberg, Versailles, 1886, p. 88; Ginzberg, *Geonica,* I, pp. 95–111; *Geonica,* II, pp. 385–386.

[82] Lewin, *Oẓar,* Yeb. ibid.

Pumbedita gained superiority over its rival academy through the influence of its last great heads, Sherira and Hai. Its authority was recognized in all the Jewish communities of the diaspora. As a result, the legality of and ethical compromise with polygamy gained general recogniton among post-gaonic scholars. It should be added, however, that the Mohammedan attitude to polygamy and its influence upon the Jews of the Orient was by no means unimportant in rendering it acceptable to the teachers of that period.

During the gaonic period, in the eighth century, the Karaite sect came into being, and in the course of its growth developed an attitude to polygamy which may be here briefly recorded. The Karaites fused into their teachings three distinct traditions. Rabbinic law was at its root. By a mysterious channel, the Zadokite teaching also entered the fabric of their law. In habits they seemed closer to the Mohammedan population than were the Rabbanites, and as a result Islamic law had a greater influence upon them than upon the main stream of Judaism. This triple combination of sources characterizes the Karaite attitude to polygamy.

Like the Zadokites, Karaites taught that the levitical law (18.18) prohibiting a man marrying two sisters does not mean two sisters literally, but two women. Like the Zadokites, too, they were forced into this artificial exegesis by the principle of "analogy" (*heḳesh*). Since the same levitical code (18.16) prohibits the marriage of a woman to two brothers, it is self-evident, by "analogy," that a man may not marry two sisters. Furthermore, as a woman may not marry a second brother even after being widowed from the first, so a man may not marry the sister of his wife even after his wife's death. Once this information is deduced, the prohibition against marrying two sisters cannot be taken literally. For one reason, there is no need for specifying the prohibition so long as it is already implied in a previous verse; for another, the Bible definitely prohibits "two sisters" only during the life of either, but by inference from the previous verse we have learned that the prohibition of marrying sisters extends beyond the life of either. Hence the conclusion that "two sisters" simply means "one and another," that is, any two women. This gives us, according to their reasoning, a biblical law against polygamy.[83]

However, they could not logically stand by the law of monogamy without claiming a new revelation, for polygamy was the Jewish tradition and abundantly supported by the record of righteous biblical personalities. Therefore, they applied an exegetical principle known in rabbinic literature [84] which brought them eye to eye with the Mohammedan law of polygamy.[85] They pronounced the word, *liẓeror,* "to be rivals" or more literally "to be vexed," in the levitical law as basis and motive for the prohibition of polygamy. That is, polygamy is prohibited because and only insofar as one wife is vexed on account of the other; but where there is no vexation, polygamy is permitted. By vexing they understand not a state of unhappiness arising out of jealousy, but primarily neglect of sexual satisfaction, and secondarily curtailment of food, clothing, and house comforts. To the Karaites, where one wife is neglected, polygamy is practically equal to incest, for it derives its prohibition from the levitical section on incest; therefore a polygamous marriage of the prohibited kind is altogether invalid, as is the rule for all incestuous marriages. Even divorcing one wife on account of another is equal to a violation of the law of incest.[86] Where there is no neglect of one wife for the other, polygamy is permitted and legally unrestricted. Ethically, however, the Karaites follow the precept of the Babylonian amora, supported by the teaching of Mohammedanism, that a man shall not marry more than four wives.

An exception to the law of monogamy is made by the Karaites in case the first wife is childless after ten years of marriage. For the sake of begetting offspring, the husband is allowed to marry another wife, even if he has to deny sexual

[83] See A. Harkavy, *Studien und Mittheilungen,* St. Petersburg, 1903, quoting 'Anan (VIII, 105, 109), Ḳirḳisani (ibid. 129), Alḳumsi (ibid. 191). See also *Eshkol ha-Kofer,* 118; *Gan'Eden,* 146d; *Aderet Elijahu,* Nashim, 5, p. 159b; A. Neubauer, *Geschichte des Karäerthums,* Leipzig, 1866, Hebrew section, p. 46; Ginzberg, *Sekte,* pp. 25–26. Other interpretations of the levitical law are mentioned and summarized briefly in *Aderet Elijahu,* ibid.

[84] Sifre ad Deut. 17.17; San. 21a. דריש טעמא דקרא.

[85] Koran 4.3.

[86] *Aderet Elijahu,* Nashim, 4, pp. 158d–159b.

satisfaction to the first or has to divorce the first. Should he choose to retain the first wife under conditions where he will have to deny her sexual satisfaction, he must establish her in a separate apartment, so that she need not be humiliated by witnessing the amours between her husband and her rival.[87]

In the main stream of Judaism at the end of the gaonic period increased resistance to polygamy became evident. It showed itself in what seemed to be a popular movement rather than a court enactment. Parents of daughters who could dictate terms to their prospective sons-in-law demanded a written pre-nuptial promise that their daughters should not be subjected to polygamy. In the course of time this demand became more popular, and almost standard for all marriages in certain localities, so that it was incorporated as a special clause in the ketubah. This read: "That he may not marry or take during the bride's lifetime and while she is with him another wife, slave-wife, or concubine except with her consent, and if he do . . . he shall from this moment be under obligation to pay her the ketubah in full and release her by a bill of divorcement by which she shall be free to remarry." [88] This clause was employed in the Orient as early, at least, as the twelfth century and has survived to this day in the sephardic ketubah.[89] The Orient never recognized the *ḥerem* (prohibition of R. Gershom) against polygamy, and this ketubah clause was the only safeguard the bride could have. By the popularity of the clause, which in the last few centuries has become practically standard, it becomes evident how much resistance the Jewish community, even in the Orient where polygamy is not offensive, has offered to polygamy.

As if this clause were not sufficient safeguard, another device was introduced later to restrict polygamy. At the time of the marriage the groom was made to take an oath that "he shall not marry another while he is married to the pres-

[87] Ibid., 159c.

[88] Epstein, JMC., p. 272.

[89] The ketubah in the Adler collection marked 4010V, cited in JMC ibid. note 5, seems to bear the date of 1155. See also sephardic ketubah, ed. Gaster, MGWJ, 54.

ent bride." The oath, like the ketubah clause, had its birth in the Orient, where there was no other restriction against polygamy. But the popularity of both reached the western Jewish communities also. They were probably employed first before the ḥerem was generally accepted in the west and continued in such localities where the acceptance of the ḥerem was late in coming; but by historical inertia, they persisted in some localities even after acceptance of the ḥerem.[90]

III

The great event in the history of polygamy among the Jews was the ḥerem or enactment of R. Gershom b. Judah, surnamed "The Light of the Diaspora," who was born at Metz in 960 and died in Mayence in 1040. The original document has not come down to us, and the circumstances connected with it are not known. In the best judgment of scholars, it was an enactment of a number of leading rabbis assembled in a synod under the presidency of R. Gershom, probably at Worms in the year 1030 in connection with one of the customary large fairs.[91] It was intended for the whole Franco-German Jewish community, and probably there were representatives from the rabbinate of the various communities in that territory. The enactment was fortified by a ḥerem, putting a ban on any transgressor. It was therefore called the "ḥerem of R. Gershom." As against the ketubah clause which prohibited polygamy *without* the wife's consent, the ḥerem prohibited it even *with* her consent, on the basis of public morality.

Historians took it for granted that the ḥerem was inspired by the monogamous standards of Western Europe under the influence of Christianity. That theory has been effectively challenged by Güdemann,[92] who points out that the moral level of family life among the Christians of the Rhineland at

[90] Responsa R. David b. Zimra (RDBZ), 221; Resp. RI Trani, 118; *Bet Shemuel* ad *Eben ha-'Ezer* (E.H.), 169, 46.

[91] See Loew, *Gesammelte Schriften* III, pp. 69–70; L. Finkelstein, *Jewish Self-Government in the Middle Ages,* N. Y., 1924, pp. 24–25.

[92] M. Güdemann, *Geschichte des Erziehungswesens,* Wien, 1888, III, pp. 115–119.

that time, and even centuries later, was not above polygamy. The ḥerem must be accounted the culmination of an inner Jewish moral development, seeing that there was moral aversion to it even in talmudic times; that this aversion had its origin and consistently grew and deepened in the Orient where polygamy was acceptable to the general population; and that the Jews, without force of the ḥerem, were employing various devices to maintain monogamous family standards.

Since the original ḥerem has not been preserved in documentary form, many doubts have arisen as to its operation. R. Solomon b. Adret, a Spanish scholar of the thirteenth century, reports from hearsay that the ḥerem expired in the year 1240, because the synod decreed it in force only to the beginning of the fifth millenium. This report, however, has no historical foundation. None of the German sources discussing this enactment know of any limit in time. Furthermore, R. Solomon himself admits it only as hearsay. Lastly, we have not even the testimony of R. Solomon himself, but of a later scholar quoting him. Yet legally, because of the great weight of Adret in Jewish law, even such uncertain testimony given in his name is granted full authority, and the ḥerem is regarded as having lesser binding force in law since the end of the fifth millenium.[93]

Soon after the enactment against polygamy, various questions arose as to its application or suspension in emergency cases. The first problem was that of the married man whose brother has died childless – when he becomes duty bound by biblical law to marry the widow. The French teachers generally held the levirate marriage in disfavor and preferred ḥaliẓah even where there was no complication of polygamy. Polygamy, therefore, did not add to the problem. In Germany, however, the levirate marriage was still practiced; there the question had to be settled, whether the ḥerem would make levirate marriage impossible if the levir was a married man, or whether it could be suspended in favor of fulfilling the biblical obligation of the levirate. There were

[93] See Finkelstein, o.c., p. 29 and p. 142 note 2; Responsa of R. Joseph Colon, 101; E.H. 1,10.

differences of opinion among the earlier authorities; some were inclined to suspend the ḥerem in such a case,[94] others taught that it was to remain in force, and that ḥaliẓah should therefore take the place of levirate marriage.[95] Later we hear of local enactments demanding that the levir yield to ḥaliẓah instead of marriage under polygamous conditions.[96] In the course of time legal opinion has become crystallized in favor of enforcing the ḥerem even where the levirate duty is involved.[97] Yet it cannot be taken as a settled matter in the law, except in the countries where preference for ḥaliẓah as against levirate marriage has become general even where there is no complication of polygamy.

A second case of emergency is that where the wife is barren. By talmudic law, if the wife remains childless for ten years, the husband must marry another in order to fulfill the duty of procreation. It was uncertain to the teachers whether the ḥerem was suspended for the duty of procreation. The view that it is suspended is given in a responsum in R. Gershom's own name.[98] This is also the view of some of the earlier scholars,[99] and many later teachers subscribe to it.[100] Yet it appears that once monogamy was accepted, the Jewish conscience on the subject became more and more sensitive, and refused to allow polygamy even if it meant that the husband would remain childless.[101]

A few other emergency situations arose where the application of the ḥerem was uncertain. If it occurred, as it sometimes did, that the wife was alienated by a gentile and converted to Christianity, would the husband be permitted to marry another wife or not? The matter was more compli-

[94] *Sefer ha-Terumah,* end of chapter on Ḥaliẓah; Responsa of R. Me'ir of Rothenburg, Prague, 866; *Nimmuke Joseph* ad *Alfasi* Yeb. 39b.

[95] A list of these early authorities is given in Responsa of R. Judah Mintz, 10, ed. Cracow, 1882, p. 18b.

[96] Responsa of R. Me'ir of Rothenburg, l.c. at the end.

[97] See E.H. 1,10, where the views of Karo and Isserles differ.

[98] Responsa of R. Me'ir of Rothenburg, ibid., 865.

[99] *Bet Joseph* ad *Ṭur* E.H., end of ch. 1, citing R. Samson b. Abraham; *Kaftor wa-Feraḥ,* ed. Luncz, p. 178; *Nimmuke Joseph,* Yeb. end of chapter 6.

[100] See Responsa of R. Me'ir Padua, 19.

[101] Responsa R. Solomon Luria, 65, giving his own view and quoting also the view of R. Eliezer b. Joel ha-Levi (REBJH); Responsa R. Judah Mintz, 10.

cated by the fact that in many cases it was not clear whether the conversion had been voluntary or compulsory. A similar problem arose if the woman was suspected of unfaithfulness or even when unfaithfulness was proven. Likewise a decision was necessary whether the ḥerem was in force when the woman's conduct was so improper as to make it obligatory on the husband by talmudic law to divorce her. In all these instances, if the woman refused to accept a divorce, could the husband marry another wife in violation of the ḥerem? The prevailing view of the authorities is to suspend the ḥerem in these instances.[102] The husband is permitted to remarry, but he must deposit with the rabbinic court a bill of divorcement for his wife and discharge whatever monetary obligations he has toward her, so that if the wife later chooses to accept the divorce voluntarily, it will be ready for her.

A similar emergency situation puzzling to the teachers of the law is afforded by the case where the wife becomes insane. Normal married life seems impossible with an insane wife, but divorce is also impossible because, in that condition, she has no legal personality to accept the divorce. R. Eliezer b. R. Joel ha-Levi, at the end of the twelfth century, cites a case where community authorities refused to free the husband, in such an instance, to marry a second wife. Some later scholars agree with this decision.[103] Yet the opposite view is well represented in the law, lifting the ḥerem in such a case and permitting the husband to marry again.[104]

Sensing the difficulties which the ḥerem would encounter in special emergency cases, the early authorities provided for the possibility of suspending it in an emergency case by joint decree of a hundred rabbis chosen from at least three territorial divisions.[105] This enactment is ascribed to Rabbi Jacob Tam of the twelfth century. It is still employed today where in the opinion of the rabbis a second marriage is

[102] Responsa R. Joseph Colon, 141; Responsa R. Me'ir Padua, 13; Responsa R. Solomon b. Adret, (RSBA), 557; Responsa R. Me'ir of Rothenburg, 1021; Isserles note to E.H. 1,10.

[103] See Responsa of Solomon Luria, ibid.

[104] See notes of Isserles and *Ḥelḳat Meḥoḳeḳ* ad E.H. 1,10.

[105] See Finkelstein, o.c., II, chapter II. He thinks, however, that this innovation is earlier than R. Tam.

morally justifiable. By this enactment, furthermore, the problem of all the emergency cases mentioned above can be solved (though it need not necessarily be resorted to) by lifting the ḥerem with the consent of a hundred rabbis. As a matter of policy, it is agreed by practically all scholars that whenever the husband is granted permission to enter into a second marriage, the annulling of the ḥerem by a hundred rabbis shall be required,[106] except perhaps where the wife is guilty of infidelity, in which case the prevalent practice is to grant the husband permission to marry another even without the decree of a hundred rabbis.

With every suspension of the ḥerem by decree of a hundred rabbis, the husband is required to deposit with the court a bill of divorcement for his wife and full payment of her ketubah.[107] In case of the wife's apostasy, and also of her proven unfaithfulness, the court not only receives the bill of divorcement from the husband for safekeeping, so that the wife may come and get it, but the court takes some action on the wife's behalf, to give her a semi-free status. It appoints an agent to act on the wife's behalf and to receive the bill of divorcement from him. In ordinary cases the court has no such power, but in these the law assumes that the wife is satisfied to be divorced, since she gets nothing out of her married state, cannot return to her husband, and is guilty of misconduct as a married woman, while in an unmarried state her misconduct would not be so grievous. Assuming that she is satisfied to be divorced, the law takes the liberty of carrying out her wishes in her absence.[108] Nevertheless, the bill of divorcement is still kept by the court, and she is not given permission to remarry until she comes and takes it herself.

The prohibition against polygamy initiated by the ḥerem

[106] *Noda' bi-Yehudah,* II,6–7, in the case of a woman who is lost; *Ḥatam Sofer,* E.H. 2, in a case of insanity; *Bet Ḥadash* ad *Ṭur* E.H. 1, at the end, for similar case; *Ḥatam Sofer,* E.H.3, for cases of conversion or unfaithfulness or other instances where the wife may not by law remain with her husband. The Karaites declare conversion equal to divorce.

[107] See *Noda' bi-Yehudah,* I,3.

[108] Responsa of R. Joseph Colon, 141; *Bet Joseph* ad *Ṭur* E.H. 1, at the end, quoting R. Israel Isserlein.

received acceptance in the Jewish communities step by step. In the thirteenth century, it had not yet been fully accepted in Venice and surrounding communities, although it was popular enough to create the legal assumption in the average marriage that it was a contract for monogamy.[109] By testimony of R. Samson b. Abraham, of the same period, the Jewish communities of France and Provence had not yet accepted the ḥerem, and polygamy was not unknown even among scholars.[110] In Italy, restriction of polygamy was not known in the twelfth century. Anatolio of the first part of the thirteenth century speaks of the moral superiority of monogamy, but seems to know no law against polygamy.[111] Some of the Italian rabbis as late as the sixteenth century permitted a second marriage to a childless husband without even the formality of officially suspending the ḥerem,[112] even though the ḥerem had then already been accepted. In such cases, however, permission of the rabbis alone for a second marriage was not sufficient; it had to be granted also by the Pope.[113] The southern part of Italy and Corfu apparently never quite accepted the ḥerem against polygamy, but plural marriage was nevertheless rare among them, for they used the above-mentioned ketubah clause and oath as the weapon against it. To this day the ketubah clause is still in use among them, more by reason of habit than because of actual need.

Neither R. Gershom nor the ḥerem was known in Spain till the thirteenth century,[114] probably because Spanish Jewry was sufficient unto itself in scholarship without having need of the German teachers. This does not mean, however, that polygamy was prevalent in Spain at that time. On the con-

[109] *Shilṭe ha-Gibborim* ad *Alfasi* Yeb. end of chapter 6; *Or Zaru'a* I, 181a. See Loew, *Gesammelte Schriften,* III, pp. 71–72.

[110] Quoted in *Bet Joseph* ad *Ṭur,* ibid. See *Iggerot ha-Rambam,* ed. Brünn, p. 3a.

[111] *Malmad ha-Talmidim,* Lyck, 1866, 101b; Shelden, *Uxor Hebraica,* p. 51.

[112] Responsa R. Me'ir Padua, 14; so also the *Takḳanot* of Farrara (1554) in Abraham, *Jewish Life in the Middle Ages,* Philadelphia, 1896, p. 71.

[113] Loew, o.c., p. 74, quoting Leon de Modena, *Historia degli Ritti Hebraici,* IV, 2, 2.

[114] Loew, o.c., pp. 78 f.

trary, R. Solomon b. Adret reports that there was hardly a case of bigamy in Catalonia, except one or two whose second marriage was prompted by the childlessness of the first.[115] A case of bigamy is reported to R. Asher, a contemporary of R. Solomon b. Adret in Toledo, of a man who is described as belonging to the vulgar class. The rabbi pronounced a special ban upon him.[116] Spanish Jewry liberally employed the ketubah clause, instead of the ḥerem, as safeguard against polygamy. On the other hand, in Castile and Navarre polygamy was practiced to some degree as late as the fourteenth century.[117] As the sanction of the Pope was required in Italy for a bigamous marriage, so was permission of the king required in Spain, and the price set was calculated to yield a considerable revenue to the ruler.[118] One of the moral decrees of the king which Spanish Jews had to obey in cases of polygamous marriages was not to divorce one wife without the other or others. That is, the polygamous husband either kept all his wives or had to divorce them all.[119]

Strictly speaking, the ḥerem was never recognized in Spain. Ethical rather than legal respect for the ḥerem grew as a result of the immigration of ashkenazic Jews into Spain, who were duty bound to honor it even after they had left the territorial jurisdiction of the ḥerem. The mingling of ashkenazic and sephardic Jews in the same community, with the former having a legal discipline for monogamy in the ḥerem of R. Gershom, made even the sephardic Jews respectful of its authority. The ashkenazic immigrants, however, concentrated in the northern part of Spain and were very sparse in the south. Therefore, southern Spain never reckoned seriously with the German enactment against polygamy.

The Jews of the Orient and North Africa never felt themselves bound by the ḥerem against polygamy. They did minimize polygamy by use of the ketubah clause and the

115 RSBA, I, 1205.
116 Responsa Asheri, 43,7.
117 Responsa R. Nissim, 48.
118 Loew, ibid., based on Kayserling, *Geschichte der Juden in Spanien und Portugal,* I,71; Joseph Jacobs, *Jews in Spain,* p. 25.
119 Loew, ibid., a decree of Theobald.

oath, but did not eliminate polygamy altogether. For one reason, the clause was not used in all marriages; for another, the clause made polygamy possible if the wife consented, and the oriental wife was easily made to consent to a second wife for her husband. The people were not altogether averse to polygamy, as was natural in a land where it was the tradition among the non-Jewish population as well. Nor did the scholars raise a positive protest against it. A case is cited of a man designated as a scholar desiring to take a second wife after he had agreed by the ketubah clause and oath not to marry another without the first wife's consent. The first wife does not give her consent to the second marriage and the scholar goes from rabbi to rabbi seeking a way out. At last he appeals to R. Levi b. Ḥabib in Jerusalem (at the beginning of the sixteenth century), who lavishes sympathy on him, because his present wife is too young to be a good housekeeper, while the woman he wishes to marry, one whom he had previously divorced, is a good housekeeper, knows his peculiarities, and can take care of his comforts. R. Levi is inclined to set aside the pre-nuptial agreement and oath, but without doing just that, he makes an appeal to the wife to consent to the husband's request for the second marriage. "If she were here," says R. Levi, "I would remind her that she did not have enough barley-bread; now she has wheat bread with full measure. . . . She worked for one piece of silver a week. I would remind her of her sister's marriage to one of the meanest men, how she suffered and how he took away her jewelry and clothing and pawned them and sold them. Is she better or of finer family than her sister? Whom would she have married here? . . . Thank God, she married a man of wisdom who supports her and gives her comforts. Gratefully she should live with him in love even though he bring to her side a rival wife. . . . How is she sure that she is entitled even to a fourth part of the husband she has?" [120]

Even with the pre-nuptial agreement for monogamy, in case the wife was childless, it was wisdom on her part not to raise objection to the husband's designs to marry another, be-

[120] Responsa R. Levi b. Ḥabib, 27, close to end.

cause the law would not sustain her protests. The law took the attitude that an agreement that interferes with the husband's duty of procreation is contrary to public policy and therefore not valid, or in the terminology of the Talmud, it is an agreement in violation of biblical law, hence lacking validity.[121]

In polygamous marriages, each wife had her own apartment, and the husband was required to divide the nights equally among all his wives. That was the usage in Mohammedan countries; in Christian lands the husband gave each wife in turn a full month of his company.[122] In the Orient, polygamy was more popular among the native Jews; the newcomers, if they were ashkenazic, observed the ḥerem of R. Gershom. In North Africa, on the contrary, the native Barbary Jews were essentially monogamous; of the ashkenazic Jews there were very few, but these were strictly monogamous, while the newcomers, Hispano Jews, were the polygamous element there.

There has been no significant change in attitude to polygamy on the part of North African or oriental Jews in the last centuries. An attempt was made lately, as a result of the westernization of Palestinian Jewry through the influence of Zionism and the influx of ashkenazic immigrants, to enforce the rule of monogamy on the sephardic settlers. The oriental Jews refused to accept the ḥerem or otherwise to restrict polygamy, and the rabbinate supported them in their position, hoping, as may well be believed, that they would gradually and naturally build up a standard of monogamy of their own by contact with the newer cultural influences now at work in Palestine.

121 Responsa R. Isaac b. Sheshet (RIBS), 97.

122 Responsa R. Solomon b. Simeon (RSBS), 624; see I. Epstein, *Responsa of R. Simon Duran,* London, 1930, pp. 88–89.

CHAPTER II

CONCUBINAGE[1]

I

THE legitimate marriage among the Jews has its roots in native national traditions; concubinage is an imported product from some foreign culture. The Hebrew term *pilegesh* is definitely foreign, and it is believed to be of Phoenicio-Semitic origin.[2] Judged by philological evidences, it may be said that the Hebrews were intermediaries between the east and west in transmitting the institution to classical antiquity, for the Greek and Latin terms for "concubine" are taken from the Hebrew.[3] Here we have a case of the Hebrews borrowing an institution from one foreign culture and then transmitting it to another. Our study, therefore, of the history of concubinage among the Jews derives its importance not only from the curiosity we have about the ancient Hebrew family, but also from the key position that the Hebrew concubine held in the development of concubinage in the civilized world of antiquity.

Concubinage originated in the Orient in prehistoric times. In historic times, the institution is recorded in its full legal development. The Code of Hammurabi (circa 2100 B.C.E.) is as definite about concubinage as about marriage, and some of its laws relating thereto are traceable to the more ancient Sumerian law. Whatever the philological evidences are,

[1] The substance of this chapter appeared in the *Proceedings of the American Academy for Jewish Research*, VI, pp. 153–188, under the title "The Institution of Concubinage among the Jews." I am glad, however, of the opportunity of presenting the subject again, because many of the conjectures that seemed to me plausible then do not seem so now, also because a composite picture of the oriental concubine, such as given in that monograph, is less desirable in a study of this nature than breaking up this unit into the Babylonian and Hebrew aspects of concubinage, as I propose to do in this chapter. Incidentally, I can add material, and recast the structure to advantage.

[2] See Gesenius, *Hebrew and Chaldee Lexicon*, s.v. פלגש.

[3] Hebrew פלגש; Greek παλλακίς; Latin *pellex*.

historical evidences show the Hebrews taking concubinage directly from the Babylonians; and it was Abraham, a contemporary of Hammurabi, who came into Canaan with a family constructed upon the legal lines established in Chaldee. In that family we find the concubine for the first time in the biblical records.[4] Evidently at the dawn of the history of the Jewish people concubinage is already found as part of the Hebrew family, and it gives the impression of being an institution already grown to maturity.

Perhaps because the institution of concubinage was foreign, perhaps also because it was not an institution for the people but for the nobility, as we shall see later, the Bible has no laws regulating concubinage. The pilegesh is mentioned in narrative portions of the Bible, where her legal status, as may be surmised, is not at all touched upon. Hence the Hebrew sources on the concubine are lamentably scanty. Added to the difficulty of lack of material is the lack of clarity. Concubinage is set into a family framework where grades of legitimacy run in the manner of spectroscopic colors, shading into one another. Besides the queen-wife[5] and the lawful wife,[6] we have the concubine,[7] the captive-wife,[8] the slave-wife,[9] and the slave-girl,[10] grading from the highest to the lowest degree of legitimacy. The ancients either did not have the acute legal mind to distinguish between them accurately, or really took no legal position on some of the details that now look vital to us, but left them to the taste or whims of the individual householder; or perhaps, having a definite legal opinion on these matters, they

[4] Gen. 22.24.

[5] Heb. גבירה, Gen. 16.4, or שרה, I Kings 11.3, or מלכה, Songs 6.8, 9; I Chron. 7.18. Babyl. *bêltu* – C.H. 146.

[6] Heb. אשה, Babyl. *aššatu* – C.H. 128, also *ḫirtu* – C.H. 138.

[7] Heb. פלגש, Babyl. *šugetu* – C.H. 144. Scholars render *esirtu* of the Assyrian, *esretum, isarti,* and *napṭarti* of the Hittite texts by "concubine." See S. Feigin, "The Captives in Cuneiform Inscriptions," in *American Journal of Semitic Languages* (AJSL) Vol. 50, No. 40, pp. 217 ff.

[8] There is no biblical technical term; the non-technical term is שבויה, Gen. 31.27. The talmudic technical term is יפת תאר.

[9] Heb. אמה, Babyl. *amtu* – C.H. 144. This describes the slave-wife the husband buys, or the one owned by the wife and put at disposal of the husband.

[10] Heb. אמה or שפחה, Babyl. *amtu* – C.H. 7. These terms are semi-technical and interchange with those of the previous group.

did not record it clearly enough in what is left to us of their writings. Lack of clarity in the sources accounts for the fact that when concubinage was taken over into the hellenic countries and therefrom into mediaeval Europe, all distinctions among the different grades of legitimacy were wiped away, except that between a wife and a concubine; and any woman was designated a concubine who had a more or less permanent agreement with a man for sexual companionship without being a full lawful wife. It included every form of sub-marital relation, slave-girls and mistresses as well.[11]

To get sharper outlines for our concepts, we must insist, in the first place, on keeping the concubine, the captive-wife, the slave-wife, and the slave-girl apart and distinct from one another. We must assume that this distinction was known to the ancients, whether we see it in all its details or not. In the second place, we must recognize that an institution of such antiquity has gone through changes of some significance in the course of its history. Even if we cannot follow each step, the more important changes can be traced. Therefore, historical tracing is necessary. The larger lines in this proposed historical chart will show us concubinage in existence in Babylonia as part of the ancient patriarchal family. It was taken over by the Hebrews, with some modifications, during a period of their history when they, too, lived under a patriarchal family organization. In the course of time the patriarchal family broke down among the Jews, and with it concubinage vanished. During that period of disintegration the Hebrews transmitted the concubine idea to the hellenic peoples. The latter converted the oriental concubine into the occidental. In the Orient she was a wife of a secondary grade of legitimacy; in the Occident she became an unmarried consort. In that transfiguration she made her way into mediaeval Europe and began assuming new

[11] Philo speaks of Bilhah and Zilpah as concubines (*Quod deus sit immutabilis*, 25,125), while Josephus (*Ant.*, I,19,8) finds difficulty describing their status. In *Wars*, I,25,6, he speaks of Herod making Archelaus a present of a concubine. He means a slave girl to be a slave-wife, because a concubine cannot be sold or given. Gen. Rab. 52.7, e.g., uses שפחה and פלגש interchangeably. Evidently, the hellenic definition of concubine dominated their understanding of that institution.

significance in the Jewish household and in rabbinic law.

The oriental concubine belongs distinctly to the oriental family structure. That family organization was a corporate household rather than a family unit. Husbandhood and wifehood indicated sex relations but not positions in the family, for there were a number of married couples within the family unit, holding various positions in it. The head of the family owned the entire household unit and he embodied within himself all the rights belonging to it. He was the *ba'al* or lord. A generic name, such as Abram, "exalted head," or "big chief," correctly described him. His children and children's children, they and their wives belonged to him.[12] All property was his, and that included all land and all chattels and all free-born females brought from the outside to be wives to the subordinate members of the household, as well as all male and female slaves and their offspring.[13]

For himself, he selected first of all a chief wife whose generic name might well be Sarai, "ruling lady," or Milkah, queen. She was the head of the women of the household and was respected by all males and females of the group. However, she addressed her husband, the head of the family, as "my lord." She was married with pomp and ceremony. Her marriage price or *mohar* was paid, her dowry came with her, and her contracts were written and sealed. In widowhood she returned to her parental home, if she had no children; or she remained the dowager queen, if she had children, especially if she was mother of the oldest son. No one dared take her to wife, not even the son who succeeded to the headship of the family.[14] In legally monogamous countries, there was only one principal wife; in polygamous lands there would be many, even the traditional seven hundred of Solomon.

In addition to the principal wife he maintained a harem of free-born or freed women who were his secondary wives, called concubines. The size of his harem was accounted a

[12] Gen. 46.8–28.
[13] Gen. 14.14; 17.27; Judg. 8.30; 12.9.
[14] C.H. 158.

token of his wealth and magnificence. Separate quarters were maintained for them, set aside from the apartment he gave to his principal wife.[15] The patriarch had the exclusive approach to these harems; no one in the family dared touch them while he was alive. At his death, the concubines might be freed to go their own way,[16] or they might remain as part of the estate to be taken over by the next head of the family. Often the new claimant to headship would establish his claim by taking possession of the harem.[17]

Wives and concubines did not exhaust the list of female possessions and sex luxuries of the oriental chieftain. Either in the harem of the concubines or in separate quarters, he kept a number of slave-wives. He acquired these either by outright purchase, or they were the property of his principal wife or wives, given him for sex indulgence and child-bearing. These, too, he kept to himself exclusively. There was no sense of marriage bond between them and the patriarch; it was only an exclusive property right. Anyone else approaching them would commit no adultery but theft. If these slave-wives were his own, not those given him by the principal wife, he could present them to other members of the family as slave-wives, after tiring of them himself.[18]

Finally, the household counted among its possessions a number of female slaves about whom there was no sense of wifehood at all. They were assigned work necessary in the household and were also used as tools for breeding the slave stock of the household. Their children were the "home-born" slaves. Usually they were paired with the male slaves in some semi-permanent form; otherwise they were free for

[15] See Feigin, o.c. pp. 232 and 240, top.

[16] C.H. 171 provides for freedom of the slave-wife after her husband's death; evidently the concubine could not be treated as if she were less independent.

[17] Inheriting the women of the head, except the chief wife (C.H. 158), is a common concept of oriental antiquity. Assyrian Code, I,43,46. However, inheriting the harem of concubines was indication of entering upon succession as head of the family; hence the case of Reuben (Gen. 35.22) and Absalom (II Sam. 16.22) and the resentment of Ishbosheth (II Sam. 3.8) as well as that of Solomon (I Kings 2.22). It is worth recording that this point was noted by Rabbi Menaḥem Schneersohn in *Ẓemaḥ Ẓedek*, E.H. 138,3.

[18] This may be the natural interpretation of Ex. 21.8–9, namely, if the master became displeased with her he must accept her ransom or give her to his son.

the approaches of the master himself or any of his sons or visiting guests.

This patriarchal family organization implied the magnificence of an oriental chieftaincy. It meant also the utter submergence of the individual into the group and the subservience of the group to the patriarch. It implied further a definition of legitimacy in social rather than legal terms, kinship in terms of ownership, and succession in terms of family government. In such a framework, the corporate household under a patriarchal head, there was room for a concubine in the oriental sense. An individual who was a subordinate member of the family did not have a concubine of his own; concubinage went with the headship. When this family organization broke down, therefore, the oriental concubine went out of existence. The individual husband, who counted merely as an individual, had a wife, not a "principal wife," and sex luxuries without marriage, but no "secondary wives" – that is, no concubines. In later times, therefore, royalty or nobility alone had concubines, for they perpetuated for a long time the original oriental patriarchal family tradition.[19]

The course of disintegration of the old time household was steady and effective as the economic life of the Jews changed from the pastoral to the agricultural, and then in turn from agricultural to commercial; as government became central, superceding tribal lines; and, above all, as religion and culture brought the individual to the position of supreme importance in the structure of human society. In post-exilic times, children were already to a large extent freed from parental authority; the age of majority as an age of independence was already recognized; and the tie between family and ancestral land was loosened by exile and by obsolescence of the jubilee and *go'el* institutions. The mature individual lived his own life. When he married, despite much meddling by his parents, he established his own home, a much simpler thing than the household of the past, a domestic center for father, mother, and children. Except for

[19] On the basis of biblical exegesis and talmudic interpretation, Maimonides comes to the same conclusion, that concubinage is permitted to kings only, not to the average Jewish citizen. See Yad, Melakim 4.4.

some different marriage laws and ideals, such as polygamy and slavery and child marriage and the mutual rights and responsibilities between husband and wife, their conception of family was not much different from our own. In such a family structure, oriental concubinage could not be continued. Therefore it is completely lost in the Apocrypha and in Mishnah and Gemara.

Though our information is as yet scant, we ought to record what we do know of the concubinage institution during the patriarchal family period, both in Babylonia and among the Hebrews.

Babylonia was a monogamous land; therefore concubinage was not permitted except where the rule of monogamy was justifiably lifted, namely, when the wife had no children or was ill with an incurable disease.[20] It is also logical to suppose that because of the rule of monogamy only one concubine was permitted but no more. The position of the concubine was inferior to that of the chief wife but superior to that of the slave-wife. She was evidently a free woman. Yet, within the circle of concubinage, the social position of one concubine was not necessarily equal to that of any other. For the concubine came from various sources and various social strata. In the ordinary family of modest parents, the girl with greater charm could bargain for a first class marriage, while her sister who was lacking in charm would be satisfied to enter a secondary marriage and become a concubine. Then, another concubine might come from a concubine caste, in that her mother was one, and her father was therefore willing to marry her off into concubinage.[21] The concubine might have an even lower social position, if her mother was a slave-wife. She was nevertheless born free and yet belonged to the slave caste. Concubinage was probably the matrimonial prospect for her. If the mother was a captive-wife, the daughter was probably likewise married off as a concubine.[22] Finally, the freed female captive or the freed

[20] C.H. 145,148.

[21] C.H. 183–184. See note 33 infra.

[22] See Feigin, o.c. p. 245; S. A. Cook, *The Laws of Moses*, London, 1903, p. 113.

female slave might herself become a concubine to some husband or even to her own master, if he retained her as a wife.[23]

In view of the fact that concubines came from various social strata, a uniform marriage ceremonial or uniform social standards for all could not be expected. The free-born concubine from a modest family or the daughter of a concubine mother had her dowry[24] at her marriage, and it stands to reason that her rights were secured by an instrument.[25] In other words, she also had a marriage contract. The purchase price was paid for her, and sometimes it was designated as *tirḫatu,* marriage price, the same as for the principal wife.[26] Logically it is possible that the husband also gave her wedding presents, called *nudunnu* by the Babylonians and *mattan* by the Hebrews; but we find no mention of this in the codes or contracts. It is more likely that instead of wedding presents, the husband assumed a "divorce price," obligating himself to pay her a certain amount at divorce over and above the standard obligations established by usage and law.[27] On the other hand, the concubine of a lower social position, such as a freed captive or freed slave, had no marriage contract[28] – which means also that she had no dowry and no wedding presents, else a contract would be necessary. *Tirḫatu* was not paid for her, but an ordinary

[23] This point will be further elaborated as we reach investigation of the ancient Hebrew concubine. The *naptartu* of the Hittites seems to correspond to just this type of concubine. She is superior to the *isarti* in that she is freed. See Feigin, o.c. pp. 232–235.

[24] C.H. 137,183,184.

[25] Kohler-Ungnad, *Hammurabi's Gesetz,* Leipzig, 1909, Nos. 2 and 3, which deal either with the case of a slave-wife or a concubine. But the inference is evident that if a slave-wife can have these specifications in the contract, a concubine surely can.

[26] Feigin, o.c. p. 238 cites a contract of a *šugetu* where the father receives *tirḫatu,* but the reading of *šugetu* is not certain. Also Koschaker-Ungnad, *Hammurabi's Gesetz,* No. 1420 has *tirḫatu* for an *amah.*

[27] So in Kohler-Ungnad, Nos. 2 and 3; Chiera in *Old Babylonian Contracts,* No. 252, cited by Feigin, ibid., p. 239, note 13a.

[28] C.H. 128. By this law we understand that it is possible for an illegitimate wife to have a contract, but it is impossible for a legitimate wife to have no contract. If there is no contract, therefore, the marriage is of inferior order. It also stands to reason that no contract is possible for a freed captive or slave, except an instrument of liberation and elevation; but not a marriage contract.

market purchase price. No special "divorce price" was stipulated, but she was entitled to the standard protection prescribed for the secondary wife in the event of divorce or widowhood.

The manner of dissolving concubinage was similar to divorcing a wife. The standard requirement was that "they shall return to that woman her dowry and shall give to her part of field, garden, and goods, and she shall bring up her children; from the time that her children are grown up, from whatever is given to her children, they shall give to her a portion corresponding to that of a son." [29] When the patriarch dies, the concubine can be taken in marriage by his successor, as mentioned above, or she can be given her freedom to go out and marry the man of her choice. It is to be supposed that if she has minor children, the same provision is made for her in widowhood as in the case of divorce – to raise her children and then depart with them and share in the gifts of parting which the family presents to the concubine's children. If her children are the only heirs, then she is probably provided for life from her husband's estate.[30]

Ordinarily her children are the only children of the husband, for a concubine can be taken only when the wife is sterile. In such a case, the children by the concubine are the legitimate heirs, else there would be no point in permitting the husband a concubine if her children would still remain illegitimate.[31] But there is a possibility in Babylonian law that the husband have children both by his wife and his concubine. That might occur in successive marriages, where the husband may have children by his first wife and may take a concubine as rival to his childless second wife. In such a case, the children are legitimate anyhow, and the father does not have to address them as "my children" in order to legiti-

[29] C.H. 137.

[30] Her right to leave the house taking her belongings with her follows from C.H. 171, granting such right even to a slave-wife. A provision for her remaining in the house of her husband without marriage to any of the heirs is not made in the Code. Only the matron has that right – C.H. 171–172. Among the Hebrews, it was a matter of honor on the part of the heirs to take care also of the father's concubines after his death, and the new head of the family became their guardian. II Sam. 3.7; I Kings 2.17 f.

[31] C.H. 105. More explicitly, Assyrian Code, I,41.

matize them, as is necessary in the case of children by a slave-wife.[32] They cannot be dismissed from the estate with empty hands, though they do not receive an heir's portion. The daughter of the concubine gets a dowry with which to be married; [33] the sons get gifts as substitutes for inheritance.[34]

[32] C.H. 170–171. More will be seen in Hebrew law, as will be shown later.

[33] C.H. 183–184 has two interpretations. Some believe that they speak of the daughter of a concubine wife, others believe that they speak of a daughter who is a concubine. The first interpretation is by now antiquated, and the second seems to be the one acceptable to most scholars. The question now arises, how is a daughter a concubine before she is married; what makes her a concubine? Landsberger and Koschaker believe that *šugetu*, the term here employed for concubine, is a minor priestess, and can therefore be a concubine before she is married. This point of view may prove more logical if we assume that female priesthood was conceived of as marriage to a god of the temple, whence that marriage can be either of the first order, yielding a *naditum*, or of the lower order, yielding the *šugetum*. On the basis of such a theory, the two sections of the Code are still not sufficiently clear. Why should the obligation of marrying the *šugetu* fall upon the father or his heirs, if she is already married to a temple god? The dowry would seem to be due to her at the time of consecration, regardless whether she marries afterwards or not, as is the case of the other temple women recorded in sections 178–182. Then again, her marriage and her begetting offspring are assumed, else the Code would provide for disposal of her dowry after her death, as it provides for it in the other cases. Apparently, a *šugetum* without marriage is not conceived by the Code.

Feigin criticises this theory (op. cit., pp. 238–243) and believes that the unmarried *šugetum* is one who belongs to the *šugetu* class even while in her father's house; that is, she is the child of a *šugetu* mother. With no knowledge of Assyriology, I have no opinion on the matter from a linguistic point of view, but the suggestion of Dr. Feigin seems to be the only logical one from a sociological view. We know that the children within the family were graded according to their mothers. Jacob groups separately the children of his wives and the children of his maid-servants (Gen. 33.2); Jephthah is recorded (Judg. 11.1–2) as belonging to his mother and sharing her status of inferiority in the family. The son of the *amah* and her daughter share the mother's status to the point where Code Hammurabi finds it necessary to declare them free after their father's death and not to be taken by the heirs as slaves. And that applies only to the *amah* who is a slave-wife; the regular slave girl who is not a wife and begets a child by her master, remains a slave after the master's death, and so do her children. If, therefore, in every social stratum, the children are exactly like the mother, there is no reason to doubt that the children of concubines have the social status of concubines. As in Jewish law there is a status of slavery, even though the slave has no master, so it is not impossible that in the ancient Babylonian law there was a status of concubinage applied to girls, even though they had no husbands.

Hence my justification in considering sections 183 and 184 as yielding information about the daughters born of concubine wives.

[34] C.H. 137 speaks of "whatever is given to her (the concubine's) chil-

The dismissal of the sons of concubines from the estate was generally arranged for by the father himself during his lifetime, or was specified in the marriage contract between the father and his chief wife; [35] else there was trouble after the father's death, because the children of concubines counted themselves as fully legitimate children and aspired to a full share.[36]

The concubine's marriage seems to have been lacking in some of the more prominent ceremonials. One of the ceremonies was the pronouncement of a marriage formula, such as "Be thou my wife" or "She is my wife." [37] Now, the term wife in a non-technical sense is used both for wife and concubine,[38] but in a legal formula it is technical and applied to a principal wife only. In Assyrian law, the concubine may be raised to wifehood by pronouncement of the formula "She is my wife," [39] which means that as concubine she is not a "wife" technically. Therefore it is fair to assume that either no marriage formula was pronounced at the marriage of a concubine or the formula was not that of the regular marriage. Another ceremonial prominent at legitimate marriages was the veiling of the bride. We have that from Assyrian and Hebrew sources.[40] A wife, among the Assyrians, was veiled at her marriage and also had to veil herself when going out in the street, in contrast with the unmarried girl

---

dren." It is also evident that if the concubine daughter gets her dowry in lieu of inheritance (C.H. 184), the concubine's son cannot be dismissed emptyhanded. More explicit information on this subject will be found in our treatment of Hebrew law.

[35] See Feigin's discussion of the status of the *naptarti* in the Hittite texts, ibid., pp. 232–235, where by pre-nuptial agreement the *naptarti* sons are excluded from first rank succession. Abraham dismissed the concubines' sons with gifts during his lifetime. Gen. 25.6.

[36] The Hittite texts, as above, show the danger of a concubine's son claiming full right of succession. Jephthah's story (Judg. 11.2) illustrates the same point.

[37] Kohler-Ungnad, No. 5; Assyrian Code, I,41. See JMC pp. 55–57 and note 8.

[38] Kohler-Ungnad, Nos. 2,3,424, and Gen. 16.3; 30.9; Ex. 21.4; Deut. 21.11, 13.

[39] Assyrian Code, I,41. Yet it is possible that the *esirtu* is lower than the *šugetu*.

[40] Assyrian Code, ibid. and Gen. 24.65; Ezek. 16.8; Ruth 3.9.

whose face was uncovered.[41] The concubine, like the wife, had to veil her face when going out, but was not veiled at her marriage as part of the ceremonial. That ceremony belonged to her elevation from concubinage to wifehood, but was evidently not afforded her in her state of concubinage. The other ceremonials of marriage, the contract, the *tirḥatu,* the *nudunnu,* we have seen were optional and were employed in some concubine marriages and not in others.

Yet, though she was a wife of inferior rank, the concubine was nevertheless a wife in the legal sense. The absence of some of the standard ceremonials did not take from her the legal position of wifehood. The fact that contract and *tirḥatu* and *nudunnu* were possible with concubinage marriage would show that she was legally a wife. We have also seen that concubinage is counted an infringement upon the law of monogamy and is permitted only when the principal wife is childless. The law of divorce makes no distinction between wife and concubine, except in a minor matter, that of a divorce price. What the Assyrian law has to say about the *esirtu,* that she has to be veiled when she goes out, must also apply to the Babylonian *šugetu;* for the *šugetu* if anything is more a wife than the *esirtu.* And veiling is distinctly symbolic of the private right belonging to the husband, in the sense that the approach of another man would be adultery. The same feeling is implied in the Code of the Babylonians, where a distinction is drawn between the principal wife and the concubine in respect to a son's cohabiting with them *after the father's death;* but no such distinction is drawn while the father is alive, for evidently it is adultery in either case.[42]

The picture here drawn is of the official Babylonian concubine, the *šugetu.* Variations from that standard are found in the large collection of deeds and contracts, yet none of these variations can be identified as distinct social institutions by themselves. The one variation we should like to follow out as a distinct social entity is the captive-wife. She

[41] Assyrian Code, I,40. Again, the *esirtu* may be lower than the *šugetu.*

[42] C.H. 157–158. Fuller information on this subject can be derived from the Hebrew sources, as will be shown later.

is necessarily different from the *šugetu,* because the latter is free while she is a captive. But unfortunately there is no such distinct class in Babylonia. She is either part of the *šugetu* group or she falls into the category of the *amtu,* the slave-wife,[43] for after all the captive is also a slave. Either is possible, and Babylonian law is non-committal. We have to turn to Assyrian and Hittite sources, where the captive-wife is a distinct legal figure, technically called *esirtu.* But the difficulty is that there the *šugetu* is not known, and hence we do not know whether *esirtu* is a substitute for *šugetu* and equal to her in position or a new type of inferior wife.

The Assyrian law lays down the rule that the wife at her marriage must be veiled, and must be veiled when she goes out in public. The *esirtu* is not veiled at her marriage but must be veiled when she goes out. The *amtu,* meaning slave-girl or slave-wife, may not be veiled when going out. The sons of the *esirtu* are not heirs by law unless there are no sons by a principal wife.[44]

That the *esirtu* is higher than the *amtu* is thus definitely recorded in the law, yet that does not give us sufficient information, for the *amtu* here referred to may mean the unmarried slave-girl. Granted that the slave-wife is referred to and our conclusion, therefore, would be that the *esirtu* is higher than the slave-wife, she still does not seem to be equal in position to the Babylonian *šugetu.* In Babylonia only one *šugetu* is permitted, in Assyria many *esirti* are permitted. The *šugetu* is, or at least may be, a freeborn woman, having the backing of a family, bringing a dowry with her, dictating property rights and divorce rights by statutory provisions or written contract; while the *esirtu,* if she really is a captive woman, is naturally thrown on the mercy of her master. The children of the *šugetu,* even when they are not

[43] Feigin, o.c., suggests (pp. 242–3) that the ideogram *šugetu* may really be read *esirtu.* That still would not change our problem where the captive-wife belongs. The *šugetu* is definitely free, if she has contracts and *tirḥatu* and definite rights, while the *esirtu* of Assyria and the Hittites is definitely not free. If *esirtu* is to be read in the Babylonian code and contracts, it must be only an indication that the original concubine came from among the captives. In the course of time her status changed but her name remained.

[44] Assyrian Code, I,40–41.

heirs, have some rights in the estate; no such rights are given to the children of the *esirtu*. Elevation to sonship in Babylonia is possible also for children of the slave-wife; in Assyria no such provision is made even for children of the *esirtu*. Evidently, even if the *esirtu* is higher than the slave-wife, she still is not the standard concubine, because she is not free and belongs rather to the slave-wife category.

The distinction is made clearer in the Hittite law. There we have two kinds of captive-wives, the *esirtu,* who is not free, and the *napṭartu,* who is a freed captive. One can have many *esirti* but only one *napṭartu*. The children of the *esirtu* can have no claim to inheritance; while it is possible for sons of the *napṭartu* to rise to the rank of equality with the children of the wife, probably by a special adoption ceremonial.[45]

The scanty sources, therefore, while yielding very indistinct information about the status of the captive-wife, permit of certain conclusions: (1) that the captive-wife, unless she be a freed captive, is inferior in rank to the standard concubine; (2) that she is always superior to the slave-wife; (3) and that of utmost importance to her social and legal position is the question whether she has been freed or not, whereby may be determined whether she is to be classed among the concubines or among the slave-wives.

The lowest level of inferior wifehood in all the records of the ancient Orient is that of the slave-wife. Both the unmarried slave-girl and the slave-wife are designated by the same term, *amtu,* which sometimes causes confusion. Additional confusion is created by the fact that the slave-wife may be one owned by the husband himself, or owned by the wife and given to the husband for the sake of begetting children. Yet despite some uncertainties we obtain a fairly clear account in our sources of the status of the slave-wife in Babylonia.

The slave-wife was a wife only in the sense of property but not of consecrated marriage. She brought no dowry, she had no contract, she had no marriage ceremony, she needed no divorce. If she had no children, she could be sold as a slave; if she had children, she could not be sold but could be reduced to slavery in her master's house, or given her freedom

[45] See Feigin, ibid., p. 233.

to go where she pleased.[46] At her husband's death, she did not remain a widow in his house, nor was she inherited by the sons as a slave, but her freedom was granted her.[47] It may be supposed that one of the heirs might propose a marriage of concubinage to her, and she was free to accept the proposal. There was no sense of adultery – just a violation of property rights – for any one cohabiting with her during the master's life; nor was there a sense of incest for a son cohabiting with her during his father's life or taking her in marriage after his death.[48] It must have been very unusual, or perhaps it was impossible by law, for the slave-wife to be raised to legitimate wifehood by pronouncement of a legitimitization formula, such as was sometimes used for children of a slave-wife or for the concubine.[49]

The children of the slave-wife were heirs by law, if there were no children by a lawful wife.[50] If there were sons by the principal wife, the sons of the slave-wife were not heirs by law but might be heirs by adoption, that is, by the father during his life calling them "my children."[51] As heirs by adoption, they shared the estate equally with the legitimate sons, but the latter had first choice. Without adoption, and where there were legitimate heirs, they were entitled to nothing of their father's estate, but at least they gained their personal freedom and the heirs could not hold them as slaves.[52]

[46] C.H. 146–147. This section deals with the wife as owner of the maidservant, but logically the same applies where the husband is owner of the slave-wife.

[47] C.H. 171.

[48] This may be derived from the Assyrian Code I, 40, where the maidservant like the harlot is not veiled; and from C.H. 158, prohibiting only the chief wife to the sons after the father's death.

[49] C.H. 170–171; Assyrian Code, I,41.

[50] This would be evident from the fact that the childless wife may give her husband a maidservant for the purpose of begetting legitimate children. But this does not prove conclusive, as we are stating further that the legal fiction may here be invoked whereby the legitimate wife becomes mother of the offspring begotten by the maidservant. Another inconclusive proof is from Assyrian Code I,41, where the sons of captive-wives are declared heirs by law, if there are no other sons. Here too the weakness consists in the fact that the captive-wife in Assyria may be the equal of the Babylonian *šugetu* and, therefore, higher in rank than a slave-wife.

[51] C.H. 170.

[52] C.H. 171.

It was said before in passing that there are two kinds of slave-wives, one owned by the husband, and another by the wife and given to the husband for begetting children, in the event the wife is childless. As for the slave-wives themselves, they seem to have the same status. But as for the children begotten by them respectively, one cannot feel sure that their status is the same. It is possible that the son of a slave-wife owned by the chief wife is born into sonship and does not have to be adopted, for the legal fiction makes the chief wife his mother, in addition to the master being his natural father. If this is so, he is always an heir by law, even though of inferior rank. We cannot derive clear information on this subject out of the theoretical teachings of the codes, because all classes of female slaves are designated by the same term, *amtu*. The Bible yields better information, because there we find the application of theoretical law in actual cases of slave-wives.

II

We turn our attention now to concubinage in the Bible. In most respects, the biblical pilegesh is equal to the Babylonian *šugetu,* for, as mentioned, the first pilegesh among the Hebrews belongs to a family definitely constructed on Babylonian traditions. Yet in some respects the pilegesh is different from the *šugetu,* the difference arising out of the influence of native Hebrew family organization.

Babylonia was monogamous; hence only one concubine was permitted and only when the wife was childless. The Hebrews were polygamous; therefore many concubines were permitted, and the wife could raise no objection, whether fruitful or childless, whether she gave her husband a maidservant or not.[53]

Hebrew concubines, like those of the Babylonians, came from various sources and various stations in life. They were daughters of lowly families, or born of mothers themselves concubines or captive-wives or slave-wives. The greater sup-

[53] Witness the case of Solomon in I Kings 11.3. Gen. 25.6 gives the impression that Abraham, too, had concubines either in Sarah's lifetime or in the lifetime of Keturah.

ply of concubines came from foreign women,[54] yet Hebrew concubines were not unknown.[55]

A considerable number of concubines came from the lower ranks of the household, the slave-wives. The slave-wife and the concubine, while not very far from each other in social rank, were contrasts in legal position. The concubine was free, the slave-wife was not. Of course, that difference is far-reaching in the law, but is not inherent in the person. It is a legal difference that can be changed by a legal formality. When the master freed his slave-wife and yet retained her in his household as a wife, she became a concubine. A case of this kind is that of Bilhah, slave-wife of Jacob. All through the biblical account she is called the *amah* of Rachel, that is, the maidservant, which was really her position. Only once, immediately after the report of the death of Rachel, is she called pilegesh.[56] It should not be assumed that the Bible confused terms; but, then, how did the *amah* become a pilegesh? The answer is: she belonged to Rachel, and with Rachel's death she became free, in accordance with old Babylonian law.[57] Yet she was retained by Jacob as wife. A freed slave-wife retaining a position of inferior wifehood could be nothing but a concubine.

A similar inference can be drawn from a levitical law which prescribes a minor penalty for lying with a female slave betrothed unto a man.[58] The law requires an investigation, and assuming that the slave-girl had not been freed, there is

[54] Sigismund Rauh in a dissertation on *Hebräische Familienrecht in vorprophetische Zeit,* Berlin, 1907, argues that all concubines of the Hebrews were foreigners. Gideon's concubine was Canaanitish; Essau's concubine, Timna, was a Chorite; so was Rizpah, the concubine of Saul; Manasseh had an Aramean. He is compelled to drive the matter too far, however, when he insists that the pilegesh of Gibeah was a foreigner to the man of Judah. See Wilkinson, *The Ancient Egyptians,* I, pp. 319 f; P. Meyer, *Das Römisches Koncubinat,* Leipzig, 1895, p. 8.

[55] Judg. 8.31; 19.1; II Sam. 5.13.

[56] Gen. 35.22. Abimelech is called "the son of his maidservant" (Judg. 9.18) although he was the son of a pilegesh, but this is no confusion of terms, only a rhetorical insult. At any rate, pilegesh may be spoken of as *amah,* but the reverse is impossible.

[57] C.H. 171.

[58] Lev. 19.20. The tannaitic interpretation of this law as referring to a half-free female slave betrothed to a Hebrew slave (Sifra ad l.c.) is peculiarly artificial.

no death penalty. This law should be understood to say that if she was freed, then she is no longer slave-wife but concubine, and contact with her constitutes adultery; but if she was not freed, there is no adultery. Because the freeing of a slave-wife and thus elevating her to the position of concubine requires no special public ceremonial, the law urges an investigation.

There is likelihood that the Hebrews had another category of concubine entirely unknown to the Babylonians. There was a time in Hebrew history when the patronymic family was fully established, and yet survivals of the metronymic family had not yet wholly vanished. At that time, the people thought of a metronymic marriage as inferior and yet a marriage, metronymic children as non-heirs and yet not slave-children. They gave the metronymic wife the name pilegesh (sometimes *zonah*) for lack of a better designation. This explains the concubine of Gideon who lived in Sichem (Judg. 8.31) and perhaps also the concubine of Gibeah (Judg. 19).[59]

From the levitical law cited above we can also infer that the pilegesh, like the Babylonian *šugetu,* was considered a married woman, and her contact with another man was treated as adultery. Even in the ancient Athenian law, a concubine could be charged with adultery.[60] For this reason, when a concubine was violated by another man, the old law required the husband to set her aside and never approach her again.[61] For this reason also, both deuteronomic and the levitical laws prohibiting marriage with a father's wife make no mention of any difference between the father's principal wife and his concubine, as does the Code of Hammurabi.[62]

Evidence to the contrary, that there is no adultery in the case of a concubine, is offered from the following. Reuben [63]

[59] See "Beena Marriage in Ancient Israel," by J. Morgenstern, in ZAW, VI, 1929, p. 95, note 4.

[60] P. Meyer, *Römisches Koncubinat,* l.c.

[61] II Sam. 20.3; Gen. 49.4. See Jub. 33.9. The expression "defilest the couch" in Gen., ibid., implies that it is now to be unclean for Jacob.

[62] Deut. 27.20; Lev. 18.8; C.H. 158.

[63] Gen. 35.22.

and Absalom[64] cohabited with their fathers' concubines without a death penalty. The pilegesh of Gibeah (Judg. 19) acted as though she could go without a divorce and was offered for rape without a thought of the crime of adultery. However, these evidences are not conclusive. The cases of Reuben and Absalom reflect the older law, when the concubine after her husband's death went over to the harem of his son, who succeeded to the headship of the family. In case of rebellion, the son showed his conquest by taking over the concubines of his father. Reuben and Absalom were both pretenders to headship of the family in their fathers' lifetimes. It was rebellion. Victory would have given them the right to the concubines in the same manner as would natural succession. If a capital crime was committed, it was in the rebellion, not so much in contact with the concubines. It was, therefore, a father's indulgence that saved them, not the pettiness of the crime. Code Hammurabi and the earlier records of the Bible still stand by this law, but the deuteronomic legislator knows the new law under which the concubine does not go with the estate, and a father's wife, after the father's death, is prohibited to the sons, whether chief wife or inferior wife.

Nor does the case of the pilegesh of Gibeah prove that the concubine was not married legally. Her being offered for outrage in preference to the host's matron is due to her inferior position, not to the choice of a lesser crime. In the same manner Lot offers his betrothed daughters for rape (Gen. 19.8), even though rape of a betrothed maiden is admittedly a capital crime. The flight to her parental home without ceremony is not to be taken in a legal sense but as a simple narrative, depicting a spoiled wife.[65]

As for Babylonia, so for the early Hebrews our conclusion is that the concubine was a married woman in the legal sense.

[64] II Sam. 16.22.

[65] The word *wa-tizneh* in Judg. 19.2 is taken by some to mean "she committed adultery," but Septuagint, Onkelos, Talmud (Git. 6b) take it in the sense of "she deserted him." Outside of this, it is not impossible that the ceremonies of divorce were not required of the pilegesh, especially a metronymic concubine whose divorce consists in her leaving her husband, since she retains her independent position.

We have no information from Hebrew sources whether the more prominent marriage ceremonials were observed at her marriage, such as contract, *mohar,* dowry, veiling, and the like. It is logical to assume for the Hebrews, as we have assumed for the Babylonians, that the public formalities were at a minimum and that the contract (if the Hebrews then had a marriage contract at all) and the exchange of marriage gifts were possible for concubines of higher social position and unusual for concubines of lower position.

If the pilegesh was married, then logically she required a divorce. But the form of divorce, even for a principal wife, other than sending her out of the house, is not known until we come to deuteronomic times, when a writ of divorcement was introduced. Therefore we can say nothing about the manner of divorcing a concubine in the earlier period, and it is not impossible that when the written divorce was introduced for wives, concubines continued to be divorced in the more primitive manner by sending them away; just as their marriages lacked public ceremonial so did their divorces. A divorce price, such as is known among the ancient Babylonians, was not known among the Hebrews of that age, whether for wife or concubine.

The concubine was entitled to maintenance and marital companionship from her husband, for this right was granted by the Hebrews even to the slave-wife.[66] In her widowhood, too, it was customary to retain the concubine in the household and provide for her support, even when she was not to be taken up as concubine of the heir.[67] But it is to be assumed that, as a widow, she could choose to leave the household and return to her parental home.[68] On the matter of property rights of the concubine, the Bible has as little to say as on the property rights of the matron. It is to be supposed that if she had any personal property her husband managed it during their married life, and at divorce or death of

[66] Ex. 21.10.

[67] So Ishboshet was the guardian of Saul's pilegesh (II Sam. 3.7) and Solomon was in charge of Abishag (I Kings, 2.17 f.).

[68] This was even the privilege of the slave-wife, according to C.H. 171, and certainly the right of a free-born concubine. There is no reason for believing that Jewish law was different in this respect.

the husband, when she left the household, she took her property with her.[69]

The offspring of concubines counted as children in the family,[70] but ranked inferior to children of the matron.[71] Their support and provision for their marriage are not specified in the Bible, but Code Hammurabi[72] will justify our conjecture that ordinarily these were provided for them in the Hebrew family. In the absence of legitimate sons, the concubine's sons are heirs by law.[73] A legal formula of adoption into sonship is not required, nor is it known in practice in Hebrew law. When there are sons of the matron, the position of the sons of the concubine is that of secondary heirs. They can claim succession, they can usurp central power in the family, unless the legitimate sons are careful.[74] By law they are entitled to a minor portion of inheritance in the form of gifts.[75]

[69] The property right of a free woman, even a concubine, as taught by the Babylonian Code, is valid in Jewish law even down to the Talmud. There is no reason for suspecting a different law in the Bible.

[70] Thus Amalek, son of a pilegesh, counts fully in the family of his father Elifaz (Gen. 36.12; I Chron. 1.36) and Zelaphehad was the offspring of a pillegesh (Num. 27.1–5; I Chron, 7.14) but carried on the family name and estate.

[71] See Gen. 33.2, 6, where Jacob arranges his sons in line of danger putting the sons of the maidservants first, even though he counts them as sons. See also the chronological tables in I Chron. 2.46, 48 and 3.9.

[72] C.H. 137, 183–4.

[73] Even Eliezer, who was a home-born slave, could be heir to Abraham, if there were no sons (Gen. 15.3). Philo, *Quis rerum divinarum heres,* 1,2, (in the MSS.), takes Eliezer as the son of Abraham, born of a slave-wife. This is the law of the Babylonian Code in respect to the slave-wife given the master by the matron. Whether it applies to any other slave-wife as well we do not know. The Assyrians apply the law to the captive-wife.

[74] Hence, Abraham sends away the sons of the concubines, so that they will not trouble Isaac (Gen. 25.6) and such trouble did arise in the case of Abimelech (Judg. 9) and Jephthah (Judg. 11), who was son of a metronymic concubine (*zonah*).

[75] Gen. 25.6. C.H. 137 also indicates that when the children of a concubine are grown up they get some gift in the form of secondary inheritance. That Jephthah was sent off empty-handed from his father's estate (Judg. 11.2) is to be taken to represent violence on the part of his brothers. Or, it may have been the rule for the son of a metronymic concubine, where the child follows the mother's family, not the father's. It should be noted that children of concubines were capable of succession in early Greece and Egypt. See Meyer, *Römisches Koncubinat,* p. 8; Seymour, *Life in Homeric Age,* pp. 149 f; Wilkinson, *The Ancient Egyptians,* I, pp. 319 f. See also I. Benzinger, *Archä-*

No less than in Babylonian and Assyrian law, the captive-wife in Hebrew law holds a place distinct from the concubine. And no less than in the Babylonian and Assyrian documents, information concerning the captive-wife derived from the Bible is meager and uncertain. The Bible speaks of the captive wife only once, in the following verses of Deuteronomy: "When thou goest forth to battle against thine enemy and Yahweh thy God delivereth him unto thy hand and thou carriest away his captive; and thou seest among the captives a woman of goodly form and hast desire unto her and wouldst take her to thee to wife: Then thou shalt bring her into thy house and she shall shave her head and pare her nails; and she shall put the raiment of her captivity from off her, and shall remain in thy house and bewail her father and her mother a full month; and after that thou mayest go in unto her and be her husband (or master) and she shall be unto thee as a wife. And it shall be, if thou have no delight in her, that thou shalt let her go whither she will; but thou shalt not sell her for money, nor reduce her to servitude, because thou hast humbled her." [76]

Her position in her captor's house after she has gone through the above ceremony, whether that of wife or concubine or slave-wife, we are not told. Logic would lead us to believe that her place is that of a slave-wife. A captive woman is generally either sold as a slave or retained by her captor as such. In the Book of Exodus the captive and the slave are represented as holding the same social position.[77] And it is striking to note that the deuteronomic legislation here, protecting the rights of the captive woman, equals in prominent features the Covenant legislation [78] in respect to rights of the slave-wife. Yet, logical as this assumption may

ologie (1907), p. 114. In Arabian law even the child of a captive woman is legitimate if the mother is of Arabian blood – W. Robertson Smith, *Kinship and Marriage in Early Arabia*, second edition, p. 90.

[76] Deut. 22.10–14.

[77] Dr. S. Feigin, o.c. p. 224, makes the interesting observation that in the parallel passages of Ex. 11.4–5 and Ex. 12.29 the phrases "the first born of the slave-girl" and "the first born of the captive" imply that the captive and the slave were of equal social position.

[78] Cf. Ex. 21.7–11 with Deut. 22.10–14.

be, we cannot be sure of it. We have seen that in Assyrian law the captive is superior to the maidservant. In the Bible, too, we find a "freeing" process provided for the slave-wife,[79] but "letting her go" is sufficient for the captive woman, evidently because she is conceived by the law as only imprisoned, not enslaved. Furthermore, the ceremonial prescribed for the captive-wife includes removing her garments of captivity, which is equivalent to saying that by this ceremony she becomes free.

We therefore remain in doubt as to the position of the captive-wife, and conjecture on this matter seems to be of no avail. We must leave it unsettled. But we permit ourselves to express the following convictions. She is definitely not a lawful wife. The ceremony is intended to raise her out of the state of captivity and to introduce her into the household. If by that she becomes free, her status thereafter is that of a concubine; if she still remains a chattel of the master, then she is no more than a slave-wife.

Fortunately we have more information from biblical records about the status of the slave-wife than about either the concubine or the captive-wife. Two types of slave-wives are recorded in the Bible, that owned by the matron and given to the husband for the purpose of begetting more children, and that owned by the master and taken by him or raised by him to wifehood. There is no difference between them as regards the social or legal position of the slave-wife herself; this arises only in respect to the legal position of the children begotten by them.

The slave-girl, generally designated as *shifḥah*,[80] was simply a slave in the household, and unmarried intercourse with her by the members of the household was quite common. But usually she was paired off with some household member, a male slave or the master's son or the master himself. If united with a male slave for enduring sex relations her status did not change; she remained a slave as before and

[79] Lev. 19.20.

[80] The slave-wife who is originally the slave of the matron is often called the *shifḥah* of the matron (Gen. 16.8, etc.) because in respect to the matron she is not an *amah* but a *shifḥah*. However, this rule cannot be stretched too far.

her children were slaves.[81] But if she was designated as companion of the master or his son, her position changed to that of a slave-wife, generally called *amah*.[82] As *amah* she had a place in the harem, but continued to perform her usual tasks of slavery.

The suggestion that a slave-girl may be elevated to the position of slave-wife is logically correct but sociologically wrong. The Bible knows of such an elevation only in the case of a female slave belonging to the matron and given as wife to the master. It knows also of a slave becoming husband of his master's daughter, which represents a similar elevation.[83] Logically, it should be possible for the master to look around among his female slaves, Hebrew or foreign or home-born, choose one to be his wife, and thus elevate her to wifehood. Yet not a single case of this kind is found in the Bible. The reason is sociological. It was considered beneath the dignity of the master to choose his consort from among his female bondwomen, who were slaves and foreigners. And if he had special desire for one of his female slaves, he was permitted intercourse with her without raising her to wifehood. As for the Jewish female slave, it seems that until we come to the deuteronomic period there were no unattached Jewish female slaves in the Hebrew household at all.

The Hebrew tradition was against Jewish slaves altogether, both for males and for females. That is why we have the limit of six years for the Hebrew male slave and the injunction to treat him as hireling rather than slave.[84] The case of a Hebrew slave occurred only when he was sold for theft or debt. Hence he is freed on the sabbatical year, because the debt is cancelled. If, then, debt was the only cause for slavery among the Hebrews at the time of the corporate patriarchal family, when the obligation was borne by the family and not the individual, the male members carried the burden of paying for the debt and not the females. The females could best be used to raise money by marriage, either

[81] This is evident from Gen. 21.4.

[82] In the technical sense *amah* is a slave-wife, but in its non-technical meaning it is interchangeable with *shifḥah*. Cf. I Sam. 25.41; II Sam. 6.22.

[83] I Chron. 2.34–35.

[84] Ex. 21.2; Deut. 15.12 f; Lev. 25.39 f.

full marriage with *mohar,* or secondary marriage as slave-wife, with a purchase price. Therefore there were no unmarried Hebrew female slaves. It is only when we come to the period of Deuteronomy, when individual responsibility developed and women under certain conditions had a reasonable amount of independence, that we find any unmarried Hebrew female slaves.[85] It was possible then for a woman to be sold into slavery, or to sell herself into slavery[86] for payment of a debt. In that case, the laws applying to the male slave also apply to the female. By this interpretation we understand why the Covenant law specifies that the female slave "shall not go out as the male slaves" and the deuteronomic law treats them both alike. For in the Covenant law we deal with the slave-wife, since there was no other kind of Hebrew female slave, and in Deuteronomy we deal with the unmarried Hebrew female slave. Likewise, in the Covenant law the female slave is sold by her father, while in Deuteronomy she sells herself or is sold by the court.

Another step in the development of slavery – to be added in passing, since we are on the subject – is that of Leviticus,[87] where the limit of six years is ignored and the jubilee year is substituted. This arose from the fact that Jewish slavery until that time had been possible only for payment of a debt, while at a later period, with the development of a more complicated economic order, it was possible for a person to sell himself into slavery on account of poverty[88] and not necessarily for debt or theft. It may have been a case of a man not earning a living for his family and deciding to go over into a position of servitude into some rich household, he and his wife and his children together.[89] Therefore, there being

[85] Deut. 15.12, 17. Cf. also Jer. 34.9 f. Evidently we deal here with the unmarried female slave; hence she is released at the end of six years or is freed by a state decree.

[86] Hence the expression *ki yimmaker* (Deut.) in place of *we-ki yimekkor* (Ex.).

[87] Lev. 25.40.

[88] Note the expression *we-ki yamuk . . . we-nimekkar* (Lev.).

[89] While in Exodus the master may give the slave a wife, in Leviticus the assumption is that he has his own wife. It is altogether unthinkable that in the time of Leviticus a man's wife and children were sold into slavery for

no question of paying a debt, the sabbatical year does not free him, except that when the jubilee year arrives "he returns to his family and to his estate" for a new economic beginning.

Returning now to the subject of the slave-wife, we find that until deuteronomic times there was no Jewish female slave except the slave-wife, and that at all times the slave-wife was not one elevated from slavery into wifehood but bought directly for the specific position of slave-wife. She is never described as "married" or "betrothed," [90] although the term wife is applied to her in a non-technical sense. She is referred to as "sold" or "assigned" or "perforated." [91] No *mohar* was paid for her but the ordinary purchase price of the slave market; nor did she receive gifts from her husband-master and most likely not even dowry from her father. No contracts were written and no mutual obligations were covenanted for. Evidently, there was no marriage ceremony whatever, and the author of the Sibylline Books records an ancient tradition when he says in proverbial form: "As a slave girl shalt thou be wedded without ceremony." [92] Even in respect to adultery, her marriage to her master was not considered a consecrated bond but a superior property right, so that anyone violating her was not guilty of adultery but of a sinful form of theft. His punishment was a minor penalty, including a sacrificial offering.[93]

Since she is not legally married to her master, the regular divorce formalities do not apply to her; either she is redeemed by her kin or she is set free. We are not informed what happens to her in widowhood. We feel certain that she is not counted among the slaves to be acquired as such by the heir, for reducing her to slavery is impossible even for the

---

payment of his debt, after centuries of teaching of individual responsibility. The situation was simply that a poor man gave himself and his family over to servitude for the sake of being supported by the master, and that is why he is treated as a servant and not as a slave.

[90] *Be'ulat ba'al* Deut. 22.22, or *me'urasah* Deut. 22.23.

[91] *Makar* Ex. 21.7, or *Ya'ad* Ex. 21.8, or *ḥaraf* Lev. 19.20.

[92] Book III, line 358.

[93] Lev. 19.20. Our interpretation agrees with the Karaite. See *Keter Torah* ad Lev. ibid.

master himself. She probably is granted full freedom. However, it is not unlikely that at the time when usage permitted the heir to take over the patriarch's harem after his death, the slave-wives were taken as concubines; for the slave-wife under her newly gained freedom ranks as a concubine, as we have seen above in the case of Bilhah.[94]

The female slave belonging to the matron and given to the master for wifehood, according to Babylonian law, could be sold as a slave if she had no children by the master, or could be reduced to servitude if she did have children. It is not improbable that this was also the law among the Hebrews of the patriarchal age, for so was Hagar treated. Probably, however, the girl originally married into slave-wifehood, because she never was a mere slave, could under no circumstances be either sold or reduced to slavery. At least, as applied to the Hebrew female slave, the Book of the Covenant teaches that she cannot be sold, and the inference is fairly certain that she could not be reduced to slavery, since that was prohibited in deuteronomic times even for the non-Jewish captive-wife.

The Book of the Covenant also establishes her right to food and clothing and marital companionship "in the manner of free daughters." If the husband denies her any of these rights, she can leave him.

The status of children born of a slave-wife is uncertain in many respects and fairly definite in others. If the mother is a slave owned by the matron and given to the master for the purpose of procreation, the son has a higher position, for he has the master as his natural father and the matron as his fictitious mother. Babylonian law and Hebrew law grant him full right of sonship, if there are no legitimate sons. He is secondary heir in both laws,[95] if there are legitimate sons; except that "adoption" is necessary in Babylonian but not in Hebrew law. He has a secondary position socially,[96] but he receives his share of the estate and counts in the gene-

[94] See p. 50 above.

[95] As evident by the position of Ishmael and the sons of Jacob by his maid-servants, Bilhah and Zilpah.

[96] See how Jacob arranges his sons along with their mothers in accordance with their position, Gen. 33.1–2.

alogical line of the family.[97] Inferior was the position of the son begotten by the slave-wife belonging to the master himself, for he could not fictitiously claim the matron as his mother. He was of superior slave stock on his mother's side, but of slave stock all the same. Probably in the absence of legitimate sons he could be admitted to succession; [98] but whether he had any share in the inheritance where legitimate issue remained behind, we do not know. It is not unlikely that the Hebrew law was no different from the Babylonian in this case, namely, that he was free but was given no share in the inheritance.[99]

The cultural development of the Hebrew people during the biblical period tended to make an end to the whole concept of inferior and superior wives or more legitimate and less legitimate children. We have said that concubinage broke down with the demolition of the patriarchal family structure. The biblical ideal of individual and family life helped to break down the patriarchal foundations. The biblical tendency was to give more recognition to the individual, more independence to the child, more personal rights to the slave. The powers of the patriarch were shorn in respect to dictating the manner of succession. The Jewish slave was only a hireling, not a slave. Kinship came to mean natural blood ties rather than legal ties with the family. Marriage became a legally sanctioned union rather than a socially stratified position against a family background. Hence all sons were sons and all marriages were marriages. And if the law did step in to deprive a son of sonship or to declare a marriage invalid, this was not a matter of gradation; it rendered the son no son and the marriage no mar-

[97] Gen. 25.8; 46.8 f.

[98] This is implied by Abraham's fear that Eliezer may inherit his property, regardless of what interpretation we give to this passage, Gen. 15.2–3. See note 73 above. Whether this means that adoption is possible or that in the absence of a legitimate son an inferior member of the family becomes the heir without adoption we do not know.

[99] When Sarah insists that Ishmael shall not inherit because he is the son of an *amah*, Gen. 21.10, or when Jotham speaks in the same manner of Abimelech, Judg. 9,18, one gets the impression that it was taken for granted that the *ben-ha'amah* does not inherit. But, of course, *amah* here may mean the unmarried slave girl, not the slave-wife.

riage. Degrees came to an end, and that was the end of concubinage in all its forms, pilegesh, captive-wife, or slave-wife.

III

Rabbinic law was altogether free from the problem of inferior marriages. No such thing existed. Concubinage was at an end because of the simpler structure of the family. Hebrew female slaves were unknown, according to rabbinic calculation, throughout the entire second commonwealth period,[100] surely at the end of it. The captive and the heathen female slave, after Ezra's time, were excluded from the Hebrew family in any matrimonial sense. Furthermore, rabbinic law actually had no room for an inferior marriage. The mating of Jew and Jewess could be either with marriage or without it. It could not be half way. The children born of that union, in or out of wedlock, were fully legitimate in every respect.[101] The mating of Jew and non-Jewess could never be a marriage, no matter what the ceremonies and guarantees gone through.[102] This applies to a free born non-Jewess, captive, or slave. The children of such a union follow their mother, but have no family kinship with their father.[103] All that the Talmud has to say on the subject of concubine, captive, or slave is merely of a theoretical nature, intended as biblical exegesis.

The Talmud half confesses that it does not know what the biblical pilegesh was. R. Me'ir says that the concubine was apparently a married woman without ketubah, which means no dowry, no guarantees from the husband, and no covenant of marriage obligations. R. Judah declares that the concubine has a ketubah without ketubah clauses, which means she may bring a dowry to her husband and he must guarantee its return by the ketubah instrument; but the duties arising from normal marriage do not apply to her, such as provision for her during her lifetime and safeguarding the interests

100 'Ar. 29a, 32b; Yad, Shemiṭṭah 10,9; 'Abadim 1,10.
101 Yeb. 22a.
102 Ḳid. 66b, 68a–b.
103 Yeb. 22a, 23a.

of her children.[104] These tannaitic views still reflect a reminiscence of the original biblical pilegesh, but probably they link up more directly with the earlier hellenic concubine, as will be explained later. Rab, one of the earliest amoraic teachers, went a step further and said a pilegesh is neither married nor has a ketubah.[105] His view suggests the Roman concubine, even though he thought he was explaining the biblical pilegesh. All this is to the rabbinic teachers of mere theoretical value. They derive from it no legal conclusion whatsoever.

The picture they had of the captive-wife, and here too only for exegetical purposes, was as follows. The soldier is licentious and cannot be bridled in his lust; therefore, though he is morally wrong, the Bible recognizes his weakness and permits him to force his captive woman and let her go. But he cannot use her as a sex tool. If he wants her he must marry her. He must bring her to his house, grant her a month of mourning for her parents, make her dress unattractively, cutting her hair and paring her nails, so as to mitigate his infatuation, convert her to his religion, and then marry her (a full legitimate marriage) as a convert to Judaism. Her conversion must be voluntary, and carried out in the proper manner with ritual immersion. Also a period of two or three months must elapse before the marriage can be solemnized. If he marries her in this manner, she is a full lawful wife and the children are legitimate Jewish children. Thereafter, if he wishes to send her away he has to write her the bill of divorcement. But if he does not marry her, either because he has lost his desire for her or because she refuses to be converted, he must set her free. He cannot sell her or keep her as a slave.[106] In other words, there is no captive-wife in the rabbinic conception; she is

[104] Yer. Ket. 29d.

[105] San. 21a.

[106] Sifre ad Deut. 21.10–14; Yeb. 48a–b; San. 21a; Yad, Melakim 8,2–9. The need of her consent to conversion is disputed by R. Simeon b. Elazar, Yeb. 47b. Also the need for waiting longer than the month prescribed by the Bible before marrying is disputed, Sifre Deut. 21.13. The need for waiting three months is urged, however, in order to identify the child to be born as conceived while his mother was gentile or Jewess.

captive but no wife before conversion and marriage, and she is wife and no captive thereafter.

The picture that the rabbis portrayed of the biblical slave-wife is most interesting in its deviation from the original institution. The gentile slave-wife was altogether inconceivable to the rabbis, for a gentile or a slave is incapable of marriage in rabbinic law. If she is freed and converted, then she is wife and no slave. Hagar, to the rabbis, was a slave and no wife; Bilhah and Zilpah, converted and freed, were wives and no slaves.[107] They encountered a biblical law which prescribes a minor penalty for lying carnally with a *shifḥah ḥarufah,* a betrothed female slave.[108] That raised a problem, for here was a case of a betrothed slave who was half slave, half wife. To the ingenuity of Rabbi Akiba is ascribed the following fantastic explanation. Supposing a gentile female slave is owned by two masters in partnership; one frees her, the other does not. Then she is half slave, half free. Supposing further she marries a Jew, or a Jewish slave, then she is half slave, half wife. The half that is slave is not wife, because a slave is incapable of marriage; the half that is wife is free and no slave.[109] Beyond this instance, there is no possibility of a gentile woman being a slave-wife.

The Jewish slave-wife of the Book of Exodus was reinterpreted in the following way, mingling much of the older tradition and much of the newer law. The newer law did not recognize a state of slavery for the Jewish girl. A Hebrew slave-wife is therefore impossible. But the newer law did recognize a state of servitude for Jews, male or female, and the father was authorized by law to sell his daughter into servitude. The newer law also did recognize the right of the father to marry off his daughter. Then, may not a father sell her into servitude with the understanding that the master or his son may have her in marriage? This is exactly how the rabbis understood the case of the *amah* recorded in the Book of Exodus. Sale and marriage are separate matters, distinct

[107] Josephus, *Ant.*, I,19,8. Philo (see note 11 above) also counts Bilhah and Zilpah as slaves and their children illegitimate.

[108] Lev. 19.20.

[109] Sifra ad Lev. ibid.; Ker. 11a; Tos. Ker. 1,16; Yer. Ḳid. 59a.

transactions succeeding each other. First she is sold and is a Hebrew female slave (or servant), then she is married and becomes wife to her husband. Once a wife, nothing of the savor of servitude applies to her.

In keeping with the older law, the father may sell his daughter for servitude. The newer law restricted his right only to the minor daughter. Hence, if the girl remains unmarried when she attains her majority, she goes out free, because the father's power has terminated. Insomuch as until marriage she is only a slave, she can be redeemed by her family at any time. After six years' service she goes free, as is the rule for Hebrew slaves; and if the jubilee year comes any time before the end of her six years' slavery, she goes free, so long as she is not married. These regulations carry out the spirit of the deuteronomic and levitical codes. The master's death also sets her free. This belongs to the oldest tradition, when the female slave was in reality a slave-wife and widowhood freed her, but it has no logic in the newer law where she is merely a slave.[110]

The marriage of the Hebrew female slave (servant), in the rabbinic conception, is like any other marriage, except that it is called "assignment," *yi'ud*. The regular marriage formula is used, "Be thou my wife" or "Be thou my son's wife . . . according to the law of Moses and Israel"; a ketubah is written and all ketubah provisions apply to her. *Yi'ud* constitutes betrothal, and after a lapse of time the nuptial ceremony is solemnized with all religious and social details.[111] This is all new to the concept of *yi'ud* in the Bible; and certainly it is new legislation to require the girl's consent for the marriage.

The distinctive aspect of *yi'ud* belongs to the older tradition, namely, that no ring or coin is necessary for *yi'ud* because the original price paid for the girl when she entered into servitude included her *mohar* or marriage price. Another element of the older tradition survived into the newer

[110] Ket. 40b; Ḳid. 14b, 16a–b.

[111] The question is raised in the Talmud, Ḳid. 18b, whether *yi'ud* constitutes betrothal or wedding. We follow the halakic conclusion. See Yad, 'Abadim 4.9.

law in the ruling that if, after selling her to the master, the father weds her to another, the master can still marry her and consider the other marriage null and void. Both these features in the new law go back to the older concept that the original sale was slavery and wifehood combined. Finally, another rule is reminiscent of biblical days – that the girl cannot be sold for servitude to one who cannot marry her because of incestuous kinship, nor can she be sold with the understanding that neither the master nor the son will marry her.[112]

We have here fine examples of the blending of the old and the new in an institution that has gone through momentous changes. Nevertheless, the changes were too radical to permit survival of the institution even in semblance. All told, there was no slave-wife in practice or in theory among the Jews of the rabbinic period, even as there was no captive-wife or concubine.

Yet that was not the end of concubinage among the Jews. It appeared again in the Middle Ages, deriving not from Jewish but from hellenic tradition. In the hellenic historical workshop a new creation in concubinage was fashioned which the Jews believed to be the one that their biblical ancestors knew. This was the occidental concubine.

IV

As the biblical period closes and the institution of concubinage comes to an end in Judea, our attention is attracted by its existence in the hellenic world. In the Homeric age as in ancient Egypt, the concubine was usually a war captive. She was, therefore, not only inferior in station to

[112] Ḳid. 19a–b. R. Jose b. R. Judah represents the newer halakah, that the original purchase has nothing of marriage in it. Therefore he rules that if the master does not give her a coin, the marriage must take place some time sufficiently prior to the end of her term of service, so that the freedom given her (by marriage) of the unexpired term of servitude will constitute the consideration for which she will be married. He also rules that the master's right does not nullify the prior marriage to another. The decision, however, is against him. See Yad, 'Abadim 4,7 and 15. In respect to the rule that sale to one of incestuous kinship is impossible, there is also an opposing view representing the spirit of the newer halakah. The traditional view, however, prevailed. Yad, 'Abadim 4,11.

the biblical pilegesh, but to an extent might be counted among the slave population of the household. Hence, while monogamy was the rule in Greece, a concubine for the married man was permitted, and he could have many of them. Yet to conclude that the concubine had no recognized position in the family would be erroneous. She was not a mere slave or harlot; she had an official legal status. She might be charged with adultery; a man violating her might be slain by her husband with impunity. She followed her husband to the sacrifices and waited on him and his guests at the table. Often the guardian who gave her into concubinage stipulated a certain divorce price or certain gifts from the husband's estate in case of widowhood. She could be raised to wifehood by the husband's pronouncement of a certain formula. Her children, not heirs by law, were free. They could be raised to full sonship by the father's pronouncement, and then they became secondary heirs, next in rank to the highborn children. Apparently, though, she had no writ and no dowry and none of the sacrificial and ceremonial observances connected with marriage.

Her standing in the beginning of Greek life is, then, very close to that of the oriental concubine. Yet she is inferior. She comes from slavery or captivity, or at best from a very inferior native family. She has no claims or rights; her children are illegitimate; she is only a shade better than a slave, probably the equal of the oriental slave-wife. In course of time her position becomes lower still. In the time of Demosthenes she can hardly be distinguished from the slave-girl; she can be given over to another for the payment of a debt.

This hellenized form of the original oriental concubine existed not only in Greece, nor did it die with collapse of the Greek states. A reflection of this form is found in Parthia, according to the brief record left to us by Josephus.[113] At a later period, it was incorporated into the Syrian-Roman Law Book of the fifth century.[114] To the Syro-Roman sect or to the Parthians, the oriental element in concubinage must

[113] *Ant.*, XVIII,2,4.

[114] Edited by Bruns and Sachau, Nos. 26, 35, 36, 93, 109.

have had a special appeal as they took over that institution intact. But it was not allowed to remain stationary at this point. The real westernization of the oriental concubine was accomplished in the next step, when the Romans took it over from the Greeks.

Rome in early republican days looked upon concubinage not, as in the Orient, as an inferior marriage, nor even, as in Greece, as slave-wifehood. Marriage was strictly monogamous and aimed distinctly at legitimate offspring. Any relation between the sexes not of such monogamous, legitimate, purposeful type was either contrary to law or of no legal consequence at all, whether of an enduring or a passing nature. To all these relations, they applied the term *paelicatus;* the woman was called *pellex,* later *concubina.* Evidently, at this point, the term alone was taken from Greece; the institution itself was radically different from its Greek counterpart. The woman was not a slave as in Greece; she was not an inferior member of the household; she was not of the household at all. Her status was not illegitimate, as in Greece; the law was either against her or completely ignored her. The Greek influence consisted mainly in the fact that it showed the Romans the possibility of making provision in the mores or the law for sexual relations outside the marriage structure.

Roman civilization at the end of the republic and throughout the time of the emperors could make good use of such legal relaxation of the marriage ties. Luxury and self-indulgence were characteristic of Roman citizenship. Monogamy was the rule of law; life made illicit love the rule, and the law had to take cognizance of it. Thus the concubine received her legal baptism and became respectable in the eyes of the Romans. The rest was merely how to extend and apply the institution and how to define its legal characteristics. By successive legislation this step was accomplished. At first a concubine was possible only for an unmarried person who wished to remain single, but had arranged with a woman for enduring sexual companionship. The custom was most popular among widowers with grown children. Later it became the custom for married men also to have concubines as mistresses. Thereafter it flourished as a substitute for persons who could not legally be united in wedlock, where difference in social rank prevented a full marriage; in the case of soldiers not permitted to marry; or later in Christian times, in the case of priests who had vowed celibacy. In all these instances, concubinage was legally recognized and freely practiced. The concubine was definitely not married; she did not enter the husband's *manus;* she joined her lover without ceremony and could leave him without legal formality. The children had no legal father, although he owed them support and they owed him respect. Some recognition of them in division of the estate after the father's death was expected, and if there were no heirs they were given one sixth. They could be legitimatized by the father or they could automatically gain their legitimacy by marriage of their father and mother. This is the ultimate development and the final legal definition of occidental concubinage: It is a legally recognized unmarried state of enduring sex companionship between a man and a woman who cannot or will not be legally married.[115]

This form of concubinage, of course, the Jew did not know from his own national tradition. But on the other hand he had forgotten his own mode of concubinage, and when this strange Roman creation presented itself to him by the same name, he thought it the same institution his patriarchs had known in biblical times. The talmudic authorities were deceived just as well, for this is certainly the basis of Rab's statement: "Wives have marriage and ketubah; concubines have neither marriage nor ketubah." It is no wonder, then, that when conditions were favorable to concubinage, when it was considered a respectable institution among the non-Jews, even among the clergy, and furthermore, when it was to their mind the institution of their patriarchs and kings, the Jews of the Middle Ages should

[115] For the treatment of concubinage in Greece and Rome, see Paul Meyer, *Römisches Koncubinat*, pp. 8–9; 14–16; 17–19; 24–25; *Encyclop. Britannica*, XIV ed. s.v. "Concubinage"; *Dictionary of Greek and Roman Antiquities*, ed. Smith, Mayte, and Marindin, London, 1890, s.v. "Concubina"; *Harper's Dictionary of Classical Literature and Antiquities*, s.v. "Concubina"; Seymour, *Life in the Homeric Age*, pp. 149 ff.

take it up in its Roman form as though they had come back to their own traditional heritage.

The moral conscience of the Jew at that time and his legal discipline were against concubinage. Contact with a woman not sanctified by wedlock was harlotry in spirit, whether the relation was of a more or less enduring nature. Professional harlotry carried a biblical prohibition under the head of *zonah* or *ḳedeshah*. Even occasional contact with an unmarried woman in a non-professional way was, according to some teachers,[116] biblically prohibited as the equivalent of *zonah*. Though this view did not prevail halakically, the moral aversion to such promiscuity is evident in the talmudic declaration that a person's life is to be imperiled rather than that he be allowed to have contact with an unmarried woman.[117] Licentious contact with slaves was combated by law and morality. Contact with a Jewish servant girl was prohibited by the law of *ḳedeshah* and *zonah*. The non-Jewish slave girl was prohibited by Hasmonean and rabbinic enactments.[118] Apparently there was no possibility of sex contact without wedlock that would not merit moral and legal reproof. Is it possible that there was a difference between occasional contact and enduring sex relations – else how was the pilegesh justified?

With characteristic determination to make the law yield to a higher moral ideal, Maimonides invents two legal principles, one having a historical, the other a moralistic semblance of truth, but neither really based on talmudic tradition and halakah. The first is that concubinage was the prerogative only of royalty in biblical times but was never permitted to ordinary Jewish citizens.[119] The second is – once the biblical pilegesh is out of the way – that any unmarried contact between a man and a woman, temporary or permanent, professional or private, is biblically prohibited as *zonah* and *ḳedeshah* and is punishable by flagellation.[120] Contact with

116 The severe view here recorded is that of R. Elazar, Yeb. 59b.

117 See Yeb. 61b and Sifra ad Lev. 19.29; San. 75a; Yer. Sab. 14a.

118 'Ab. Zar. 36b.

119 Yad, Melakim 4,4.

120 Yad, Ishut 1,4; Na'arah Betulah 2,17. In the latter section Maimonides draws the distinction between one who is willing to cohabit in an unmarried

a Jewish maidservant, a common evil in his day,[121] is no exception. Contact with a non-Jewish maidservant, although accounted by Onkelos as a case of *ḳedeshah,*[122] he admits has not the severity of a biblical prohibition. But he makes strong denunciation of such a practice in the words: "Let not this sin seem light in thine eyes because the Bible did not prescribe the penalty of flagellation for it, for by that, too, the offspring is caused to turn away from God. For the son of a slave woman is a slave and not an Israelite; thus one causes holy seed to be profaned and be slaves." [123]

Maimonides' view was a little too rigorous for the populace and not wholly convincing to his contemporaries and successors. Rabbi Abraham b. David protested: "A *ḳedeshah* is one who gives herself freely to any man; but one who is permanently at the disposal of one man belongs neither to the category of flagellation nor of biblical prostitution. She is the pilegesh of the Scriptures." [124] Naḥmanides, too, took the position that there is no prohibition against concubinage. In a reply to R. Jonah Gerondi he says: "I know not why the doubt; surely she (the concubine) is permitted so long as one has reserved her for himself." [125] Yet the opponents of Maimonides contested only the question of legality. They agreed with him in moral sentiment. Naḥmanides concludes his communication with the warning: "But thou, O master, may God grant thee life, in thy place thou shalt restrict the people against concubines, for if they be informed of the permission, they will fall into prostitution and licentiousness and will visit them during menstruation." The general public, too, sensed the immorality of concubinage. They had found from sad experience that the unmarried consort was unfaithful, just because the sense of adultery was missing.[126]

---

state, whether by temporary or permanent arrangement, and the respectable girl who succumbs to a momentary impulse. This answers the question of *Maggid* ad Ishut 1,4.

[121] Resp. R. Nissim, 68.

[122] Onkelos, Deut. 23.18.

[123] Yad, Issure Bi'ah 12,13.

[124] Notes of R. Abraham b. David (RABD), Ishut 1,4.

[125] Resp. RSBA, ascribed to Naḥmanides, 284.

[126] *Ẓedah la-Derek,* 3,1,2.

A strange desire to give a Jewish touch to a Roman institution produced an occidental concubine in oriental garb, namely, the married concubine. The unmarried concubine, of course, was not wholly given up, but the married concubine came on the Jewish scene as a concession to people with higher sensibilities. A concubine in position, she was a wife in law. She was betrothed and not wedded; that is, the marriage coin was given to her and the formula of marriage was pronounced, but the home-taking ceremony, the *ḥuppah,* was not solemnized, and the ketubah was not written. Her status in respect to the marriage bond was that of any other wife; unfaithfulness was adultery and a bill of divorcement was necessary for her release. But the husband assumed no obligations to her, such as are contained in the ketubah. She was in a perpetual state of *arusah.*

This kind of concubinage may or may not have had its counterpart in the non-jewish family of that day. But it had its theoretical basis in Jewish sources. We have seen above that the tannaim described the concubine as one who was evidently married, while her ketubah provisions were either lacking or inferior to those of a wife. The report that Rab had declared the concubine not even betrothed was challenged by a reading based on the authority of Rashi,[127] making it appear that Rab, like the tannaim, considered the concubine a betrothed mistress. Naḥmanides corrects Rashi as to the reading,[128] stating that according to Rab, the concubine is not even betrothed. But apparently the authority of Rashi was sufficient to lead people to the conclusion that the teachers of the Talmud considered the bethrothed mistress the pilegesh of the Bible, Hence, if the unmarried concubine is morally objectionable, the betrothed pilegesh is permissible and proper for the ordinary Jewish citizen, whose standard of morality need be no better than that of the biblical personalities. Thus, two concubines existed side by side in the mediaeval Jewish family, the unmarried for the less scrupulous, and for the more rigorous the married concubine.

[127] Rashi ad Gen. 25.6.

[128] Naḥmanides Commentary ad Gen. ibid.

The betrothed concubine was either a Jewess or a freed and converted female slave. She was the concubine of an unmarried or a married man.[129] The unmarried man might have had his own reasons for concubinage; the married man generally tried to adjust his conscience to a promise he had made his wife that he would take no other wife in addition to her.[130] She was either kept in an apartment of her own,[131] or remained in the husband's house in the guise of a servant.[132] The legal objection to her is very indefinite, even according to Maimonides,[133] but moral objections came to the foreground, such as that the man thereby became estranged from his family; [134] that he enjoyed marital pleasures without the nuptial benediction; [135] or that she would be ashamed to observe ritual cleanliness, and he would therefore approach her in time of impurity.[136] These objections sounded more ethical than legal and people did not mind them.[137]

The position of this concubine, from the point of view of the law, was definite. She was a full wife in respect to adultery, incest, and divorce.[138] Being only betrothed and not wedded, she had no claim to maintenance or burial or ransom. Even *mohar* or the standard obligation of two hundred *zuzim* was not due her, even though betrothal alone in ordinary marriages imposes this obligation, because the pilegesh was betrothed with the understanding that she was never to be wedded.[139] The husband was not entitled to her earnings and, according to a ruling of Asheri – contrary to talmudic law for the betrothed – he did inherit her goods if she lived in his house.[140] The children begotten by the

[129] RSBA, I,1205; II,363; Resp. R. Nissim, 68; *Ẓedah la-Derek,* III,1,2.

[130] *Ẓedah la-Derek,* ibid.

[131] Resp. R. Nissim, 68.

[132] Resp. Asheri, 37,1; RSBA, IV,314.

[133] See *'Azmot Joseph,* Introduction; Benvenisti, *Dine d'Hayye,* negative command 222.

[134] *Ẓedah la-Derek,* ibid.

[135] RSBA, VIII,284; Resp. Asheri, 37,1.

[136] Resp. Asheri, 32,13.

[137] RSBA, V,242.

[138] *Ẓedah la-Derek,* ibid.; RSBA, V,242.

[139] Resp. Asheri, 35,9.

[140] Resp. Asheri, 37,1.

betrothed concubine were fully legitimate and of equal standing with children of regular marriages.[141]

The betrothed concubine found her most favorable territory among oriental and Spanish Jews, to whom polygamy was legally permitted. In Central Europe, where polygamy was prohibited by the ḥerem, the objection to a betrothed concubine was that she too was legally a wife and was prohibited to the man who already had a wife.[142] On the other hand, the free concubine, unbetrothed, therefore not a wife, hence not an infringement against the law of polygamy, was acceptable to Jews everywhere – in Germany, Spain, or the Orient.[143]

The unbetrothed concubine was the mistress of a married man or *chère amie* of an unmarried man.[144] She was kept in the house or maintained in a private apartment.[145] Her children were fully legitimate in respect to succession to their father and in respect to consanguinity, as it affects incest, testimony, levirate duties, and mourning.[146] But she had no legal standing in relation to her lover; she was like the betrayed maiden.[147] After her lover tired of her he could send her away without formality of a divorce, and she could be taken back even after she had in the meantime been married to another. For that matter, she could be taken in marriage by his brother or his son, for she had not been legally married to him. And, for the same reason, she could never be charged with adultery.[148] She had no claim on her husband for maintenance, and the husband had no right to her property during her lifetime, nor succession after her death.

The original controversy as to whether concubinage is

[141] RSBA, IV,315; II,363.

[142] RSBA, I,1205.

[143] RSBA, VIII,284; Resp. Asheri, 32,1; *Ẓedah la-Derek*, III,1,2; Resp. R. Nissim, 68; RIBS, 217; Resp. R. Me'ir Padua, 19; Resp. Benjamin Ze'eb, 111; *Yam Shel Shlomo*, Yeb. II,11.

[144] R. Me'ir Padua, ibid.; R. Nissim, ibid.; RSBA, I,1205.

[145] RSBA, R. Me'ir Padua, R. Nissim, ibid.

[146] RSBA, II,363; IV,315.

[147] Resp. Asheri, 32,1.

[148] Resp. R. Me'ir Padua, 19; RIBS, 395. R. Menaḥem Schneersohn in responsa *Ẓemaḥ Ẓedeḳ*, E.H., 138 opposes this view, and requires divorce.

permitted in Jewish law centered around this unbetrothed concubine. The leaders in the controversy were, Maimonides prohibiting, and Naḥmanides permitting the concubine legally but not ethically. The teachers of the law in succeeding generations generally followed Maimonides.[149] Yet Naḥmanides' view is represented by such scholars as R. Nissim, R. Menaḥem b. Zeraḥ, R. Me'ir of Padua, and others. The codes of R. Jacob b. Asher and R. Joseph Karo prohibit concubinage in accordance with the Maimonidean view.[150]

Yet an impulsive and eccentric talmudist, in the person of Rabbi Jacob Israel Emden of Altona in the early eighteenth century, dared defy the authority of Maimonides and the codifiers and went even beyond the teaching of Naḥmanides in declaring that concubinage was not only legally permitted but even ethically respectable. He is opposed, first of all, to the prohibition against polygamy. He is interested in increasing the population of the holy people. Only the Shabbethaians wish to bring to an end the souls together with the bodies, in order to hasten the coming of Messiah. But his own view, he says, is: "It is a *miẓwah* to proclaim publicly the permission of concubinage." But he adds: "I do not wish that anyone rely upon me except if it be with consent of the scholars of the day. But if these words of mine find favor in their eyes, may I share in their reward. I shall join them and be counted among them for a meritorious undertaking. Still I warn anyone who wishes to rely upon my legal decision that he consult the rabbi of his community, who shall see to it that permission be granted on the condition of complete exclusiveness, safe from corruption, namely, that he (the lover) set aside a separate room for her and command her not to have dealings with other men; that if she disobey he will immediately send her out of his house. He shall also command her to take the ritual bath at the proper time and shall convince her that she has no cause for shame. He shall also explain to her that the children which she shall have by him will be without blemish, like those of pure blood in Israel; that she should keep her

[149] See RDBZ, IV,225, giving a summary of the attitude of legal authorities.
[150] *Ṭur* and *Shulḥan 'Aruk,* E.H. 2,6.

covenant and be faithful to him. And on these conditions there is not the slightest fear of stumbling into sin. On the contrary, it shall be accounted meritorious to eliminate the stumbling block from the way of the wicked. Even scholars have great need of it, for 'the greater the man, the stronger his passion.' "[151]

Apparently, this liberal appeal fell on deaf ears. The Jews disliked concubinage even in defiance of such eccentric scholars. Private and public measures were taken against it. For a while they inserted in their marriage contracts special clauses providing against concubinage;[152] then they enacted local community ordinances;[153] but in the course of time neither was necessary. The practice was very uncommon, and when it did occur, it was looked upon as a violent infringement upon decency.

[151] *She'elat Ya'abez*, II,16.

[152] RIBS, 395; Asher Gulak, *Ozar ha-Shetarot*, Jerusalem, 1926, No. 43, p. 47. See JMC p. 272.

[153] RSBA, V,242.

CHAPTER III

LEVIRATE MARRIAGE

I

AMONG many primitive peoples in the western as well as eastern lands, a woman continues in a certain sense to be married even after the death of her husband. Widowhood is not a release from matrimonial ties but a married state under the misfortune of having no husband. The ancients conceived of such a condition in the following way. In marriage the wife joined not only her husband but also his family. In fact, it was not the husband alone who espoused her as wife, but more the head of the family who took her for one of his members. She was owned, therefore, by the family first and by the husband next. This does not mean that any one in the family outside the husband could live with her. Marriage was at the same time an assignment of the bride to one and only one member of the family; and he was assigned private right over marital relations with the bride, as he was also assigned to a separate tent of which he had exclusive use. Yet her companionship with one man did not remove the rights the corporate family held over her. The family had paid for her and the family owned her. Therefore, if the husband died she was a widow, but she was still owned by the family.

What was her status then and what to be done with her? Her fate was entirely in the hands of the head of the family, for she was still its property, and the head had full and final control over family possessions. In the second place, family property with value and usefulness was not allowed to lie fallow; someone in the family must put it to use. This woman, therefore, bought and paid for and capable of wifehood and of childbearing, could not be allowed to be without a husband; someone in the family must take her as wife and succeed the deceased husband. This primitive form of thinking gave rise to the ancient levirate custom, requiring the widow of the deceased member of a family to be married to another member of the same family. Where this logic alone prevailed, one may reasonably expect to find that custom required full marriage and not mere cohabitation between the widow and her husband's successor. It may also be expected that the levirate duty would fall upon the widow whether she had children by her deceased husband or not. Furthermore, logic would require that the levirate duty should not be limited to the brother of the deceased, though he might have priority, but that the father or the son or a more distant relative might be designated as the levir to marry the widow.

In the special instance where the husband died without issue, a new consideration arose and with it a new logic. The deceased should have a child to bear his name, else he would be "cut off" from the family estate here and from the celestial estate hereafter. Wherever ancestor worship existed, saving the soul of the childless brother became of primary importance in the logic of levirate marriage. Where ancestor worship did not assume the undue significance, the foremost consideration in the levirate process where the brother had died childless was to perpetuate his name in the family estate, that is, not to have him "cut off" from the estate of the living. The patriarchal family was considered like a branched tree, the head of the family being the trunk and the children the branches. When one of the children died childless it was as if one branch were cut off. It had to be re-rooted into the trunk in some semi-artificial way. That was accomplished by the levirate act, for the child born of cohabitation between the widow and the surviving kin of the husband would be counted as a son to the deceased husband, and thus his branch of the family would continue. Such a motive is expressed in the primitive concept of "raising seed for the deceased brother." By this logic marriage between the levir and widow, while possible, is not necessary; cohabitation between them would be sufficient. The child born of the union would be fictitiously counted as son of the deceased husband. Where, however, the levir actually married the widow and more than one child was born of the union, law and custom declared that the first-born alone be the fictitious descendant of the deceased.

These motives for the levirate rite, preserving the family's property right in the widow and raising up seed for the deceased brother, are widely different. By reason of the first motive, levirate marriage is a privilege enjoyed by the surviving members of the family; by the second motive, it is a duty on the family rather than a privilege. The first requires marriage, the second requires only cohabitation between levir and widow. The first motive seems to be the more original and the more primitive, the second seems to belong to a later and more refined stage in the development of primitive life.

Some scholars seek to penetrate even beyond these early primitive stages in development of the levirate institution and believe that levirate marriage goes back to an original condition of polyandry or group marriage;[1] but the evidences offered to prove these theories are not convincing.[2] The two primitive concepts, that the woman is family property and that the childless person is cut off from the family tree and must be artificially regrafted, are the main motives transmitted to us in the records of history, and are in themselves sufficient to explain the origin of the levirate custom.

Another motive for the levirate rite should be added which seems to belong to a later stage in development of primitive life than the two previously mentioned. This is to provide for the childless widow a place in the family, where, as during her husband's lifetime, she may continue to receive protection, care, and sustenance and retain the social advantages of membership in her husband's family. The position of the widow at best was one of insecurity and helplessness; she was one of the unfortunates in ancient society, an object of compassion. Doubly unfortunate and pitiful was the childless widow who might be ejected from her husband's home and

1 McLennan, "Levirate and Polyandry," in *Fortnightly Review*, N.S., XXI, pp. 703 ff. J. Kohler, "Zur Urgeschichte der Ehe," ZVR, XII, p. 321.

2 Westermarck, HHM, III, pp. 207–20; 261–3; Sigismund Rauh, *Hebr. Familienrecht*, pp. 39–40.

become an unwelcome burden in her paternal home. The levirate rite, if not established entirely upon an altruistic and charitable basis, found support in the altruistic social benefits which the institution offered. This third motive has more in common with the second than with the first mentioned above, in that it presents levirate as a duty rather than a privilege. But it adds to the second motive an important element, in that it requires the levirate obligation to be fulfilled by marriage, not by mere cohabitation.

A combination of all three motives accounts for the biblical institution of levirate. There are reminiscences of the most ancient concept that by the levirate rite the woman is inherited, the surviving kin of the deceased being admitted into a property privilege. Then, the motive of raising seed for the deceased is quite prominent; and in that connection, as in the case of Judah and Tamar, a suggestion is offered that one productive intercourse is sufficient for its fulfillment. Finally, the rite becomes stabilized into levirate marriage, which means marriage of the brother-in-law, upon whom the obligation is put to take the place of his deceased brother both in providing a "name" for him and in caring for his widow.[3] The historic process of the levirate institution has been gradually moving further away from the first motive and closer to the third, until every motive is lost in oblivion and the institution survives only by force of social habit.

Uniformity in the levirate observance as practiced by the Jews uninterruptedly for a period of fifty centuries is certainly too much to expect. Even within range of the biblical period, there are definite and radical changes in the institution. The first case of levirate, known in Hebrew as *yibbum,* is recorded in Genesis,[4] in the story of Judah and Tamar. While the brother-in-law is first considered, it is the father-in-law who actually performs the levirate act, although unwittingly. Levirate is obligatory on the widow and the levir, and its evasion is punishable by death. Property succession

[3] Cf. K. H. Rengstorf's introduction to Mishnah Yebamot, and Israel J. Mattuck, "The Levirate Marriage in Jewish Law," in *Studies in Jewish Literature in Honor of Kaufman Kohler,* Berlin, 1913.

[4] Gen. 38.

does not come into question; the motive is "to raise seed for the (deceased) brother." Deuteronomy[5] limits levirate to the brother-in-law, and adds the motive of "perpetuating the name of the (deceased) brother in Israel" — still without reference to succession in respect to property. It ignores the death penalty for evasion, but prescribes public censure for the brother-in-law in the ḥalizah ceremony, performed by the widow pulling off the shoe of the levir. The Book of Ruth[6] continues the record of levirate marriage. Here, however, there is no surviving brother-in-law, and the duty goes over to the next of kin. Neither the widow nor the next of kin can be forced into the levirate marriage. The motive is "to establish the name of the deceased upon his estate" and succession to the estate plays a prominent role in the negotiations.

Leviticus and Numbers at times ignore the levirate institution and at times legislate it out of existence. A widow who has no children is told to go back to her father's house,[7] without thought as to the possible childlessness of the husband, consequently the levirate duty. If a man dies childless, according to the ruling of the Book of Numbers,[8] his estate goes over to the brothers or uncles, as if a levirate institution did not exist at all. But the Levitical author makes bold to say, "And if a man shall take his brother's wife, it is impurity: he hath uncovered his brother's nakedness: they shall be childless."[9] Samaritans, rabbis, and Karaites, accepting the whole Pentateuch as a unified code of legislation, sought to explain the discrepancies in various ways. Critical scholars[10] see historical development in the institution and successive biblical legislation in respect to it.

[5] Deut. 25.5–10.

[6] Ruth 3.9, 12–13; 4.1–17.

[7] Lev. 22.13.

[8] Num. 27.8–11.

[9] Lev. 20.21; 18.16.

[10] Benzinger, *Hebräische Archäologie,* pp. 288–9; J. Scheftelowitz, "Leviratsehe," in *Archiv f. Religionswissenschaft,* 1915; Abraham Menes, *Die vorexilischen Gesetze Israels,* Giesen, 1928, pp. 122–3; Julius A. Bewer, "Die Leviratsehe im Buche Ruth," in *Theologische Studien,* 1903; M. Guttmann, "Über die Leviratsehe," *Zeitschrift f. jüd. Theologie,* Stuttgart, 1839; Wechsler, "Die Leviratsehe," *Jüd. Zeitschrift f. Wissenschaft u. Leben,* 1862.

Geiger [11] believes that the contradiction between the law of levirate of Deuteronomy and the law of succession in Numbers can be explained on the basis of geographical differences between one legislator and the other. Levirate, he believes, was known only in Judah, in the south, probably as a tribal tradition, but was not known or not heeded in the north. The legislator of Numbers belongs to the Kingdom of the North, where he was free to establish rules of succession in utter disregard of levirate regulations. Most scholars [12] differ with Geiger on limiting the area where the levirate rite was practiced, and they rightly maintain that in the earlier biblical period the rite was observed among the Hebrews generally, north or south. But they say, and Geiger agrees, that the institution was ruled out of existence by post-exilic legislators through an official act of abrogation, declaring it to be incest.[13] Yet this theory, too, cannot be taken without some serious doubt. It is not likely that a post-exilic legislator would, out of personal moral convictions, sweep away an institution so deeply rooted in Hebrew life and formulated in no uncertain terms in such a highly regarded code as Deuteronomy; and that he would defiantly term it incest, contrary to the conscience of his age.[14] And why was not his legislation on the levirate obeyed by the Jews of the Second Commonwealth, as they followed him in other innovations concerning the law of incest? We cannot escape successive legislation, but the sociological foundations of these changes in law must be sought. Viewed sociologically, our difficulties seem to dissolve.

The marriage of a widow to a surviving heir is possible in one of three ways, by succession, by redemption, or by levirate. We call succession that condition when the estate of the deceased remains in its original status, and an heir steps in to take his place. In redemption the estate goes

[11] "Die Leviratsehe," in *Jüdische Zeitschrift*, I, pp. 19–39.

[12] See Jacob Mittelmann, *Die altisraelitische Levirat*, Leiden, 1934, pp. 35–37.

[13] K. H. Rengstorf in his introduction to Mishnah Yebamot pp. 28 ff. advances the theory that levirate was not practiced during the Second Commonwealth. J. Jeremias in ThLZ 54, 1929, p. 583 disproves this theory.

[14] See Wechsler, o.c. pp. 48–49.

over to another owner to become part of another estate. Levirate designates no immediate movement of the estate but a provision for the future.

In the nomadic period of the ancient Hebrews, the family was a fairly large group, including several brothers and their respective descendants. The oldest brother was the patriarch, and when he died the one next in age became head of the family. He did not inherit the possessions of his deceased brother but succeeded him. That succession included taking over his brother's wives together with the estate.[15] This is marriage by succession. It represents a very primitive condition of which there are hardly even vague memories in the Bible.

Under pastoral and later under agricultural conditions, the Hebrew family became smaller. Brothers belonged to one family unit only so long as their father was alive to head the group. When the father died, the family broke up into smaller households, each son receiving a parcel of the family estate, establishing a household of his own, and becoming the patriarch of his own family unit. The sons did not succeed their father but were his *heirs.* Only the oldest son *succeeded* the father, for he took his father's place on the original estate. He became trustee of the shares belonging to the minor unmarried sons; he disposed of the hands of his unmarried sisters and provided dowries for them out of the estate; he also disposed of the wives left widowed by his father. His own mother remained on the estate as queen mother, holding a position of dignity and retaining some persuasive authority. The mothers of the rest went with their respective sons, to become queen mothers of the new estates to be established by their own offspring. The childless widow normally returned to her parental home. It is not illogical to believe that sometimes she would not wish to go back, but would remain either as a client of the estate or as wife of the oldest son, new head of the family. How-

[15] This seems to be the earliest sociological source for making the brother of the deceased the preferred levir. Herein, too, we have the origin of the feeling that the father's brother is the nearest of kin in the family, designated especially as *dod,* beloved.

ever, there are no records to confirm this logical conjecture. The inferior wives went with the estate, and the son who succeeded as patriarch took over the harem as part of his right of succession. In this stage, too, therefore, the heir's marrying one of the widows was succession, not levirate.

Marriage by succession is very primitive and lost ground with the advance of the agricultural civilization of the Hebrews. In the first place, as early as deuteronomic times succession came to an end altogether, and the first-born was given a double portion of the estate in lieu of succession – which means he was made an heir like the other sons, with special privileges. Second, the Book of Deuteronomy already prohibits sons marrying their fathers' wives.[16] What would happen, then, to the childless widow who did not want to return to her parental home? Of course, a brother of the deceased patriarch could be persuaded to take her. If he did, he was in a sense a *go'el,* a redeemer, not permitting his deceased brother's property (wife) to go into strange hands. He had no obligation to do so, because, as we shall see later, *ge'ullah* is never obligatory, especially where there are heirs and the brother has not died childless. Nor was there any property inducement for the brother to marry the childless widow, because the property went to the surviving sons.

But, assuming the patriarch has died leaving no sons, then the same brother will be persuaded to marry the childless widow, on two considerations. First, he will be told that it is his duty to do so in order to perpetuate his brother's name. Second, he will be offered the inducement that with the widow he also is given the estate. This is still optional with him, and also with the widow, for she can return to her parental home if she chooses; but if he does marry her, he has done so by the principle of *ge'ullah,* the estate being transferred from one family to another. This would be a case of a brother-in-law marrying the childless widow of his deceased brother under the head of *ge'ullah,* not under levirate.

Supposing, again, that there is no surviving brother, then the *ge'ullah* privilege goes over to the next of kin. This is

[16] See Deut. 21.17; 27.20.

the case recorded in the Book of Ruth. The date of the book is a matter of controversy among biblical scholars, the majority placing it in the post-exilic period. But evidences and arguments offered by a minority group seem to prove that it belongs to the pre-deuteronomic period and perhaps even to the time of the immediate successors of King David.[17]

The circumstances connected with this romance are important for an understanding of the *ge'ullah* marriage. Elimelech and his two sons died; no direct heirs remained. Naomi, wife of Elimelech, becomes head of the now all female family. She holds the estate, and whoever would claim it as next of kin must negotiate with her.[18] Her first act of authority is to dispose of her daughters-in-law, who are childless widows. Custom permits them to go to their paternal homes, but they are so attached to their mother-in-law that they wish to stay in the family and follow her to Bethlehem. Naomi is also a childless widow. If she were of the childbearing age, she might be persuaded to submit to a *ge'ullah* marriage for herself. If she did that, there would be a chance for the daughters-in-law, for a child born of that marriage would count as son to Elimelech and brother-in-law to the younger widows, who could marry them on the principle of succession or levirate or *ge'ullah,* which ever it might be. But Naomi is too old.[19] In truth, also, she was not childless,

[17] See Mittelmann, o.c. pp. 16–27; L. B. Wolfenson, "The Character, Contents and Date of Ruth" in AJSL, XXVII; J. A. Bewer, "The Ge'ullah in the Book of Ruth," AJSL, XIX.

[18] Ruth 4.3. The word *makerah* is rendered by scholars in the sense of "she is about to sell" by manipulation of the vowels. One feels tempted to translate with Septuagint "which was given (sold) to Naomi," indicating that Naomi's possession of the property is considered an alienation because she is not of the Elimelech family. The *go'el,* according to verse 5, is supposed to take it "from the hand of Naomi" apparently, Naomi being the *de facto* owner of the estate.

[19] Ruth 1.12. The implication that if Naomi could be married and have sons these sons could marry Orpah and Ruth raises difficulties. If she married a stranger, and that might be justified because at the time of her husband's death there were surviving sons and she was therefore not obligated to enter a levirate marriage or a *ge'ullah* marriage, the sons born of that union would be maternal brothers-in-law of Ruth and Orpah; how could they marry the latter under the head of levirate? Our suggestion is that Naomi could enter a levirate or *ge'ullah* marriage because her husband, posthumously, became childless through the death of his sons — of course, contrary to later law. If

because two sons had survived her husband's death. Should her daughters-in-law enter into a *ge'ullah* marriage, the names of her own husband and children would be perpetuated. She, therefore, wants no marriage for herself.

There being no evident prospect for marriage in the Elimelech family, Orpah is discouraged and leaves her mother-in-law, returning to her parental home in accordance with the law of the day. Ruth clings to her mother-in-law and remains a client on the Elimelech estate with Naomi's permission. Ruth finds a *go'el* in the person of Boaz. He is willing to marry her and take the estate, to hold in trust for the first child born of the union. But *ge'ullah* belongs to the nearest of kin, and there is one closer to the Elimelech family who must first be offered the right of *ge'ullah.* The latter refuses, because it does not profit him to take on the burden of another wife and the old Naomi, and raise a child who would later take the estate from him. He transfers the *ge'ullah* right to Boaz by the ceremony of taking off his shoe. Boaz becomes the *go'el* and marries Ruth. This *ge'ullah* marriage, like the levirate, has its social sanction in the motive to perpetuate the name of the deceased; therefore, in the benediction at the marriage ceremony the story of Judah and Tamar is recited, and the child that is born, Obed, is accounted as continuing the name of the Elimelech family.[20]

Levirate marriage is different from succession in the fact that there is no estate to be inherited. It is different from *ge'ullah* in that the childless widow remains in the original family household and does not, as in the case of *ge'ullah,* go over to another. The levirate situation arises while the patriarch is still alive and heads his corporate family. It is one of the sons who has died childless and left a widow. There is no question of disposing of an estate, because the patriarch is still alive. It is a matter of conserving property right in the childless widow and perpetuating the name of the deceased.

---

she were not old, therefore, she could beget *ge'ullah* sons or levirate sons, who would count as sons of Elimelech and therefore paternal brothers-in-law of Ruth and Orpah. See Mittelmann, o.c. pp. 17–19.

[20] Ruth 4.12–17.

Both the property right in the widow and the duty to raise seed for the brother are concentrated in the corporate family. Therefore levirate is limited to members of the patriarchal family unit, which rule the Bible expresses in the words "If brothers dwell together." [21] This means that a son who has left his parental estate and set up his own household is excluded from the levirate scheme, either as the deceased or as surviving brother.

The first child born of the levirate union is accounted in the older records fictitiously as a son of the deceased brother.[22] For him is reserved a share in the estate after the patriarch's death in place of his deceased uncle, fictionally his father. In Deuteronomy the levirate child is not the fictitious "seed" of the deceased but bears his name.[23] What "bearing his name" means is not definite. Probably it refers to the anticipation that, when the patriarch dies and the estate is divided among the sons, he, the levirate child, will take the place of the deceased son. In the Book of Ruth the motive of Deuteronomy, that of bearing the name of the deceased, is applied to transfer of the estate,[24] for here we have an estate to be conveyed as well as a widow to be married. Here the *ge'ullah* child bears the name of the Elimelech family[25] in that he is called "a son of Naomi" and becomes possessor of the Elimelech estate. In a sense, the child is the ultimate *go'el* of the estate,[26] for he takes it out of the hands of the kinsman and sets it up in possession of one bearing the original family name. The Chronicler, who lived in post-exilic times, when the solidarity of families on family estates had suffered

[21] Deut. 25.5.

[22] Gen. 38.8–9: "raise seed . . . " Herein is the significance of the scarlet thread that was tied on the hand of Perez, Gen. 38.28, "saying this one came out first." Probably primogeniture was also granted to the levir child if his fictitious father was the first born of the family.

[23] Deut. 25.6–7. The expression, "to raise a name . . . in Israel," does not definitely imply the right of succession. The Talmud also doubts it. Yet the probabilities are that this biblical expression does imply some form of succession, so that the levir-child, after the death of the patriarch, is given some part of the estate on which he bears the name of the deceased. See Mittelmann, o.c. p. 33.

[24] Ruth 4.5: "to establish the name of the deceased upon his estate."

[25] Ruth 4.14, 17.

[26] Ruth 4.14 seems to indicate that the child himself is a *go'el*.

much weakening, no longer took seriously even the perpetuation of the name of the deceased, and simply records the *ge'ullah* child as a son of Boaz, his real father.[27]

In deuteronomic days levirate and *ge'ullah* existed side by side. Where within the family one brother died and another married his widow, that was levirate; where a brother, having established his own family, was called upon to take charge of the estate and to marry the widow of another, who was head of another family, that was *ge'ullah*. In other words, brothers dwelling together performed levirate; when not dwelling together, they performed the *ge'ullah* courtesy. But at the end of the biblical period both levirate and *ge'ullah* were falling out of use through sociological forces. "Dwelling together," which alone permits the levirate situation, presupposes a patriarchal family structure, and where there is no patriarchal family there is no levirate. But the patriarchal family was becoming antiquated and was yielding to the individual family where the sons, generally as soon as they married, established independent families of their own. It was at that time that the laws of inheritance became direct and immediate upon a person's death.[28] To be sure, the levirate law was not changed. Wherever there was a patriarchal family and brothers did "dwell together," the levirate rite was performed. But such cases were rare. The only other thing that could apply in a non-patriarchal family organization was the *ge'ullah* marriage. *Ge'ullah* marriage, too, receded before newer sociological conditions. The woman attained a measure of legal independence and could not be counted as a mere chattel going with the estate. If she was childless, she went back to her parental home and from there married the man she or her father chose. *Ge'ullah* continued in respect to property,[29] but *ge'ullah* marriage, only optional to begin with, was becoming unsavory and out of keeping with the newer position of woman. In fact, other than in the Book of Ruth, there is no mention of *ge'ullah* marriage in the Bible.

Now, the author of the levitical code did not attack the

[27] Ruth 4.21; I Chron. 2.12; also Gen. 46.12 and I Chron. 2.4.

[28] Num. 27.6–11.

[29] Lev. 25.25, 48.

law of levirate commanded by the deuteronomic legislator. If there was still a survival of a patriarchal family where brothers did "dwell together," the levirate rite was performed in accordance with old tradition. But such cases were rare. His condemnation was aimed at *ge'ullah* marriage, which had outlived the patriarchal family. In this assault he did not abrogate any previous law, for *ge'ullah* was altogether optional, and he had on his side the newer independence gained by woman. He therefore declared a *ge'ullah* marriage between brother-in-law and sister-in-law incest.[80]

In the breakdown of the patriarchal family, we have said, levirate came to an end. Almost so, but not entirely. The exceptional case was that of the betrothed son who, not yet wedded, had therefore not yet left his parental home. When the patriarchal family was altogether lost, he was still "dwelling together" with his brothers. If the levitical law did not abrogate levirate, his was the only case where levirate applied even according to levitical legislation. It is not impossible, therefore, that post-exilic Jews for a time knew of no levirate rite except in case of the betrothed son who was the only one still "dwelling together" with his brothers. The Samaritans preserved that tradition.

To Geiger[81] this Samaritan tradition represents a mixture of the North-Israelitish antagonism to levirate and a new acceptance of the authority of the Book of Deuteronomy, where the levirate rite is made mandatory. To Mittelmann[82] it appears a totally foreign tradition brought by this alien group into Judea. This latter theory has considerable merit, for we know that the Samaritans were dominated by foreign influences, and we know also that the Assyrian law, according to the best interpretations,[83] required levirate marriage

80 Lev. 18.16. The *ge'ullah* marriage, even where there was no incest, was evidently abandoned, and the Karaites and Samaritans (as we shall see later) who substituted *ge'ullah* for levirate revived an institution that was long dead. The law requiring a daughter who comes into an inheritance to marry within her family also has the *ge'ullah* motive, except that it applies in the reverse order, for here the estate goes with the girl instead of the girl going with the estate. However, that too was soon abandoned.

81 Geiger, "die Leviratsehe," in *Jüdische Zeitschrift,* I, p. 27.

82 Mittelmann, o.c. p. 49.

83 P. Koschaker, "Quellenkritische Untersuchungen zu den altassyrischen

for the betrothed widow only; and, furthermore, where levirate emphasizes the aspect of the property right in the widow, as did practically all foreign cultures of the Orient, it is logical that the betrothed should be more subject to levirate than the wedded, for she is an object paid for and not yet used. But, with our sociological interpretation, there is no need to look for foreign influences; in the sociological development within Judea itself and in the original Hebraic tradition there is sufficient basis for the practice of limiting levirate to the betrothed.

Suspicion has been raised that the Samaritan teaching was also adopted by the Sadducees,[34] that even the more ancient pharisaic halakah accepted it,[35] and that it was generally employed by the foreign hellenistic Jewish communities at the end of the Second Commonwealth.[36] We wish, naturally, that there were sufficient proof to establish these conjectures, for it would then make our sociological interpretation more compelling. But the proofs offered are inconclusive, and the Samaritan practice may be a distinct deviation from the historic tradition of the main stream of Judaism. Our assumption that levirate for the betrothed only is a genuine Jewish tradition of the early post-biblical period offers no proof save that of logical plausibility.

Gesetzen," in *Mittheilungen der vorderasiatischen Gesellschaft,* 1921, pp. 48 ff; P. Cruveilhier, "Le Levirat chez les Hebreux et chez les Assyriens," in *Revue Biblique,* 1925, pp. 19 f.

[34] Geiger, *Ḳebuẓat Ma'amarim,* p. 159; *Jüdische Zeitschrift,* l.c. This suggestion is denied by Ginzberg, *Sekte,* p. 83, note 4; and a case of levirate marriage among the Sadducees for the *wedded* is given in Josephus, *Ant.,* XIII,12 f, that of Alexander Janaeus marrying his sister-in-law, the wedded wife of Aristobulus.

[35] Geiger, ibid. In Yer. Yeb. 3a we have the amoraic statement that the Shammaites accepted the Samaritan interpretation of the word *ha-ḥuẓah,* but they did not apply it to the limiting of levirate to the betrothed.

[36] Samuel Belkin, *Philo and the Oral Law,* Cambridge, 1940, pp. 251–55, concludes that the Alexandrian Jews at the time of Philo and probably all Jewish communities under hellenic influence outside of Palestine accepted the Samaritan view, else he cannot see why levirate law is omitted in the hellenistic writings including the Apocrypha. I should imagine that a more logical explanation would be, if it is granted that levirate was not practiced in the hellenic countries, such as maintained by the Karaites, that levirate applies only in Palestine because it is connected with the ideal of preserving inheritance within the family.

In the later centuries of the Second Commonwealth further development took place in the mental horizon of the Hebrews on the subject of levirate. The last memories of the patriarchal family were gone and distinctions in the law based upon patriarchal concepts had lost their meaning. Levirate should have been completely lost to the Jews then, were it not for the fact that the Orient had been habituated to the levirate practice and that new eschatological beliefs gave point to the biblical motive of "establishing a name for the deceased." Therefore complete abandonment of the old institution was impossible. But "dwelling together" could no longer have the sociological interpretation, for reference to patriarchal family structure no longer had any meaning. And to declare levirate to apply in all cases seemed contrary to levitical law. The Samaritans too, therefore, like the rabbis and the Karaites, had the problem of adjusting Deuteronomy with Leviticus and of setting down legal rules where levirate does and does not apply. But these respective adjustments and the rules proceeding from them were now no longer of a sociological nature, but rather of an exegetical character.

The Samaritan exegesis of the law of levirate in Deuteronomy, as reported by the rabbis,[87] ignores the expression "dwelling together" and emphasises that word *ha-ḥuẓah,* which they take in the sense of *ha-ḥiẓonah,* the one who is outside the family, that is, the betrothed bride. They read verse five thus: "If brothers dwell together and one of them die without issue, the *betrothed bride* of the deceased shall not be married unto a stranger; her husband's brother shall go in unto her and take her to him to wife and perform the duty of levirate." The levitical law declaring the marriage of a sister-in-law to be incest is taken by the Samaritans to apply only to the wife who had been *wedded* to a brother, not one who had been only betrothed. Although in respect to adultery the Bible accounts the betrothed equal to the "wife," [88] this is because adultery is based on property rights, hence on contract. Incest, however, is based on "uncovering the nakedness" and has reference to marital union between

[87] Ḳid. 75b–76a; Yer. Yeb. 3a; Yer. Giṭ. 43c at bottom; Kuthim, at the end.
[88] Deut. 22.24.

husband and wife. This interpretation of incest has its logic in the Bible itself, was sometimes introduced into sectarian and rabbinic arguments as well,[39] and had its parallel also in the practice of a number of other ethnic groups in antiquity.[40]

Apparently the rabbis do not complain of any other deviation of the Samaritans from rabbinic halakah in performance of the levirate rite. We must assume, therefore, that they agreed on the other essentials, two of which should be mentioned here – that there was no levirate duty if only female issue remained and that the childless widow was free from the levirate duty if the husband had issue by another wife.[41] But the basic interpretation of the Samaritans, both of the levirate law and the law of incest, disturbed the rabbis, who saw therein a danger to family purity; and on that account they excluded them from marriage with Jews.[42]

[39] See Jubilees 41.27; Yoma 13b; Tosafot Yeb. 2b, s.v. *bitto.*

[40] Code Hammurabi 156; Hittite Code 27; Roman and Greek law cited by Belkin, p. 249, in the name of Gulak; ancient Arabs, specifically in respect to incest with a step-daughter, cited by Samuel Bialoblocki in *Materialien zum islamischen und jüdischen Eherecht,* Giesen, 1928, p. 39.

[41] Yer. Yeb. 3a raises the question according to the Samaritan interpretation, what is the meaning of the biblical statement in connection with levirate, "he has no issue," if only for the betrothed is there the levirate rite. The amoraim answer properly, that even the betrothed does not have to undergo levirate marriage unless the husband had no issue at all, not even by another wife. This argument is logical, and seems to indicate that the Samaritans agreed that if there is issue by another wife there is no levirate marriage. As to annulling the levirate duty where female issue has remained, we shall see later that it goes back to post-exilic legislation in respect to the right of daughters to inherit in the absence of sons and that such was the conception also of the Septuagint.

[42] The charge against the Samaritans in the matter of levirate is made by R. Johanan (Ḳid. 75b), and, of course, we assume that the older halakah accounted the child born of a woman who did not go through the levirate rite a mamzer, as we shall see later. On the other hand, Rabbah b. Abahu (Ḳid. 76a) charges them with two kinds of incest, taking sisters and taking sisters-in-law. Taking a sister-in-law is based on their misinterpretation of the law of incest as not applying to the betrothed, which means that even if there was no need for levirate marriage they allowed the brother to marry the wife of the deceased so long as she was only betrothed and not wedded. In other words, R. Johanan complains of their misinterpretation of Deuteronomy; Rabba complains of their misinterpretation of Leviticus.

The charge that they take sisters sounds rather strange. This certainly does not mean that there was an admixture among them of an immoral group of Jews who married sisters or lived with sisters and if it refers to a non-Jewish group the result is not mamzerut. Again it must refer to a certain teaching of

The implications of their theory of incest, rendering the betrothed not incestuous to her husband's relatives, seem to have been too radical for the Samaritans themselves. The Karaites, whose views on levirate we shall discuss later, began with a similar theory of incest and soon discarded it, even evidencing shame that they had ever subscribed to it. It must have been shocking to the morals of civilized orientals to teach that the betrothed, after leaving her husband, could marry one of his near kin. That superior morality caused the later Samaritans also to abandon the teaching that there was any difference between the betrothed and the wedded in the matter of levirate marriage, since there was no difference in respect to incest, and they interpreted the word "brother" in the levirate law to mean a "kinsman," a more distant relative. Thus levirate marriage to them came to mean *go'el* marriage.[43]

II

The rabbinic tradition drew no distinction either in incest or in levirate between the betrothed and wedded,[44] and the rabbis were more correct historically when they insisted that levirate marriage was different from *ge'ullah* and required marriage of the surviving brother and no one else. They adjusted Deuteronomy with Leviticus not in a critical nor sociological way, but in their own exegetical manner. The levitical law declares contact with a sister-in-law to be incest *only if there is no levirate duty;* i.e., when she has been

---

the Samaritans. Possibly the Samaritans taught that a natural daughter, one born of prostitution, is no daughter to the father and no sister to her brother, since this law is based on hermeneutic inference (Yeb. 22b) and the possibility of such a view by a rebellious judge, *zaken mamre,* is suggested in the Talmud (San. 87b). Perhaps the Samaritan view is referred to in this talmudic passage. The matter, however, is uncertain, and if we assume that the Samaritan view on this subject agreed with the rabbis, the charge of mamzerut from a sister must be accounted an exaggeration for rhetorical effect, as if to say the worst kind of mamzerut.

[43] See Geiger's articles in *Jüdische Zeitschrift* and *Kebuzat Ma'amarim,* ibid.

[44] In respect to incest, the subject will be discussed in the next chapter; in respect to levirate see Yoma 13b and Yeb. 13b: "*lerabbot ha-arusah.*"

divorced or when the brother has died leaving issue behind. The levirate duty applies only when there are no children, and *then the Bible suspends the incestuous prohibition against a sister-in-law.*[45] In other words, a sister-in-law either *must* be married, where there is a levirate situation, or *must not* be married, under the stringency of incest, where there is no levirate situation; there is no middle point between the positive and the negative imperative.

The rabbis were conscious that their teaching held in balance a situation which by the slightest turn of a technicality might be either the fulfillment of a biblical commandment or a violation of the law of incest, and therefore they dealt with the law of levirate in its most minute details and defined its terms with meticulous accuracy. As a result, they produced a whole tractate of the Talmud devoted to the complexities and intricacies of the levirate law. It would hardly be possible for us to reproduce in full the rabbinic law of levirate. Let it suffice to give the broader outlines of the law and to indicate wherever possible its historical background and development. We shall treat it under the following headings: (A) The levirate situation; (B) The state of *zikah;* (C) Levirate marriage; (D) Ḥaliẓah; (E) Imperfect dissolution of *zikah;* (F) Enforcement of the levirate; and (G) Succession to the estate.

(A) THE LEVIRATE SITUATION is established by the presence of a few essential conditions: first, that the marriage between the deceased brother and the widow was valid and was expected to be productive; second, that there be no offspring; third, that there be a surviving brother; fourth, that a physically productive and legally valid marriage between the levir and the widow be possible.

Our first requirement, that the deceased brother and his wife be married, includes the betrothed as well as the wedded according to rabbinic interpretation, as we have already mentioned. According to no interpretation known to us does it include the concubine or the slave-wife or the unwedded consort. By definition, therefore, a marriage that is not legally valid cannot create a levirate situation. If the deceased hus-

[45] Targum Jonathan ad Lev. 18.16; Yeb. 55a; Yer. Yeb. 2b.

band was a minor [46] or insane or a deaf-mute,[47] or if the widow was a minor and acted without her father's authority,[48] or if she was of age but was insane [49] or a deaf-mute,[50] there was no levirate situation because the marriage had no full legal validity. For the same reason, if the marriage was a violation of the biblical law of incest, there was no levirate duty.[51]

The valid marriage, in order to produce a levirate situation in rabbinic law, must have the possibilities of being productive. We have no reason to suspect that this limitation set upon the law of levirate antedates the rabbinic period. Whether the economic motive of levirate is invoked or whether emphasis is placed upon the perpetuation of the name of the deceased, we cannot say, in the biblical spirit,

[46] Yeb. 69b; 96b. The Talmud does not cite any biblical derivation for this rule, but Maimonides, Yad, Yibbum 6,8 cites a tannaitic midrash, the source of which is not known to us.

[47] Yeb. 112b. Rabbinic law considers the deaf-mute as incapable of contracting marriage. Yet the marriage of a deaf-mute is rabbinically valid. Hence, there is no levirate situation from a biblical viewpoint. But a rabbinic levirate situation does exist.

[48] Yeb. 2b. A minor daughter married by her father comprises in every sense a full biblical marriage. Here we refer to a minor girl who had no father, or who gained her independence from her father through a previous marriage. And here, as above, there is no biblical levirate situation but a rabbinical levirate duty.

[49] If she was a minor and was married by her father there is a biblical levirate situation, Tos. Yeb. 2,5. But an insane woman who has attained majority cannot be married. Yeb. 112b.

[50] Here, too, we deal with the major, but the minor deaf-mute woman can be married by her father in a biblically valid marriage. However, in our case, the marriage is rabbinically valid and therefore creates a rabbinic levirate situation.

[51] Various talmudic derivations are offered; see E.H. 173,4; but the matter is evident and is definitely included in the last mishnah of the first chapter of Yeb.

If the prohibition of the marriage of the deceased brother was less than incest, there is a full levirate situation and either levirate marriage or ḥaliẓah is possible. Yeb. 84a; Yad, Yibbum 6,13.

There are two exceptions to the rule. In the case of a woman who committed adultery while with her husband, after his death there is no levirate duty, because the "defilement" was considered almost equal to divorce. Yeb. 11a. In case the woman has been divorced, married to another, and remarried to her husband in violation of the biblical prohibition, after the husband's death there is no levirate marriage, but ḥaliẓah is necessary. Yeb. 12a.

that the widow of a brother who was incapable of begetting children is not to be conserved in the family as an economic good, or is not required to establish seed for the deceased. The restriction is entirely rabbinic, by a method of hermeneutics characteristic of the rabbis, and evidently for the purpose of excluding from the levirate situation as many cases as possible. The rabbinic reasoning is that the levirate rite is intended to give offspring to one disappointed in his childlessness, not to one by nature destined to be childless.[52] Thus, if the deceased brother was a natural eunuch or hermaphrodite, even if the widow be capable of childbirth, there is no levirate duty.

The second requirement for establishing a levirate situation is that the deceased brother has died without issue. Although the levirate law in Deuteronomy states this condition explicitly, yet our statement cannot go unchallenged. The levirate circumstances given in Genesis permits the interpretation that Tamar's childlessness was the important element in the levirate situation, and that her condition impelled her to remain in her father's house as a widow, in the manner reflected by the Book of Leviticus, and furthermore, that her childlessness rendered her an object of pity and drove her to subterfuge. Again, if we go back to the original motive in levirate, that of preserving the economic value of the widow, her childlessness, more than that of her husband, should be emphasized; for if she had children she would remain in the family even without marriage, but having no issue, she would leave the family unless retained by levirate law. Such an interpretation is given by Josephus[53] when he says: "If a woman's husband die and leave her without children, let his brother marry her . . . . and this will be for the solace of wives under their affliction, that they are to be married to the next relation of their former husbands." And peculiarly enough, 'Anan, founder of Karaism, formulates this interpretation into a law, that if the wife have

[52] Tos. Yeb. 2,5; Yeb. 79b. If the deceased was castrated, the levirate situation is not destroyed because there was a time in his life when he had expected issue. Yeb. ibid.; E.H. 172,3.

[53] *Ant.*, IV,8,23.

children by another husband, (even if the husband be childless) she is not subjected to the levirate rite.[54]

The rabbinic tradition does not take into account the wife's childlessness at all. Her having children by another husband would not at all alter the levirate situation, so long as the husband died without issue. The rabbis do not find it necessary to show reason for this interpretation, nor do they indicate any biblical derivation therefor. Apparently, the interpretation was too well known in earliest tannaitic times to require support. And surely the biblical sentiment of "raising seed" for the *brother,* or to "establish a name for the *brother* in Israel," or "to establish the name of the dead upon his inheritance" indicates that the point of emphasis is on the man's childlessness, in full support of the rabbinic teaching.

The brother's childlessness, as defined by the rabbis, means no children whatever, male or female, from one wife or another. This interpretation, it is said,[55] while in conflict with the specific statement in Deuteronomy, "and he has no *son,*" goes back to an earlier stage in the law, when the term *seed* was employed, not *son.* So it is in Genesis that Judah commands his son to beget *seed* for his brother, with the implication that if the brother had had *seed* of his own, son or daughter, there would be no need of levirate marriage.[56] The inference is interesting but by no means conclusive. If it be true, however, that originally if the husband left a

[54] *Sefer ha-Mizwot,* ed. Harkavy, Nashim, sec. 35, p. 108.

[55] Zevi Karl, "Ha-Yibbum we-ha-Ḥaliẓah," in *ha-Mishpat,* 1927, pp. 266 f, concludes that originally any child made the levirate unnecessary, later only a son. The older halakah was practiced in hellenic communities; Palestine for a time followed the new law, but later yielded to the old law because it produced fewer cases of *yibbum.* The old law is represented by the expression "seed" in the Judah-Tamar case and in the Septuagint. Now, to me the word "seed" in the negative does mean neither son nor daughter, as in Lev. 22.13, but "seed" in the affirmative, as is the case in the passage in Genesis — "establish seed for thy brother" — is only a general expression for offspring and may be used even when one has in mind only sons. So is the term "seed" employed in connection with circumcision, Gen. 17, or in connection with Torah, Isa. 59.21. It simply means that even when you have only sons in mind, you can speak of offspring; but you cannot say "without offspring" when you know that there are daughters.

[56] Gen. 38.8.

daughter there was no levirate duty, that law had a totally different foundation from the rabbinic law. It was at that early stage of Jewish history when metronymic marriage was still practiced, and in such a marriage the daughter remains in the family and her children perpetuate the name of the deceased.

The foundation of the rabbinic law is the patronymic family, which was the standard family organization in the entire biblical period. In that system sons alone remain in the family; they alone can perpetuate the name of the deceased; and they alone can carry on the chain of succession in an estate. This was the background of the law of Deuteronomy, whereby the absence of male issue is the only basis for the levirate situation. In the next step of biblical legislation, however, daughters were granted the right of succession in the absence of male offspring.[57] From that moment the levirate duty applied only when neither male nor female remained behind, and likewise, the childless widow returned to her parental home only if she had neither male nor female children.[58] This change of law may have been known even to some of the later biblical authors, for not very long after the biblical period, in the Septuagint translation, the deuteronomic expression "and he had no son" is rendered "and he had no children." [59] Josephus, who corroborates the Septuagint reading,[60] is probably not citing a pharisaic tradition but takes the Septuagint as his text, the only text of the Bible known to his readers, and expounds the law in Septuagint terminology.[61]

By the term childless, the rabbis understood that the de-

[57] Num. 27.8.

[58] Lev. 22.13.

[59] Septuagint, Deut. 25.5.

[60] *Ant.*, l.c.

[61] A similar case is found in the Mishnah, which Karl took too literally and too seriously. M. Yeb. 22b reads: A son of any sort frees (his mother from levirate duty). Karl believes that here the rabbis go back to the deuteronomic tradition that only sons but not daughters count. In reality, this mishnah submits a tannaitic midrash in comment upon the word "son" in Deuteronomy, and teaches that "son" in the text means any son. It does not give the halakah in terms of "sons." Josephus, here, stands in the same relation to the Septuagint as the tannaim stood to the Hebrew text.

ceased had no children at the time of his death, even if he had had children who died before him. However, if those children left sons or daughters, that is, if the deceased left grand-children, there was no levirate duty upon the widow.[62] To continue – if the widow is pregnant at the time of the husband's death, the posthumous child will count for him if it be established that he is normal.[63] Every child counts for the deceased father, even if born out of wedlock, from harlotry, from incest or adultery, because a natural child, even a *mamzer*, is heir to his father and therefore perpetuates his name.[64] On the other hand, a child born of a gentile or slave mother does not count, because he is reckoned after his mother and does not become heir of his father.[65] In connection with the Bustanai story,[66] the geonim declared that a man who lives with his own female slave and begets children by her proves by his action that he has not treated her as a slave but as a freed woman. Therefore the law assumes, without evidence, that he had freed her. As a consequence, the child born of the union is not the issue of a slave but of a free woman. Hence he is accounted legal heir to his father; and is reckoned as a son to free his father's wives from the levirate rite.[67] Adoption is a process not recognized by rabbinic law, and the adopted child, therefore, does not count as a child.[68]

The third requirement, that there be a surviving brother in order to establish a levirate situation, is in keeping with

62 Yad, Yibbum 1,3.

63 Yeb. 35b; Yad, Yibbum 1,5. Biblically, if the child lived for a moment after his father's death there is no levirate duty. Rabbinically, if there is suspicion of abnormalcy in the birth, and that suspicion always exists in the law unless the child has lived thirty days, there is a rabbinic duty of ḥaliẓah, but *yibbum* is impossible.

64 Yeb. 22a.

65 Yeb. ibid.

66 Bustanai, *Rosh Galuta* in the seventh century, lived with a gentile slave woman, by whom he had sons who occupied prominent positions in Jewish communal life. Their legitimacy was challenged because their mother was a gentile and slave. See Jewish Encyclop. "Bostani."

67 Yad, Gerushin 10,19; E.H. 156,2.

68 Dr. Belkin in *Philo and the Oral Law* suggests (p. 254) that the hellenistic Jews may have evaded levirate in case of childlessness by means of adoption. It was certainly never accepted by rabbinic halakah.

biblical law, but reveals a deviation from the pre-biblical usage permitting the father of the deceased to perform the levirate rite, as in the case of Judah and Tamar. The possibility of a *ge'ullah* marriage, as in Ruth, is not eliminated, but to the rabbis *ge'ullah* and levirate are two distinctly different things, for *ge'ullah* is optional and levirate is mandatory. In this tradition, too, the rabbis are close to biblical standards. They probably also follow biblical tradition when they teach that only brothers of the same father count as such in respect to levirate, not maternal half-brothers; for the levirate duty is part of the chain of succession, and since maternal brothers are not heirs to one another, they have no reciprocal levirate obligations.[69] In another ruling, however, the rabbis seem to have deviated from the biblical norm, in that only a brother who was alive at the time of the death can perform the levirate duty; one born after the death of the brother cannot marry the widow.[70] Biblical evidences are to the contrary,[71] and this must be recorded as rabbinic legislation made necessary by the consideration that otherwise the widow would never be free to remarry when there are no surviving brothers, so long as the father was alive and might beget children at some future time.[72]

The legitimacy of the surviving brother does not come into consideration. Even if he be a mamzer, the levirate duty falls upon him.[73] However, if he be born of a gentile or slave mother, even if the deceased brother was also born of the same mother, the surviving brother cannot perform the levirate rite.[74] In gaonic times there was a serious attempt to declare the convert not accountable as a brother to the other sons in the family. According to this ruling, if a converted brother has remained the only levir, there is no

[69] Sifre Deut. 288; Yeb. 17b; Yer. Yeb. 2d. Since the difference between the patriarchal family and the individual family was not sensed by the later tannaim, they interpreted "dwelling together" to mean having a right of succession to each other. The sense that levirate is based upon succession (Yeb. ibid.) is thoroughly historical.

[70] Sifre Deut. ibid.; Yeb. 2b; 18b.

[71] See Ruth 1.11 and Rashi and Ibn Ezra thereto.

[72] Yer. Yeb. 3c.

[73] Yeb. 22a.

[74] Yeb. ibid.; 97b.

levirate situation. But this gaonic ruling was not accepted by the later authorities, consistent with the general principle of rabbinic law that a converted Jew is accounted a Jew nevertheless.[75]

We complete the picture of the levirate situation by presenting the last requirement, that the marriage between widow and surviving brother be physically productive and legally valid. The term "physically productive" is defined by the rabbis in the most limited sense, that neither the widow nor the levir be *congenitally* sterile. It does not exclude from the levirate rite the castrated, the barren, or the aged,[76] of whom it cannot be said that they were *never* capable of procreation. But it does exclude the *ailonit*,[77] the hermaphrodite, or the congenital eunuch, who were born sterile.[78] Again, the term "legally valid" is interpreted by the rabbis in a most narrow sense. It does not exclude from levirate marriage the minor or insane or deaf-mute,[79] who are incapable of contracting a legally valid marriage. For the levirate marriage is not a contractual marriage, so as to require legal personality; it is a *Heaven-made* marriage, similar in character to the acquisition of property by inheritance, of which the minor and the insane are also capable. Therefore, whether the levir or the widow be minor or insane or deaf-mute, levirate marriage is possible and required.

This rule, however, is directly intended to exclude from the levirate picture cases where the levir and the widow are of a grade of kinship to make their marriage incestuous[80] and therefore legally invalid. Of course, the levirate law itself is an infringement upon the law of incest; but while the specific incest of marrying a brother's wife is suspended in the case of levirate, according to the rabbis, no other incestuous prohibition is similarly superceded by the levirate duty.

[75] Yad, Yibbum 1,6 and *Maggid* thereto; E.H. 157,4.

[76] Tos. Yeb. 2,6; Yeb. 20b; 79b. Ḥaliẓah is prescribed; marriage is prohibited but valid.

[77] Yeb. 79b; Tos. Yeb. 2,5; Yeb. 24a.

[78] Sifre Deut. 289; Tos. ibid.; Yeb. 79b.

[79] Tos. Yeb. ibid.; Yeb. 111b. Ḥaliẓah is ineffective in these cases, because ḥaliẓah represents a transaction of which the minor and the insane are incapable. Yeb. 119a.

[80] Sifre Deut. 289–290; Jeb. 3b; Yer. Yeb. 2b.

Thus in the matter of two brothers marrying two sisters, – when one dies, the widow cannot be married by the surviving brother, because she is sister of his own wife. Or as often occurred, a man married his brother's daughter; when he died the widow could not be married by the surviving brother, because he was her father. In all such cases there is no levirate situation; it is destroyed by the situation of incest.

In our portrayal of the levirate, we have assumed that there is only one surviving brother and one widow. This was necessary for clarity, but it need not necessarily be true. Many surviving brothers may be expected in any family, and many surviving widows may be expected in a polygamous family. How does that condition affect the situation? Let us recall that the deceased husband, the children, the widow, and the levir, all played a part in making up the levirate complex. Logic compels the conclusion that where the levirate situation is destroyed by a physical or legal difficulty in the husband, the destruction is complete. Likewise where there are children recognized by law as legitimate heirs to the deceased. Where, however, the defect is in the widow, the other widows remain under obligation of performing the levirate rite. Similarly, where the bar to levirate marriage is due to the levir, the other brothers come under the levirate duty.

The case of a widow who is of an incestuous degree of kinship to the levir partly conforms to this principle and partly forms an exception to it. In conformity with the above principle, the rule is that if there are other brothers to whom she is not of an incestuous degree of kinship, she is subject to levirate marriage by one of them.[81] As exception to the principle, rabbinic law teaches that if one of the widows is of an incestuous degree of kinship to the levir, none of the other widows may be married by him either. The exception, however, is more apparent than real. It does not mean that the entire levirate situation is destroyed for all widows; it simply means that the levir to whom one of the widows is of an incestuous degree of kinship is en-

[81] M. Yeb. 2a. See Rashi Yeb. 2b, s.v. *halekah.*

tirely eliminated. In other words, if he cannot marry one, he cannot marry any;[82] and the levirate situation goes on without him. Once it is agreed that he cannot marry any of the widows, then all of them become prohibited to him as incestuous, because they are his brother's wives. Hence it follows that one of the co-wives or co-widows (*Ẓarah*), if taken in levirate marriage by another brother, when again widowed without issue from that brother, will be accounted of incestuous kinship to him; and again he will be eliminated from the levirate situation in respect to all the widows remaining.[83]

The basic principle in these rules, that the incestuous kinship of one of the widows renders the other widows also incestuous to the same levir, was formulated by the Hillelites at the end of the Second Commonwealth. The Shammaites contested the principle and permitted the levir to marry the co-widows who were not of an incestuous degree of kinship to him.[84] The Shammaites represented the older halakah and the older practice;[85] the Hillelites, by their teaching, introduced a reform in the law. This reform was combated bitterly down to the middle of the second century,[86] and both views were acted upon by various courts. The innovation on the part of the Hillelites must have had some pressing motive. One would suspect that it had to do with the economic condition of the Jews after the conquest of Judea.[87] But exact information on the subject we have not, and the student is free to conjecture about it as he may wish. Later tannaim based the difference between the Shammaites and the Hillelites on a certain hermeneutic interpretation of

82 Yeb. 3b; 8b.

83 M. Yeb. 2a; Yeb. 13a.

84 M. Yeb. 13a–b.

85 Yeb. 14a–16a, despite an attempted denial by the amoraim.

86 Yeb. 16a, in the generation of R. Akiba.

87 It is difficult to conjecture about this matter, yet we make bold to suggest that the motive back of this reform was that whereas in the case of a man marrying his brother's daughter and dying childless the father is obligated to take care of his widowed daughter, as in Lev. 22.13, it was considered too much of a burden to ask him to take care also of the second childless widow. The Shammaites were richer and of higher economic standards. That is the reason why the controversy originally concerned the co-wife of a *daughter*. The other cases of incestuous kinship were derived

a biblical verse.[88] Although it is true that the Hillelites made freer use of hermeneutic interpretations, it does not seem true that the interpretation created the law, but rather that the law created the interpretation. Besides, the interpretation really belongs to a later date. All that does seem certain is that the Hillelites sought to contract application of the levirate law to a narrower circle. The law favored the Hillelites' view in declaring the co-wife of one who was of incestuous kinship to the levir to be accounted as if she – the co-wife – herself was of incestuous kinship to him, and therefore free from the levirate duty; and the law also accepted the Hillelite tendency of contracting the levirate situation to ever narrower limits, and ruled that when the co-wife is married to a second brother and he in turn dies childless, her co-wives, like herself, are also free from the levirate duty.

(B) THE STATE OF ZIḲAH describes the legal status of the widow from her husband's death to the time of her marriage to the levir, or to the time of obtaining a release by ḥaliẓah. The term is rabbinic and means "being chained." The law finds it difficult to give an exact definition of the state. The widow, on the one hand, is freed from her husband by his death, yet she is chained to him; on the other hand, she is given by Heaven to the levir, yet he has not come into possession of her. This duality of status is felt in the Bible itself, when Tamar is asked to return to her parental home and yet remains wholly under control of her father-in-law. Ziḳah nearly approaches the status of the betrothed bride, and yet seems to be inferior legally. Betrothal represents actual legal ownership, while ziḳah represents a *right to ownership*. Upon the exact definition of ziḳah hinge a number of laws dealing with the rights and duties of the widow in respect to the estate and surviving brothers of her deceased husband.

---

from the case of the daughter. The tradition cited (Yeb. 16a) in the name of the prophet Haggai mentions *ẓarat ha-bat,* tithes for the poor on the sabbatical year, and foreign proselytes. Probably all three were legislation in interest of the poor, although the direct benefit to the poor of the third item is not very clear.

[88] Sifre Deut. 288, cited in Yeb. 8b in the name of Rabbi Judah the Nasi.

Thus the Hillelites, contrary to the views of the Shammaites, teach that the betrothed bride is under control of her groom in respect to her personal property, so that she can sell none of it without his consent. They agree with the Shammaites, however, that the levirate widow in the state of ziḳah can sell her personal property without interference from the brothers. An amora explains that this view defines ziḳah as "doubtful betrothal."[89] It follows that if the widow die in the state of ziḳah, her own family and her levir's family have equally doubtful claim to her personal possessions.[90] The right of the levir to annul the vows of the widow can also be determined on the basis of the definition of ziḳah. R. Eliezer believes that the widow is by the gift of Heaven the wife of the levir, and he can annul her vows;[91] R. Akiba says, "The levirate woman does not so definitely belong to the levir as the betrothed bride belongs to her husband," and therefore he cannot annul her vows.[92]

This principle is also invoked in the following contingency. A man dies childless; his brother marries the widow. During the period of ziḳah another brother is born. R. Simeon maintains that ziḳah is equal to betrothal, hence the newly born brother has nothing to do with the death of the first brother. When the second brother dies childless, he may marry the

[89] Yeb. 38a. It should be remembered that during the period of the Hillelites the law granted the husband the right of succession to his *betrothed*. See JMC p. 137. 'Ula, who interprets the first part of the mishnah as referring to the betrothed and the last part as referring to the wedded, was forced into that position by the law of his (amoraic) day, which denied succession to the husband until the nuptials.

[90] Yeb. ibid. The disposition of these doubtful claims is also discussed by the Shammaites and the Hillelites, but that is irrelevant to our subject. See JMC pp. 95–99; 108–11.

[91] Ned. 74a. One may take for granted that the *shomeret yabam* is no better than the *arusah*. R. Eliezer's view may, therefore, have been properly interpreted by the amoraim: יפר בשותפות. Or, R. Eliezer, being he who maintains (Ned. 73b) that the widow who is betrothed to a second husband falls under his power for the annulment of her vows from the time he begins to support her, may grant that right to the levir – exclusive of the father – because she is widowed and, therefore out of her father's jurisdiction, and because she is supported by the levir.

[92] The halakah accepted the view of R. Akiba in keeping with the tendency to give more independence to the levirate woman. See Yad, Nedarim 11,23–24.

widow under the levirate law.[93] R. Me'ir believes that zikah is not like betrothal.[94] The newly born brother, therefore, finds himself included in the levirate situation. He, however, cannot marry her because he was born after the brother's death. On that account she becomes incestuously prohibited to him forever. Hence, should the second brother die childless, he would not be able to perform the levirate rite because of the incestuous prohibition.

The most direct question involved in this doubtful character of zikah is whether the widow in a state of zikah having contact with a man outside the family commits adultery or not. It will be remembered that in the case of Tamar she was sentenced to death by burning on the charge of unfaithfulness to her levirate bond. The deuteronomic law did not consider the offence so severe as to merit a death penalty. Surely the Talmud would not raise the question of capital punishment for violation of the levirate bond. But if the widow's contact with other men is equal to adultery of a kind, even though of a milder nature, the conclusion should be that the levir could no longer marry her after her unfaithfulness, in the same manner as a husband is not permitted to live with an unfaithful wife. The amoraim are divided on this question; one maintains that the unfaithful widow is prohibited to the levir, another that there is no prohibition.[95]

If adultery is brought into the question, we must also raise the question of incest. Can the levir marry the widow's mother or sister while the widow is in the state of zikah? Or can he marry the mother after the widow's death? Rab believes zikah is not like betrothal; therefore the law of incest does not apply to her relatives. Samuel contends that

93 Mishnah and beraita Yeb. 28b. The amoraic interpretation of this mishnah is given on p. 19a. The amoraic argument (Yeb. 18b at bottom) that R. Simeon accounts zikah as a doubtful status is not conclusive where the woman has zikah towards two surviving brothers (as in the case of the mishnah cited by them); the zikah itself is discounted; the *ma'amar* alone comes into question, and it is the effect of the *ma'amar* that R. Simeon finds doubtful. According to this view, R. Oshayah's interpretation (יבם ואח״כ נולד), while not conclusive, is quite logical.

94 Yeb. 18a.

95 Sotah 18b; Yer. Sotah 18d.

ziḳah is like betrothal and the widow's mother is an actual mother-in-law to the levir.[96]

The halakah does not decide this principle but takes a practical view on the question of incest and adultery. It teaches that ziḳah establishes affinity between the widow and the levir similar in character to the affinity between husband and wife. Therefore all incestuous degrees of kinship that apply between husband and wife apply also between levir and widow. Yet while similar they have not the same severity in law. They do not constitute actual biblical incest but a rabbinical prohibition patterned after biblical law.[97] Rabbinical incest is a familiar concept in talmudic law, and that concept fits the state of ziḳah. But there is no concept of rabbinical adultery, and since ziḳah is at any rate inferior to betrothal, adultery for the widow in a state of ziḳah is impossible. Hence the unfaithful widow does not become prohibited to the levir.[98]

The logical assumption is that during the ziḳah period the widow lives in her former husband's house, even though the regularly betrothed woman does not reside in her groom's house. This is because she belongs to her husband's family not so much on account of her bond of ziḳah to the levir, but because she is the widow of the deceased. In the case of Tamar, she was asked to return to her parental home, and we do not know definitely why.[99] Ruth was emphatic about continuing in her husband's family while awaiting *ge'ullah* marriage. Whether the law in Leviticus, prescribing that the childless widow shall return to her parental home, also includes the widow in a state of ziḳah, we do not know. However, in rabbinic law, dating back to Temple days, the ketubah provided by special clause that the widow should dwell in her husband's house and be supported out of his

[96] Yeb. 17b–18b.

[97] Yad, Yibbum 1,13.

[98] Yad, Yibbum 2,20.

[99] We do not know whether that was the older custom of which the law in Lev. 22.13 is a later echo; whether Tamar remained throughout her marital experience in the status of *arusah,* perhaps being only betrothed to Er; whether Shelah's being a minor had anything to do with her returning to her parental home.

estate during her widowhood, and no distinction was drawn between the widow under ziḳah or under no ziḳah bond.[100] Later law set down a period of three months of waiting before the levirate woman could be either taken in marriage by the levir or released by ḥaliẓah, and her support out of her husband's estate was limited to that period.[101] Beyond that she had no claim for support from the estate. The levir, on the other hand, assumed no obligation for support of the widow on his own until he married her. Realizing, however, that the widow was wholly dependent upon the levir either for marriage or for ḥaliẓah and that he might unduly delay performance of his duty by her, the court sometimes imposed upon him the duty of supporting her even before he married her or (declining marriage) before he gave her release by ḥaliẓah.[102] If the delay was due to no fault of the levir, as for instance if he was a minor, and especially if due to the

[100] JMC. pp. 175–80. Of course, the view (Ket. 81a) יבם כאחר דמי is later and artificial.

[101] Yeb. 41b. This question involves the Talmud in the very problem on which the levitical law legislates, namely that the childless widow goes back to her father and eats of his food; i.e. if he is a priest, she eats of the heave offering; if he is an Israelite, even though she was married to and widowed from a priest, she cannot eat of the heave offering. The levirate widow, when her husband was a priest and she of an Israelitish family, according to *Mishnah Aḥaronah,* cannot eat of the heave offering as if she were an *arusah.* Whether she was permitted to eat *terumah* according to the *Mishnah Rishonah* is a matter of controversy between Rashi and Rabbenu Tam, and one feels like siding with the latter on the basis of his evidences. See Tosafot Yeb. 67b, s.v. *ḳinyan* and Tosafot Ket. 58a, s.v. *wa-afilu.* But I wish to draw attention to one point of confusion in Rabbenu Tam's argument. All his evidences prove only that as long as the levirate widow is supported out of her husband's estate, *terumah* is permitted to her, according to the *Mishnah Rishonah.* That proves in no way when the husband's alimentation duty comes to an end, and the widow is thrown upon the levir for support, that she can eat of *terumah* because of her ziḳah to the levir. In this respect the Talmud is right in saying that ziḳah to the levir, even according to the *Mishnah Rishonah,* does not constitute a bond equal to betrothal. My own conclusion would be that she may eat *terumah,* according to the *Mishnah Rishonah,* as long as she is supported out of her deceased husband's estate, not when the levir is charged with her support; according to the *Mishnah Aḥaronah,* the woman cannot eat *terumah* under any circumstances until she is taken in full levirate marriage. See Tos. Ket. 5,1; 4,3.

[102] Yeb. 41b; Tosafot ibid., s.v. *'amad.* See Yer. Ket. 29d and commentators on the principle of: האומר איני חולק כאומר איני מגרש.

widow herself, the levir was not required to support her.[108]

The widow's earnings during the period she is supported out of her husband's estate go to the estate, whether she be maintained all her lifetime, as in the original law, or for a period of three months, as in the later law.[104] If she is supported out of the levir's own property, the levir is not entitled to her labor or her earnings [105] or to usufruct or to inheritance,[106] for she is supported not on the basis of the ziḳah bond but as a matter of penalty or discipline. In return, the levir does not owe the widow ransom [107] if she is made captive, or medicine if taken sick, unless the medicine belongs to the category of support.[108] If she dies, the husband's estate or the levir must pay her burial expenses in return for her unpaid ketubah.[109]

Most important in the ziḳah state, however, is not the status of the widow in respect to her husband's family, but the implications of the ziḳah bond as to marriage prohibitions arising out of it. There are two types of such prohibitions. One is based on ziḳah kinship and yields a series of prohibitions which we may call ziḳah-incest. We have mentioned above that these are only rabbinical, not biblical. We shall treat this subject more fully in a succeeding chapter. The other type is of the very essence of the whole levirate law, that forbidding the widow to marry anyone but the levir. This holds the center of interest to the rabbis in a levirate situation, and ziḳah has become practically synonymous with this marriage prohibition in their minds. They forget the deceased husband; they lose sight of the chain of succession from the deceased to the child not yet born; they make little of the levir's own interest in the ziḳah situation. To them, above everything else, the ziḳah

[103] Yeb. ibid.
[104] Tos. Ket. 5,2.
[105] Ket. 107b.
[106] Tos. Ket. ibid.; Yad, Ishut, 18,8 and *Maggid* thereto. That the levir inherits her ketubah is a case of inheritance of the deceased brother, not of the widow.
[107] Yer. Yeb. 29a; Yad, ibid. 5.
[108] As is the case with any widow. Ket. 52b.
[109] Ket. 80b–81a.

bond is similar to the marriage bond in that the widow cannot marry an outsider while she is "chained" to the levir.

We have mentioned that in earlier biblical times, the violation of the ziḳah bond, that is, the widow's marrying an outsider, was penalized by death. Deuteronomy emphasizes the violation, implies perhaps some form of corporal punishment, but prescribes no death penalty. The early tradition among the tannaim no doubt was that the marriage of the levirate widow to an outsider was not valid and the children born of such a union were mamzerim.[110] This tradition persisted even among the early amoraim.[111] But the majority opinion of the amoraim, and therefore the accepted halakah, is that the violation of ziḳah rates as violation of any negative biblical command, punishable by flagellation but not invalidating the marriage or rendering the offspring illegitimate.[112]

Now, there are four grades of intensity of ziḳah. It may be

[110] M. Yeb. 92a implies that a child born of *yebamah leshuḳ* is a mamzer. Later tannaim having a different legal view stated (beraita ibid.) that this mishnah records only the view of Rabbi Akiba. Tos. Yeb. 1,8 also (inconclusively) seems to indicate that the offspring of *yebamah leshuḳ* is illegitimate. Tos. Yeb. 1,9 as given in Zuckermandel and quoted in Babli Yeb. 14b would seem to indicate that the offspring is only unfit for marriage to a priest, but the reading as given in Yerushalmi Yeb. 3a expressly declares the offspring a mamzer. Ḳid. 75b–76a, which gives the reason for excluding the Samaritans from marrying with Jews because they permitted the wedded wife to marry outside the family even where a levirate situation existed, also indicates that *yebamah leshuḳ* was cause for mamzerut, and here, too, the Gemara seeks to escape this inference by saying this is only according to the view of R. Akiba. Rab is of the opinion that the marriage of a levirate widow to a stranger is not valid; other authorities are quoted as holding the same view; a mishnah (Ḳid. 62a) is cited to prove that point; but again the Gemara (Yeb. 92b) seeks to ascribe this mishnah to R. Akiba. One can see that only by forced interpretations and sometimes by emendations in the older texts was it possible to maintain the view that the violation of the ziḳah bond neither invalidates the marriage nor causes mamzerut.

[111] Rab is the leading exponent of this view. Samuel half agrees with him, yet requires a divorce for the *yebamah* who marries an outsider. Other amoraim are quoted following the view of Rab. See Yeb. 92b.

[112] It is not unlikely that R. Elazar is the first of the tannaim to pronounce the rule that *yebamah leshuḳ* does not cause mamzerut, reporting his view to be an admission of the Shammaites to the Hillelites (in the case of *ẓarah*) — Tos. Yeb. 1,10. This view seems to be accepted in the halakah. See Yad, Issure Bi'ah 15,1. However, the validity of the marriage is doubtful, in accordance with the view of Samuel, cited in previous note. See Yad, Ishut, 4,14 and Tosafot, Yeb. 92a, s.v. *abal*.

biblical or doubtful biblical ziḳah; it may be rabbinical or doubtful rabbinical ziḳah. Biblical ziḳah is the normal case, in a regularly constituted marriage. The doubtful biblical cases are those where there is doubt as to the validity of the marriage [113] or where there is no way of determining whether the deceased left either children or brothers.[114] Rabbinical ziḳah exists where the widow is a minor orphan whose marriage to the deceased brother was only of rabbinical validity.[115] Another case of rabbinical ziḳah is given in the Talmud, where a woman married a second husband on the report that her first husband had died, thereafter proven false. Her second marriage, while not valid, still has the effect that when her second husband dies childless, his brothers have to free her by ḥaliẓah; for by rabbinical enactment she is in a state of ziḳah in respect to her second husband's family.[116] Doubtful rabbinical ziḳah exists where a widow remains pregnant at the death of her childless husband, and the child is born posthumously but dies a few days after birth. In that case there is no biblical ziḳah because a child has been born to the deceased husband. However, if the child should be prematurely born there would be rabbinic ziḳah, because he does not count as a child in rabbinic law. If he died soon after birth, it remains doubtful whether the death was or was not due to premature

[113] Tos. Yeb. 2,6. It would also be biblically doubtful ziḳah if the husband before his death gave his wife a divorce of doubtful validity. Yad, Yibbum 6,7.

[114] The doubt as to brothers is possible when the husband's parentage cannot be established. A similar doubt may exist as to the husband's childlessness, when a surviving child may or may not be his — in the case, for instance, when the child is born of a prostitute but claimed by the deceased as his (Yad, Yibbum 3,7) or when the widow gave birth to a child after being married only a little after six months to him, while it was within nine months since she had been divorced from a former husband. In that case, it is doubtful whether it was a pregnancy of six months and the child belongs to the later (the deceased) husband or a pregnancy of nine months and the child belongs to the former husband. See Yad, Yibbum 1,23. Another possibility of a doubtful child is when father and child died together in an accident and it cannot be ascertained whether the father died first or the child. If the father died first, there is no ziḳah; if the child died first, the ziḳah situation does exist.

[115] M. Yeb. 109a at bottom.

[116] M. Yeb. 87b and Rashi ibid. s.v. ḥoleẓin.

birth. The ziḳah in that case is of doubtful rabbinical validity.[117]

The law has imposed penalties on the woman who, in defiance of the bond of ziḳah or unwittingly, marries an outsider. In the same manner as if she had violated an actual marriage bond,[118] she must be divorced by her husband, is not permitted to return in levirate marriage to her levir, and has no ketubah claims on either. A gaonic tradition sought to soften the penalty by ruling that if the woman had children by the husband whom she married in violation of the ziḳah bond, she did not have to leave him, but was given ḥaliẓah by the levir in order to legalize life with her husband. But the halakah does not recognize that compromise.[119] The severe penalty is applied in cases violating positive biblical ziḳah. The law is not clear whether it would be applied also in violations of rabbinical ziḳah or doubtful biblical ziḳah. However, if there was only an offense involving doubtful rabbinical ziḳah, the law rules that the woman can remain with her husband even if she has no children, except that ḥaliẓah from the levir is necessary. And if the husband is a priest, who may not be married to one who has been given ḥaliẓah, the ḥaliẓah requirement is also waived.[120]

The state of ziḳah includes every widow left of the childless husband and every surviving brother; that is, every widow is "chained" to every brother-in-law. However, the law does not require nor does it permit that the levir marry all the widows or give them all ḥaliẓah, but accounts the marriage or the ḥaliẓah of one sufficient to free all the others from the ziḳah bond.[121]

Because the levirate law in Deuteronomy is couched in terms of monogamy, we do not know what the biblical law was in cases of polygamy, whether it required levirate for all the widows or only for one. There are arguments on both sides. On the motive of "raising seed" for the deceased,

[117] Yad, Yibbum, 1,5.
[118] M. Yeb. 92a; M. Giṭ. 80a.
[119] Tosafot Yeb. 92a, s.v. *abal;* Yad, Yibbum 2,18. See also 2,20.
[120] Sab. 136a; Yad, Yibbum 2,21.
[121] Yeb. 24a; 39a; 44b–45a.

only one marriage should be satisfactory; but in the matter of preserving the property right in the widow, every widow should be taken in levirate marriage. The third motive, that of providing for the widow, may justify marrying all the widows, and yet may equally justify the argument that marrying one is all the burden that a brother should be expected to carry out of loyalty to his deceased kinsman.[122]

As in our discussion as to [123] whether the Bible took into consideration the woman's childlessness also or only the man's in establishing a levirate situation, we have projected the belief, by conjecture only, that the Bible supports the rabbinic tradition that the woman's childlessness did not matter; so too in our present problem we are inclined to believe that the rabbinic tradition has its origin in the Bible, namely, that the levirate marriage of one of the widows is sufficient for any levirate situation. Logic will not permit us to ignore the woman's childlessness and yet require levirate marriage for every widow. The rabbis themselves believed this law to have biblical origin, but their biblical influence is by artificial hermeneutic derivations which are by no means convincing.[124]

[122] It seems that this consideration was wholly in accord with the sentiments of the rabbis, certainly those following the view of the Hillelites freeing the levir from marrying the *ẓarat ha-bat* which, as above in note 87, had the same motive of freeing the levir from carrying too big a load in his levirate duty.

[123] See above pp. 96–97.

[124] Deut. 25.9 – "So shall be done to the man who buildeth not his brother's house" is taken by the rabbis to indicate that "only one house" is he expected to build but not more. At first sight it would seem as if, in spite of this biblical derivation, the rabbis did not consider that the Bible actually removed all ziḳah from the other wives by the marriage of one, for rabbinic law teaches that if the levir did marry more than one of the widows the marriage is valid. That would be impossible, if the second widow had no ziḳah at all, for then she would be prohibited to him on the basis of incest, as a brother's wife where there is no ziḳah. On second consideration, this argument is not conclusive. The legal logic of the rabbis is that a brother's wife who has been fit for levirate cannot be incestuous to the levir, even after she has been freed from ziḳah. This rule applies also to the case of the levir marrying the widow after he has freed her by ḥaliẓah. See Yeb. 10b. Therefore, the marriage of one widow frees the others (even biblically), as if the others had been given ḥaliẓah, but yet does not make them incestuous to the levir, so long as they come within the ziḳah state. See Yeb. 11a. The logic is that of R. Johanan, Yeb. 10b.

If our assumption is correct that only one levirate marriage was required by the Bible to make an end to ziḳah, we still remain in doubt as to whether one ḥaliẓah likewise freed all the brothers and all the widows from the ziḳah bond. By talmudic logic this is necessarily so, for ḥaliẓah is only an alternative of levirate marriage. But this reasoning does not apply to the Bible. There ḥaliẓah does not seem to have the character of a substitute for marriage and may not constitute a release from ziḳah altogether. It is primarily intended as ostracism of the brother from the family circle and perhaps also from the family estate, as penalty for not doing his duty by his deceased brother. It is possible, therefore, that after the widow pulled off the shoe of one brother she turned to the younger brother for levirate marriage. The levir whose shoe was pulled off was definitely out of the levirate involvement, but we have no right to assume that ziḳah was dissolved for all the widows and for the other brothers.

Yet we have certain flimsy logical grounds on which to base a judgment that in the Bible as in the Talmud one ḥaliẓah was sufficient to undo the entire ziḳah situation. Removing the shoe is recorded in the Book of Ruth as a means of legal conveyance of rights. In Ruth, the *go'el* gives the shoe to Boaz and thereby conveys his own rights to him. If the removal of the shoe in the levirate ceremony of Deuteronomy intended to convey the levirate right to a younger brother, it should be the younger brother, not the widow, who removes the shoe from the older levir. When the woman takes off the shoe, it is apparently intended to make her possessor of herself, to give her her freedom. That means that she does not have to go back to the other brothers. Again, in the ḥaliẓah ceremony as described in Deuteronomy, the levir is reproved for not building his brother's house. That would seem to imply that the possibility that he might consent to marry another one of the widows is excluded. True, the Bible has in mind a monogamous marriage, but the conclusion is inescapable either that the deuteronomic legislator thought polygamy impossible, or he meant to have no ḥaliẓah at all or a different formula for ḥaliẓah in the case of polygamy, or he considered one ḥaliẓah sufficient no matter how many wives remained behind. One of these four conclusions must be true, and it is an easy choice to accept the last one as most logical. Conscious that we are after all in the realm of conjecture, we still feel inclined to say that in biblical as in talmudic law one marriage or one ḥaliẓah completely dissolved the ziḳah bond for all the brothers and all the widows.

To add the last touch in delineating the state of ziḳah, it should be recorded that under certain legal abnormalities it is possible for a widow to have a double ziḳah bond, to be "chained" twice, so to speak. This particular situation arises when the levirate woman was taken into marriage by one of the levirs but the marriage was not consummated or imperfectly consummated. Should this levir-husband now die, the widow would now be "chained" doubly to the surviving brother, as widow of the first childless husband and as widow of the levir-husband. A double ziḳah, therefore, exists, and by rabbinic law in such a case, no levirate marriage to the third brother is permissible, but ḥaliẓah is necessary to dissolve the ziḳah.[125]

We have presented an account of what in rabbinic law constitutes a levirate situation. We have carried the account further by showing that in rabbinic law where there is a levirate situation a state of ziḳah develops, and we have attempted to describe that state in rabbinic legal terms. Our next step is to present the rabbinic views as to dissolution of ziḳah in whole or in part. There are three methods of dissolving the ziḳah bond. Two offer total dissolution — levirate marriage and ḥaliẓah. The third offers only a partial dissolution. Let us call it "imperfect dissolution of ziḳah." To these and to their legal effects we now turn our attention.

(C) LEVIRATE MARRIAGE is the fulfillment of the purpose of ziḳah, and, naturally, when the purpose has been attained, ziḳah comes to an end. Until the levirate marriage was performed, all the widows were not free to remarry, and all the brothers were restricted against marrying the kin of

125 Yeb. 31b. See Yad, Yibbum 6,27 and 30.

these widows under the rule of ziḳah-incest. But with marriage of one of the brothers to one of the widows, the ziḳah is completely dissolved. The widow has become a married woman, like any other wife, without a trace of ziḳah in her status. The other widows are free to marry any man they desire, save any of the brothers themselves, because only one levirate marriage is permitted.[126] The restrictions of ziḳah-incest upon the other brothers in respect to kin of the levirate widows terminate with the marriage.[127]

Rabbinic law teaches that the essence of levirate marriage is sexual intercourse between the levir and the widow. No marriage formality is necessary prior to intercourse, no coin, no ketubah, no contract, no blessings; cohabitation alone makes the widow the wife of the levir.[128] In this respect, the law has continued the historic background of the institution, for originally the levir did not enter into a new marriage transaction but took over the marriage rights of his deceased brother. The law further teaches that the first cohabitation is the only one that counts in the levirate rite.[129] This, too, has its clear historic background in the Bible. The motive of property right in the widow, as we have seen above, is less prominent in the Bible than the motive of raising seed for the deceased. But raising seed is possible by only one intercourse. As a matter of fact, among some primitive tribes the levirate duty consists only of one intercourse, and contact thereafter is prohibited.[130] The Bible nowhere refers to one intercourse as the essence of levirate. Even though, in the Judah-Tamar story, the expression "come in unto thy brother's wife" is used and Judah himself accounts only the one intercourse he had with Tamar as fulfillment of the levirate duty, the Bible nevertheless speaks of levirate as marriage (Gen. 38.14) even in this early account, and makes marriage a specific requirement in the deuteronomic law. Yet the rabbinic law may be taken as a comment upon the Bible; and the comment is historically correct, that in the

[126] Yeb. 11a.

[127] M. Yeb. 41a on top.

[128] M. Yeb. 53b; M. Ḳid. 2a; Yeb. 52a.

[129] Yeb. 20b.

[130] See Westermarck, HHM, III, p. 216. This is also the law of Manu.

scheme of levirate marriage the first intercourse constitutes its fulfillment.

Although intercourse is the essence of levirate marriage legally, and although it would seem evident that in the entire biblical period there was no other formality connected with levirate marriage, it was not likely that the Jews would for long, with their growing moral sensibilities, permit a new husband to approach a bride as if she were a mere chattel inherited from a deceased brother. Rabbinic practice, therefore, has established a set of formalities for the levirate marriage similar to those of other marriages. And just as marriage by intercourse, without the formalities of betrothal, was penalized by flagellation, so also was levirate intercourse without the betrothal formalities established by the rabbis.[131] The levirate betrothal, like the ordinary betrothal, consisted of the levir giving the widow a ring or an object of value in the presence of witnesses, or writing an instrument of betrothal containing the formula: "Be thou betrothed unto me according to the law of Moses and Israel." [132] Legally, this is sufficient to constitute any espousal, but social formalities above the mere legal requirements grew up in connection with ordinary betrothals; and levirate betrothal kept pace with them. In post-talmudic times the benediction over a cup of wine, the *ḥuppah,* and the seven benedictions in connection therewith over a second cup of wine were added to the levirate ceremonies.[133]

Levirate betrothal is not called *erusin* or *ḳiddushin,* terms which imply "conveyance" or "sanctification," for the levirate widow is not conveyed, since the original conveyance is partly in effect; nor is she sanctified anew, the prohibition against her contact with others being a mere continuation of her former state. The technical name is *ma'amar,* which means promise or pronouncement. The name really indicates its legal character. It does not represent a change of status of the widow; it merely settles her status to a certain

[131] Yeb. 52a; 50a–b; 29a; Yad, Yibbum 2,1.

[132] Yeb. 52a: Rashi ibid., s.v. *natan,* has the following formula: *Hare at meḳuddeshet li bema'amar yebamin.*

[133] Yad, Yibbum 2,2; Isserles ad E.H. 166; *Yam Shel Shlomo* Yeb. 5,2.

scheme of action, a promise of being taken in levirate marriage by a certain one of the brothers. This *ma'amar* innovation seems to belong to the last days of the Second Commonwealth, for the first generation of scholars after the fall of the state employ the term with apparently long standing familiarity and deal with its legal details quite extensively.[134]

Since levirate betrothal, or *ma'amar,* is post-biblical, it can not have the legal effect of a biblical marriage. While betrothal makes the bride the wife of her husband, levirate betrothal does not make the widow the wife of the levir.[135] In respect to adultery with other men, her status is no different after betrothal from before – it is only a violation of ziḳah. Furthermore, after levirate betrothal she can still be betrothed to another man; and the second betrothal would be more valid than the first, because the first has only rabbinic validity, the second biblical.[136] *Ma'amar* has a legal effect not dissimilar to betrothal of a minor orphan girl. It has rabbinic validity and no more. Except that the minor orphan girl can free herself by *mi'un;* the dissolution of *ma'amar* is by divorce. But the divorce, in that case, must also be considered rabbinic.[137] The *ma'amar* does not dissolve ziḳah; the woman still remains under ziḳah to all the brothers, even to the levir-groom. Hence, to free the widow completely, after she has gone through levirate betrothal, both divorce and ḥaliẓah are necessary, divorce for *ma'amar* and ḥaliẓah for ziḳah. The one effect that the *ma'amar* has is to make it impossible for any of the other brothers to take her in levirate marriage. Not that the marriage would be invalid, but it would be rabbinically prohibited.

By the *ma'amar,* the levir declares his intention of performing the levirate marriage. Thereby he attains no more rights in the widow or the property than he had before on the basis of mere ziḳah. Nor does he gain more rights than

134 M. 'Eduy. 4,9; M. Yeb. 29a; 50a; etc.

135 Yeb. 29a–b.

136 No specific statement in the sources to this effect is given but the logic is compelling, otherwise there could be no *ma'amar* after *ma'amar.* See *'Aruk ha-Shulḥan,* E.H. 166,8.

137 Yeb. 52a: *geṭ yebamah derabbanan hu.*

the other brothers. Even after his *ma'amar,* the other brothers can also perform the *ma'amar* or give her ḥaliẓah, and any one of them may take her in full levirate marriage, even though it would be in defiance of rabbinic law.[138]

The nuptial ceremony in ordinary marriages has a definite legal effect. This corresponds to the home-coming of the bride and admitting bride and groom to private seclusion in the manner of husband and wife. That instant is recognized by the law as the final step of the marriage. From that moment, even though intercourse has not taken place, the full effects of marriage have been attained. But the nuptial ceremony in the scheme of levirate marriage has no legal effect whatever. It remains no more than *ma'amar* until there is actual cohabitation between the levir and the widow. Nothing less than this and no mere symbol of it concludes the levirate marriage.[139] The nuptial ceremony is introduced into the levirate scheme merely as a social formality in connection with the first levirate intercourse.

A widow is always required by rabbinic law to allow a lapse of three months before her second marriage, so that when pregnancy is recognized it may be known whether she be pregnant by her former or her latter husband.[140] The importance of this matter in other marriages is merely genealogical. In the case of levirate marriage, too, three months must elapse between the husband's death and the nuptials,[141] but here it is of great importance, for should the widow be pregnant by her former husband, and should the child be born alive, the whole ziḳah situation would be destroyed, and the widow would prove to be incestuously prohibited to the levir.

With the first intercourse, the levir enters upon all rights and assumes all obligations of a husband to his levirate spouse. There is only one exception, the ketubah, which guarantees payment of *mohar,* gifts, and dowry. The levir writes no new ketubah; the old one remains in force. The

138 Yeb. 29b; 50a.
139 Yeb. 111b–112a.
140 Yeb. 41a.
141 Yeb. 35b–37a; Yeb. 41a.

historic logic is evident; the levir simply continues the marriage contract of his deceased brother. All property liens, therefore, attach to the estate of the deceased; the levir's own property is not encumbered.[142] However, the ketubah obligations were later conceived of as a deterrent to divorce, and by an enactment the rabbis imposed the ketubah obligations on the levir for protection of the woman, in case she could not get her ketubah from the estate.[143] In keeping with this enactment, it has been the custom since later tannaitic times to have a ketubah written by the levir in all cases. The instrument reads: "On this date and in this place came to us so-and-so and said to us, My brother by the same father died leaving no son or daughter, and he left this woman whose name is so-and-so whom I am to take in levirate marriage according to the command of the Torah of Moses . . . and she consented to the levirate marriage in order to raise a name in Israel (for the deceased), as it is written. . . . Therefore now, he, so-and-so, has written for his levirate bride, so-and-so, (a ketubah of) two hundred zuzim, the amount which was inscribed in the ketubah of her former husband, and has added gifts and dowry. . . ." [144]

Because the lien for payment of the ketubah obligation attaches primarily to the property of the estate, the levir cannot sell any property of the deceased's estate even after

[142] Yeb. 38a.

[143] Yeb. 39a. What situation the rabbis had in mind when they spoke of the woman's not being able to get her ketubah from her deceased husband is a matter of controversy among later authorities. It includes the case where the estate is insufficient for the payment of the ketubah (Rashi, ibid., s.v. *we'ee*) or where the widow sold or cancelled her ketubah (Yad, Yibbum 2,17). Where the widow has no ketubah because her marriage to the deceased was contrary to law, the widow does not even get a ketubah from the levir, according to Maimonides (Yad, ibid.). Other authorities, on the other hand, impose a ketubah obligation upon the levir even in such a case. See *Maggid* ad Yad, ibid. and Isserles ad E.H. 168,8.

[144] Yad, Yibbum 4,32; *Sefer ha-Shetarot*, ed. Halberstamm, p. 55; *Ginze Kedem*, ed. Lewin, II, p. 42; *Tikkun Soferim*, Livorno, 1789, p. 5b. *Sefer ha-Shetarot* mentions a *mohar* of one hundred *zuzim* as a substitute for the two hundred *zuzim* of the standard ketubah, in keeping with the law that if the old ketubah is paid out of the estate, the ketubah amounts to two hundred *zuzim*, as originally given by the deceased husband; but if the levir has to pay out of his own he pays only one hundred *zuzim*, because he married not a virgin but a widow.

his marriage to the widow, and even if he is willing to take over the lien on his own property, unless she consents to release the estate from that lien.[145] The greater restriction on sale of the estate than is imposed on other husbands in the sale of property encumbered by a ketubah-lien, may be variously explained.[146] But probably the historic explanation is the most logical. Originally there was no property transfer in connection with levirate, as mentioned above, because the property continued in possession of the patriarch. Later the transfer of property came into the levirate complex, and then it was understood that the property went from the deceased to the first son born of the levirate union. The levir was then only the custodian on behalf of the unborn child. Hence the restrictions against his meddling with the estate, even where the child's interest is not in question but that of the widow, and even when the law recognized the levir himself as the heir.[147]

Where there are more than one levirate widow of the same deceased brother, the levir can choose any one of them for levirate marriage. Where there are several surviving brothers, the levirate duty falls primarily upon the oldest. If the oldest refuses, or if he is gone to a distant land, the duty goes over to the one next in age.[148] No compulsion is exerted by the court on any one of the brothers to marry the widow, since the alternative of ḥaliẓah remains to them.[149]

145 Ket. 81a–b.

146 Tosafot Ket. 81a, s.v. *haroẓeh*.

147 The lien on property for payment of the ketubah was restricted to realty, unless movable property was specifically mentioned in the ketubah. According to this, therefore, the levir was not limited in his freedom of selling the movable property of the estate. A later gaonic enactment made all ketubot payable also out of movable property. Yet according to Maimonides, Yad, Ishut 22,13, the enactment did not include a restriction against the levir selling the movable property of the estate.

148 Yeb. 39a; 24a. Rashi and Tosafot (Yeb. 24a) and RABD (Yad, Yibbum 2,12) give priority according to age; Maimonides (Yad, Yibbum 2,7–13) maintains that if the oldest refuses there is no priority among the other brothers.

149 Yeb. 39b. Rashi, s.v. *amar,* and Maimonides, Yad, Yibbum 2,7, differ in their interpretation of this amoraic teaching. The difference is due to the fact that Maimonides follows the tradition that *yibbum* is preferable, while Rashi teaches that ḥaliẓah is preferable. I follow the Maimonidean interpretation of the talmudic text because it is more logical.

Has the widow any choice in the matter? In respect to levirate betrothal, *ma'amar,* she has full choice to accept or refuse betrothal. If the *ma'amar* is carried out without her consent or that of her legal representative, it has no validity whatever.[150] But in regard to levirate marriage she has no arbitrary choice, yet she has a reasonable decision. According to the view that ḥaliẓah is preferable to marriage, which we shall present later, she always has the right to demand ḥaliẓah in preference to marriage on any pretext whatever.[151] Those who hold the view that marriage is preferable, leave her some voice in the matter nevertheless. If the oldest brother offers her marriage, she must accept it at the penalty of being declared a "rebellious wife" and losing her ketubah.[152] Yet, if she has a reasonable explanation for her refusal, the court will give it full recognition.[153] If the oldest brother does not wish to marry her, she may have her choice from among the other brothers.[154] However, she cannot refuse to marry any one of them even if she be willing to remain forever in a state of ziḳah, for the brothers too have a right to demand the dissolution of the ziḳah bond.[155]

(D) ḤALIẒAH, or the ceremony of taking off the shoe,[156] is a creation of the deuteronomic legislator as a form of release of ziḳah, but was not known in pre-deuteronomic times. The rabbis retained all the features of the biblical "taking off of the shoe," but changed the spirit of it radically. In rabbinic times it was no longer a token of disgrace to the levir for not marrying the widow, such as is the spirit in Deuteronomy; it was the proper thing for the levir to do, in order to free the widow from the ziḳah bond and thus afford her opportunity to marry the man of her choice. Even in the Book of Ruth it is represented as a mere symbolic

150 Ḳid. 44a.

151 See Rashi Yeb. 39b, s.v. *amar.*

152 Yad, Yibbum 2,10–11; Ket. 64a. See JMC, pp. 145 f.

153 If he is repulsive (Yeb. 4a) or if he has a repulsive profession (Ket. 77a) or if there is great disparity between the levir and the widow in age (Yeb. 44a).

154 Yad, Yibbum 2,12. See note 148 above.

155 Yad, Yibbum 2,13; 2,16.

156 The significance of the removal of the shoe in ḥaliẓah and other transactions is dealt with by Jacob Nacht in J.Q.R., N.S., VI, 1: "The Symbolism of the Shoe," and by Jacob Mittelmann in *Der altisraelitische Levirat,* pp. 22–23.

release, without blame. The levitical law against marrying a sister-in-law has added to the unpopularity of levirate marriage and made ḥaliẓah quite acceptable. The tragedy of a man's name being lost because of childlessness became less alarming than in former days either from an eschatological or patriarchal point of view. What remained of the whole levirate situation in rabbinic times was the prohibition against the widow marrying a stranger – that was the essence of ziḳah to the rabbis – and, for the dissolution of ziḳah, ḥaliẓah was as satisfactory as levirate marriage.

Within the rabbinic period itself there have been definite changes of attitude to ḥaliẓah. The tannaim began with the tradition that ḥaliẓah is satisfactory only if marriage is impossible; that is, marriage is preferable to ḥaliẓah. They gradually developed a feeling that since sister-in-law marriage is incestuous and is permitted only for the fulfillment of the biblical command of levirate, any levirate marriage that is not entered upon with that pious feeling but because the levir is fond of his widowed sister-in-law savors of incest. This sentiment was expressed by Abba Saul, a tanna of the third generation. In his day, during the second century, the majority scholars still contested that view, and said that, no matter what the intention of the levir, levirate marriage was still preferable. Early in the third century, this sentiment of Abba Saul found full and authoritative expression in the verdict of the Mishnah: "Now that the levir's intention is not for the fulfillment of God's command, it is decided that ḥaliẓah is preferable to marriage.[157]

The Palestinian amoraim consistently maintained this attitude.[158] The Babylonian amoraim cite a tradition that there was a reversal of attitude to ḥaliẓah in their generations, namely, that marriage was still to be preferred to ḥaliẓah.[159] But apparently, this view was not crystallized into halakah in amoraic days. In gaonic times, the Babylonian academies were divided on the subject; the Sura academy taught that marriage was to be preferred, while the Pumbedita academy

[157] Bek. 13a; Yeb. 39b; Yeb. 109a.
[158] Yer. Yeb. 12d, 13a.
[159] Yeb. 39b.

termed ḥaliẓah preferable.[160] Following the decline of the Babylonian academies, the sephardic communities, Spain and the Orient, led by Alfasi and Maimonides,[161] preferred marriage to ḥaliẓah, while French Jewry, under the influence of Rashi and R. Jacob Tam, avoided levirate marriage and gave preference to ḥaliẓah.[162] The legal authorities in Germany were not unanimous on the question. We have seen that they were not of one opinion whether levirate marriage might be performed in defiance of the ḥerem against polygamy. The indecision there may also be ascribed to their wavering attitude whether marriage or ḥaliẓah was generally to be preferred.[163] However, as where marriage would involve polygamy, so where marriage entailed no violation of the law, the tendency in Germany has gradually come to be one of antagonism to levirate marriage and preference to ḥaliẓah under all circumstances.[164]

In a number of cases the law leaves no choice between marriage and ḥaliẓah, but either requires marriage and permits no ḥaliẓah, or calls for ḥaliẓah while declaring marriage impossible or improper. Marriage has the advantage over ḥaliẓah because it is "Heaven-made." In the case of levirate marriage, this is to be taken in the severest literal sense; the widow is made wife of the levir by decree of Heaven. The levir does not have to acquire her; he only has to take her, for she is his. Therefore persons who have no legal power of acquisition can enter into a levirate marriage. Ḥaliẓah, on the other hand, is a plain act of release, similar in nature to conveyance. Consequently legal maturity is necessary for ḥaliẓah. Hence, if the levir is a minor or insane, likewise if

160 See a note on the subject by Prof. L. Ginzberg in *Ginze Schechter,* II, pp. 270–71.

161 Yad, Yibbum 1,2, and *Hagahot Maimoniyot* thereto.

162 Rashi and Tosafot Yeb. 39b s.v. *amar.*

163 Professor Ginzberg, l.c., suggests that the ḥerem was perhaps the reason for their preference of ḥaliẓah. I do not think this plausible, as Dr. G. himself doubts it, because R. Gershom himself provided for lifting the ḥerem in the case of childlessness. If *yibbum* was so important to him, he would not have hesitated to make an exception in the case of a married levir. Rather I think the reverse is the order. Those authorities who insist on the ḥerem even in the face of a levirate duty, do so because they consider marriage less preferable than ḥaliẓah.

164 Note of Isserles, E.H. 165,1.

the widow is a minor or insane, ḥaliẓah is impossible; but the pair can be united in levirate marriage with sufficient temporary validity.[165]

There are more cases, however, where marriage is impossible and ḥaliẓah is the only alternative. These include every instance where marriage would involve a biblical or rabbinical prohibition,[166] every case of doubtful ziḳah or double ziḳah,[167] certain cases of rabbinic ziḳah,[168] and that where the levir is definitely impotent because of castration or injury or old age.[169]

There is at least one case where ziḳah is allowed to remain forever, neither marriage nor ḥaliẓah being permitted to dissolve it — where the deceased was king of Israel or the only surviving brother is king.[170] The dignity of the king's office,

[165] Yeb. 112b; Tos. Yeb. 2,5–6. See also Yeb. 96a, 104b, 105b. There are different tannaitic views expressed as to the effect of ḥaliẓah both if the levir was a minor or where the widow was a minor. Where the levir was a minor, the majority view has it that the ḥaliẓah is altogether invalid, while R. Me'ir gives it some validity. Where the widow is a minor, R. Jose maintains that the ḥaliẓah is valid, but R. Me'ir accounts the ḥaliẓah defective. It does not seem that according to R. Me'ir it is entirely invalid, and the reading in the Yerushalmi Mishnah (12,5), *ḥaliẓatah kesherah,* is more correct than the Babylonian reading. See Yad, Yibbum 4,16; *Maggid* ad Yad, Yibbum 1,17; and E.H. 169,43, 49.

[166] Tos. Yeb. 2,5. If the widow's marriage to the deceased was contrary to law but valid, either levirate marriage or ḥaliẓah is possible, so long as there is no legal prohibition against marriage of the widow and the levir. There is only one exception to this rule. If the prohibition was due to the fact that the deceased had previously divorced his wife and then remarried her after she had been married to another, the levir may not marry her and ḥaliẓah alone is possible. See Yad, Yibbum 6,13.

[167] See notes 113, 114, 117. A part exception to this rule is where the marriage of the deceased to the levirate widow had doubtful validity. Marriage in that case is possible, for either she is not at all a sister-in-law or she is a full levirate widow. We may add to instances cited in the notes here referred to a few other cases, such as the *ẓarah* of a marriage that was of doubtful incestuous kinship either to the husband or to the levir.

[168] The case given in note 115 does not come under this head, since if the marriage be looked upon as biblically not valid, the levir can marry the minor widow because she is not his sister-in-law. The case cited in note 116 above is typical of rabbinic ḥaliẓah.

[169] Tos. Yeb. 2,6; Yad, Yibbum 6,4.

[170] San. 18a. Two additional cases (cited Yad, Yibbum 3,15–16) can have no dissolution of ziḳah either by marriage or ḥaliẓah, but there the reason is that there is a lack of testimony as to facts. As soon as the facts are established, the cases become normal levirate cases.

the rule that the king's widow may not remarry, the position of honor accorded the king's widow, and the historic sense that ḥaliẓah is intended as an insult to the levir, account for this law.[171]

Where there are many surviving brothers, the ḥaliẓah is to be performed by the oldest. If he refuses, the other brothers in order of age can offer to perform it.[172] If they all refuse, the obligation reverts to the oldest brother, who is forced by the court either to marry the widow or to free her by ḥaliẓah.[173] The widow has no choice. Even if she be willing to remain unmarried the rest of her life, she is compelled to undergo ḥaliẓah in order that the brothers may be freed from the ziḳah bond.[174] Where the deceased has left several widows, the brothers can choose any one of them for the performance of ḥaliẓah, thereby freeing all the others.[175]

Ḥaliẓah cannot be performed before three months have elapsed from the husband's death, in the same manner as marriage is impossible prior to that time.[176] Should it be performed before then according to talmudic law the ḥaliẓah is valid, but the widow is still not permitted to remarry regularly until the three months' period has passed.[177] Post-talmudic authorities, however, declare such ḥaliẓah "an imperfect dissolution of ziḳah." [178] Certain physical deformities constitute hindrances to ḥaliẓah. The widow and the levir must both make certain declarations before the court; therefore, if either is mute, the ḥaliẓah cannot be performed.[179] Likewise, deformities in the levir's right foot or its amputation up to the knee make ḥaliẓah impossible, because it is

[171] See *Kesef Mishneh* ad Yad, Melakim, 2,3.

[172] The rule for ḥaliẓah is the same as that for *yibbum,* treated previously; see note 148 above.

[173] M. Yeb. 39a and Gemara, ibid.

[174] Ket. 64a; Yad, Yibbum 2,16.

[175] If, however, of two widows left, one is able to marry a priest and the other is not — then ḥaliẓah is to be given to the one who is already disqualified for marriage to a priest, not to spoil the chances of the other to marry a priest. Yeb. 44a.

[176] Yeb. 41a; 35b.

[177] Yeb. 41b at bottom.

[178] Isserles ad E.H. 164,1. The meaning of an "imperfect dissolution of ziḳah" will be given later.

[179] Yeb. 104b; Yad, Yibbum 4,13.

the levir's right foot from which the shoe is to be loosened in the ceremony.[180] Although the rite requires the widow to loosen the shoe, which evidently is manipulated by the hands, one who has no hands can perform ḥaliẓah by use of her teeth.[181] If the widow is blind, there is no interference with ḥaliẓah, but the levir's blindness matters to the extent that, if there are other brothers, one who is not blind shall perform the rite.[182] Finally, we have already mentioned,[183] both levir and widow must be of age and of sound mind to make the ḥaliẓah valid.

Ḥaliẓah is described in the Bible as an official public ceremony; therefore rabbinic law requires a full court for its performance, consisting of three judges according to one opinion, or of five judges, according to another.[184] The judges are either those officially ordained, or substitute deputy judges, able to conduct the ceremony in Hebrew.[185] Ḥaliẓah performed in private or before improper judges or in the presence of an insufficient number of arbiters is valid, but defective in its dissolution of ziḳah.[186] Performance of the rite need not be in the regular court house, but definite temporary quarters for the court must be designated in advance, and any place is satisfactory, generally in the city where the levir has his domicile.[187] Like all court actions in Jewish law, ḥaliẓah is performed in the daytime, not at night. If performed at night it is defective.[188]

The court proceedings arc as follows. The judges sit and the levir and widow stand before them. The court ascertains that they are of age and that three months have passed since the husband's death, and they call witnesses to testify to the identity of the levir and the widow. The levir is asked

[180] Yad, Yibbum 4,17. See *Maggid* thereto.

[181] Yeb. 105a.

[182] Yeb. 103a; Yad, Yibbum 4,8.

[183] See note 165 above.

[184] Yeb. 101a–b. The halakah accounts three satisfactory but five preferable. See E.H. 169, 3.

[185] Yeb. ibid. For the requisite of Hebrew see M. Yeb. 106b and M. Soṭah 32a.

[186] E.H. 169,2.

[187] San. 31b; Yeb. 101b.

[188] Yeb. 104a; E.H. 169,6.

whether he consents to the ḥaliẓah rite, and on his answer in the affirmative, he is placed in position for the removal of his shoe, leaning against the wall or an indoor post. The shoe is of a special ceremonial kind, made all of leather, even seams and strings. The levir's right foot is washed before the ceremonial shoe is put on; the shoe is donned, laced up, and tied below the knee. When thus ready with the ceremonial shoe, he presses his foot on the floor. The woman, facing the levir, audibly recites in Hebrew, prompted by the head of the court, the biblical phrase: "My husband's brother refuseth to raise up unto his brother a name in Israel; he will not perform the levirate duty unto me." The levir also replies audibly in Hebrew, reciting after the head of the court the biblical phrase: "I do not wish to take her." Then the woman, bending down, loosens the strings of the shoe with her right hand; thereafter, holding up his foot with her left hand, she pulls off the shoe with her right and throws it on the ground. She straightens up and spits upon the ground before the levir's face in sight of the court, and exclaims in Hebrew as prompted by the head of the court: "So shall it be done to the man that doth not build up his brother's house, and his name shall be called in Israel, the house of him that had his shoe loosed." Those present at the ceremony all exclaim together in Hebrew, *Ḥaluẓ hana'al!* (he that hath his shoe loosed) three times.[189]

There are a number of superstitious beliefs about details in the ḥaliẓah ceremony. The dead brother, it is believed, is invisibly present. That makes the ceremony not only sad but also gruesome. Some people think the water prepared for washing the levir's foot represents ceremonial oblations for the dead. Others insist that the screening of a corner in the courtroom for privacy for the removal of the levir's shoe and stocking before replacement by the ceremonial shoe is intended as a place reserved for the dead brother who cannot or will not mingle with the living. It is generally believed that when the ceremony is over, the widow should sprinkle water over the levir to assure an easier task in finding

[189] Yad, Yibbum 4,6–9; E.H. 169, *Seder Ḥaliẓah.*

a new husband. The law, of course, ignores these extraneous assumptions.

The ceremony is concluded by a few prayers that have no talmudic origin. One, recited by the judges when the levir returns the shoe to them, reads as follows: "May it be Thy will (O, God) that the daughters of Israel be not in need of ḥaliẓah or levirate marriage." When the court is dismissed, its head offers the benediction: "Blessed art Thou, O Lord, our God, who hast sanctified us by Thy commandments and statutes, even by the commandments and statutes of Abraham our father." [190]

Writing an instrument of ḥaliẓah is not part of the ceremonial, but a certification from the court that the woman is free to marry again. It may or may not be issued, according to local custom. Yet the ḥaliẓah instrument is recorded in tannaitic literature and its details are given fairly completely in amoraic records.[191] It is to be signed by two witnesses, preferably those who were of the court of five, but any two present at the ceremony may serve. The instrument reads:

"On this day and month and year of Creation as counted in this place (NN), we judges, some of whom are signed at the bottom, were sitting as a court of three when NN, widow of NN, came before us, and NN spoke to us as follows: NN is a brother of one father to my husband, to whom I was married and who died and left no son or daughter, heir or successor, one who shall establish his name in Israel, and it is proper for this NN that he marry me. Now, may the masters speak to him that if he wishes to marry me let him marry me, and if not let him hold out to me his right foot in your presence that I may loosen his shoe from his foot and spit before him. Thereupon, we established by investigation that NN is a paternal brother to NN deceased, and we said to him: If you wish to marry her, marry her, and if not, hold out your right foot to her in our presence and let her loosen your shoe and spit before you. He answered and said: I do not wish to marry her. Thereupon we recited with this

[190] E.H. 169, *Seder Ḥaliẓah,* 56.

[191] Tos. Yeb. 12,15; B.M. 20a; Yeb. 39b; Yer. M.Ḳ. 82a.

woman: My husband's brother refuseth to set up for his brother a name in Israel; he does not want to do the levirate duty by me. And with him too we recited: I do not wish to take her. Then he held out his right foot and she loosened his shoe from his foot and spat before him spittle that was visible to us from the mouth to the ground. Thereafter we recited with her: Thus shall be done to the man who doth not build up his brother's house and let his name be called in Israel, 'He of the house of the loosened shoe.' And we judges and all who were with us answered after her: Loosened shoe, loosened shoe, loosened shoe, three times, and when this was executed before us we permitted her (NN) to go and be married to whomsoever she may wish and no one may prevent her from this day and forever. Now NN asked from us this instrument of ḥaliẓah, which we have now written and attested and given to her for possession according to the law of Moses and Israel. Signed .... (two or three witnesses)." [192]

(E) IMPERFECT DISSOLUTION OF ZIḲAH results when severance of the ziḳah bond is attempted by defective means. A full discharge of ziḳah implies that all widows and all brothers are free from ziḳah by an act of one brother toward one of the widows – marriage or ḥaliẓah. Freedom from ziḳah implies several things in the law. To the other widows it means freedom to remarry without ḥaliẓah; also freedom to marry a priest, for they are widows, not divorcees or *ḥaluẓot;* and in respect to all the brothers they are now total strangers, so that marriage with their kin is not prohibited under the law of ziḳah-incest. To the brothers it means the end of all duty to the widows and freedom to marry the kin of these widows without restriction of the law of ziḳah-incest. In an imperfect dissolution of ziḳah this total freedom does not exist. Either additional ḥaliẓot are necessary to the same widow or separate ḥaliẓot are needed by the other widows. Ziḳah is not at an end and yet levirate marriage is impossible. Ziḳah-incest still exists between all

[192] The instrument is the one given in Yad, Yibbum 4,30. Variations in other texts are slight and of little significance. See *Sefer ha-Sheṭarot,* ed. Halberstamm, p. 26; *Tiḳḳun Soferim,* p. 15; Gulak, *Oẓar ha-Sheṭarot,* p. 92.

the levirs and all the widows, and marriage to a priest becomes prohibited where divorce or ḥaliẓah becomes necessary on account of the imperfect manner of dissolution of ziḳah.

An imperfect dissolution of ziḳah arises from a defective levirate act, that is, defective marriage or defective ḥaliẓah. The defect may be inherent in the act itself or may be due to circumstances; let us call them internal and external defects. A marriage that is internally defective is that of a minor levir. Levirate marriage being "Heaven-made," the minor levir has some power of acquisition by his levirate act, but his intercourse is accounted immature, and, it will be remembered, intercourse alone counts in the levirate marriage. The first mature intercourse will conclude the full levirate marriage, if no complications develop, but until then ziḳah continues,[193] and none of the widows can remarry. Another instance is that of the levir being the high priest, who is by law prohibited from marrying a widow, therefore unable to enter a levirate marriage. True, the marriage is valid, but the violation of law is so severe that it is still accounted defective. The co-widows, therefore, would have to obtain ḥaliẓot for themselves.[194] Again, in cases of rabbinical ziḳah, it follows logically that levirate marriage there has only the character of dissolution of a rabbinical ziḳah. In that sense, therefore, it has only rabbinical validity and is defective to the extent that it cannot free the other widows who may be under a biblical bond of ziḳah to the levir; they must obtain their own separate ḥaliẓot.[195]

Also ḥaliẓah may be internally defective. Thus a ḥaliẓah that dissolves only a rabbinical ziḳah, like marriage in rabbinical ziḳah, does not free the remaining widows who may be under a biblical ziḳah bond. Unlike marriage,

[193] Yeb. 111b, etc.; Yad, Yibbum 1,16.

[194] Yeb. 20a; Yad, Yibbum 6,11. This case is an exception to the rule, that in all prohibited marriage, except incest, the marriage nullifies ziḳah for the other widows. See Yad, Yibbum, 6,10.

[195] Rabbinic ziḳah has been described above in notes 115, 116. See M. Yeb. 110a. However, if the co-widows are also only under rabbinical ziḳah, their ziḳah is removed. They must all be of the same quality of ziḳah to have the marriage of one remove the ziḳah of the others. But if the one married is a minor and the others are deaf-mutes, or vice versa, the ziḳah is not removed from the co-widows. See Yeb. 110b–111b; Yad, Yibbum 5,23–25.

however, which even if prohibited dissolves ziḳah, ḥaliẓah, where marriage cannot be performed either because of a biblical or rabbinical prohibition, is considered internally defective, and does not remove the ziḳah of the other widows.[196] Ḥaliẓah is also defective when performed prior to three months after the husband's death,[197] while the widow is pregnant,[198] or while the widow is a minor.[199] Likewise, the ḥaliẓah is defective when there are technical faults in its performance, as when done before an improper court or witnesses;[200] when there has been irregularity in the ceremonial;[201] or when proper execution of the ceremonial has been impossible because of physical deformities in levir or widow.[202] In these cases, so long as the ḥaliẓah is not alto-

[196] E.H. 174,1.

[197] This law is disputed by the authorities. Maimonides, Yad, Yibbum 1,19 maintains that if there is no pregnancy after three months from the time of the husband's death, the ḥaliẓah is valid and no other ḥaliẓah is necessary for her; evidently the co-widows are also free. Isserles in E.H. 164,2, cites Mordecai declaring the ḥaliẓah performed prior to three months invalid under all circumstances and ineffective in freeing the co-widows. See *'Aruk ha-Shulḥan,* Yibbum, 164,8.

[198] Yeb. 35b; Yad, Yibbum 1,20. The question raised here is if the child was still born. If the child was born and lived to the age of thirty days, the whole levirate situation is destroyed, because the deceased has left a child. In our case, where the child did not live after birth, it is agreed that the ḥaliẓah is defective; another is necessary. But it is disputed between authorities whether the second ḥaliẓah is not in itself defective and would therefore require a separate ḥaliẓah from every brother. See *'Aruk ha-Shulḥan,* Yibbum, 164,12.

[199] Yeb. 105b; Yad, Yibbum 1,18. Another ḥaliẓah, of course, is necessary when the widow becomes of age. Whether the second is not a *ḥaliẓah pesulah,* requiring ḥaliẓah from every brother, is not specified in the law.

[200] This includes many details; ḥaliẓah at night, before a court of fewer than three judges, if the judges were related to one another or to the levir or widow (Yad, Yibbum 4,16), under misrepresentation or under compulsion by gentiles, or under compulsion by Jews not justified by law, or over the levir's declared protest, *mesirat moda'ah* — Yad, Yibbum 4,24–25.

[201] Under this head we include: when the whole ceremony was performed but the shoe was not pulled off (Yad, Yibbum 4,14); when the lace was tied above the knee, or when he assisted in the pulling off of the shoe (Yad, Yibbum 4,16); when the shoe was made of the wrong material or sewn together with the wrong thread, or when the shoe was too large or too small, or when the shoe was torn in the process of pulling off, or when the shoe was not on the levir's bare foot but on a stocking (Yad, Yibbum 4,18, 20, 21).

[202] Here we include: if the levir or widow be mute (Yad, Yibbum 4,13); deformity of the levir's right foot (Yad, Yibbum, 4,17); and to this we ought

gether invalid, the rule is that if the widow has remarried she does not have to leave her husband, but requires another ḥaliẓah nevertheless; and the co-widows must look for separate ḥaliẓot for themselves.[203]

Betrothal as substitute for marriage and divorce as substitute for ḥaliẓah may also count as levirate acts that are defective in the dissolution of ziḳah. Biblically, neither betrothal nor divorce has any place in the levirate situation, and each, if executed, is as if nothing had taken place – entirely without legal effect. Rabbinic law, however, recognizes these acts as having some validity in the levirate complex. Betrothal is valid enough to require a divorce in addition to ḥaliẓah; divorce is valid sufficiently to make marriage to a priest impossible; both have sufficient validity to make levirate marriage impossible for all brothers and all widows;[204] finally, both are valid to the extent of interfering with the regular process of levirate, as we shall soon see. Yet they do not dissolve ziḳah; they corrode it, so to speak; they upset its regular function; but they leave a residue of ziḳah to be dissolved by a later ḥaliẓah.[205]

These internally defective acts in a levirate situation, namely, defective marriage, defective ḥaliẓah, betrothal, and divorce, have the effect of interfering with the full validity of an otherwise proper levirate marriage or proper ḥaliẓah. They create circumstances wherein the regular marriage or ḥaliẓah becomes externally defective. After an improper ḥaliẓah, a proper ḥaliẓah or proper marriage may follow, but neither the ḥaliẓah nor the marriage following would remove ziḳah from the other widows. Likewise, after a divorce or after betrothal by one of the levirs or after intercourse with a minor levir, there

---

to add the need for both levir and widow to have intent to perform ḥaliẓah; lack of such intention on either side makes the ḥaliẓah unsatisfactory.

203 Yad, Yibbum 4.26–27. To what extent the second ḥaliẓah will free the other widows or whether the second must be performed by all the surviving brothers is not given in the sources nor in the codes. This will depend upon our law requiring a separate ḥaliẓah from every brother in all cases of *ḥaliẓah pesulah*, which we shall discuss in note 206.

204 Except of course, that the levir who performed *ma'amar* can consummate the marriage, if there was no other interference.

205 Yeb. 50a ff.; Yeb. 29a–b.

is no full dissolution of zikah either by marriage or halizah. It is possible, therefore, for a levirate widow to have intercourse with a minor levir, to be divorced by his brother, to be betrothed by a third, to have mature intercourse with a fourth, to be given halizah by a fifth, and yet to leave a residue of zikah, so that none of the widows, even by a combination of all these levirate acts, are freed from the zikah bond and have to find their freedom in separate halizot from all the brothers.[206]

(F) ENFORCEMENT OF THE LEVIRATE LAW has a simple but direct history of its own, running along a straight line from maximum enforcement to minimum. In the Judah-Tamar story, the duty is enforced inescapably by a divine death penalty. Onan refuses to perform the levirate act and God slays him. When it was thought that Tamar had violated the levirate duty her penalty was projected as death by burning. Deuteronomy was milder in the matter of enforcement. It knew of no death penalty either for the levir or for the widow. It employed the halizah ceremony as a means of penalizing the levir for refusing marriage, for in Deuteronomy halizah is a public disgrace of the levir and possibly also entails ostracism from the family estate. To compel the widow to undergo levirate marriage, the deuteronomic legislator satisfied himself with prohibiting her marriage to any one else. The possibility that the levir might refuse both marriage and halizah is not contemplated in Deuteronomy any more than that of a thief retaining his stolen goods. The court evidently had sufficient power to compel the levir to

[206] Yeb. 26b–27a. The last halizah, after all these complications, frees the widow who received it, according to Samuel, but does not free the other widows. According to Rab, even this widow must get halizah from all the surviving brothers. Maimonides decides in accord with Samuel, requiring only halizah from one brother. However, he teaches, the other widows cannot be freed by the halizah of one widow unless this one has gotten halizah from all the levirs. Else, they all have to have separate halizot from at least one levir. Adret maintains that even halizah given by all brothers to the widow, involved in divorce and *ma'amar* and cohabitation, will not free the other widows; on the other hand, if one halizah is given to one of the co-widows who had none of those complications, even though she was rabbinically affected by them, the one halizah is enough to free all other widows. See *Maggid* and *Kesef Mishneh* ad Yad, *Yibbum* 5,11, and *'Aruk ha-Shulhan,* 170,6–16.

perform ḥaliẓah, if he was not willing to marry the widow.

In post-biblical times, down to the end of the Second Commonwealth, enforcement of the levirate duty upon the widow remained the same as in Deuteronomy. Forcing the levir to perform the levirate duty, however, assumed a different character from that in the Book of Deuteronomy. Perpetuating the name of the deceased was no longer of paramount importance; the stress was laid on freeing the widow from the levirate bond. Ḥaliẓah was therefore as good as marriage, even though marriage was given undisputed preference. And probably the sense of disgrace or ostracism was already insignificant in the ḥaliẓah ceremony. Hence we hear of no method or penalty then employed by the court to compel levirate marriage. He was evidently free to marry the widow or to liberate her by ḥaliẓah. The supposition that he might do neither does not seem to trouble the teachers of that period. The court, of course, had its own method of seeing that justice was done the widow. One was to compel the heirs of the deceased brother to support the widow out of the estate of her husband, until she was freed to remarry, in accordance with a standard ketubah clause.[207]

In tannaitic and subsequently in amoraic and gaonic times, we recall there were two attitudes to levirate marriage, one favoring it and one that favored ḥaliẓah. Yet it is a generally accepted principle among teachers of those periods that no compulsion was exerted on the levir to marry the widow, even among those who considered marriage preferable to ḥaliẓah.[208] These teachers, like their predecessors, viewed the levirate situation as a question of freeing the widow more than that of perpetuating the name of the deceased; therefore ḥaliẓah was quite satisfactory and compulsion for levirate marriage unnecessary. If the levir consented to a levirate marriage, however, the widow, under original tan-

[207] The clause read: "Thou shalt dwell in my house and be supported out of my estate. . . ." See JMC p. 177.

[208] M. Yeb. 39a — *o ḥaleẓ o yabbem.* Rab's statement (Yeb. 39b) that no compulsion is employed for marriage (misinterpreted by Rashi), like the statement of the Mishnah, makes no assumption that ḥaliẓah is preferable. Indeed, Sura, the academy founded by Rab, maintained that marriage is preferable.

naitic law, had no choice but to accept marriage, even according to the view that ḥaliẓah is preferable.[209] Down to the time of the grandson of Rabbi Judah the Nasi, when sentiment in Palestine was already crystallized in favor of ḥaliẓah, we find the penalties of *moredet,* "the rebellious wife," applied to a widow who refuses to accept her levir in marriage.[210] These consisted of public announcement in the synagogue on four successive sabbaths of her "rebellion," followed by court warnings that punitive measures would be applied to her, if she did not yield, followed finally by cancellation of her ketubah. Samuel, of the first generation of Babylonian amoraim and contemporary of the grandson of Rabbi Judah the Nasi, deviated from this tannaitic tradition, and ruled to the contrary that the widow could not be treated as a *moredet* for refusing to accept levirate marriage.[211] Among post-talmudic authorities, there is a division of opinion on the subject, based generally on the question whether ḥaliẓah or marriage was preferable. Those who preferred ḥaliẓah employed no compulsion on the woman to accept levirate marriage, and those who preferred marriage treated her as a *moredet* if she refused the marriage proposal of the levir.[212]

In this period, the possibility of neglecting the levirate duty and letting ziḳah continue undissolved either by marriage or ḥaliẓah is not overlooked. If the levir and the widow both agree to have neither marriage nor ḥaliẓah, the court will not interfere. Apparently, the court does not concern itself with the dead man's claim to perpetuation of his name.

[209] M. Yeb. 111b — *hanoderet hana'ah.* The statement of *rabbotenu* Ket. 63b, referred to in the next note seems to indicate that the question of the preference of ḥaliẓah had no bearing on the subject, for *rabbotenu* represent a Palestinian tradition, where ḥaliẓah was preferered.

[210] Ket. 63b. The remark by the Gemara, Ket. 64a, that this is in keeping with the older tradition making marriage more desirable than ḥaliẓah is not entirely convincing. See previous note. Rather I take it as a residue of the old tradition, even though the sentiment may have changed.

[211] Ket. 64a. Here it may have been Samuel's preference for ḥaliẓah, for the Pumbedita academy, successor to Nahardea over which Samuel presided, was rather in favor of ḥaliẓah.

[212] In accordance with *stam gemara,* Ket. ibid., it was assumed by post-talmudic teachers that enforcement is a question depending upon whether marriage or ḥaliẓah is preferable. See Yad, Yibbum 2,10, and *Maggid* thereto.

But if either the widow or the levir demands freedom from the ziḳah bond, ḥaliẓah, if not marriage, is made compulsory, enforced by certain penalties,[218] imprisonment or flagellation. Compulsion for the widow was usually unnecessary, except when she was determined not to remarry, for the ziḳah gave her every disadvantage in prohibiting her to remarry under severe penalties, while she derived no advantage from it. For the old clause in the ketubah which gave the widow support out of her husband's estate was modified in amoraic times in such a manner as to give the heirs choice at any time to pay her the ketubah and send her out of the house. Therefore the levirate widow, too, could be paid out her ketubah and have her claim on support thus cancelled. It was the levir generally on whom the court had to impose penalties for refusing to marry the widow or to give her ḥaliẓah. By giving ḥaliẓah to the widow he gained no advantage for himself, for the law afforded him no special rights in the estate of his brother for his trouble in freeing the widow. Often, again, the widow's ketubah was so large or the estate so small that none of the brothers could expect anything out of the estate for themselves. Disadvantages because of the ziḳah bond the levir had none, for he was permitted to marry another wife, regardless of the ziḳah bond to his sister-in-law. It was on the levir that the law had to use physical compulsion to make him free the widow by ḥaliẓah.

Physical compulsion, however, was not always the most pleasant treatment of a levir who defied the law. Monetary inducements to the levir were sometimes deemed necessary. These were originally privately arranged between the levir and the widow, consisting generally of a settlement of the widow's ketubah claims for a fraction of their just value; and in course of time the monetary inducements took on the nature of community enactments. In one place we hear of an enactment that the levir who performs the ḥaliẓah is granted outright half the estate of the deceased. Out of the

[218] Yeb. 39a; Ket. 64a; Yad, Yibbum 2,16. *Maggid* ad Yad ibid. cites an opinion that in those places where marriage is preferred, the widow can refuse to accept ḥaliẓah and demand marriage.

other half, the ketubah is paid first and the residue divided among the other brothers.[214] If there is not enough in half the estate to pay the ketubah in full, the woman has to take what she can and the brothers get nothing. In other localities it was the custom at the time of marriage for the groom's brothers to make out an instrument for the bride obligating themselves, by oath or by property security, to grant her ḥaliẓah in the event the groom should die childless.[215] Sometimes the father-in-law would issue such an instrument, guaranteeing ḥaliẓah by a lien on his property.[216] It read approximately as follows:

"We, the undersigned, do hereby testify that the brothers NN and NN have authorized us to write an instrument and to attest it and to convey same to NN the bride of NN their brother, stating that . . . they submit all their property and possessions as security for the fulfillment of their promise that if NN remains a widow under levirate obligation they will free her by ḥaliẓah . . . without payment or gift or reduction of her ketubah . . . and that neither one of the two brothers can refer her to the other, but that whichever one of them will be first approached will free her by ḥaliẓah without protest or hesitation, so that the property of both remains under lien until NN shall have been freed by proper ḥaliẓah, as herein stated . . . date . . . signatures." [217]

A special problem of enforcement was faced by the law in the case where the levir was an apostate, and therefore out of jurisdiction of the Jewish court. That problem was often anticipated at the time of marriage, when the groom had only one brother who had already renounced Judaism. There was a gaonic ruling that an apostate did not count as a brother and his ḥaliẓah would therefore not be required; [218] but the halakah decided to the contrary, counting the apos-

[214] Note of Isserles, E.H. 165,3. If half of the estate was not enough to pay the ketubah, the widow had to lose part of her ketubah. Special enactments on this matter are treated of in Finkelstein's *Jewish Self-Government,* pp. 55–58.

[215] *Naḥalat Shib'ah,* I, 22; *Tikkun Soferim,* p. 31.

[216] *Nahalat Shib'ah,* I, 23.

[217] This is an abbreviation of a manuscript instrument cited in Gulak, *Oẓar ha-Sheṭarot,* p. 95.

[218] See *Maggid,* Yibbum 1,6.

tate as a Jew.[219] Should the husband, then, die childless and the apostate refuse to give ḥaliẓah, the widow would remain an *'agunah* for life. In such a case, therefore, the law permitted a conditional marriage, specifying in the marriage contract that if the husband died childless the marriage became null and void.[220] With decline of the power of the Jewish court to enforce its authority, there has arisen a movement to arrange all marriages on a conditional basis, so that if the levir refuse to grant the widow ḥaliẓah, even if he be a loyal Jew, the marriage shall be invalid. General rabbinic opinion opposed introduction of a conditional clause in all marriages, and to our knowledge Algeria is the only Jewish community that maintains a general conditional marriage over protest of the rabbis. In other communities, the problem of enforcing ḥaliẓah forms part of the larger problem of *'agunah,* to which the law as yet has no solution. To a certain extent, the ḥaliẓah problem is severer than the *'agunah* problem, because the law requires that the levir and the widow meet in the same rabbinic court; and that is often impossible where they reside in different and distant lands.[221]

(G) SUCCESSION TO THE ESTATE of the deceased brother will conclude our study of the levirate institution under rabbinic law. We have noted above [222] that the problem of immediate succession did not occur in the levirate situation as contemplated in the Judah-Tamar story or in the Book of Deuteronomy. Deuteronomy singles out the first-born levirate-child as the one who will "establish the name" of the deceased. By tannaitic exegesis, this expression means that he enters upon the inheritance of the deceased, and proof is given from the fact that Jacob uses the same expression in respect to the sons of Joseph (other than Manasseh and Ephraim), for whom he specifies a certain manner of succession in the family estate.[223] This tannaitic

219 Yad, Yibbum 1,6; E.H. 157,4.

220 See note of Isserles ad E.H. 157,4 and references quoted in *Pitḥe Teshubah* thereto.

221 Rabbi Yudelewitz of New York at the beginning of this century made an attempt to permit ḥaliẓah through a *shaliaḥ* but could not get the consent of the rabbis.

222 See p. 86 above.

223 Gen. 48.6. See Yeb. 24a; Targum Jonathan and Sifre ad Deut. 25.6.

interpretation of the text in Deuteronomy is vaguely implied in the text itself, and by it we obtain a definite concept of the rule of succession in a levirate situation, applicable probably to Genesis as well as Deuteronomy. The law is that the first-born levirate-child, but none of the other children,[224] is heir of the deceased. And this means theoretical heir, or potential heir. That is, while the patriarch does not part with his property during his lifetime, he counts on turning over his estate to his sons at the time of his death; and in this case he accounts a grandson, the first-born levirate-child, as one of his sons, taking the place of the one who died childless.

Direct succession from the deceased to the levirate-child came with the breakdown of the patriarchal family, and its pattern was taken from the Book of Ruth, even though the latter was a case of *ge'ullah* and not levirate. In the Ruth story there is an immediate problem of disposing of the estate of the deceased, and the *go'el* together with the *ge'ullah*-child play a confusing role. It is hard to fathom the mind of the author, how he conceived of the rule of succession to the estate of the deceased in his *ge'ullah* situation. But according to the best interpretation, and approximating his mind as closely as we can, we get the following picture. As *go'el,* Boaz becomes immediate owner of the estate. His ownership, however, is "directed," that is, limited to a specific purpose, to the ultimate possession of the estate by the yet unborn *ge'ullah*-child. When this *ge'ullah*-child is born, the *go'el* loses his ownership and becomes guardian of the estate on behalf of the child. Whether the child becomes outright owner at his majority or at his father's death, we do not know. The tendency in later time was to believe that the *go'el* held the estate for his lifetime.

This was the pattern for levirate succession, the levir was the immediate successor, the child the ultimate successor. But it was natural that the child's part as ultimate successor should gradually be submerged and lost. With loss of the patriarchal family structure, with the weakening of the fiction that the child was actually the offspring of the de-

[224] See a full discussion of this point in Mittelmann, o.c. p. 13.

ceased, and with the acknowledgment, even as by the Chronicler during the biblical period,[225] that the child really belonged to his natural father, the levir, the child lost every claim to the estate of the deceased in the post-biblical period. The first-born levirate-child, in rabbinic law, had nothing to do with his deceased childless uncle. He belonged to the levir like the rest of his children. To adjust this law with Deuteronomy, the rabbis had to resort to the highly artificial biblical interpretation, that the "first-born" referred to in Deuteronomy did not mean the levirate-child but the oldest levir.[226]

When the levirate-child was out of the way, there were only two ancient traditions to follow in the matter of succession, both referring to immediate succession. In Genesis and Deuteronomy the father was the immediate successor; in the Book of Ruth the levir (*go'el*) was immediate successor. Both views are represented among the tannaim. An anonymous tanna in the Mishnah teaches that under all circumstances, the levir is the sole heir of his deceased brother; but R. Judah b. Ilai maintains that if there is a surviving father, he is the sole heir and not the levir.[227] Whichever opinion we follow, levirate succession is an exception to the rule of succession given in Numbers[228] – for the levir, it is admitted by all, does not share the estate with the other brothers, as indicated in the Book of Numbers. The rabbis, of course, would say that the law of succession changes in a levirate situation, as does the law of incest. There are a number of amoraim who support the view of R. Judah, but the final halakah ruled that the levir is the sole heir, whether the father be alive or not.[229] The law, however, restricts his

225 See note 27 above.

226 Yeb. 24a.

227 Yeb. 40a.

228 Num. 27.8–11. Brothers are equal heirs (even where there are neither sons nor daughters); father is not mentioned as heir, probably because this legislation was issued at that last stage of the patriarchal system when children's property was controlled by the father while brothers were already out of the patriarchal family with the death of the father. See a peculiar twist given to the text by A. Wolff in *Das jüdische Erbrecht*, Berlin, 1888, pp. 24–26.

229 See Yeb. 40a and Yer. Yeb. 5d. But the final law is given in E.H. 163,1, in accordance with gaonic ruling. See B. Lewin, *Ozar*, Yeb. 40a.

right of succession to only the estate actually in possession of the deceased at the time of his demise; any later additions from whatever source are divided equally among the brothers in accord with the standard law of succession.[230]

If the levir does not perform the levirate duty by marriage but frees the widow by ḥaliẓah, according to biblical law he certainly loses all rights of succession to the estate of the deceased. He may even lose his right of succession in the general family estate after the father's death, for the name *Ḥaluẓ hana'al* which is attached to him seems to indicate ostracism. But in rabbinic law ḥaliẓah is not an offence, and no penalty attaches to the levir who performs ḥaliẓah. "He is like the rest of the brothers," and the estate is divided according to the standard law of succession.[231] This law has been in operation from tannaitic times to the present day, except for the local enactment cited above giving the levir half the estate as an inducement to free the widow by ḥaliẓah.

III

Having concluded our study of the main features of the levirate institution under rabbinic law, we shall now briefly summarize its fate and fortune in the hands of the Karaites. To them the levirate applies only in Palestine, for outside the land the biblical interest in conserving family estates within the family does not apply, and therefore it has no purpose.[232] A levirate situation exists only when the husband has no son or daughter, even as is the rule among the Rabbanites,[233] but the Karaites add two additional limitations — one, that the marriage of the deceased be monogamous, so that if more than one widow remains of the same husband, there is no levirate situation; [234] two, that the widow herself have no children by any former husband, else there would

230 Bek. 51–52.

231 Yeb. 40a.

232 *Eshkol ha-Kofer,* 324; *Gan'Eden,* Nashim 13; *Aderet Elijahu,* Nashim 5.

233 'Anan, *Sefer ha-Miẓwot,* Nashim 41; *Keter Torah,* Deut. 25.5; *Aderet Elijahu,* Nashim, end of 5.

234 *Sefer ha-Miẓwot,* Nashim 43. Later Karaites differ with 'Anan and demand levirate even in polygamous marriages. In such a case, one marriage or

be no "first-born" in the maternal sense and levirate marriage would be impossible.[235]

To the Karaites, zikah has no legal significance whatever. The levirate widow stands in relation to the levirs, whoever they be, as though there were no levirate situation at all. She is just the widow of a relative. There are no zikah rights, no zikah duties, no zikah-incest. The levirate situation, however, prohibits her marrying one outside the family, and to the Karaites this prohibition is severer than to the Rabbanites, for they declare such a marriage totally invalid.[236]

Levirate marriage, to the Karaites, is in no respect different from any other. The account of the *ge'ullah* marriage in the Book of Ruth serves them as the standard marriage ceremonial both in levirate and in any ordinary union.[237] Following the example of the Book of Ruth, they consider levirate marriage optional both with the levir and the widow; again, because they permit no coercion in any marriage.[238] If none of the levirs is willing to marry the widow, the Karaites prescribe ḥaliẓah, according to biblical law, and the ceremony is just as described in Deuteronomy.[239] While in rabbinic law there are cases where ḥaliẓah alone is possible and some where marriage alone is possible, the Karaites know of no such cases, for the Bible prescribes either marriage or ḥaliẓah without exception.[240]

As to who is the proper levir, the Karaites have two teachings. The older school declares that actual brothers are the proper levirs. But in order to adjust the levirate law with the law of incest, this school teaches that levirate applies only to the betrothed and incest applies only to the wedded. The later school rejects that distinction and maintains that both levirate and incest apply equally to the betrothed and

one ḥaliẓah is sufficient for all the widows. The one married first is first in line of levirate duty and the others next, in order of the time of their marriage. See *Keter Torah*, Deut. 25.7.

235 *Sefer ha-Miẓwot*, Nashim 35. Here, too, *Keter Torah*, Deut. 25.6, differs with 'Anan and prescribes levirate even if the woman had children before.

236 *Gan'Eden*, Nashim 13, etc.

237 *Sefer ha-Miẓwot*, Nashim 46, 48.

238 Ibid. 47; *Aderet Elijahu*, ibid.

239 *Sefer ha-Miẓwot*, ibid. 50–55.

240 *Gan'Eden*, ibid.

the wedded. As a consequence they permit no levirate marriage of an actual sister-in-law, and levirate to them means *ge'ullah* marriage. They take the term "brother" in the sense of "kin." The nearest of kin, next to the brothers, becomes the levir, and if he refuses to marry the widow, the one next in order of kinship takes his place.[241]

The Karaites, apparently, would agree that the levir-child is the ultimate heir of the deceased,[242] but the question of the immediate heir raises some difficulties in their minds. The later school of Karaites, who teach that a relative other than the brother becomes the levir, could not have succession to property of the deceased follow in line with levirate marriage; for succession, as given in the Book of Numbers, goes to brothers in the absence of children, while levirate, according to their interpretation, goes to the next of kin after the brothers. They therefore divide succession into two parts, succession to property and succession to the wife of the deceased. They are independent of each other. Succession to property goes to the brothers, but succession to the wife, for the purpose of establishing a name for the deceased, goes to the next of kin, the levir.[243]

241 Geiger, *Ḳebuẓat Ma'amarim,* pp. 59 f; *Sefer ha-Miẓwot,* Nashim 31,42; *Eshkol ha-Kofer,* 322; *Keter Torah,* Deut. 25.5; *Gan'Eden,* Nashim 13; *Aderet Elijahu,* Nashim 5.

242 *Keter Torah,* Deut. 25.6; *Aderet Elijahu,* ibid.

243 *Aderet Elijahu,* Nashim 5, p. 157 d.

CHAPTER IV

INTERMARRIAGE

I

THE prohibition of intermarriage derives its moral force from one of five motives or from a combination of several of them. The first and most primitive is the rule of endogamy, demanding marriage within the tribe. Second, in course of the historic experiences of the tribe, it often happens that it develops friction with another tribe and expresses its enmity by prohibiting marriage with the other's members. Third, if the difference between one tribe and another is religious, that may form a strong barrier against intermarriage. Fourth, more often racial differences and the desire of each to keep its blood pure and free from adulteration give valid basis to the prohibition. Finally, a tribal group weakened by untoward political conditions and in danger of disintegration, or more especially when uprooted from its soil and forced to live among other racial or cultural groups as a minority element and subject to the disintegrating forces besetting a minority, builds up an outer wall of separation, a kind of compensating resistance to the outside world, as a means of self-preservation; and therein it finds its motive for prohibiting intermarriage. The prohibition in Jewish law has followed this pattern throughout Hebrew history, emphasizing sometimes one motive, sometimes another, and often finding justification in several in combination.

Among the primitive oriental tribes endogamy was the general rule, requiring marriages to be made within the family group rather than outside. With the larger patriarchal family, it meant actual marrying within the family; with reduction of the size of the family unit, it meant marrying within the clan, bride and groom being of kindred family units. Endogamy held out many advantages. It gave the bride's family a sense of security that the girl would be treated with consideration by the groom and his people, because she was no stranger to them. It made possible intimate and advantageous negotiations between both sides on the terms of the marriage. Negotiations could be made for exchange of brides, one family taking a bride from the other and giving one of its daughters in return, thereby saving bride price for both. Mistrust of strangers intensified the motive of endogamous marriage.

The Hebrews, like their neighbors, from time immemorial tended to endogamous marriages. Abraham married his half-sister;[1] his brother, Nahor, married a niece.[2] Isaac and Esau and Jacob married cousins.[3] Amram, father of Moses, married his aunt,[4] and Caleb gave his daughter to his nephew ʿAthniel.[5] In the numerous cousin marriages recorded in the Bible, one can see, in fact, a definite biblical standard of marriage between near relatives. That standard, however, never rises to the level of a law prohibiting marriage with non-relatives, but is definite and firm enough as a social usage in biblical times. It should be understood in the sense in which the Arabs of Palestine have continued this old tradition in their practice today.[6] They recognize the cousin, particularly the son of the father's brother, as having first claim on the girl; if it is not pressed or if for one reason or another the cousin is not acceptable to the girl's family, she marries a more distant relative or a stranger. That cousin marriage was not actually required by biblical law is evident from the many marriages between strangers recorded without explanation or apology. Furthermore, if marrying a stranger, even a Hebrew, were prohibited, there would be no need for special legislation against espousing a Canaanite, Ammonite, Moabite, or Egyptian.[7] The incident of the rape

[1] Gen. 20.12.
[2] Gen. 11.29.
[3] Gen. 24.15; 28.9; 29.12.
[4] Num. 26.59.
[5] Jos. 15.17.
[6] H. Granquist, *Marriage Conditions in a Palestine Village*, Vol. I, pp. 67 f.
[7] Deut. 7.3; 23.4–9.

of the concubine of Gibeah, on which account the tribes of Israel covenanted not to give their daughters to the sons of the tribe of Benjamin,[8] evidently implies that intermarriage among tribes was a common occurrence, necessary under ancient conditions and proper according to ancient law.

The law raises objection to marriage between man and woman of different Hebrew tribes only where it becomes the cause of conveying property from one tribe to another. This law was enacted in connection with the daughters of Zelaphehad. The older law gave no inheritance to daughters under any circumstances. Zelaphehad died without male heirs and his daughters demanded that they be given their father's estate. Moses granted their demand and ruled that in the absence of sons, daughters be given the estate of their father; but he specified in his new legislation that a daughter who inherits her father's estate must marry within his family so that it be not transferred from one tribe to another.[9] This new legislation, according to biblical critics, is of post-exilic origin, and seems to have been in force down to the second century before the Common Era, for the Book of Tobit still reckons with it.[10] It was probably abrogated at an early rabbinic period, at least before the end of the Second Commonwealth; and the rabbinic tradition has it that its abrogation was officially proclaimed on the fifteenth day of the month of Ab and that it received such full popular approval that the day was declared an official holiday in the Jewish calendar.[11] There are also rabbinic traditions to the effect that Zelaphehad's daughters were not affected by this legislation, that is, that the ruling was introduced after marriage to their cousins in anticipation of similar cases in the future, or that this marriage restriction was intended only for the first generation of Hebrew settlers in Palestine.[12] These traditions are amoraic in origin, exegetical and casuistic in nature, and can claim no historic validity. The one conclusion we seek to draw, and that is evident from talmudic accounts, is

[8] Judg. 19–20.
[9] Num. 36.
[10] Tobit 4.12; 6.10–12.
[11] Ta'anit 30b; Yer. Ta'anit at the end; Introduction to Ekha Rabbati, 33.
[12] B.B. 120a.

that the restriction was no longer in operation in rabbinic times, so that even its exact nature was no longer known in the later rabbinic period.

This is not to be wondered at, for tribal distinctions had vanished from the Jewish consciousness, and likewise, attachment to family estates meant very little. Yet the social tradition of marrying within the family continued in part even down to the rabbinic period. If the motive of preserving family estates had lost its meaning, a new motive arose, that of preserving family purity. The Jews of the post-biblical period made much of the aristocracy of blood, free from the taint of foreign admixture or from illegitimacy. They kept family records tracing descent for generations back to show the purity of the family stock. The priests were leaders in this, and the aristocratic Israelitish families emulated them. Mistrustful of other families, they married, as far as possible, within their own. Those Israelites who had no record of family purity were naturally limited to their own group, and within the group alliances with their own relatives were the most logical, because all controversy on possible taint of a serious nature could be avoided, and negotiations on the terms of the marriage could be more informal and more intimate. Inbreeding, therefore, while not a law, was the accepted social standard for the Jews of the two centuries immediately preceding and immediately following the beginning of the common era. The apocryphal books of Tobit and Jubilees [13] consider it most meritorious to marry cousins or, at least, within the family. The propriety of marrying a niece was the subject of a heated controversy among the sectaries, the Pharisees insisting not only that this was permissible but that it was an alliance of special merit.[14] The heat of the controversy and the attitude of the Pharisees can be explained only if the general tradition of marrying within the family is assumed. The tannaim have a tradition that priestly families, and likewise pure-blooded Israelitish families, set up a standard *mohar* of four hundred zuzim, double

[13] Tobit, ibid.; Jubilees 4.15; 19.24.

[14] Yeb. 63a; Tos. Ḳid. 1,4. The subject will receive fuller treatment later on under the heading of incest.

that of the normal *mohar*, as a mark of family distinction; [15] and the amoraim remark that it was so instituted by them "in order to cause people to marry within their tribe and within their family." [16] The development of priest cities, of which we hear in early tannaitic times, is probably due to inbreeding of the priestly families; and, strangely enough, according to reports of travelers, such priest cities still exist among the Berber Jews of North Africa.[17]

In the two centuries following collapse of the Second Commonwealth there were sufficient time and good reason for the aristocracy of priesthood to decline, for family records to be lost or destroyed, hence for family purity to become an insignificant factor in marriage alliances. Therefore, during the amoraic period, the desire of Jews to contract marriages within their own families waned almost to extinction. What remained to keep up the tradition of marrying relatives was only the natural sociological circumstance of relatives living closer together, affording their youth opportunity to mingle more freely, also enabling the parents to discuss marriage terms more frankly. This alone accounted for a certain proportion of kin marriages among Jews of the middle ages; and when the *shadkan*, match-maker, made his appearance in the mediaeval Jewish community and took from parents the task of marriage negotiations and meetings, the number of such alliances was probably reduced. The free mingling of the sexes in modern times and the congestion of Jews in larger cities have all but made an end to the preference for marrying relatives. In fact, it seems to be a rare occurrence today for husband and wife to be cousins, and when this does occur it attracts special notice.

If the rule of endogamy among the Hebrews accounted for the primitive standard of marriage within the family, it becomes obvious that the same rule set up a barrier against intermarriage with other racial groups. In fact, in the earliest biblical records, endogamy is the only motive for the tendency against intermarriage. No political enmity, no religious

[15] Ket. 12a–b.
[16] Yer. Ket. 25c.
[17] N. Slouschz, *Travels in North Africa*, Philadelphia, 1927.

antagonism is harbored toward the heathen neighbors. The sentiment against marrying them is no different from that of marrying within the family, and, like the latter, it did not formulate itself into a definite law, prohibiting intermarriage, but amounted to a social standard which was heeded as a matter of propriety. The breach was common enough, yet there was no sense of outrage. This is all that intermarriage meant to the Jews prior to the deuteronomic period.

The aversion to marriage with alien races is definite enough in the pre-deuteronomic family records. It is basic in Abraham's choice of a wife for Isaac,[18] as well as in Rebecca's sending Jacob away from his parental home.[19] Esau's marriage of Hittite women gave grief to his parents,[20] and the sons of Jacob spoke truthfully that they considered it a disgrace to their family to marry their sister to one not circumcised.[21] Samson falls in love with a Philistine woman and his parents dissuade him from marrying her by the argument: "Is there no wife among the daughters of thy brothers or among all my people that thou goest to take a wife from the uncircumcised Philistines?"[22] This general condemnation of foreign marriages probably accounts for the surprising fact that the kings of Judah and Israel, numbering thirty-nine and reigning for three hundred and ninety-three years, had only two and possibly three who married foreign wives.[23] Yet the sentiment was not strong enough to deter Judah[24] and Simeon[25] from taking Canaanite wives, Joseph[26] from marrying an Egyptian woman, and Moses from espousing one Midianite[27] and one Cushite.[28] For, as remarked, a legal prohibition against intermar-

[18] Gen. 24.3.
[19] Gen. 27.46.
[20] Gen. 26.34, 35; 28.8.
[21] Gen. 34.14.
[22] Judg. 14.3.
[23] This fact is pointed out by Leopold Loew in *Gesammelte Schriften*, III, 138–9.
[24] Gen. 38.2.
[25] Gen. 46.10.
[26] Gen. 41.45.
[27] Ex. 2.21.
[28] Num. 21.1.

riage did not yet exist; it was still in the stage of an endogamous social rule that permitted exceptions. Evidently that was the judgment conveyed by the author of the twelfth chapter of the Book of Numbers, who recounts that Aaron and Miriam condemned Moses for taking a Cushite wife, and God was wroth against them and punished Miriam with leprosy. This chapter is pre-deuteronomic and deals, therefore, not with a legal prohibition against intermarriage but with a social standard that might under certain conditions be overlooked. Hence the author offers no apology or explanation for Moses, but demands confidence in his judgment and conduct.[29]

A peculiarly favorable attitude to intermarriage is implied by the author of the Book of Ruth. Ruth the Moabite is praised for her fine character, her devotion to her mother-in-law, Naomi, and her loyalty to the God and people of Israel, and she is recorded as mother of the royal house of David. An argument in favor of intermarriage is taken to be the intent of the author. As we have noted above, scholars are inclined to judge this book a product of post-exilic times and to consider the author an antagonist of Ezra's severe condemnation of intermarriage. We find it difficult to follow this view. We hear from no other source, neither the levitical code nor the Chronicler nor the early apocryphal writers, of such a teaching being officially acceptable to Judaism during the Second Commonwealth. No doubt there were intermarriages and even schools of thought that defended it, but so far as we know, Ezra's attitude to intermarriage in severer or milder form remained the attitude of Judaism, officially, throughout the period. Permitting an argument favorable to intermarriage to remain part of the Canon seems to us unthinkable. The more so, since the argument involves a reflection against the purity of stock of the Davidic family. We are forced, therefore, on ideological bases alone to conclude that the Book of Ruth is pre-exilic and even pre-deuteronomic, as mentioned in the previous chapter, belonging therefore to a time when the Jewish attitude to inter-

[29] Moses' marriage to the Cushite woman is variously explained by Josephus, Midrash, and commentators. See Loew, o.c., pp. 131–2.

marriage was totally different from what it was after Ezra's days. The author had only the rule of endogamy before him, a rule which was not binding and the breach of which raised no scandal. Furthermore, the idea of a taint of blood was altogether unknown; therefore even if Boaz was wrong in marrying the Moabite, this had no bearing on the purity of the Davidic family. But Boaz was not wrong, even under the severest interpretation of endogamy, for he was in duty bound to marry her according to the rule of *ge'ullah,* and *ge'ullah* supercedes endogamy. Elimelech was wrong in breaking the rule of endogamy in marrying his two sons to foreign women, but Elimelech was not the ancestor of David. At any rate, the author of Ruth did not feel himself called upon to express an opinion in the matter. He took intermarriage as lightly as the endogamous sentiment and its frequent occurrences warranted, and gave his attention to the beauty of soul of the loyal foreign woman. If he implied any judgment on the subject of intermarriage, it was this. Intermarriage has social disapproval, and as a social standard, it does not distinguish between one kind of foreign woman and another. That, says the author, is unfair: Ruth is different from other foreign women by her character and by her fine loyalty. If he had completed his picture, he would have drawn a contrast between Jezebel, wife of Ahab, of the Kingdom of the North, and Ruth, great-grandmother of David, of the dynasty of the South, and would have concluded: We of the South, when we marry foreign women, marry women like Ruth.[80]

Such a mild attitude to intermarriage was natural for the Jews during the early settlement in Palestine. The nation was just being formed out of tribal groups, and the distance between a Hebrew and a heathen was merely an extension of that between a Hebrew of the tribe of Judah and one of the tribe of Benjamin. Religious formulation was still in process. Political and social mingling between the Hebrews and their neighbors was inevitable; covenants of friendship and mutual assistance were necessary for political security

[80] See our brief remark on the Book of Ruth in the chapter on levirate marriage, p. 86 and note 17.

and peace. Non-Jewish clients were joined to Hebrew households; foreign slaves and home-born slaves often attained their freedom and grew naturally into the Jewish population. It could not be otherwise but that intermarriage should take on large proportions.[31] Innocent of political treachery and of cultural dangers, the Hebrews of that period saw little objection therein save breach of the general rule of endogamy.

With the deuteronomic period, in the days of the later kings of Judah, intermarriage entered into its second phase. No longer a matter of social standards, it now became a matter of law, prompted by certain political frictions with neighboring nations and by antagonism to the ethically degraded cultures of the heathens. Thus, in the legislation of the Book of Deuteronomy and in passages found in other sections of the Pentateuch emanating from the same period we have for the first time a legal ruling against intermarriage, the motive for which is sometimes political, based on enmity to a certain nation, and sometimes religious, aversion to the religious cults of certain peoples and a fear lest the Hebrews fall victim to their abominations. Racial purity does not come into consideration in deuteronomic legislation against intermarriage; it is all motivated by a desire for political and religious solidarity.

Important social, religious, and political changes must have taken place to account for the new legislation, and perhaps we can penetrate beneath the surface of biblical records to gain a fuller understanding of them. In the first place, there were various elements in Judea divided on their attitude to their heathen neighbors. Those residing in the outlying provinces, having closer contacts with the tribes living across the boundary, were inclined to accept intermarriage; those in the interior, coming into little contact with the heathen population beyond the border, harbored definite prejudices against it. It is said, in the second place, that the Hebrew population was divided into strata, according to cultural level. The peasant, uncultured element, on their

[31] See W. Nowack, *Lehrbuch d. Hebräischen Archäologie*, Leipzig, 1894, I, pp. 343–44; Benzinger, *Hebräische Archäologie*, 1907, p. 286.

first immigration into Canaan, struck root into Canaanite life, absorbed rather than moulded their environment; while, on the other hand, there was the so-called Mosaic element that came into Canaan to master their new world and to subject it to the culture and ideals of their monotheistic religion. The former accepted intermarriage with equanimity, the latter condemned it.[32] Perhaps, also, two influences within the Hebrew nation were opposed on the question of intermarriage, and both had followers among the people. One standard of life and ideals was set up by royalty; they favored foreign manners and alliances and therefore welcomed intermarriages. The other standard was held by the spiritual personalities, priests and prophets, who were zealous for the purity of their monotheistic faith and who on moral grounds held the heathens in contempt. They and their followers opposed intermarriage.[33] With this composition of the Hebrew population, it is understandable how the development of the people brought into power the better element, the interior or Mosaic or prophetic, and gave rise to the deuteronomic legislation against intermarriage. But, in the fourth place, there was probably another general influence at work. In the days of Solomon, with national glory at its highest, there was no need for building inner solidarity or fearing foreign influence. But when Judah was declining politically, and through foreign influence also religiously, the fear of its own weakness prompted the people to set up a wall of separation between itself and competing heathen cultures, in the belief that this outer fortress might take the place of inner strength.[34] But probably, and finally, the most effective and immediate cause of the deuteronomic legislation was the reformation movement begun by Hezekiah under the influence of Isaiah the prophet, continued, after some interruption, by Josiah under the influence of Jehoiada the priest.

Reformations are initiated as a means of retrenchment

[32] Cf. R. H. Kennett, *Hebrew Social Life and Customs*, London, 1933.

[33] Sigismund Rauh, *Hebräisches Familienrecht in vorprophetischer Zeit*, Berlin, 1907.

[34] Heinrich Ewald, *Die Alterthümer des Volkes Israel*, Göttingen, 1866, p. 259.

during or at the end of a national crisis. Their purpose is to counteract the sense of defeat, to bolster up national courage, and to tighten inner bonds in order to offset the weakening of national solidarity. They take the form either of a religious revival or an intensification of national sentiment; and in either case a sense of national or cultural exclusiveness and superiority, an antagonism to foreigners, a zeal for national or cultural purity is certain to be the result. And thus the stage is set for prohibition against intermarriage as a national policy. Four definite attacks upon intermarriage are to be found in Jewish history, and all of them came in the wake of a reformation movement consequent upon a national crisis. The first was the deuteronomic reformation, the second came with the Restoration under Ezra, the third with the Maccabean victory in the War of Independence, the fourth with the final fall of the Jewish State.

The reformation of Hezekiah and Josiah resulted from the political national crisis in their day and yielded the deuteronomic restrictions against intermarriage. The great power threatening the Hebrew people was Assyria. The Kingdom of the North fell in the eighth century and the Kingdom of the South waited in despair for the overhanging doom. Under such outer political conditions, the inner life of the people suffered great demoralization. It would have taken little to crush Judah's spirit by the mere fear of Assyria, had not Isaiah kept pouring new faith and hope into his people, and had not the Assyrian hosts been miraculously decimated by a plague while besieging Jerusalem. New courage was gained; Hezekiah's reformation began. But Assyria was not quite defeated. It was still strong enough to exact tribute from Judah. The fear of Assyria continued to weigh heavily on the Jewish spirit. Many resigned themselves to eternal vassalage to the mighty foreign nation. Then, in the time of Josiah, the Assyrian power was broken for good, and Judah, while still beset from other quarters, was for the moment free of the Assyrian yoke. With the new freedom came new courage and the reformation begun by Hezekiah, was now continued and extended by Josiah. The reformation, true to pattern, attacked everything foreign, cleansed the land of its idolatrous importations from heathen neighbors, aroused religious zeal against pagan practices, reawakened certain national enmities, and set up a barrier against friendly contacts with the hateful heathens. And here the deuteronomic legislation against intermarriage had its beginning.

We shall consider first the deuteronomic prohibition against marriage with the native tribes of Canaan, the "seven nations," Hittites, Girgoshites, Amorites, Canaanites, Perizzites, Hivites, and Jebusites.[85] ,The severest attack on these nations finds expression in the following passage: "When thou comest nigh unto a city to fight against it, then proclaim peace unto it. And it shall be, if it make thee answer of peace and open unto thee . . . that all the people that are found therein shall be tributaries unto thee . . . So shalt thou do to all the cities that are very far off from thee . . . but of the cities of these people which the Lord thy God giveth thee for an inheritance, *thou shalt save nothing alive that hath breath*. But thou shalt utterly destroy them."[86] This rule, thou shalt save nothing alive that hath breath, was evidently taken seriously and literally in earlier, pre-deuteronomic wars, for this was the manner in which Joshua is recorded to have dealt with the cities he conquered in Canaan, "as the Lord God of Israel hath commanded,"[87] and Samuel so instructed Saul to deal with the Amalekites.[88] But this law, though part of our deuteronomic code, was apparently not subscribed to whole-heartedly as a practical,

[85] Ex. 23.23; 34.11; Deut. 7.1–3. I have followed the accepted opinion of biblical scholars who consider the verses in Exodus of deuteronomic origin. I am not convinced of this assumption, and at any rate I am not convinced that the deuteronomic author did not draw these injunctions from older sources. If the prohibition of marriage with the "seven nations" is to be considered pre-deuteronomic, it must be recognized to be different in nature from the other intermarriage prohibitions in Deuteronomy. The natives of Canaan were marked for extinction as part of the program of conquest. The Ammonites, Moabites, Edonites and Egyptians were not. Hence Ruth the Moabite was acceptable to pre-deuteronomic Jews.

[86] Deut. 20.15–18.

[87] Jos. 10.40.

[88] I Sam. 15.3.

operative command by the deuteronomic legislator, and was even less heeded in post-exilic times. The deuteronomic legislator permits taking captive-wives in war, and it is fairly evident that he had in mind no distinction between war captives of the Canaanite tribes and other heathen tribes.[39] In the battle against the Midianites, Moses permitted the minor captive girls "who had not known men" to be taken as war booty.[40] The Priestly Code permits even buying slaves from "the nations that are about you,"[41] which seems to be in contrast to "the cities that are very far off from thee."

The conflict between these laws and the law, "thou shalt save nothing alive that hath breath," has troubled commentators, who have offered various adjustments.[42] But two things seem evident to us about this rule, and with these the conflict is dissolved. First, the rule is one that the deuteronomic legislator took from an older source, for we have seen that it was known and observed before deuteronomic times. Second, it had nothing to do with peace time relations between the Hebrews and the Canaanites; it lay down a war regulation and war program at the same time, namely, that the conflict against the natives was not to be for conquest but for extermination. The deuteronomic legislator and surely the legislator of the Priestly Code did not worry any more about wars against the natives. "Thou shalt save nothing alive that hath breath," therefore, had no practical application to them. It must have been to them the ideal of an exaggerated chauvinism which fitted in with their national crisis psychology and with their religious aversion to the heathen practices of their neighbors. For their peace time relation with Canaanites living beyond their borders or for

[39] Deut. 21.10–14.

[40] Num. 31.18.

[41] Lev. 25.44.

[42] Rashi ad Deut. 21.10, explains that this refers to the tribes other than the seven nations. So also Andreas Eberharter, *Alttestamentliche Abhandlungen, Das Ehe- und Familienrecht der Hebräer*, München, 1914. Benzinger, p. 287, and Nowack, I, p. 344, believe that this legislation considers the case of an Israelite taking the captive to wife contrary to the law. Against the first explanation our objection is that the Bible makes no distinction between captives of one tribe and another. Against the second, our objection is that the law would not legislate for a law violation.

those who lived among them, the rule had no practical bearing.

The practical, peace-time attitude of the Hebrews to the "seven nations" in deuteronomic days was to permit no alliance or covenant with them, based upon enmity, hatred of their degrading heathen idolatry, and fear lest they mislead the children of Israel and cause them to turn away from their God. Any pact was prohibited, whether a trade covenant or one of friendship, even fraternizing at a feast table,[43] but especially a marriage covenant. Thus Deuteronomy commands: "Thou shalt utterly destroy them, thou shalt make no covenant with them nor show mercy unto them. Thou shalt not enter into marriage with them, thy daughter thou shalt not give unto his son nor shalt thou take his daughter unto thy son; for he will turn away thy son from following Me, that they may serve other gods." [44]

From this command we learn that the motive of the prohibition against intermarriage with the seven nations was partly political but mainly religious, and that it was prohibited only as a form of covenant or alliance with them. An inferior marriage, such as taking a slave-wife or a captive-wife (perhaps exclusive of concubines, for some covenant was necessary there),[45] was permitted. Therefore the law permitting captive-wives from these nations.[46] In a later record we find that Moses did not permit captive-wives from among the maturer women of the Midianites, fearing the influence of their idolatrous sex orgies, but he accepted the minor girls "who had not yet known men." [47] In keeping with this spirit of the deuteronomic legislation, distinguishing between an alliance with and a mastery over members of the seven nations, the legislator probably had no objection

[43] Ex. 34.15. Cf. Ex. 23.32–33.

[44] Deut. 7.3–4. Cf. also Ex. 34.16 and Jos. 23.12.

[45] One might suspect, though, that concubines were not prohibited, for in reproof of Solomon the First Book of Kings (11.3) says that his wives turned his heart, but lays no blame on his foreign concubines, but this matter remains uncertain.

[46] Deut. 21.10–13, Sifre thereto recognizes that Canaanites are included in this law.

[47] Num. 31.18.

to Hebrews having Canaanite slaves, male or female, even as later specifically permitted by Leviticus, nor did he have objection to Canaanite clients in the Hebrew community. In all these instances, it was not a covenant on a basis of equality; and the inferior position of the Canaanite, as captive or slave or client, made it necessary for him to accept in greater or smaller amount the cult of the Hebrews rather than be in a position to impose the heathen cult upon the Hebrews.

Deuteronomy prohibits marriage with other nations, not of the group of seven. The motive, however, is somewhat different. The religious motive is most prominent in the case of the seven nations; in others the political comes to the front. Traditional hostility to certain peoples is awakened by the intensified nationalism of the deuteronomic reformation. The Amalekites are the traditional enemies of the Hebrews, and the enmity goes back to a battle fought with them under the leadership of Moses, when Israel was a weak and weary wanderer in the wilderness. The deuteronomic code commands never to forget or forgive the Amalekite but to track him down to the end of days and blot out his memory from under the heavens.[48] Not even a command forbidding intermarriage with them is deemed necessary. It is taken for granted. And the prohibition against marrying an Amalekite was at least as severe as that against marriage within the seven nations, perhaps even more so, for it excluded even inferior marriages. Ammon and Moab are next in line as traditional enemies of the Hebrews, "because they met you not with bread and water in the way when you came forth out of Egypt and because they hired against you Balaam . . . to curse thee."[49] Therefore the law commands, "An Ammonite and a Moabite shall not enter (marry) into the assembly of the Lord; even unto the tenth generation shall none of them enter into the assembly of the Lord forever." The mamzer, too, who in this connection seems to represent a certain primitive tribe whose identity is not known, cannot enter the assembly of the Lord even unto the tenth genera-

[48] Deut. 25.17–19; Ex. 17.8–16; I Sam. 15.
[49] Deut. 23.5.

tion.[50] Milder is the hostility to the Egyptian and the Edomite, the former "because thou wast a stranger in his land," the latter "because he is thy brother." These nations are excluded from marriage with Jews only for three generations: "The children that are begotten of them shall enter into the congregation of the Lord in their third generation."[51] The author of I Kings adds the Zidonians to the nations with whom intermarriage is prohibited by the deuteronomic law, and the objection is religious, because of their Ashtoreth worship.[52] Later documents include Midianites[53] and Ashdodites,[54] again with emphasis on the danger of their heathen cult to the Jewish religion.

Three additional concluding statements may be made to characterize the deuteronomic prohibition against intermarriage. First, the question of the validity of an alien marriage is never raised, as in later Hebrew law. As yet the legal concept of a marriage that has no validity did not exist. Marriage was home-taking for marital union; as such it was fact, right or wrong, that no law could undo. Second, the status of the children born of mixed marriages is not a problem to the legislator. This was determined, as in regular marriages, by the family structure of the time; in patronymic families the child followed the father, in the metronymic he followed the mother. A mixed marriage raised no problem.[55] Third, the foreign marriages which the deuteronomic legislator prohibited included marrying foreign men or foreign women. The talmudic teachers, as we shall see later, believed that of certain tribes the men alone were prohibited but not the women. We can have no doubt on the subject, since the reproof of King Solomon by the author of I Kings is spe-

[50] Deut. 23.2. In that sense is the word mamzer used in Zech. 9.6, according to the Septuagint translation.

[51] Deut. 23.8–9.

[52] I Kings 11.1.

[53] Num. 31.15–17.

[54] Neh. 13.23. It should be suggested, however, that the Ashdodites here may be the same as mamzer in Deut., for mamzer and Ashdod are connected in Zech. 9.6.

[55] Geiger, *Urschrift*, Breslau, 1857, p. 54, maintains that mamzer in Deuteronomy means a child born of a mixed marriage, and he sees in this word a combination of two Hebrew words, *m'am zar*, of a strange nation. This interpretation, however, is not acceptable to us. See remark on the Davidic dynasty on p. 152, above.

cifically directed against his taking foreign women, "Moabite, Ammonite, Edomite, Zidonite, and Hittite women, of the nations concerning which God said to the children of Israel ye shall not go in to them, neither shall they come in unto you, for surely they will turn away your heart after their gods." [56] Later Nehemiah makes reference to this passage and imposes an oath on his people once more to marry neither foreign men nor foreign women.[57] If the emphasis was at all placed on one kind of marriage over another, it was that with a foreign woman that was most condemned, because the alienation of a son from his religion through strange contacts was more serious than turning a daughter away from God, since the woman had no standing in the religious community.[58]

The deuteronomic restriction against intermarriage did not entirely eradicate that evil. It is not improbable that during the reign of the last kings of Judah there was abundant intermarriage between the Hebrews and their heathen neighbors,[59] though no definite mention thereof is made in the Bible. It is definite, however, that with the destruction of the State intermarriage grew into dangerous proportions. The consequent demoralization, with the burning of the Temple, weakened the moral fibre of the people. The conquest by Babylonia extended beyond the borders of Judea, subjecting neighboring tribes as well. Mutual sympathies between the Hebrews and the other unfortunate tribes developed, which brought them closer together, at first socially and thereafter in matrimonial alliances. When the deporta-

[56] I Kings 11.2. This passage mentions the Ammonites and Moabites, of whom the rabbis make a distinction between the men and the women. They admit that there is no such distinction among the seven nations, and this, of course, is evident from Deut. 7.3, etc.

[57] Neh. 13.23.

[58] Ex. 34.16; Num. 25.1–2; Deut. 7.4. The Talmud, Yeb. 23a, seems to take the words "thy son" in the last named passage to refer to the child of the mixed marriage, implying that the marriage most severely criticized here is that of a Hebrew woman with a man of the seven nations; the child of the mixed marriage will be misled by his heathen father. The evident meaning of the passage is that in a marriage of a Hebrew to a heathen woman, there is danger that the Hebrew "son" be turned away by the influence of his heathen father-in-law.

[59] See Loew, III, p. 143.

tion took place, the nobility and learned men of the community were exiled and the lower classes remained behind in Palestine without leadership, save for Jeremiah's brief stay. Nothing was more natural for these lowly Judeans under such influences than to relapse into foreign worship and intermarriage on a large scale.[60] With the first Restoration under Zerubabel, a better group of Jews was added to the Palestinian community. They brought from the exile a zeal for their national sanctuary and a pride in their national heritage. Nevertheless, among these too there were many of doubtful origin, of mixed stock, and the priests were no exception.[61] Having joined their brethren in Palestine and having settled in the land comfortably, they emulated their Palestinian correligionists in foreign marriage alliances, especially with the Samaritans.[62] Upon this scene came the reformation inspired by three leading figures, Zerubabel, Ezra, and Nehemiah, which aimed to make an end to intermarriage. The real reformer in that group was Ezra the Scribe; therefore history has designated the new nationalism at the time of the Restoration as the Ezra Reformation.

With the Ezra Reformation, the prohibition against intermarriage enters the third stage. If endogamy was the motive of the first and the politico-religious motive accounted for the second, the third was characterized by racialism; political and religious motives, important as they were, were included in the racial ideology. The racial teaching was not altogether new to the Jewish people; it was part of the original endogamous sentiment, and of the national religion of the Hebrew people. But Ezra gave it point and extreme emphasis as a basis for the prohibition of intermarriage. The Jewish community was "holy seed," the heathens belonged to the "uncleanness of the nations." Hence, intermarriage was defilement. The racialism expressed in the term holy seed will be understood, of course, to express a religious racialism, for to Ezra purity of blood and purity of the Hebrew monotheistic religion were inseparably bound together. In

[60] See Graetz, *History of the Jews* I, chapters XVII–XIX.
[61] Ezra 2.59–62; Neh. 7.61–64.
[62] Ezra 9.1.

other words, mixing Hebrew blood with that of the heathen was to him synonymous with adulterating the ancestral faith. Ezra's racial teaching had two effects on the law concerning intermarriage. One, that not only was marriage with heathens prohibited but also marriage with children born of such unions; in fact all who had the stain of foreign blood, even if followers of the Jehovah worship, were not to be admitted into the congregation of pure-blooded Hebrews. Of this particular innovation, we shall treat later when we consider proselytes and Hebrews of uncertain ancestry. The second innovation of Ezra was to prohibit marriage with all non-Hebrew races, be they those prohibited in Deuteronomy or any other alien group.

Ezra rode on the wave of the new reformation psychology. With the restoration edict of Cyrus, the crushed national spirit of the exiles reawakened into an exalted national hope. The nobler spirits led the way and the rest of the population followed. A pure Jewish nation in blood and culture was the aim of the new nationalism. They were determined to rid themselves at all costs of the mixture of foreign blood and foreign cultural influences which the national defeat had brought in its wake. Proselytes, children of mixed marriages, foreign wives, *nethinim,* and descendants of Solomon's foreign slaves had to be separated from pure-blooded Israelites. Zerubabel began the task. Of old, the Jews had maintained family records, preserved both in their home country and in exile. These records were now drawn from the vaults and made the basis of judgment as to purity of blood. Those of pure blood constituted the national body. Doubtful cases were investigated by a special court set up by Zerubabel. If their pure origin was established, they joined the main body; otherwise they were recorded and set aside as of doubtful descent. They were eliminated from the priesthood, but their status as Israelites was not affected, except that the pure-blooded Israelites would not marry them.[68] However,

[68] Ezra 2.59–66. From vv. 62–63 it is evident that discredited priests still remained in good standing in the community, simply as Israelites of inferior descent. Likewise, nothing was done about the other families whose descent was found to be impure, except that they were so recorded. See Levi Freund,

if they were wholly of non-Jewish origin or children of mixed marriages, they were separated from the congregation entirely and their status was like that of the proselyte.[64] They shared in all the religious and civil rights of the community, but married within their own group or within a group of a similar inferior position, and they felt themselves fortunate if admitted to marriage with a Jewish family of doubtful record.

The task, however, was too much for Zerubabel. Intermarriage was too firmly rooted in the community to be eliminated easily, and too much resistance was offered to the purification process. Then Ezra came to Palestine with an enthusiastic delegation of nationalists from the Exile. Learning of the sad state of affairs, he made a new and determined effort to purge his people. He staged a dramatic assembly, and arising in their midst out of fasting and praying and weeping, he brought the people to tears with a stirring address. He reminded the congregation that it was for their sins that evil had befallen them; that they and their kings and their priests had been given to slaughter and to captivity; that God had shown them mercy in turning the hearts of their Persian rulers with favor to them, permitting them to return to their land and to rebuild the ruins of their sanctuary; that of old the merciful God had asked them by the mouth of their prophets to keep themselves free from the abominations of the nations of the land, not to give their daughters in marriage to them nor to take their daughters in marriage for their sons. And now, he continued, if after all this, should they again break God's command and join in marriage with the people of these abominations, He would surely pour His wrath upon them and utterly destroy them,

---

"Über Genealogien und Familienreinheit in biblischer und talmudischer Zeit," in *Festschrift Adolph Schwartz*, Berlin, 1917, p. 168 and note 5.

[64] This was the only possible status of children of mixed marriage whom Ezra later separated from the community. Ezra 10.3. Freund, ibid., is right in saying that this ruling concerning children of mixed marriage indicated the special rigor of Ezra, not consistent with earlier law or later law, especially since he applied that rigor also to the proselytes, who in later law are set up on a footing equal to the Jew by birth, in practically all matters. But of that later.

so that there should be no remnant or escape.[65] The congregation was deeply moved. Whereupon some arose and exclaimed to Ezra: "We have trespassed against our God, and have taken strange wives of the people of the land: yet now there is hope in Israel concerning this thing . . . Let us make a covenant with our God to put away all the wives and such as are born of them according to the counsel of my Lord and of those that tremble at the commandment of our God: and let it be done according to the law. Arise! for this matter belongeth unto thee: we also will be with thee: be of good courage and do it." The people and the elders took an oath to send away their foreign born wives and the children begotten by them. Then Ezra appointed a commission to carry out to the letter the terms of the oath and to free the community once and for all of its foreign blood. Yet the task was still too large even for Ezra.

Nehemiah came later with governmental power to enforce Ezra's teaching. He still found mixed marriages tolerated in the Jewish community and children so estranged from their people's culture that they did not know the Judean tongue and spoke only the Ashdodian language. Mixed marriages with Samaritans were particularly prevalent, and of these families some had gained prominent political position and considerable influence. They penetrated into the official life of the returned exiles and even into the priesthood and the sanctuary. Nehemiah, with the zeal of Ezra and with the determined practical leadership of a military governor, used his authority and the physical force at his command to drive the offenders out of communal life, to clear away all foreign mixtures from the Hebrew family, and finally to establish a purified Jewry in the new Judea.

Ezra's attitude to intermarriage is reflected in the literature of that period. Some maintain that the genealogical tables in the Books of Chronicles and elsewhere in the Bible were written for the purpose of testifying to the purity of blood of the prominent Jewish families.[66] A scribe of that period

[65] Ezra, 9–10.

[66] Graetz, *History*, German ed. II, 2, note 15, p. 420. It may be supposed, though, that some genealogical glosses belong to a later period, when the

blames the tribulations of Israel during the reign of the judges upon assimilation with the native tribes.[67] Likewise, Solomon's decline is ascribed to his foreign marriages, leading to his general moral degeneration.[68] A case of blasphemy is reported in Leviticus with the significant remark that the offender was the son of a mixed marriage; [69] the murderers of Joash are also presented to us as children of mixed marriages, one an Ammonite, the other a Moabite on their mothers' side.[70] More direct, in the traditional spirit of Ezra, is Malachi's attack upon intermarriage in the words: "Judah hath dealt treacherously and an abomination is committed in Israel and Jerusalem. For Judah hath profaned the holiness of the Lord which He loveth and hath married the daughter of a strange god. May the Lord cut off to the man that doeth this him that calleth and him that answereth out of the tents of Jacob and him that offereth an offering unto the Lord of hosts." [71]

A few details about Ezra's teaching may be added in conclusion. He prohibited intermarriage with either sex, but like the deuteronomic legislator, emphasized the prohibition against marrying a foreign woman. His reason, however, was somewhat different. Deuteronomy sought to preserve the purity of the religious community, and women did not count greatly in the community. Ezra, on the other hand, had in mind the purity of Hebrew stock; by marriage of a Jew with a heathen woman the stock became adulterated, since the child would count in the father's family as a Jew, while by marriage of a Jewess with a heathen, the child would not be counted as a Jew but would follow his heathen father. Again, as in Deuteronomy, inferior marriages were not attacked by Ezra, else he would have spoken in modification of the law of the captive-wife to which the deuteronomic legislator had given full approval. Although there was less reason for Ezra to approve the law than for Deuteronomy,

---

righteous proselyte was given a place of equality with the native Jew. To that period must be ascribed the last five verses of the Book of Ruth.

[67] Judg. 3.4–6.

[68] I Kings, 11.8.

[69] Lev. 24.10–12.

[70] II Chron. 24.26.

[71] Mal. 2.11–12.

since Ezra's objection was against mixing of blood, still he needed not oppose it, insomuch as children born of such marriages belonged to an inferior social class, perhaps with the status of freedmen, and thus socially separated from the pure blooded Israelites.[72] Finally, as in Deuteronomy, a foreign marriage was not declared void by Ezra's teaching. When he bade the people put away their foreign wives, he did not mean annulment of their marriages but simply to send the wives away. The concept of a marriage being null because prohibited did not yet exist in Ezra's time.

II

The period between the restoration and the Hasmonean revolt, a period of close to three centuries, was rich in spiritual development. The priestly legislator, the last of the biblical prophets, and the Men of the Great Synagogue were active in creating new religious concepts. How did Ezra's doctrine of racialism fare during that time? It seems that ideologically it was losing ground, for during that period there was a large accretion of proselytes, a more favorable attitude to them on the part of the community; and, most important, the post-exilic prophets indoctrinated the people with the progressive teaching of the universality of Judaism. On the other hand, the influence of the priest-teachers had the effect of preserving the tradition of racial exclusiveness in practical life, so that purity of stock continued as the token of aristocracy, family records were guarded jealously, and the separation of classes by reason of blood taint as established by Ezra remained in effect for centuries thereafter. Nevertheless, whatever were the fortunes of the racial doctrine during those three centuries, the prohibition against intermarriage with non-converted heathens was recognized and, in fact, established for all time. Only a milder attitude to intermarriage with proselytes than that of Ezra was gained by the new teaching of universalism.

[72] Slight evidence for our deduction is the fact that female slaves of the heathen tribes came with the people into Palestine, Ezra, 2.65, even though sex contact with female slaves was taken for granted in those days. We remain in doubt here, as in the legislation of Deuteronomy, whether foreign concubines were permitted.

But the rigor of the law against intermarriage was attacked and endangered by forces of life which began with the Greek period and concluded with the Hasmonean revolt. These were the assimilative forces which were crystallized into the Jewish hellenist movement. The spread of Jewish colonies in foreign lands, Alexandria and Antiochia, for example, the growth of Greek colonies on Judean soil, the disloyalty of the influential Tobiad family to the faith of their fathers, paved the way for the penetration of Greek culture into Judea with a dazzling lure that almost overpowered the people spiritually. The last link of this process was the physical compulsion exerted by Antiochus Epiphanus to alienate the Jews from their ancestral worship. Certain elements among the Jews were consumed by the sweeping force of Hellenism; they turned traitors to their own traditions and embraced the idolatry and lust of the Greeks.

The so-called progressive philosophy of that assimilative movement was: "Let us go and make a covenant with the nations that are round about us; for since we separated ourselves from them many evils have come upon us." [73] And the Maccabean Chronicler reports of them, among other things, that "they joined themselves to the gentiles and sold themselves to do evil." [74] That philosophy surely protested the restrictions set up by the law against marriage covenants with heathens. But there was no use worrying about intermarriage when the very foundations of the law were attacked. Between the enemies without and the traitors within, the ancestral faith of the Jews and their very national existence were all but destroyed. The faithful were powerless against the onslaught; their only escape was in the rocky hillside, abandoning the sanctuary and the God who dwelt therein to the fate decreed by the Hellenists.

The doom was averted by the Hasmonean victory; and with victory, true to pattern, came a reformation psychology. The broader scope of the reformation program aimed to reestablish the purity of Judaism in worship and its potency in law. But to counteract the assimilationist teachings of the

[73] I Macc. 1.11.
[74] I Macc. 1.5.

Hellenists, the Hasmonean reaction was to set up anew walls of separation between Hebrew and heathen. And just as intermarriage was the logical focal point of the hellenist teaching, so was the prevention of intermarriage the goal and purpose of the separatist teaching of the Hasmoneans.

A number of ordinances have come down in the law which have been ascribed to "legislative councils of the Hasmoneans," whose purpose was to discourage intermarriage. Among them are the prohibitions against feasting with the gentile,[75] against using his wine or oil,[76] and a special ordinance prohibiting sexual contact with heathens even though it be of a promiscuous, temporary nature.[77] This latter prohibition evidently existed prior to the Hasmonean period, for it comes into play in a story about Joseph, a tax farmer for Ptolemy III at about the year 229 B.C.E., as told by Josephus.[78] This Joseph fell in love with a heathen actress in the king's court and asked his brother's assistance in obtaining her and keeping the matter secret so as not to create scandal, for it was unlawful for a Jew to consort with a foreign woman. The brother dressed up his own daughter in the guise of the actress and gave her to Joseph. The latter thinking her to be the actress lavished affection upon her and

[75] Jubilees 22.16–18.

[76] Daniel 1.8; Esther's prayer in the Septuagint, Esther 5.17; M. 'Ab. Zar. 35b; Gemara, ibid., 36a–b. That the prohibition was intended to prevent intermarriage is correctly stated in Talmud, ibid., 35b and 36b. See Yad, Ma'akalot Asurot 17,9. I. H. Weis, *Dor Dor Wedoreshav*, I, p. 122, maintains that the prohibition against gentile bread was of later date; that the Hasmonean ordinance referred only to Samaritans, who were more hateful to the Jews than the heathens. M. Sheb. 8,10, and Pirke de Rabbi Elazar 31 are taken by him as embodying a Hasmonean law. We cannot agree with this view. It seems more logical to assume that any restriction against Samaritans followed a similar restriction against heathens, and not vice versa. The restrictions against intercourse with the Samaritans seem definitely to belong to the "eighteen ordinances" of the Shammaites and Hillelites. The amoraim who in their time treated the Samaritans as heathens were led to believe that the term *kuthi* in the tradition meant gentile, not Samaritan. Hence their difficulty in explaining the need of an ordinance by the Shammaites and Hillelites on a matter that had already been settled before. On this assumption, we believe that all enactments against Samaritans imply older prohibitions of similar nature against gentiles in general. See also the separatist exhortations of Tobit, 4.12.

[77] 'Ab. Zar. 36b; San. 82a; Prayer of Esther, Septuagint, ibid.

[78] Jos., *Ant.* XII,4,6.

finally married her, to the satisfaction of all concerned. Probably the pre-Hasmonean prohibition was, under the influence of the Hellenists, disregarded as time went on and was revived by the Hasmonean council.

The Book of Jubilees shows undue severity toward intermarriage in that it prescribes a death penalty for it: "If there is any man in Israel who wishes to give his daughter or his sister to any man who is of the seed of the gentiles, he shall surely die, and they shall stone him with stones . . . and they shall burn the woman with fire because she hath dishonored the name of the house of her father and she shall be rooted out of Israel." [79] The main stream of Jewish law never penalized intermarriage with death. It was a sectarian teaching based upon certain points of biblical exegesis. The first part of the law was derived from Leviticus 20.2, prescribing the death penalty for one who gives his daughter to Molech, which they interperted to mean to a gentile.[80] The second part was drawn from the levitical law prescribing the death penalty for a priest's daughter who surrenders herself to harlotry, and they applied that law to the members of their sect for whom they set up priestly standards.[81] Yet, this sectarian teaching, though not acceptable to the official halakah, reveals the reformation psychology of that day in its sharpened antagonism to intermarriage.[82]

Further development of the law in respect to intermarriage with proselytes took place during the Hasmonean period and more especially at the end of it, which we shall discuss in a later section. In respect to marriage with heathens, the development from Ezra to the end of the Hasmonean period can be summarized briefly. In a practical sense, the various ordinances gave potency to the prohibition of intermarriage; in a doctrinal sense, the racialism of Ezra was rejected and

[79] Jubilees 30.7.

[80] Jubilees 30.10; so also Targum Jonathan, Lev. 18.21; also the view of R. Ishmael, Yer. Meg. 75c; Meg. 25a. Mishnah, ibid., rejects this interpretation.

[81] It was not unusual for sectarians to emulate priestly restrictions.

[82] The zealots who executed offenders without trial when they caught them in sexual converse with a gentile ('Ab. Zar. 36b) had that tradition from earlier zealots.

in its place came religious nationalism as a basis for the prohibition of mixed marriage as well as for the separatist psychology of the latter part of that period.

The separatist tendency on a national religious basis dominated Jewish life up to the fall of the state and rabbinic law thereafter. But the years of struggle against Rome, the final collapse of Judea, and the adjustment of the Jewish people to an organized existence without statehood made a new orientation to the Jew-gentile relation necessary, as part of a practical program of facing the crisis. This crisis had a peculiar development, unlike that which came in the wake of the destruction of the first Temple. It took a comparatively long time to develop, beginning with the revolt in 66, through the destruction in 70 and ending with the failure of the Bar Kokba revolt in 135. There was no demoralization of the Jewish national spirit either before the crisis or during its development. There was no deportation to break up the unity of the national body or the continuity of the national history on its own soil. The crisis was weathered courageously and intelligently, because at no time before had the people been so rich in leadership of great personalities, patriots, scholars, sages. There was one inner problem, that of finding a spiritual substitute for the Temple, and R. Johanan b. Zakkai settled it by the establishment of the Jabneh academy. When a center of study took the place of a center of worship, also the inner problem of authority was solved, the teachers becoming the rulers in the place of priests. Under the wise leadership of the scholars, there was hardly an inner problem that could baffle them. The only problem they had to face seriously was the outer problem: How would the Jews preserve their solidarity among the nations of the world? Roman domination was bad enough, Roman destruction was worse, but still worse would be the scattering of the Jews to the four corners of the earth which seemed inevitable as a consequence of the loss of statehood. How would the Jew continue his existence under these conditions? This crisis, therefore, was not one of reaction but of adjustment. There was no turning against the past, no revolutionary psychology; there was just the simple and steady effort to build national solidarity on national religious foundations independent of statehood. And here the antagonism to intermarriage enters upon its final phase as a bulwark for group solidarity made the stronger as the political unity of the people becomes the weaker.

The motive of national religious solidarity of Hasmonean days was a good beginning for the tannaim of the post-Hasmonean period, but the tannaim emphasized the religious element above the national. They were religiously keener than the Hasmonean authorities, and could not help but develop a horror of paganism much sharper than that felt by their predecessors. The teachers of the law saw paganism in all its ugliness, filth, superstition, and sensuality. Imbued with the lofty ideals of Judaism, they hated paganism with all their souls – not a national hatred but a religious hatred, not the pagan but paganism. The pagan who was decent, who observed the seven Noahide laws of morality, was treated with kindness. The one whose life was truly pagan was hated, because he personified immorality.

This attitude to paganism found expression in a series of laws passed at about that time. Any service helpful to the spread of paganism or to its rooting itself in the world was prohibited.[83] No quarters might be rented to the heathen where he might shelter his idols, and no land might be sold to him in Palestine in order that he might not root himself in the holy land.[84] A Jew was not permitted to deal in materials used for heathen rites or feasts.[85] A heathen wedding feast was considered ritual in character and a Jew was not permitted to attend it.[86] Thus, on purely religious grounds and in matters purely religious was a considerable wall of separation set up between Jew and heathen by these tannaitic ordinances.

Naturally, marriage with heathens was most obnoxious to the tannaim, and therefore the wall of separation was consciously strengthened by them with the object of discourag-

[83] 'Ab. Zar. 26a.
[84] 'Ab. Zar. 20b–21a.
[85] 'Ab. Zar. 2a.
[86] 'Ab. Zar. 8a.

ing social mingling and thereby preventing intermarriage. They accepted the Hasmonean prohibition against heathen bread and wine and oil,[87] and added to it the further restriction that a Jew may not drink wine touched by a heathen[88] or food cooked by him.[89] The heathen, man or woman, young or old, was declared in a state of defilement, so that his touch alone caused ritual impurity.[90] In addition to prohibiting unmarried contact between Jew and heathen on the authority of the Hasmonean council, the tannaim made it a dangerous business, for they sanctioned the practice of the zealots who, following the example of Phinehas (Num. 25.7–8), meted out punishment to the offender without court trial, if caught in the act.[91] They further added a very significant law, requiring chaperonage between the sexes of Jews and heathens.[92] Finally, they established the prohibition of intermarriage as a biblical law, and prescribed for the violation of it the standard penalty of flagellation.[93]

87 'Ab. Zar. 36b.

88 'Ab. Zar. 57a.

89 'Ab. Zar. 35b, 37b, 38a. Tosafot, ibid. 37b, s.v. *veha-shelakot* dates this prohibition earlier than the "eighteen ordinances" and also notes its relation to intermarriage. See Yad, Ma'akalot Asurot, 17,9.

90 Nid. 34a; Sifra Lev. 15.2, 74d; Sab. 16b, 17b; 'Ab. Zar. 36b. The ordinance applied to males and to females (Sab. 16b; 'Ab. Zar. 37a); hence the ostensible explanation of the Talmud that it was meant to prevent sodomy is not quite correct. Rather was the reason the prevention of intermarriage. It is assumed by all scholars that the ordinance as it applies to heathens belongs to the "eighteen ordinances" of the Hillelites and the Shammaites, and was formulated in 65–66. See Zeitlin, "Les Dix huit Mesures," R.E.J., 1914, and "Studies in the Beginnings of Christianity," J.Q.R., N.S. XIV (1923) and Büchler, "The Levitical Impurity of the Gentile," J.Q.R., N.S., XVII (1926). The latter contends that certain levitical impurity was ascribed to the gentile prior to this date, and that is the impurity due to his contact with his wife during menstruation. That, however, applied only to his touch of sacred objects not to his touch of ordinary Israelites. The story (Yer. Yoma 38d) that Simeon b. Ḳimḥit was disqualified to minister in the Temple because the spittle of a gentile fell on his garment, which belongs to the year 17–18, is taken by him to represent the earlier law. The later law extended the levitical impurity of the gentile to the point of affecting any contact with a Jew, and that is the law of the "eighteen ordinances."

91 'Ab. Zar. 36b, etc. The Talmud gives this law Sinaitic authority, but it evidently goes back only to the last days of the Second Commonwealth, when the zealots took the law in their own hand.

92 'Ab. Zar. ibid. and 22a.

93 Ḳid. 68b. 'Ab. Zar. 36b. That the biblical prohibition applies to all

But the most significant ruling of the tannaim was to declare marriage between Jew and heathen not only prohibited but legally invalid. Declaring a marriage invalid was a novel point in Jewish law. Natural as it sounds to us that a marriage prohibited by law should be invalid, such a principle was not at all taken for granted in Jewish law and would have seemed strange to the predecessors of the tannaim. The difference is this. General law today considers marriage a covenant whose validity is rooted in state sanction; the state can make it and the state can unmake it. Therefore it is logically inconceivable that the state should prohibit a marriage and at the same time sanction it. In Jewish law, on the contrary, marriage is in the first place a private covenant without state interference, and secondly it is a fact, that of home-taking and intercourse, which the state cannot undo. Therefore invalidating a marriage has no logic in Jewish law. The tannaim learned this, evidently, from Roman law, even though they offer an unconvincing biblical derivation,[94] and the logic is Roman logic. An intermarriage is invalid not because it is prohibited, but because the heathen (also the slave) is incapable of contracting marriage within Jewish law, like the barbarian and slave in Roman law.

After the days of bitterness against the heathen consequent upon destruction of the Temple and the Hadrianic persecutions, the rabbis became more lenient toward the gentiles, for one reason because the memory of the hurt had been weakened, for another because the gentiles had developed more acceptable standards of morality. It is reported that Rabbi Judah the Nasi protested the prohibition of gentile bread, and even though he did not lift it, he introduced various extenuations.[95] His grandson, R. Judah

---

heathens, not only to the "seven nations," is the teaching of R. Simeon b, Yoḥai. Whether this view is final is not quite settled. See Yad, Issure Bi'ah 12,1, and *Kesef Mishneh* thereto.

[94] Ḳid. 66b; 68b.

[95] 'Ab. Zar. 35b; amoraic discussion of Rabbi's intention yields the law that bread of a commercial gentile baker or bread of a gentile by chance meeting, not as a neighbor of a Jew in the city, is permitted. See Yad, Ma'akalot Asurot 17,12.

Nesi'ah, abrogated the prohibition against gentile oil.[96] The ban on gentile cooking was modified to permit it when a Jew provides the slightest help in the cooking.[97] The Talmud also reports laxity in certain localities in the matter of drinking wine touched by gentiles,[98] but the law continued firm in this prohibition, except that under certain circumstances it was permitted for the Jew to sell the wine and use the money for his own benefit.[99] The interdiction against dealing with gentiles was limited to the day or days of their sacred festivals and only to those who participated religiously therein.[100] A disregard of this law is reported of the same R. Judah Nesi'ah and two other leading personalities among the amoraim.[101] These leniencies toward the gentiles, however, did not alter the opposition of later tannaim and the amoraim to intermarriage, except for two amoraic statements which were noted legally but had no practical effect. One, by Rab Asi, declared that the frequent mingling of Jews and non-Jews raised the suspicion concerning any gentile that he might be a descendant of Jews, at least of the Ten Lost Tribes. This would mean that marriage between a gentile and Jew would have doubtful validity.[102] The statement was entirely disregarded by the halakah. The other was made by Raba, that the biblical restriction of intermarriage with the "seven nations" referred not to the time when they were idolators, for then marriage could not be valid, but when they had been proselytized.[103] This means that the biblical prohibition against intermarriage refers only to proselytes of the "seven nations"; marriage with a gentile of whatever nationality, who is not converted, is mere prostitution. It is therefore not biblically prohibited, and is punishable not as

[96] 'Ab. Zar. 36a. R. Judah Nesi'ah, as reported there, wanted also to abrogate the prohibition against gentile bread.

[97] 'Ab. Zar. 38a–b. The same leniency was applied to gentile bread.

[98] 'Ab. Zar. 59a.

[99] 'Ab. Zar. 57a, referring to unintentional touch by the gentile; an additional leniency is reported (ibid. 58b), that unintentional handling of the vessel, without actually touching the wine, is permitted, even for drinking.

[100] 'Ab. Zar. 11b; Yad, 'Akum 9,1; 'Ab. Zar. 8a; Yad, 'Akum 9,5.

[101] 'Ab. Zar. 6b; 64b–65a.

[102] Yeb. 16b–17a.

[103] Yeb. 76a. See *Kesef Mishneh* ad Yad, Issure Bi'ah 12,1.

a matter of law but of discipline, according to local usage or court traditions. In the final halakah, this view of Raba was rejected by Maimonides but accepted by two leading codes, *Ṭur* and *Sefer Miẓwot Gadol.*[104] Discussion on the theoretical points of the law continued among later teachers, but in practical terms there is hardly a difference between one view and the other. The marriage of any gentile to a Jew is invalid in any case, and the Jewish culprit is given severe corporal punishment for his violation, whether because of biblical law or by authority of the court.

There have been a few liberal views on the general subject of Jewish-gentile relations among teachers of the law, talmudic and post-talmudic, that should be mentioned here, even though they did not lead to relaxation of the prohibition against intermarriage. First, we should mention that a distinction between the "seven nations" and other heathens was always in the minds of the tannaim, and the tosafists insisted that all restrictions in the Bible against friendship and covenants with the heathens, and laws derived therefrom by the tannaim, should not apply to other nations.[105] The Book of Ezra, apparently extending these prohibitions to other nations, is accounted, of course, of rabbinic but not biblical authority.[106] Second, even in talmudic times there was evidence of a growing feeling that not every gentile was an idol worshiper. R. Judah expressed this feeling in respect to an individual gentile;[107] R. Johanan formulated a general principle that "The gentiles outside of Palestine are not idolators but follow (blindly) the habits of their fathers."[108] Perhaps taking their cue from R. Johanan, post-talmudic authorities taught, in the third place, that Christians and Mohammedans count not as idolators, despite the differences between their religions and Judaism. Maimonides,

[104] Yad, Issure Bi'ah, ibid.; *Ṭur,* E.H. 16; *Sefer Miẓwot Gadol,* negative command No. 112.

[105] Tosafot 'Ab. Zar. 20a s.v. *de-amar,* etc.

[106] See Yad, Issure Bi'ah 12,1, quoting Ezra to prove his contention that all gentiles are prohibited biblically. Ezra does not rate as a biblical legislator but proves the biblical exegesis of R. Simeon, which Maimonides follows.

[107] 'Ab. Zar. 65a. See further, ibid., where the same is said of Raba.

[108] Ḥullin, 13b.

living in the Orient, speaks for Mohammedanism,[109] while Rashi and the tosafists, living in the West, speak for Christianity.[110] These views have been generally accepted by the halakah in respect to practically all restrictions against social intercourse between Jews and gentiles; but not the slightest attempt has been made to relax the prohibition against intermarriage between Jew and gentile, whether Christian or Mohammedan, by any of the teachers of the law.

III

For approximately eight centuries of fuller communal Jewish life in Europe, this attitude to intermarriage remained stable and unchallenged because it was consonant with the political and social position of the Jew. The Jew was set apart from the non-Jew by social discrimination and the ghetto. He had to live among his own and had to conform to the standards of his community, where intermarriage, by general Jewish sentiment and by Jewish law, was condemned. His separateness was no cause for complaint from the gentiles, who wanted no social contact with the Jew. Politically, too, the Jew was kept apart from the other citizens of the state by the very logic of the state organization. The state was a Christian state governed for the most part by Church laws. The Jew, or any non-Christian, could not logically be a full citizen. Marriage, which is now considered a state sanction, was then a Church matter; therefore, but for the instrument of self-government, the Jew could not marry at all. Surely he could not marry a gentile, for he would find in the Church-controlled state laws prohibiting intermarriage between gentiles and Jews.

The political situation and ostensibly also the social condition of the Jew were changed in the beginning of the nineteenth century. The state became secular, divided from the Church, and the Jew became a citizen thereof. The last remains of the ghetto walls were torn down, and the Jew began to mingle with his non-Jewish fellow citizens. To be sure,

109 Yad, Ma'akalot Asurot 11,7; See *Torat ha-Bayit*, 5,1.

110 Tosaf. 'Ab. Zar. 57b, s.v. *la-afuke;* Tosaf. 'Ab. Zar. 2a, s.v. *asur; Ṭur,* Yoreh De'ah, 148; RIBS, 119.

political and social distinctions between Jew and Christian were not completely wiped away, but the liberal program, in theory at least, of equality and fraternity among all citizens became the progressive philosophy of the day. Henceforth there was to be such a thing as civil marriage, with mere secular state sanction, wherein the religion of the marrying parties would be a matter of total indifference. The Jew was happy in his new citizenship and the liberal tendencies of the time; but he faced a new orientation. Social contacts under the new spirit of equality would encourage intermarriage; the state now would allow it; and, furthermore, it was considered antagonistic to the liberality of the state to inject questions of religious differences in a matter, such as marriage, which the state sanctioned on the basis of equality of all citizens without reference to religion. And for whom was that liberality meant, if not for the Jew? How could he be the one to oppose it? The formulation of a new Jewish attitude to intermarriage was a need of the moment, and the task was a difficult and delicate one — to be not disrespectful to the Jewish tradition nor ungrateful to the liberality of the state.

This task was faced by the Assembly of Notables convened by order of Napoleon in 1806, whose deliberations formed the basis for the Great Sanhedrin. To this Assembly Napoleon put the question: "Can a Jewess marry a Christian or a Jew a Christian woman? Or has the law ordered that Jews should only intermarry among themselves?" Apparently, an analysis and evaluation of the Jewish law on the subject did not receive first consideration by the Assembly. The matter was discussed rather from the point of view of expediency and propriety. Two opposite views were represented. One by a rabbinic member is described by the reporter as follows: "A rabbi thought that marriages with Christians were forbidden. He requested the Assembly to consider that when Moses forbade those unions with the proscribed nations, he gave, as the motive of this prohibition, the fear . . . lest men should be led astray from the law of God in whose name he spoke; that, consequently, the probability of seduction still existing in unions with other nations, the prohibition still existed likewise." The opposite view was given by a lay member: "Why should we apply to Christians the prohibitions contained in these verses (Deut. 7.1–4)? Are we commissioned to destroy them, not to give them any quarter? Do they not worship the same God we adore? Surely if God were to send us a second Moses, far from tracing a line of separation between us, he would tell us, 'Love the Christians; cherish them as your brothers; unite with them; consider them as children of the same family. You all acknowledge that they are no idolators; that they worship, as you do, the Creator of heaven and earth; that they are your brethren and your benefactors.' What more is necessary to make marriages lawful between Jews and Christians?"

The final answer to Napoleon's question, after every side was given a hearing and a chance to introduce its modifications, was formulated as follows:

"The law does not say that a Jewess cannot marry a Christian nor a Jew a Christian woman; nor does it state that the Jews can intermarry only among themselves. The only marriages expressly forbidden by the law are those with the seven Canaanean nations, with Ammon and Moab and with the Egyptians. . . . The prohibition in general applies only to nations in idolatry. The Talmud declares formally that modern nations are not considered as such since they worship, like us, the God of heaven and earth. And, accordingly, there have been at several periods intermarriages between Jews and Christians in France, in Spain, and in Germany; these marriages were sometimes tolerated and sometimes forbidden by the laws of those sovereigns who had received Jews into their dominions.

"Unions of this kind are still found in France; but we cannot dissemble that the opinion of the rabbis is against these marriages. According to their doctrine, although the religion of Moses has not forbidden the Jews from intermarrying with nations not of their religion; yet as marriage, according to the Talmud, requires religious ceremonies called *ḳiddushin* with the benedictions used in such cases, no marriage can be *religiously* valid unless these ceremonies have been performed. This could not be done towards persons who would not both of them consider these ceremonies as sacred; and in that case the married couple could separate without the *religious* divorce; they would then be considered as married *civilly* but not *religiously*.

"Such is the opinion of the rabbis, members of this assembly. In general they would be no more inclined to bless the union of a Jewess with a Christian, or of a Jew with a Christian woman, than Catholic priests themselves would be disposed to sanction unions of this kind. The rabbis acknowledge, however, that a Jew who marries a Christian woman, does not cease on that account to be considered as a Jew by his brethren any more than if he had married a Jewess *civilly* and not *religiously*." [111]

This formulation of the Jewish attitude to intermarriage with Christians has all the merit of tactfulness, but hardly the full measure of historic accuracy. Unless one is willing to wipe off the records of the development of the law after Deuteronomy, it is not correct to say that the prohibition applied only to the "seven nations" and only to idol worshippers. While the sentiment is expressed in authoritative sources that modern nations are not idol worshippers, and that sentiment is applied specifically to Christians and Mohammedans by post-talmudic authorities, never was it expressed in respect to permitting marriage between Jews and Christians or Mohammedans. Social and commercial contacts alone were intended, not intermarriage. Nor is it correct to say that the main obstacle to intermarriage is the inability of the rabbi to employ the religious ceremonial in such a marriage; that it therefore has the status of a civil marriage. Of course, the rabbis cannot undo the civil status of such a marriage, but that is not the whole story. Jew and Jewess can be married legally, according to Jewish law, without sanctification by the rabbi; while Jew and Christian cannot have a legally valid marriage even with rabbinic ritual and sanctification. However, if presentation of the law was not quite correct, the attitude of the Assembly of Notables to intermarriage could not be called a defiance of tradition and law, because in sentiment it expressed an opposition to inter-

[111] Tama, *Transactions of the Parisian Sanhedrin*, translated by F. D. Kirwan, London, 1807, pp. 154–6.

marriage and in practice it ruled that no rabbi should officiate at an intermarriage.

Different was the attitude taken by the early leaders of the Reform movement at a conference held at Braunschweig, Germany, in 1844. For the basis on which it rested was different. The Assembly of Notables in France had no theological quarrel with tradition; the Braunschweig Conference arrived at a new attitude to intermarriage by way of a new attitude to the Law. With the new freedom gained by western European Jewry, the restrictive measures of rabbinic law became an unbearable burden to the liberals of that day, and the wall of separation between Jew and non-Jew which that law set up became to them a prison wall. The Reform movement, therefore, aimed at abrogation of traditional law and complete demolition of the wall of separation. A conscious movement toward assimilation, unhampered by any restriction of a valid and authoritative religious law, was the basis of the deliberations at Braunschweig. The Conference concluded: "The intermarriage of Jews and Christians, and, in general, the intermarriage of Jews with adherents of any of the monotheistic religions, is not forbidden, provided that the parents are permitted by the law of the state to bring up the offspring of such marriage in the Jewish faith." [112] And if anyone wished to square this resolution with traditional law – not that there was any reason therefor, since traditional law had been abrogated – he might say that the traditional prohibition against intermarriage was based on Jewish national sentiment, but Jewish nationalism was at an end, and Jews had the same nationality as the Christian citizens of the land in which they lived.[113]

The extremists at the Braunschweig Conference wished to press the matter further and to specify in the resolution that "the rabbi is permitted to solemnize such marriages," but the Conference refused to go so far.[114] Individual members of the Reform rabbinate, such as S. Holdheim in Germany and

[112] *Protokolle der Rabbinerversammlung in Braunschweig*, p. 73.

[113] S. Holdheim, *Gemischte Ehen zwischen Juden und Christen*, Berlin, 1850, Introduction, p. v.

[114] M. Mielziner, *The Jewish Law of Marriage and Divorce*, Cincinnati, 1901, p. 48, note 1.

E. Hirsch in America, held firmly to this radical position, but the general tendency among the Reform rabbis was to be satisfied with the statement of the French Assembly. The Braunschweig resolution, even in its moderate form, did not find enough support to be confirmed by the Augsburg Synod of 1871. Even Ludwig Philippson, author of the resolution, later modified his views on the subject and demanded that "Religion must pronounce against intermarriages." [115] And such pronouncements came in abundance, from Geiger and Aub and Einhorn and Isaac M. Wise. Dr. M. Mielziner, a student of the subject and member of the faculty of the Hebrew Union College in America, characterized the attitude of Reform Judaism to intermarriage in the following words: "The position of modern Judaism, in general, regarding the question of intermarriage is similar to that taken by Protestantism or Roman Catholicism, both of which discountenance mixed marriages on purely religious grounds." [116]

The emancipation of the Jew from the ghetto, his new political status, and the consequent assimilative tendency, had the opposite effect upon the Jews of eastern Europe from that upon western Europeans. They saw the danger of extinction through assimilation, and therefore intensified their opposition to intermarriage even above the restrictions of traditional law. There was the intensity of a struggle against national doom. They considered intermarriage little less than apostasy. It was not unusual for parents to observe seven days of mourning with all its dramatized sorrow for a son or daughter who married out of the Jewish faith, and thereafter to consider that child as physically dead. Even in the new world, it is not unusual for congregations to write a clause in their constitutions to the effect that one married out of the faith cannot be admitted to or retain membership in the organization. Intermarriage is not unusual,[117]

[115] Mielziner, l.c.

[116] Mielziner, ibid. p. 49.

[117] Statistics on the subject of intermarriage are inadequate, but we have the following figures. Dr. Arthur Ruppin in *Jews of the Modern World*, London, 1934, pp. 317–32, cites statistical reports that in Germany in 1929 there were 22.79 intermarriages out of every hundred Jewish marriages. Local reports of big cities for the same year read 23.47 for Berlin, 33.83 for

and many people make their peace with it *ex post facto,* and yet even among people otherwise indifferent to tradition an intermarriage is considered a family tragedy. No doubt, Christians take no kindlier to intermarriage with Jews.[118]

IV

The problem of intermarriage involves the question: What is the legal or social status of the child born of a mixed marriage? Until we come to Ezra's reform, we find hardly a mention of the question in the Bible. Whether intermarriage was a violation of the rule of endogamy, as in pre-deuteronomic times, or a breach of religious law proclaimed by the deuteronomic legislator, the offspring of such a marriage were not affected in the least. In the patronymic family system, which was general throughout the biblical period, the child of an intermarriage followed his father and was equal to his brothers in all respects. We infer this not only from absence of any instructions to the contrary, but also from a number of family records in the Bible where children by heathen mothers rank as fully legitimate members of their fathers' families, without any discrimination whatever.[119] The law in Deuteronomy (23.9) declaring the third genera-

---

Hamburg (1928), 16.52 for Budapest, 14.83 for Amsterdam, and 12.95 for Vienna. Unusually large figures are given for Copenhagen and Trieste. In the former, the general rate of intermarriage is 31.76%, but in the older families the rate is over 50%. In Trieste, the figure for 1927 was 56.10 mixed marriages out of every hundred Jewish marriages.

Some statistics for the New World are given by Dr. Julius Drachsler in *Democracy and Assimilation,* New York, 1920, pp. 121–2. The general rate of intermarriage in N. Y. is only 1.17 per hundred Jewish marriages. But native American Jews whose parents are American-born intermarry at the rate of 4.26 per hundred. The figures are insufficient and the rate is progressively advancing.

[118] Christianity was as a rule severer on the matter of intermarriage than was Judaism. Constantius (339) decreed the death penalty, the Council of Illiberis (Spain) excommunication; and the Council of Toledo (Spain, 589) took the children of such marriages into forcible baptism. The yellow badge was introduced by a decree of the Fourth Lateran Council at Rome (1215) to prevent intermarriage. See Graetz, *History* II, pp. 567, 620; III, pp. 46, 545, 595.

[119] Rehoboam, son of Solomon, had an Ammonite mother, I Kings 14.21; Ahaziah, son of Ahab, king of Israel, had the wicked Jezebel of Zidonia as mother; also his brother Jehoram, I Kings 22.52; II Kings 3.1.

tion offspring of Edomites and Egyptians fit to enter the congregation of the Lord should not mislead us into believing that the legislator was conscious of the half-Jew or quarter-Jew as legal concepts. It is not the measure of blood that the legislator had in mind, for since the law prohibits intermarriage until the third generation, there could be theoretically no mixing of blood. He considered only the degree of naturalization, and he intended that an Edomite or an Egyptian whose father and grandfather had been Palestinian residents under the status of *ger,* circumcised, participating to an extent in the Hebrew cult, and under the friendly protection of the Hebrew people, might marry a Jew or a Jewess.

Geiger believes [120] that the mamzer who by deuteronomic law (23.3) is not permitted to enter the congregation of the Lord even unto the tenth generation is the child of mixed parentage. His main proofs are the Septuagint translation of the word mamzer in Zech. 9.6, and the tradition in rabbinic law that a child born of contact between Jew and heathen is a mamzer. His view is supported by other scholars [121] who add further proof. To our mind, however, it is highly improbable. The term mamzer in Deuteronomy, by its context, seems to imply a person of some alien group similar to the Edomite and the Egyptian, and the passage in Zechariah gives the same impression. That race lived or overran Ashdod and was known to Nehemiah as Ashdodians, whom he counted among those prohibited to intermarry with Jews.[122] Possibly this was a race that lived in promiscuity among themselves and also mingled freely with other races, so that when the race itself no longer existed, their name remained a symbol for irregular marriage relations. At any rate, the offspring of mixed marriages could not logically be prohibited by the deuteronomic legislator so long as he had not yet issued a general prohibition against such marriages.

We have reason to believe, however, that social discrimination against a child of a mixed marriage existed in Israel

[120] Geiger, *Urschrift,* pp. 54 f.

[121] A. Büchler, "Familienreinheit und Familienmakel in Jerusalem," in *Schwartz Festschrift,* p. 144, and Levi Freund, "Über Genealogien und Familienreinheit," ibid. p. 183.

[122] Neh. 13.23.

even in pre-exilic times, and this accounts for the existence of family records tracing purity of Jewish descent which Ezra and Nehemiah used in the process of purification of the race. Purity of descent in deuteronomic days, like the earlier rule of endogamy, was not observed as a marriage law but as a token of aristocracy. The priestly and the royal families were particularly given to this distinctiveness. Yet royal personages of foreign blood were not rare among the later kings, and priestly families of foreign taint were brought to light by Zerubabel. As the matter stood until the time of the Restoration, the aristocracy of pure Jewish descent was recognized as a social distinction, and records of such pure families both among priests and laymen were carefully preserved; no child of a mixed marriage had any chance of marrying into one of these pure-blooded Jewish families, but that was all on a social basis and no more.

Ezra's intensified nationalism and his zeal for racial purity led him to raise this social standard to one of law. He was the first to prohibit all intermarriage with any and every foreign race, and therewith he introduced the prohibition against marrying the child of mixed parentage. In the reformation process, he caused the people to put aside not only their foreign wives but also those born of them.[123] By this we are to understand, not that he drove them out of the community, but that he set them apart from the pure-blooded Jewish community and prohibited marriage with them.[124] The community was classified by Ezra in three groups, those of pure blood, those of doubtful blood, and those of definitely foreign descent. The children of mixed marriages could not marry with the first class, and probably could not marry with those of the second class, but apparently joined the third group among whom were the proselytes, the Nethinim, and the slaves of Solomon. What distinctions may have been drawn within the third group itself we do not know, but it is likely that there was no distinction at all, for Ezra nowhere suggests that there be a difference in status between one who has more of foreign blood and one who has less. From that

[123] Ezra 10.3.
[124] See Levi Freund, ibid. p. 168, note 5.

point of view, therefore, it is evident that to Ezra not only the children of mixed marriage but also their children and children's children to all generations, so long as their records or the memory of men could trace them to foreign parentage, could not marry into the first two classes. Only when the records did not reach far enough or when memory could not trace back to a foreign ancestor could the offspring join the second class of Israelites – though never the first.

Ezra's teaching prevailed for the greater part of the Second Commonwealth both in form and in content. The exact date is hard to determine, but it may be said safely that it penetrated far into the Hasmonean period. From then on, under the influence of pharisaic teaching and rabbinic halakah, much of the content of Ezra's law was changed, but a great deal of its form remained, and persisted down to the end of the Second Commonwealth and for some time thereafter. The general division of the Jewish people into three groups in respect to their purity of blood was so persistent a feature of Jewish life that it survived the breakdown of the Jewish State.

Priests and aristocratic Israelites belonged to the first group, priding themselves on their purity of stock and supporting their claims by carefully guarded records of family descent, even according to Ezra's standards. Josephus tells [125] us that even in his time the priests, both those at home and those in foreign lands, maintained records of family purity, and when these were destroyed as a result of war or other circumstances, the priestly courts made up new rosters on the basis of reliable documents and testimony. A statement in the Tosephta relates that the High Court at Jerusalem would devote sessions to examination of the family records of the priests, to determine who was fit for the Temple service and who not.[126] The Israelites of aristocratic families, desiring to emulate the priests, likewise maintained their family records to prove the purity of their stock and thereby justify their position in the first group established by Ezra. They were known as *meyuḥasim* or were described as "those who marry

[125] Josephus, *Contra Apion*, 1,7.
[126] Tos. Hag. 2,9; Ḳid. 76b.

into priestly families." These families generally ranked high politically and socially and from among them were generally drawn the responsible administrative officers of the community. A priest in Temple service or a layman holding high office was beyond suspicion of any taint of foreign blood. So teaches a mishnah: "No investigation is necessary beyond the altar or the choir or the sanhedrin, or beyond the fact that one's ancestors served as public administrators or as trustees of charity funds." [127]

The second group, those of beclouded ancestry, also remained within the general outer limits set for them by Ezra, and continued to maintain a secondary position in the social strata of the Jewish people. In the time of Ezra, this group numbered six hundred and fifty-two persons, divided into three families, but at the end of the Second Commonwealth they constituted substantially the bulk of the Jewish population. They gained in numbers both from above and below. Records after a long while become uncertain, and those of the upper class with a shadow of uncertainty about their genealogy must go down a step into the second class. Aristocracy always has the tendency to diminish in numbers to the gain of the middle class. Of the group below, that is of those who had definite foreign origin, there were two types that were acceptable to the Israelites of the second group, by pharisaic halakah – proselytes and freed slaves. In the later part of the Hasmonean period, proselytes and freedmen formed quite an addition to the Jewish population, and they ingrained themselves into the Jewish people by marrying into the second group. Zerubabel's account (Ezra 2.60), giving their number and the families to which they belonged, suggests that this second group, like the first, also maintained family records, partly by compulsion from the authorities representing the upper class and partly to be distinguished from the class below them. It is likely that up to the end of the Hasmonean period they continued to preserve their family records, for this seems to be evident from the writings of the Damascus sect and a report of Africanus.[128]

[127] M. Ḳid. 76a.

[128] Cf. Ginzberg, MGWJ 1912, p. 666; *Sekte,* pp. 124–5. See also Levi

The lowest class, composed in Ezra's time of the Nethinim, descendants of Solomon's slaves, the proselytes, and the children of mixed marriages, apparently did not have registers of their own in Ezra's time. Their separation from the rest of the community was physical; the Nethinim had quarters of their own, as did the proselytes. In course of time, though, Jewish elements of technical taint were added to this group, such as the mamzer, the *ḥalal,* i.e., one born of a union prohibited for priests, the foundling, and the "hush child." These being of Jewish stock and mingling with the Jewish population, constituted a danger of ultimate impurity within the Jewish family. Likewise the proselytes, who by rabbinic law were permitted to intermarry with Israelites, offered a problem of ultimately adulterating Jewish purity. It may be conjectured, therefore, that at some time during the latter part of the Hasmonean dynasty, an additional family record was established for Jews belonging to the third group, marriage with whom was prohibited either for Israelite laymen or priests; and for proselytes, marriage with whom was prohibited to priests only.[129]

If in outward form Judaism of the Second Commonwealth remained true to the standards of Ezra in respect to family purity, in content it was radically changed so soon as pharisaic halakah began to exert an influence on the Jewish people. Under pharisaic influence, the mind of the people was turned from racial to religious nationalism. Therewith the concept of aristocracy tended to be altered so as to give first place to the teacher, though he belong to the common people, rather than to the *meyuḥasim* in high places. In addition, the concept of purity was changed from racially unadulterated to religiously or legally proper. Certain historic incidents favored the pharisaic as against the view of Ezra as to racial exclusiveness. During the Maccabean conquests, large numbers of new converts were added. These, in addition to "those who

---

Freund, o.c., p. 175 and note 1, opposing the view of Ginzberg on insufficient ground, but admitting that it may have been the older usage to register those of the second class also.

[129] The Zadokite text, 14.4–5 expressly states that the proselytes were entered in a register. See Ginzberg, *Sekte,* ibid. M. Yeb. 49a records a register giving the name of a mamzer.

fear the Lord" of previous generations and of later proselytes, intermarried with Israelites and became part of the Jewish people. Religious nationalism did not discourage the process. Then came Herod, himself of foreign descent yet ruler of his people and married into the Hasmonean family. His influence was on the side of the religious rather than racial view of purity. At last came destruction of the Temple, dealing a death blow to priestly traditions of exclusiveness, and in its place came the academy of Jabneh, setting up a nobility of learning in place of that of birth. And throughout that period, as may be surmised, records were lost and confused, so that the documentary evidences of racial purity were no longer sufficient. It is even reported by Africanus that Herod burned the archives of family registers, so as to create general confusion as to descent, and make it easier for himself to bear the stigma of foreign origin.[180] With insufficient records, the memory of men and court investigations had to be resorted to,[181] both of which were conditioned to the newer concept of purity. All these facts left the field practically free to rabbinic halakah.

Rabbinic halakah tried to eliminate all marriage prohibitions that were not based upon pentateuchal law. Deuteronomy knows marriage prohibitions under the heads of intermarriage, incest, mamzer – these applying to all Jews. Leviticus has additional prohibitions applying to priests only – divorcee, *zonah,* and ḥalalah. Through laborious discussions and with accuracy of definition, the rabbis grouped all marriage prohibitions under these heads. We need not treat them here, but shall take them up under separate headings in their proper order. Here we are interested in the first category, intermarriage, and more especially the status of offspring of such unions. One thing the rabbis knew, that intermarriage was a category applying to priests and laymen

[180] Eusebius, *Hist. Eccl.* 1,7,5. See Rosenthal, MGWJ, 1881, p. 118. Freund, *Schwartz Festschrift,* p. 173 note 3 argues against the authenticity of this report, but to my mind without success.

[181] The memory of men is typified by the *keẓaẓah* ceremony cited Ket. 28b; Tos. Ket. 3,3. Court investigation is cited in Tos. Hag. 2,9, mentioned above. Freund, ibid., believes that all these uncertainties belong to a date later than destruction of the Temple, but his arguments are inconclusive, and Tos. Hag. proves the opposite.

alike. Any distinction between priest and layman in a marriage whose basis was the problem of foreign blood evidently had no biblical sanction. Either it should be prohibited to all or permitted even to priests. Perhaps that was the goal of the Pharisees and the rabbis following their tradition, for they essentially disliked the exclusiveness of the priesthood. But they could not reach that goal for two reasons. First, family tradition was even according to the Bible the very essence of priesthood. If descent from Aaron was important, then certainly some thought should be given to Jewish descent. In the second place, the deep-rooted exclusiveness of the priest was too difficult for the rabbis to overcome. We have on record several instances where the Pharisees tried to interfere with the marriage restrictions of priests so as to bring them closer to the standards of ordinary Israelites, but gave up the attempt because of too stubborn priestly resistance.[132]

They conceded the priests certain special restrictions and at the same time negated a number of unreasonable rules of exclusiveness long maintained. The rabbis did not wish to recognize foreign blood as a hindrance to marriage, if the foreigner accepted Judaism. The proselyte and his descendants were admitted into the congregation of the Lord.[133] But it was granted that they should not be admitted into the caste of priesthood. The taint of foreign blood could not serve as reason for this prohibition – since it is no hindrance to marriage with Israelites, it can be no basis for exclusion from marriage with priests. The rabbis, therefore, found another basis. They declared the proselyte woman a statutory *zonah* [134] and the daughter of a proselyte a ḥalalah.[135]

However, to uproot the traditional prejudice of the priests to foreign blood required a number of steps on the part of

[132] One case is the one of *'issah*, 'Eduy. 8,3, the other is that dealing with priestly marriage to a proselyte, Ḳid. 78b.

[133] M. Ḳid. 69a, which according to Samuel, ibid. 75a, goes back to Hillel. Freund denies this tradition with injustice.

[134] M. Yeb. 61a, beraita, ibid. 61b. See Yad, Issure Bi'ah 17,1 and 3, and *Maggid* thereto.

[135] The view of R. Judah, which seems to be the older tradition, in M. Ḳid. 77a. The final halakah is against this view, yet the child is a ḥalalah, even according to the final halakah, if she was born of a priest and proselyte.

the rabbis. They began by attacking the old idea that foreign blood was a taint carrying over from generation to generation unto perpetuity. They felt there must be a time when a foreigner could be so welded within the Hebrew people as to be counted in every respect as a native Jew. Granted even that the proselyte could not reach this level, being a Jew by adoption only, his children should, being born into Judaism, and surely his grandchildren born of native Jewish parents. The assimilative process, they felt, must be reckoned with, so that at least the third or fourth or fifth generation of proselytes, even with the strain of foreign blood, should be counted as full-blooded native Jews. That had not been the priestly tradition since the days of Ezekiel, who ruled that priests might marry only "virgins of the seed of the house of Israel," and certainly not since Zerubabel, who demoted from priestly dignity all those who could not show an uninterrupted record of Hebrew origin. The sadducean courts, following the priestly tradition, would have ruled to the very end that no person could be accounted a native Jew for any religious purpose if he had non-Jewish ancestry, no matter how remote.

The pharisaic attack upon this tradition came not in connection with the legal restrictions against priestly marriages but in connection with a political issue; and it was dramatically staged in the Jerusalem Temple on the Feast of Tabernacles, during a sabbatical year when thousands upon thousands of pligrims were assembled in the Temple court to hear the king recite the specific scriptural section prescribed for the occasion. It was Agrippa II, great-grandson of Herod, a follower of the Pharisees, who mounted the rostrum to recite the Law. When he reached the verse (Deut. 17.15), "One from among thy brethren shalt thou set king over thee; thou mayest not put a foreigner over thee, who is not thy brother," he halted with tears in his eyes. He was a foreigner by descent in the traditional sense and therefore unfit for the royal position he held. But the Pharisees had a different view of the matter. To them three generations of Hebrew blood were enough to end the foreign strain. They took that occasion to proclaim their view and to declare

Agrippa, a third generation Hebrew, a native Jew in the eyes of the law. In the midst of that vast congregation they shouted: "Fear not, Agrippa, thou art our brother, thou art our brother!" [136]

At that stage of the development of pharisaic law, it probably was still assumed that at least three generations of Hebrew ancestry were necessary to give a foreigner the status of a native Hebrew. But this was later reduced to two generations, to one generation, and finally to the sole requirement that at least one parent must be a native Jew. Fifty percent Jewish blood, then, according to the final halakah, is enough to give a person of foreign origin the status of a full-blooded native; he can be king of the Jewish people, or judge of any of the courts, or hold any office of responsibility in the community; he may recite the confession in connection with the offering of the first fruit which reads (Deut. 26.3), "I profess this day unto the Lord thy God that I am come unto the land which the Lord swore to *our fathers* to give us"; and in his prayers he may follow the regular formula for native Jews, "Our God and God of *our fathers.*" [137]

By slow degrees the Pharisees forced this teaching upon the priesthood in respect to their marriage laws. First they prevailed upon them to accept the ruling that three generations of Jewish blood constituted sufficient purity for priestly marriages, regardless of the record beyond the third generation.[138] We hear of a more liberal concession by the priests, accepting in marriage also those who could trace their genealogy only

[136] Sifre Deut. 17.15; M. Soṭah 41a; Büchler, *Die Priester*, pp. 13 f. A view opposing the ruling of the Pharisees has been recorded in tannaitic texts, asserting that it was mere flattery to Agrippa. See Tos. Soṭah 7,15; Yer. Soṭah 22a; Soṭah 41b. Levi Freund in *Schwartz Festschrift*, pp. 184–5, believes that the charge of mamzerut was involved in this case, but this appears to be a misinterpretation.

[137] M. Bik. 1,4; Ḳid. 76b; Yeb. 45b. From the texts themselves it would seem that the important thing is that his mother be Jewish, but in reality where the father is a native Jew the mother may be a proselyte. See Tosafot Yeb. 102a, s.v. *le'inyan*.

[138] This stage is recorded in M. Ḳid. 76a. According to Rashi the investigation is intended to eliminate mamzerut. This does not seem logical, for mamzerut is not a priestly disqualification and does not terminate after three generations. Tosafot takes the investigation to aim at the elimination of ḥalalut. Belkin in *Philo and the Oral Law* agrees. But that, too, is impossible,

two steps back to parents and grandparents of Jewish blood.[139] Then there must have followed a stage where grandparents did not matter at all, but both parents had to be of Hebrew birth in order to permit a daughter to marry into the priesthood, but we have no explicit record of this in our sources. We have, however, a clear record of the next stage, where the law did not require even that both parents be of Hebrew birth, but that one parent a Jew and one a proselyte was enough to permit their daughter to marry a priest. The halakah of the Pharisees goes further and permits priests to marry a girl both of whose parents are proselytes, but on this point the priests did not follow the leniency of the halakah and did not permit marriage with the daughter of proselyte parents.[140] A leading scholar of the second century wanted proselyte women accepted into the priestly families, if con-

---

because ḥalalut is eliminated before three generations if one of the parents is of the Israelitish caste, as the tosafists themselves observe. To my mind, the original problem of *yoḥasin* was that of eliminating foreign blood; the other problems were added as secondary matters of interest. This mishnah records an old tradition (contra Freund, ibid. pp. 176–7, who believes that it belongs to a later period), and is interested primarily in the problem of foreign blood. On this basis we can more easily understand why the mishnah teaches that the female ancestors should be investigated and not the male. The Talmud has a highly artificial answer to this question, but in the light of our interpretation it can easily be understood. The family followed the male line. A male proselyte could not easily be lost because the male line of all his descendants converged toward him. A female proselyte could be lost in any one generation. Even in the case of the immediate parents of the person in question, if the father should happen to have two wives, one a native Hebrew and the other a proselyte, there would be immediate need of finding out which children were born of the Jewess and which of the proselyte. This stage is also recorded in Philo, *Spec. Leg.* I.19,101 requiring a record of three generations.

139 This stage is recorded in Josephus, *Contra Apion,* 1,7. In the Talmud we find a reflection of this view at a later date. Yer. Ḳid. 66a reports that Rabbi Judah the Nasi investigated a family as to its right to priestly marriage; discovering that the grandmother had been a minor below three at the time of her conversion he permitted the grandchild to marry a priest. Yeb. 60b has a different reading, that the mother was converted before she was three years old and the daughter was permitted to marry a priest.

140 According to R. Elazar b. Jacob it makes no difference which parent is Jewish. See M. Bik. 1,5; M. Ḳid. 77a, and the remark of Yer. Bik. 64a and Yer. Ḳid. 66a, explaining that to R. Elazar either father or mother of native Jewish stock was satisfactory. According to R. Judah, M. Ḳid. 77a, the father, not the mother must be of native Hebrew stock. If the father is a proselyte the daughter has the status of ḥalalah. According to R. Jose (in M. Ḳid.

verted before three years old,[141] but the halakah did not support him and the priests did not follow him. By this slow and laborious process, the rabbis succeeded in breaking down the idea of a perpetual taint of foreign blood, and established the law that the convert woman might marry an Israelite, and that the daughter of such a union might marry even a priest.

These rabbinic leniencies apply only, however, to children of proselytized parents. The child of an intermarriage (without conversion) naturally stands lower than the child of a proselyte, even than the proselyte himself, because — if foreign blood is in itself not reckoned as a blemish — the proselyte was born without sin, while the child of a mixed marriage was born of a sinful union. What, then, is his status; is he Jew or gentile; is he fit for marriage with Israelites, priests, or neither?

We have mentioned that in translation of Zech. 9.6, the Septuagint indicates that the child of mixed blood is a mamzer. If that be no proof that Deuteronomy really used the term mamzer in that sense, it gives at least a suspicion that at the very dawn of rabbinic halakah the child of mixed blood was so designated. Apparently no distinction was made between the child who had a heathen father and one who had a heathen mother, nor whether the child was born of a mixed marriage or from unmarried contact between Jew and heathen. Nor did it matter whether the child was by the current rule of descent considered ethnically a Jew or not; in other words, the child could be a non-Jew and a mamzer at the same time.[142] Earlier rabbinic halakah and agadah also speak of the child of a mixed marriage or of a free union between Jew and heathen as mamzer, regardless whether the father or the mother was heathen. R. Zadok, when taken captive and brought to Rome, was given a heathen consort,

---

77a, which the halakah accepts as final, Ḳid. 78b, but which the priests refused to follow), even if both parents are proselytes, the child can marry into priesthood.

141 Ḳid. 78a; Yeb. 60b.

142 So last mishnah of third chapter in Ḳid. (69a) cites the opinion of R. Eliezer that the child of a mamzer and slave is both slave and mamzer, which amounts almost to saying gentile and mamzer.

but refused to cohabit with her, because as he put it rhetorically, "I am descended from high priests, from a noble family; if I come in unto her I will bring into the world mamzerim." [143] Whereas the case here is one of a heathen mother, we have a general assumption in the earlier law that the child of a Jewish mother and heathen father was likewise considered a mamzer. A discussion of the last days of the Temple, whether converts might be accepted from Kardu and Tadmor, was decided in favor of their acceptance by R. Dosa b. Hyrcanus.[144] According to amoraic interpretation the question involved the admissibility of Karduans and Tadmoreans into Jewish marriage, because of the prevalence of mamzerim among them as a result of their contacts with Jewish women captured in their wars of conquest.[145] There is no reason to doubt this interpretation, in the absence of any other explanation for their exclusion, and it yields the inference that a child born of a Jewish mother and heathen father was accounted a mamzer.

Under the tannaim in Jabneh two general legal principles were evolved, which had a bearing on the status of a child of mixed parentage. The term mamzer came to be applied only to offspring of adultery or incest. Hence there can be no mamzerim among heathens, who can commit neither adultery nor incest in the sense of biblical law, for biblical law is for Jews only. Another principle evolved was that a child born of a union where marriage was legally impossible followed the ethnic group of the mother.[146] One aspect of this law was not new, that where the parents were unmarried the child belonged to the mother. The other aspect was new, of Roman origin — that there was such a thing as a marriage which the law counted as none at all, and that the marriage

[143] Ab. R. N., ch. 16. Büchler, *Festschrift,* p. 146, remarks that R. Zadok's view is not in agreement with the older halakah implied also in Jubilees 30.10 and in Targum Jonathan ad Lev. 18.21 that the child of a gentile mother is gentile, but there is no contradiction, if we assume that in the older halakah it was possible to be a mamzer and gentile at the same time.

[144] Yeb. 16a. See Büchler, *Festschrift,* pp. 149–51, arguing conclusively that this tradition goes back to Temple days.

[145] Yeb. 16b. The correctness of this interpretation is supported by Büchler, ibid., and by Obermeyer, *Die Landschaft Babyloniens,* pp. 132 f.

[146] M. Yeb. 49a and M. Ḳid. 66b.

of a Jew and a heathen had no validity. With these principles, the law yielded the following results for the child of a mixed marriage. If the union, married or unmarried, was between a Jew and a heathen woman, the child was heathen; if between a Jewish woman and a heathen, the child was a Jew.[147] With this, the child whose mother is gentile is no longer a halakic problem; he is a gentile and no mamzer, and may convert to Judaism if he wishes. The child of a Jewish mother and gentile father still remains a problem. He is a Jew, but nevertheless bears the blemish of one foreign parent. Some tannaim, followed by certain amoraim, would prohibit him marrying into the congregation of the Lord, giving him the status, as in the older law, of a mamzer.[148] Others permit marriage with Jews, because he is a Jew by law, and would not apply the blemish of mamzer to him.[149] They would exclude him only from marriage into priestly families, as though he were a convert.[150] The final halakah accepted the latter view, that the child is a fully legitimate Jewish child, fit for marriage with Israelites but not with priests.[151] Nevertheless, Israelites of distinction thought it socially improper to marry a half-Jew, despite the leniency of the halakah. An incident told of Rab is typical of this attitude. A young man born of a Jewish mother and gentile father asked him in apparent innocence whether he was permitted to marry a Jewish girl. When Rab answered in the affirmative, the young man made bold to ask the master,

147 Yeb. 22a; Ḳid. 66b; 68b; Mek. 21.4. The rabbis seek to derive this rule from the Bible (Ḳid. 68b) but without success. However, the rule that a child whose mother is Jewish counts as a Jew goes back to Temple days, and seems to be a principle invoked for the first time by the Pharisees in declaring Agrippa II a Jew because his mother was Jewish (M. Soṭah 41a). Yet Tos. Soṭah 7,15 cites R. Nathan as taking exception to this ruling. It is for the same reason that Paul circumcised Timothy (Acts 16.3), who would not otherwise require circumcision according to Paul's teaching but for the fact that his mother was Jewish.

148 M. Yeb. 69b; Tos. Ḳid. 4,16; Sifre Lev. 22.13; Yeb. 44b–45a, 46a, 70a, 99a; Ḳid. 75b; Yer. Yeb. 6c, 8b; Yer. Ḳid. 64. This view is ascribed to R. Akiba, R. Ishmael, R. Me'ir, Rabbi, R. Johanan, R. Ami, R. Haninah, R. Simeon b. Lakish, and R. Eliezer.

149 Yeb. 45a.

150 Yeb. ibid.: *pagum likehunah*. See also Ḳid. 68b.

151 Yad, Issure Bi'ah 15,13; *Ṭur* and *Shulḥan 'Aruk*, E.H. 4.

"Will you give me your daughter?" Rab turned down the proposal. His pupil remarked sarcastically, "In Medea a camel dances on a disk, people say. Here is Medea, here is the camel, here is the disk, and no dancing." Rab insisted he had a right to choose a son-in-law regardless of the law; the young man pressed his proposal on the ground that he ought to be encouraged. The master was angered, with results fatal to the persistent young man.[152]

V

Thus concluding with the gentile and the child of mixed marriage in respect to Jewish marriage laws, we may now examine the position of the proselyte, and begin with a general statement of his background.

There were always foreigners living among the Jews in Palestine. The independent foreigner was the *nakri*, the stranger. Whatever obligations the law of the land imposed upon him and whatever protection the state gave him, he was never part of the Jewish body politic. He did not settle in the land but was there as a sojourner, for a temporary stay. The foreigner who remained in the land for a more enduring stay and sought residence and protection in Palestine, was the *ger*, or resident alien. His rights and obligations were determined by the rules of clientage, for he was a client either of the people as a whole or of a particular family, and as such counted in the body politic. At first he had no standing in the religious community, his relation to the people being of a social and political nature only. Then a peripheral position was assigned him in the religious structure of the household to which he was attached. Gradually he approached closer and closer to the cult of the household, until permitted to participate in sacred feasts, required to circumcise himself, to keep the Sabbath, to abstain from certain forbidden foods, and to honor God and the sanctuary. In the meanwhile, the cult expanded from a household discipline to a national religion, from family altars to a Temple, and thereafter the national religion itself broadened out into

[152] Yeb. 45a.

a comprehensive universal faith. The national God became the One God, the Only God, and Zion, His abode, the light of the nations. The *ger* then was no longer a client in territorial contact with the people, but an adherent to the faith of the people, a correligionist. His former politico-social standing was changed into a religious status. He did not even have to live in Palestine. It was conceived that a person or a group that would cleave unto the Lord of Israel and observe His statutes and commandments, in whatever abode, would belong to the religious commonwealth of the Jewish nation. In early post-exilic times they constituted a separate unit in the Jewish community and were designated as "those who fear the Lord." Ezra's teaching of separateness did not help them to become part of the people; marriage between them and the native Jews was forbidden; but their numbers were considerable and they formed a smaller community within the larger.

They were apparently discouraged by the inferior position they held socially and by their inability to marry Jews, and felt there was no future for them and that they had no share in the religious structure of Judaism. Isaiah (56) encouraged them with a message of hope for the future and an equal share in God's love. "Also the sons of the stranger, that join themselves to the Lord, to serve Him and to love the name of the Lord, to be his servants, every one that keepeth the Sabbath from polluting it, and taketh hold of my covenant; even them will I bring to my holy mountain and make them joyful in my house of prayer; their burnt offerings and their sacrifices shall be accepted upon mine altar; for mine house shall be called a house of prayer for all people." The date of this prophecy is uncertain, nor does it mean that it offered proselytes intermarriage with Jews. It gave them standing in the Jewish community which they did not have under Ezra. At this time the proselytes were not yet "converts" in the rabbinic sense; that is, they were not "naturalized," as we might say, into the Jewish people, but belonged to the nations of their origin, in a legal sense, but they cleaved unto the Lord and were faithful clients of His people. According to Bertholet,[153] the word *ger* is used in the rabbinic, technical sense as a convert or naturalized Jew for the first time by the Chronicler of II Chronicles, 30.25, which he dates somewhere close to the Hasmonean period.

The proselyte as the halakah knew him was a full Jew by religion, and though of foreign origin was conceived as a "new-born" member of the people. His initiation ceremony consisted of ritual baptism, circumcision, and a sacrifice upon the altar. The first represented purification from his heathen uncleanness, the second was the standard form of naturalization, amounting to a union with Israel by covenant of the flesh, the last was expressive of his incorporation into the religious fellowship of Israel.[154]

We have already recorded that Ezra's teaching concerning the taint of foreign blood and its perpetual effect as a hindrance to intermarriage was opposed by pharisaic halakah; that the priestly families alone held to that tradition, as well as certain aristocratic Israelites, down to the end of the Second Commonwealth; that by rabbinic influence the priests finally accepted the rule that if only one parent was Jewish, the offspring could marry into a priestly family; that Israelites, under the same influence, long before the destruction of the Temple permitted marriage with proselytes.[155] The first pharisaic statement permitting Israelites to marry proselytes is given by Hillel, according to an amoraic tradition.[156] But this ruling evidently was not new in Hillel's time, for not even the Shammaites, who often preserved older traditions, cast doubt on its validity. If the tradition of Abtalion's foreign origin be correct,[157] it is hardly thinkable that he would be permitted to hold the office of Ab-Bet-Din if his admission into the Jewish people had been by a

[153] Alfred Bertholet, *Die Stellung der Israeliten und Juden zu den Fremden*, Leipzig, 1896, p. 178. See also G. F. Moore, *Judaism in the First Centuries of the Christian Era*, Vol. I, pp. 323–53.

[154] For the subject of proselytization, cf. Bertholet, ibid. section 5, pp. 123–178; Moore, ibid.; B. J. Bamberger, *Proselytism in the Talmudic Period*, Cincinnati, 1939, ch. 4, pp. 38–60.

[155] See above, pp. 188–90.

[156] M. Ḳid. 69a. See note 133 above.

[157] Giṭ. 57b; Yoma, 71b; Pes. 66a; 70b. See Bamberger, ibid. pp. 222–3.

sinful union between his ancestors, no matter how remote — especially since such a union, if then prohibited, would result in branding the child as a mamzer. Probably even at the beginning of the first century B.C.E. it was already accepted as pharisaic halakah that an Israelite might marry a convert.

It should be assumed that the convert, having equal standing with the native Jew in all religious matters and having been admitted to marriage with Jews, would be subject to all Jewish marriage laws. To a certain extent this is true; he may not marry a heathen or a slave. Yet some of the laws restricting marriage for native Jews do not altogether apply to the proselyte. These exceptions have been made more for the benefit of native Jews than out of disregard of the proselyte's duty to observe biblical marriage restrictions. Thus, the proselyte may marry a mamzer or mamzeret, while the native Jew may not. This was a definite teaching in the time of Hillel,[158] when his right to marry a Jewess was still remembered as an innovation. Two centuries later, however, the matter came up for discussion in the academy. It appeared strange to the tannaim that a convert should be permitted to violate a biblical marriage law. R. Jose supported the Hillelite tradition, explaining that a mamzer could not enter the *congregation* of the Lord, but proselytes could not be designated as a *congregation*. R. Judah opposed Hillel's ruling, and would not permit a convert to marry a mamzeret, on the ground that proselytes were a *congregation* like native Jews.[159] The halakah accepts the traditional view that a proselyte may marry a mamzeret, it being understood, however, that the child would have the status of a mamzer, in the same manner as if a Jew married a mamzeret.[160] The proselytes did not like this ruling, for it was a token of their inferiority. When an amora announced it in Mehuza, a

[158] M. Ḳid. 69a.

[159] Tos. Ḳid. 5,1; Ḳid. 72b. In Yer. Ḳid. 64c two teachers by the same names as those of Babli are given, holding opposite views, R. Jose prohibiting marriage between proselyte and mamzeret and R. Judah permitting. These teachers are probably Palestinian amoraim and not the tannaim mentioned in Tosephta. See Bamberger, p. 116, note 90.

[160] Tos. ibid.; Yer. ibid.; Ḳid. 73a, 67a; Yad, Issure Bi'ah 15,7.

Persian city which apparently had many proselyte residents, he was pelted with citrons.[161] To soothe their feelings, another amora told them at the same time that they were permitted to marry the daughters of priests. Both laws are correct; they may marry daughters of priests because the females in priestly families have no special priestly restrictions, and they may marry mamzerim because they are not included in the term *congregation* used by the Bible in connection with marriage prohibitions. On the same basis, though it is not specifically stated, a female proselyte may marry a castrated Israelite,[162] and according to some opinions even a castrated priest, though such a marriage is biblically prohibited for Jews.[163]

The racial origin of the convert, however, was of great importance to the halakah, for certain specific racial groups are excluded by the Bible from marriage with Israelites even unto the third or tenth generation, and it remained for the halakah to determine what effect conversion would have on these prohibitions.

No limit is set by the Bible on the prohibition of marriage with the "seven nations." It is a matter of speculation whether from the biblical point of view conversion, as later conceived, would lift that prohibition or not. We have suggested[164] that the prohibition was based primarily on religious grounds. It would seem logical to conclude, therefore, that whensoever a member of the "seven nations" accepted Judaism, and the danger of being misled into idolatry was thus eliminated, there would remain no ground for prohibiting intermarriage with him. On the other hand, would not conversion itself represent a covenant with a representative of the race with whom covenants of any kind were prohibited? Until we come to talmudic law, we have no evidence to go by. In the Talmud we have a second century tanna, R. Simeon b. Yoḥai, who implies that after proselytization there is no prohibition against marrying a

161 Ḳid. 73a.

162 M. Yeb. 76a. See Rashi ibid. based on the statement of R. Ami, Yeb. 79b.

163 Yeb. 76a; Yad, Issure Bi'ah 16,1; E.H. 4,1.

164 See p. 158 above.

member of the seven nations, for he points out that the prohibition is based specifically on the danger of idolatry.[165] This is also a general assumption in the Gemara.[166] Raba, a third century amora, however, believes that a proselyte of the seven nations may not marry Jews, under a biblical prohibition.[167] We have referred to Raba's statement above and we have mentioned that Maimonides agreed with R. Simeon b. Yoḥai and *Ṭur* with Raba. Thus we have a difference of opinion in the final halakah whether a convert of one of the seven nations may or may not marry a Jew. It seems to be agreed by the halakah, however, that the child of a Canaanite convert born in the Jewish faith is permitted to marry a Jew.[168]

One particular Canaanite nation, the Gibeonites, has acquired a specific standing in Jewish law. In Joshua, Nehemiah, I Chronicles, and the Talmud they are called "Nethinim." Their acceptance by the Jewish people is told in the Book of Joshua (ch. 9) in the following story. Hearing of the victories of Israel and fearing lest they be conquered and exterminated like the other Canaanites, they disguised their identity, claiming to have come from a distant land, and asked Joshua to accept them under a covenant of protection. The covenant had been made and confirmed by an oath – when their deception was discovered. The Jews would not recall the covenant, but permitted the Gibeonites to remain among them under protection as perpetual servants of the sanctuary to draw water and hew wood. Ezra (8.20) records the Nethinim as having been reduced to servitude by King David. The Talmud adds the following account.[169] Even Moses in his time anticipated their position of servitude as drawers of water and hewers of wood (Deut. 29.10), and as such he wished them to be set apart from the Jewish people, legislating, however, for his own generation only. Joshua, in making them servants of the sanctuary, intended to keep them in that servitude only as long as there

165 Yeb. 23a; Ḳid. 68b.
166 'Ab. Zar. 36b. See *Kesef Mishneh* ad Yad, Issure Bi'ah 12,1.
167 Yeb. 76a. See note 103 on p. 175 above.
168 See *Maggid* ad Yad, Issure Bi'ah 12,22.
169 Yeb. 79a.

be a Temple in existence. David condemned them forever as a slave group, because he saw special cruelty in their nature, in connection with the revenge they exacted on the house of Saul (II Sam. 21).

A plausible historical account of the Nethinim is given by Ezekiel Kaufmann.[170] Different from the other Canaanite groups, they did not resist the Israelites in the conquest of Canaan but concluded a peace treaty with them – probably without deception. They lived as a free people in their cities and mingled freely with the Israelites, assimilating with them religiously and culturally, yet remaining apart as a separate ethnic group. From the time of Joshua, who concluded the peace pact with them, to the time of Solomon, their position became steadily worse. They were driven out of their cities and scattered over the entire Jewish territory. Saul was particularly unfriendly to them, probably for political reasons, and sought their extermination. Solomon, we are told (I Kings 9.20–21), reduced to slavery all the Canaanites in Palestine who had not been exterminated by the wars of conquest; and among these were the Gibeonites. They became slaves of the state, not owned by private individuals. The other Canaanites were designated as Solomon's slaves; the Gibeonites formed a special group among them, retaining their identity and coming to be known as Nethinim. Their acceptance of the Jewish religion was natural and gradual throughout their contact with the people, and in the time of Ezra they belonged to the proselyte group of those who returned to Palestine, or as they were then known, "those who fear the Lord." The author of the Book of Joshua knew of the position of servitude to which Solomon had reduced them, and justified the act by showing deception on their part in the covenant. The Chronicler credits David with reducing them to servitude in the Temple because he believed it was David who had formulated all plans for the Temple structure and service.

They formed a separate community among the Jews down to the second century of the common era, and intermarriage with them was prohibited throughout that period. From

[170] Ezekiel Kaufmann, *Toledot ha-Emunah ha-Yisraelit*, pp. 647–49.

talmudic sources it would seem that the prohibition was based on the fact that they had the status of slaves, and being slaves of the state rather than of individuals, could not be freed. However, the matter is not altogether clear, and the post-talmudic authorities are divided on whether they are prohibited as slaves or as Canaanites.[171] Likewise, it is not altogether clear in the halakah whether the prohibition against marrying them is biblical or rabbinical.[172] The Talmud reports that Rabbi Judah the Nasi sought to lift the prohibition altogether, but encountered legal and probably also social difficulties.[173] Nevertheless, the hope is expressed that in messianic days the Nethinim might obtain full equality with Jews.[174]

Having the status of proselytes, their marriage with Jews, although prohibited, is not invalid. The offspring of a marriage between a Nathin and a Jew, regardless which parent is the Nathin, is a Nathin,[175] which means, of course, that the blemish is perpetual unto all generations. They may marry proselytes, freedmen, mamzerim, and foundlings; [176] in other words, all those who possess some kind of disqualification for free marriage with Jews. The offspring of such a marriage, having a double disability, have the legal status of the parent with the severest blemish, the Nathin and the mamzer sharing the honor of having the worst because both perpetuate their failings to eternity. Socially, the Nathin stands below the mamzer, the latter being a Jew by birth, and above the proselyte, for the proselytization of the Nathin is of such long historical standing.[177]

Proselytes of the Ammonites and the Moabites, by the plain injunction in Deuteronomy (23.4), should forever be excluded from marriage with Jews. The restriction was not always observed, it is true, but it cannot be said that it was ever abrogated or otherwise interpreted till the last days of

[171] See Tosafot Yeb. 79a, s.v. *unetinim*.
[172] See Yad, Issure Bi'ah 12,22–23 and *Maggid* thereto.
[173] Yeb. 79b.
[174] Ḳid. 72b.
[175] M. Ḳid. 66b.
[176] M. Ḳid. 69a.
[177] M. Hor. 13a.

the Second Commonwealth. Rabbinic halakah, however, by successive interpretations, practically nullified this biblical prohibition. The tannaim had an old tradition that only male Ammonites and Moabites were prohibited to enter the congregation of the Lord, but the females carried no such prohibition, provided they accepted Judaism.[178] The tradition is said to go back to the authority of the prophet Samuel, in order to explain the legitimacy of King David and his grandson Rehoboam, the former a descendant of Ruth the Moabite, the latter son of an Ammonite mother.[179] We need not take this agadic statement too literally. We do know that to the Chronicler, to Ezra and Nehemiah, the deuteronomic prohibition against marrying Ammonites and Moabites included both males and females.[180] However, such an agadic statement indicates that the rabbis believed the tradition to be very old, and by internal evidence we can see that it goes back at least to Temple days.[181] The halakah accepts it without a single dissenting opinion, and so it remains as the final rabbinic ruling that Ammonite and Moabite female converts may marry Israelites. That they may not marry priests goes without saying, since no other proselyte women may, but the daughter of an Ammonite or Moabite proselyte mother by a Jewish father may marry into the priesthood.[182]

178 M. and Gemara Yeb. 76b–77a.

179 Yeb. 77a.

180 I Kings 11.1–2; Ezra 9.12; 10.2; Neh. 13.23.

181 The tradition is reported in the name of R. Akiba, Mid. Tan. ad Deut. 23.4. Again, R. Simeon wishes to apply the same principle to Egyptians, Mishnah Yeb. 76b, assuming application to Moabites and Ammonites as well rooted in tradition. Furthermore, M. Yadayim, 4,4 decides that Ammonites cannot be identified any longer. That decision came immediately after destruction of the Temple. It is hardly likely that the distinction between males and females would be halakically of interest to the rabbis after the whole question was of no practical value. Hence we judge that the principle of "Ammonites and not Ammonitesses" must have been formulated before, which brings it to Temple days.

182 This is evident from the fact that if the mother can marry an Israelite the daughter can marry a priest. An opinion is expressed in the Talmud that even if Ammonite or Moabite converts marry, their daughter may marry a priest, Yeb. 77a–b. This ruling is based, of course, on the assumption that the view of R. Jose prevails, that a daughter both of whose parents are converts (*giyyoret mikkannah*) is fit for marriage with priests. But we

Theoretically, the biblical prohibition against marrying Ammonites or Moabites continued in the rabbinic halakah in respect to the males, and the prohibition was considered perpetual on the male line, as the Bible has it, "even unto the tenth generation." That means that the son of a son of a son and so on of an Ammonite or Moabite male convert cannot marry a Jewish woman. The marriage is not invalid but prohibited, as is the case with any marriage prohibition except incest and adultery. The halakah, however, raises an interesting question in respect to the daughter of an Ammonite or Moabite male convert. Is she to be counted as a first or second generation convert? As a descendant of a convert, she is second generation, but in respect to marriage with Jews, she is the first to achieve that permission. This question has no bearing on her fitness to marry an Israelite, but it does have on her fitness to marry a priest, because priests may not marry first generation converts. The matter is discussed between R. Johanan and Resh Lakish. The former permits it, the latter prohibits; and the halakah accepts the view of R. Johanan and permits her to marry even a high priest.[183]

This discussion, however, must be considered as only theoretical, for in the early days of the Jabneh academy, soon after destruction of the Temple, it had already been decided that the Ammonites and Moabites could no longer be identified and no special disqualification could be imposed upon them because of their origin. A mishnah reports that "on that day" Judah, an Ammonite convert, came before the academy and asked whether he was permitted to marry a Jewish woman. R. Gamaliel thought the biblical prohibition

---

have stated above that, though this is the halakah, the priests refused to accept the ruling and insisted on one parent being a native Jew.

[183] Yeb. 77a–b. The Babylonian Talmud speaks only of a priest, but the Palestinian Talmud speaks even of a high priest and properly so, because R. Johanan's inference is from Lev. 21.14, which deals with the laws governing marriage of high priests. Resh Lakish ascribes the prohibition to the fact that the marriage of the Ammonite and the Jewish woman is prohibited; therefore, the daughter is unfit for marriage with priests. Apparently, if it was a case of an Ammonite male convert married to an Ammonite female convert, even Resh Lakish would admit that the child is fit for marriage with a priest. See previous note.

should apply to him, but R. Joshua was of the opinion that he should be permitted, arguing that, "Sennacherib has long since come and mixed up all the peoples, as it is said (Is. 10.13), 'I have removed the bounds of peoples,'" and their identity was therefore no longer known. R. Joshua's view prevailed in the academy and Judah was admitted into the congregation of the Lord.[184] The halakah recognizes this decision and accounts proselytes of the Ammonites and Moabites as not different from other proselytes.[185]

The Egyptians and the Edomites are placed in one category in Deuteronomy (23.8–9), prohibiting marriage with them until the third generation. There is no accepted tradition that the females of these nations were more acceptable to the Jews than the males. R. Simeon desired to set the female converts of the Egyptians and the Edomites on the same footing as those of the Ammonites and Moabites, and permit them to marry Israelites upon conversion. He cited tradition, he argued logic, but his view was not accepted.[186] The halakah decides therefore that first and second generation converts of Egyptians and Edomites, both male and female, cannot marry Jews.[187] Also, the principle uttered in the academy of Jabneh, that the old races had become confused and could not be identified, was brought into question in respect to Egyptians and Edomites. R. Gamaliel proposed to apply it also to the Egyptians and Edomites, R. Joshua argued against, and we do not know whether the academy reached any decision.[188] The Tosephta reports that R. Akiba declared Egyptian converts fit to marry Israelites, on the ground that they could not be identified as the same race as the biblical Egyptians.[189] The Babylonian and the Palestinian Talmuds apparently did not know this Tosephta text or did not reckon with it.[190] Nor did the tosafists see the text, for they quote

[184] M. Yadayim 4,4; Tos. Yadayim 2,17; Ber. 28a.

[185] Yad, Issure Bi'ah 12,25.

[186] M. Yeb. 76b; Beraita, ibid. 77b.

[187] Yad, Issure Bi'ah 12,19.

[188] Tos. Yadayim at end.

[189] Tos. Ḳid. 5,5.

[190] Babli quotes Minyamin's question twice (Yeb. 78a and Soṭah 9a) but omits R. Akiba's answer; but in quoting the question, the Gemara seeks to prove that Egyptians can be identified, contrary to the alleged answer of

it only in the name of Rashi,[191] the latter having had unusual texts before him. Its origin is hard to trace, nor can we say that it is not an authentic statement of R. Akiba. We feel confident, however, that the amoraim – at least those of Palestine – did not recognize this reported view of Rabbi Akiba as halakically valid.[192] Maimonides, nevertheless, relying on this Tosephta text, decides that Egyptians cannot be identified, and their proselytes, even of the first generation, may marry Jews.[193] Naḥmanides, on the other hand, stands by the biblical prohibition against marriage with Egyptians unless they are third generation converts.[194]

What constitutes the third generation? R. Johanan is cited by one amora to have said that the child of a second generation proselyte father by a first generation proselyte mother is a third generation proselyte. Another amora quotes him as deciding in such a case that the child is only a second generation proselyte, because his mother is only of the first generation. The third, and probably the final report of R. Johanan's view is that "among converts, the child follows the parent who is most unfit for marriage with Jews." Which means that the child does not count as third generation convert unless both parents are second generation converts.[195] The Palestinian Talmud submits a report in the name of R. Johanan that R. Akiba, in answer to a question of a certain Minyamin, an Egyptian proselyte, also required two generations of converts on the side of both parents before the Egyptian proselyte might marry a Jewess.[196]

R. Akiba. Yerushalmi quotes R. Akiba's answer also in two places (Yeb. 9b and Ḳid. 65d) but gives the answer as follows: "No, my son, thou shalt marry him to a second generation convert, so that he (the child) may be third generation on both sides."

[191] See Rabbi Samson's commentary to Yadayim 4,4; Tosafot Soṭah 9a, s.v. *Minyamin*, quoting Rashi, Soṭah, ibid., s.v. *asi*.

[192] The discussions in both Talmuds on the marriage laws of Egyptian converts go back to Palestinian sources, especially R. Johanan. These laws could not have been of such vital interest to them, if the Egyptians could not be identified.

[193] Yad, Issure Bi'ah 12,25.

[194] *Maggid*, ad Yad ibid. *Ṭur* E.H. 4, sides with Maimonides in respect to Edomites, and with Naḥmanides in respect to Egyptians.

[195] Yeb. 78a–b.

[196] Yer. Yeb. 9b and Yer. Ḳid. 66a. An interesting concession is made in

The application of R. Johanan's principle, that the offspring of convert parents follow the parent with the worse disqualification, is simple enough in the ordinary case. If one parent is a convert of the non-prohibited nationalities and the other an Egyptian convert, the child reckons as an Egyptian convert. If one parent is first generation Egyptian convert and the other second generation convert of the same nationality, the child counts second generation Egyptian convert. The principle becomes more complicated when an Ammonite male convert marries an Egyptian female convert; the Ammonite is under lesser disqualification than the Egyptian in respect to females but under severer disqualification in respect to males. In such a case the female offspring count as Egyptians, while the male children count as Ammonites.[197]

Another group of people stands in contrast to these mentioned here. They are the Samaritans. The Ammonites and Moabites and Edomites were ruled out of existence by history and by law. The Samaritans have remained to this day. In respect to those others, the law has progressively softened down their exclusion; in respect to the Samaritans, the law has stiffened the lines of separation. The Samaritans, we are told in the Second Book of Kings (17.24–41), are a group of heathens who were settled in the north of Palestine by the Assyrian kings after destruction of the Northern Kingdom in the eighth century B.C.E. They came under the influence of Judaism through the missionary efforts of Jewish priests, established their own religious center at Samaria, worshipped Jehovah, but did not abandon their former idolatries. The Book of Kings gives a miraculous account of their conversion. Beset by lions who were devouring their population, they recognized that the God who inhabited the land of Palestine had employed this scourge to impose upon them the "law of the God of the land." They told this to the king

---

the Talmud: if an Egyptian woman converts during pregnancy, the child born is a second generation convert. It would appear that this ruling holds good even if the father remains an idol-worshipping Egyptian. See Yeb. 78a, lines 17–18; Yad, Issure Bi'ah 12,20.

[197] Yeb. 78b.

of Assyria, who sent them priests from among the captives of Israel whom he had deported, to teach them the law of the God of the land. Their conversion, however, was not very successful. They worshipped Jehovah and also offered sacrifices to their idols. Concentrated in the north and thus politically segregated from the Jews, worshipping in Samaria and thus religiously alienated from Jerusalem, a foreign group that adulterated its Judaism, the Samaritans had poor chance, to begin with, to be accepted on a footing of equality with native Jews. Their political activities were for the greater part directed to the injury of the Jewish people. During rebuilding of the Temple under Zerubabel, Ezra, and Nehemiah, they put obstacles in the way by intrigue as well as by physical force.

Jewish sentiment toward them was anything but friendly. The Chronicler (II Kings 17.34, 41) condemns their religious confusion. The Book of Ezra (4.1) calls them "the enemies of Judah and Benjamin" and speaks of them, in common with the heathen population, as "the peoples of the land." While no direct ban against marriage with them is found in earlier sources, Ezra prohibited this under the heading of "the peoples of the land," that is, both as foreigners and as heathens. The older converts, the Nethinim, were at least taken up in the Jewish community as an inferior and distinct group; the Samaritans did not count in the community at all. As long as foreign blood constituted a bar to marriage with Jews, their exclusion was self-evident. But, as we have seen, rabbinic halakah did not recognize foreign blood as a hindrance to marriage with Jews, and therefore a new explanation had to be found for exclusion of the Samaritans. The natural explanation might have been that the rabbis considered their religion not sufficiently Jewish. But that was not and could not have been the rabbinic mind. In those days sectarian deviations from standard Judaism were quite numerous — Sadducees, the Damascus sect, Judeo-Christians, and the various sects whose writings have been included in the Apocrypha. Yet the rabbis never prohibited intermarriage with them on the basis of sectarianism. Marriage prohibition, to the rabbis, had to have a biblical basis, not sectarian antagonism. This broad-mindedness of the rabbis gives the Samaritans a standing as "genuine converts" in the older halakah,[198] and they are generally accounted equal to Jews, except in ceremonial observances in which they differ. The new explanation that the rabbis offered for exclusion of the Samaritans was to give them the status of doubtful mamzerim.[199] The bases for the mamzer charge against them are offered by the amoraim. One, that the Samaritans permitted childless widows to marry without ḥaliẓah, if they were widowed after nuptials.[200] Another, that among them there were children of mixed marriages, whom the older law counted as mamzerim.[201] Still another charges them with permitting cohabitation between brother and

[198] M. Ber. 45a, in respect to *zimmun* counting as a Jew; M. Ket. 29a, in respect to the fifty shekels to be paid for rape of a Samaritan woman; M. Giṭ. 10a, recognizing the validity of an instrument bearing the testimony of Samaritans; beraitot B.Ḳ. 38b and San. 85b placing Samaritans equal, or approximately equal to Jews in the matter of injury; M. Nid. 56b, accounting the Samaritans subject to menstrual defilement like Jews; beraita Ḥullin 3b, declaring slaughter by a Samaritan kosher; Tosephta Pes. chapter 2.

[199] M. Ḳid. 74a. Loew, in *Gesammelte Schriften,* III, p. 163, argues that in Hillel's time intermarriage with Samaritans was permitted, else he would have mentioned the Samaritans also in his mishnah, wherein he reckons the various grades of purity in respect to marriage. The argument is weak from many points of view. On the contrary, if marriage was permitted to Jews but not to priests, Hillel would have had more cause to mention the Samaritans. He does not mention them because they did not count in the Jewish community. Furthermore, Josephus, *Ant.* XI,8,2, indicates that he knew of the prohibition against marrying Samaritans for Israelites as well as for priests, and we have no record of a change in the attitude to Samaritans from the time of Hillel to that of Josephus.

[200] Ḳid. 75b; Yer. Giṭ. 43c.

[201] Yer. Ket. 27a; Yer. Giṭ. 43c (in the name of R. Elazar); Yer. Yeb. 8b (in the name of R. Ishmael). Kuthim, at the end, cites R. Ishmael that Samaritans are *gere ẓedeḳ* and their exclusion is due to mamzerut and to freeing the wedded levirate widow. However, Babli supports the report of Yerushalmi, ascribing to R. Ishmael the view that Samaritans are *gere arayot,* Ḳid. 75b, and at the same time supports the reading of R. Elazar, because R. Elazar too is supposed to have the same view (ibid.). According to these Yerushalmi texts, the marriage prohibition of Samaritans depends on the view that they are *gere arayot* and the prohibition exists, so to speak, because the child born of the union of a Samaritan and a Jewish woman will count as a mamzer. I cannot accept this interpretation, because it is unusual that a marriage should be prohibited because a mamzer *will be born.* Furthermore, this reasoning would account only for the prohibition of a Samaritan male marrying a Jewish woman, but would not account for the prohibition of a Jew marrying a Samaritan woman, where the child would

sister or sister-in-law.[202] One more explanation is offered, which would make them not doubtful mamzerim but doubtful slaves, suggesting that, mixed population as they were, they had among them also an admixture of slaves.[203]

In the next stage of development of rabbinic law, a new logic developed which operated in practically every respect to the detriment of the Samaritans, but in one respect, at least, it led to their advantage. The older law made it impossible for the Samaritan ever to be accepted by Judaism even if he followed the rabbinic teachings in full. The newer law made it possible for the Samaritan to convert to Judaism and become a full Jew. This new advantage came as a result of the added disqualifications which the law gradually imposed upon him. Already in Jabneh, R. Elazar had pronounced: "He who eats of the bread of Samaritans is as if he ate swine flesh." [204] Later on Rabban Gamaliel and his court pronounced the *sheḥiṭah* (slaughtering) of the Samaritans prohibited.[205] Then R. Me'ir decreed that their wine be prohibited. The Talmud adds in connection with this prohibition that on investigation R. Me'ir learned that they worshipped the image of a dove in their Temple on Mount Gerizim.[206] Among the last of the tannaim, it is reported that Rabbi Judah the Nasi was of the opinion that Samaritans should count as out and out gentiles.[207] To account for such an attitude, ascribed to other tannaim of his generation as well, it was said that the Samaritans were really not true converts but "lion-converts," since the fear of lions had made them accept Judaism and their conversion was

---

be a Samaritan, not a mamzer. Of course, the Yerushalmi used this casuistically for its purposes, but in reality the prohibition is based on the conception that the Samaritans themselves are mamzerim because they are children of mixed marriages.

202 Ḳid. 76a. See my interpretation of this amoraic statement in the chapter on levirate marriage, note 42.

203 Ḳid. ibid.

204 M. Sheb. 8,10.

205 Ḥullin, 5b. Rashi maintains that this R. Gamaliel was the son of Rabbi and not his grandfather. Tosafot argues the point. See Tosafot ibid. s.v. *Rabban Gamaliel.*

206 Ḥullin 6a.

207 Yer. Demai 23c; Yer. Sheḳ. 46b; Yer. Ket. 27a.

never sincere.[208] The amoraim, however, did not act upon this principle of Rabbi Judah, arguing among themselves whether the Samaritans were to be considered "genuine converts" or "lion converts," until R. Ammi and R. Assi, among the last of the Palestinian amoraim, formally decreed that they be accounted full gentiles.[209] This decree of R. Ammi and R. Assi, backed by the theory that the Samaritans were only "lion converts," while it reduced them to the position of gentiles, offered them one advantage in that it opened for them the door for proselytization. Hence Samaritans were thereafter declared eligible for conversion if they renounced loyalty to Mount Gerizim, accepted Jerusalem as the place of sanctity, and adopted the belief in resurrection.[210] Whether such conversion would entail permission for them to marry Jews is not definitely stated. Reason seems to lead to such a conclusion. Yet the Palestinian amoraim take it for granted that Samaritans even after conversion have no chance for marriage with Jews.[211] It is not impossible that the suggestion for the acceptance of Samaritans into the fold by proper conversion was intended as a halakic reform of post-talmudic times. The codes have no decision on the subject, except that they class Samaritans with gentiles, the assumption being that conversion is possible and thereafter marriage may be permitted. In fact so closely have the terms

208 The view is ascribed to R. Ishmael and doubtfully to R. Elazar, Ḳid. 75b (see note 201 above); the Talmud, B.Ḳ. 38b, withdraws a suggestion that R. Me'ir holds this view, for there are, in the mind of the amoraim, sufficient evidences that he holds the opposite view. In Yer. ibid. R. Me'ir is the opponent of Rabbi and maintains that Samaritans are like Israelites. Also the anonymous sages in M. Nid. 56b are credited with the view that Samaritans are not full Jews because they are *gere arayot*. All these are interpretations of the Mishnah on the basis of a principle developed later. So far as I know the whole concept of *gere arayot* is not found in tannaitic writings. Among the amoraim, R. Johanan is prominent in the pronouncement of the principle that the Samaritans are *gere arayot*, therefore like heathens, and explains the prohibition of marrying them on this basis. See Yer. Giṭ. 43c.

209 Ḥullin 6a.

210 End of Tractate Kuthim.

211 Yer. Giṭ. 43c, fifth line from the bottom. To R. Johanan's view that marriage with Samaritans is prohibited because they are *gere arayot*, the Talmud asks, why should not conversion be satisfactory? Evidently they stood firm by the tradition that even after conversion marriage with them is prohibited.

gentile and Samaritan been identified that one rabbinic term, *Kuthi,* covers them both. The question of Samaritan converts has not come up in centuries, but if it did so now, it may be adjudged that the final halakah would not stand in the way.

VI

Pharisaic halakah began with a thoroughly generous and liberal attitude to the sectaries, who were of Jewish birth and origin but who differed with the teachings of the Synagogue in dogma and practice. Until the days of Jabneh we hear little of any condemnation or invective against the sectaries. The Pharisees sought the power to establish their teaching and to guide Jewish life thereby, and once their official law was established, they had no desire to persecute the vanquished sects. With destruction of the Temple, however, and loss of the State, no victory over a sect was deemed complete and final, for it could still carry on its teachings and gradually undermine the authority of the pharisaic teachers. At that time, too, the new sect of Christian-Jews had come into being and they were more dangerous because they had allies among non-Jewish Christians. They not only deviated from the standard halakah but also placed themselves half within the Jewish community and half outside it. Then the rabbis felt it necessary to invoke measures of discipline against them. Their main desire was to suppress heterodoxy and to eliminate dangerous heretics from the Jewish community. It was then that the daily prayers introduced the curse upon heretics, in the twelfth section of the Eighteen Benedictions.[212] It was also then that the tannaim taught that heretics have no share in the world to come, and they specified those who deny resurrection, meaning the Sadducees, those who deny the divine authority of the Torah, probably referring to the Judeo-Christians, and the Epicureans – a general term for those who deny divine providence and retribution.[213] Sectarian antagonism in later tannaitic

[212] *Birkat ha-minim:* Cf. Ber. 28b; see Elbogen, *Der jüdische Gottesdienst,* pp. 36–39.

[213] M. San. 90a; see Yad, Teshubah, 3, 8.

times went so far as to say concerning "sectarians" that "they are lowered down [into a pit] and are not pulled out," in contradistinction to "heathens," of whom, as also of "shepherds of small cattle," it is said that "they are not pulled out but neither are they lowered down." [214]

It is hard to tell whether these tannaitic teachings represent halakah or preachment. If they record halakic principles, it is surprising to find nowhere in the Talmud any practical application of them either in civil or criminal litigation. Certainly, never in the Talmud is the inference drawn that marriage with a sectarian heretic is prohibited. The contrary is taught in the beraita: – if a thoroughly wicked man marries a woman with her understanding that he is righteous, the marriage is valid, for he may have repented.[215] Violation of religious law is not even a ground for divorce, unless it interfere with the peace of the home.[216] These anti-sectarian statements, therefore, must be taken as propaganda material against the sects, not even intended to be formulated into law. No doubt they had the effect of Jews discriminating against them in all dealings, and in marriage in particular. For that matter, such social discrimination was applied also to the ignorant and ritually careless rustic, the *'am ha-areẓ,* who was not dangerous as a sectarian. But never in talmudic time was any reflection cast on intermarriage with sectarians. As mentioned, prohibition of marriage, in the minds of talmudic rabbis, had to have biblical bases, either the barrier of gentile or of mamzer, neither of which could be charged to the sectarian heretics.

The ethical impropriety of marrying a heretic, or for that matter any wicked man or woman, is sufficiently established in rabbinic writings, but talmudic law knows of no legal restrictions against it. The law recognizes even the marriage of an apostate as fully valid. And when the geonim proposed to exclude an apostate from levirate marriage, their suc-

[214] Tos. B.M. 2, at end; 'Ab. Zar. 26b and parallels. Some readings in Tosephta omit *minim* and *mumrim.* Cf. Yad, Mamrim 3,1–2.

[215] Ḳid. 49b.

[216] JMC, pp. 212–13.

cessors overruled them, declaring him a Jew in every respect of Jewish marriage law.[217] Naturally, before the law would *approve* marriage to a heretic or renegade, it insisted that he do penance and reaffirm his loyalty to Judaism; but the door of penitence was always open to him, provided he was not under suspicion of illegitimate birth.[218]

In post-talmudic times, there was only one sect to be dealt with officially in respect to intermarriage, the Karaites. Down to the twelfth century, there were marriages between Karaites and Rabbanites, without protest from either side.[219] Maimonides in his code and Mishnah commentary does invoke against the Karaites the non-legal pronouncements of the tannaim against heretical sects, excuses them in part because they have been misguided by a tradition not of their own making,[220] but significantly omits mention of any prohibition against intermarriage, even while they retain their practices and loyalties.

Maimonides' softness toward the Karaites was not shared by a younger contemporary of his, a French tosafist, R. Samson of Sens, who being unacquainted with them and having little sympathy for their religious views, was the first to pronounce a ban on any Rabbanite to marry a Karaite. He deals specifically with the Karaite unconverted to Rabbanism. Admitting that such a marriage is valid in the law, he argues its prohibition on the ground that they are to be treated like gentiles because of the many violations of law which their teaching permits them. He hints also that they are to be considered mamzerim, for their marriages are valid but their divorces are not legal.[221]

R. Samson's ḥerem was effective either by his authority or because it reflected the antagonism which the Rabbanites at

217 See pp. 100–101 above, under subject of levirate, and note 75.

218 That is the spirit of a legal decision on the question rendered by R. Naṭronai Gaon, *Sha'are Ẓedeḳ*, 6,7, p. 24a.

219 See JMC, pp. 279–80. R. Solomon Troki reports that 'Anan had prohibited the Karaites to marry Rabbanites, (see S. Pinsker, *Liḳuṭe Ḳadmoniyot*, p. 8) but the report is not substantiated.

220 Yad, Mamrim 3,2; Mishnah Commentary of Maimonides on Ḥullin 1 and San. 11. See Responsa of Maimonides, 371.

221 The ḥerem of R. Samson is quoted in RDBZ II, 796, MABIT I,38, *Ohale Yacob*, 33, etc. *Bet Joseph* ad *Ṭur* E.H. 4 quotes it briefly.

that time already felt toward the Karaites. After this date we have no further records of Karaite-Rabbanite marriages, and while we have no evidence that such marriages did not occur, we have reason to believe that they were less frequent or perhaps unusual. R. Samson's suggestion, however, that mamzerut can be charged to the Karaites seems to have fallen on deaf ears. Karaites who accepted Rabbanite teachings had no difficulty in being admitted to the fold and marrying among the Rabbanites. The Nagid R. Abraham of Egypt, a great-grandson of Maimonides, accepted into Rabbanism a whole community of Karaites,[222] and they attained full equal standing with the Rabbanites.

But it is the nature of sectarian antagonisms that they become sharper and bitterer with the passage of time. Thus, at the close of the fifteenth century popular sentiment was in favor of a total break with the Karaites, to the extent even of imposing a ban on any one who might teach them sacred literature, philosophy, or science.[223] As part of that spirit, the question of marriage was raised to great prominence. Many famous oriental rabbis threw themselves into the controversy, such as Elijah Mizraḥi of Turkey, David b. Zimra of Egypt, Moses di Trani and Jacob Berab of Safed, Samuel b. Ḥakim ha-Levi, and later two less famous personalities, R. Jacob Castro and R. Solomon Gabison. There was no serious attempt on the part of any one of them to permit marriage with Karaites who did not accept Rabbanism. To marry an unconverted Karaite, it was evident, was to subject a Jewish woman to temptation of neglecting her own observance of rabbinic law and to put her in a position to help her husband violate the law. Less objectionable seemed to be the marriage of a Rabbanite to a Karaite woman, because the temptation there would be, on the contrary, for the woman to follow the law of her husband. R. Samuel ben Ḥakim does argue for such permission, but the counter argument is offered that karaitic law does not provide for proper ritual purity for women in menstruation, and the husband would subject himself to the danger of defilement.[224]

[222] *Kaftor wa-Ferah*, p. 70 and quoted by RDBZ ibid.

[223] Responsa of Elijah Mizraḥi, 57.

[224] Responsa of RDBZ ibid.

The main subject of the controversy, however, was whether a Karaite who was converted to Rabbanism might be admitted into marriage with a Jew; and here the suggestion of R. Samson played a most prominent part, that members of the sect might be counted as mamzerim because their marriages are valid and their divorces invalid. R. Elijah Mizraḥi [225] in a veiled manner, and R. Moses di Trani[226] and R. Solomon Gabison [227] more explicitly, account the Karaites as doubtful mamzerim and prohibit marriage with them even after conversion to Rabbanism. R. David b. Zimra [228] and R. Jacob Berab,[229] followed by R. Jacob Castro,[230] ignore the charge of mamzerut against the Karaites on the uncomplimentary basis that Karaite marriages are also invalid, because Karaites do not qualify as legally acceptable witnesses, and where there is no marriage there is no mamzerut. Hence they permit marriage to Karaites converted to Rabbanism. The matter would still remain unsettled, if not for the fact that sectarian cleavage continued to widen the breach, and for the additional fact that R. Joseph Karo and R. Moses Isserles, codifiers of Jewish law, threw the weight of their authority on the side of severity, prohibiting marriage with Karaites on the ground that they were doubtful mamzerim.[231] In the last few centuries there has been little desire on the part of Karaites to accept Rabbanism and to marry Jews. The general principle of the law as formulated in the codes, therefore, has not been challenged. But in individual cases, when they did occur, the teachers of the law were not quite as severe as the codifiers.[232]

In the heat of controversy between standard Judaism and

225 Responsa, 58.
226 Responsa, I,37.
227 *Ohale Yacob*, 33.
228 RDBZ I,73; II,796.
229 Quoted in MABIT I,37 and *Ohale Yacob*, l.c.
230 *Ohale Yacob* ibid. at end.
231 *Bet Joseph* ad *Ṭur* E.H. 4 and notes of Isserles ad E.H. 4 at end.
232 *Noda' bi-Yehudah*, I, E.H. 5. He proposes a lenient view in that particular case on consideration that the majority of the Karaites are not mamzerim, and the individual Karaite bride should be considered as belonging to the majority rather than the minority, according to the principle: *Kol deparish merubbah parish*.

any of its heretical groups, the rabbis did not hesitate often to threaten non-conformists with a ban against marrying them. Such a ban was pronounced in 1665 against the Shabbethaians,[233] and the threat was hurled at the Reform Jews at the beginning of their movement.[234] In neither case was the ban carried out effectively. The Shabbethaians, of course, are by now forgotten. The Reform Jews are probably still a problem to many devout orthodox Jews, but a halakic decision against their intermarriage surely does not exist. Sentiment on the subject is not clear. Many pious orthodox Jews would definitely oppose entering into a marriage alliance with Reformists. Some orthodox rabbis would not regard a Reform marriage ceremonial of sufficient religious sanctity and would insist on an additional orthodox rite. On the other hand, it would be unusual for a rabbi today to refuse to marry a pair, one of whom was orthodox and the other Reform. The closest we can get to an analysis of the sentiment is to say that the orthodox Jew considers the Reformist not a sectarian but as a transgressor of rabbinic law.

[233] *Torat ha-Kena'ot* 41a; *Teshubah me-Ahabah,* 1,8.
[234] See Trier, *Rabbinische Gutachten* . . . Frankfurt, 1844.

CHAPTER V

INCEST

I

THE rule of endogamy and the law of incest exert their respective forces in opposite directions. The former sets up a line beyond which marriage is prohibited; the latter marks the line within which marriage is prohibited. The former is around the tribe, the latter is around the family.

Whatever the psychological reason may be,[1] practically every primitive group has some set of rules prohibiting marriage with close kin. Such rules, constituting the law of incest, always have the severest moral sanction of the group and are most rigorously enforced, generally by death penalty. There is wide disagreement between group and group as to what constitutes incest. Even in one clan the definition is not constant, but varies and develops in the process of history. Our study of the laws of incest among the Hebrews, therefore, must first follow their historical development. This implies not merely the passage of time, but also the play of forces in historic succession. It becomes the burden, therefore, of our investigation also to uncover the forces that brought about changes in the laws of incest.

There are five main stages in the development of the Hebrew law of incest. We shall call our first the pre-deuteronomic stage; in deuteronomic legislation we find the second; the levitical code presents the third; the Talmud offers the fourth. So far as the main stream of Judaism is concerned, the matter ends with rabbinic law in which the Talmud is the source of authority. But the sectarian law of the Karaites also has its roots in the Hebrew tradition, and by no justification can it be ignored. We shall call the karaitic law of incest the fifth stage of development. Not knowing the mode

[1] See Westermarck, HHM, II, Ch. 19.

of life of the Hebrews prior to biblical records, even though we sometimes permit ourselves certain conjectures, we take the early sections of the Bible, dating about the tenth century before the Common Era, as starting point. This represents our pre-deuteronomic stage, and we may briefly characterize it in the following manner. The incestuous restrictions are at a minimum and are based on a concept of kinship which has three distinct features: tribal, predominantly maternal, and natural.

In those days the sense of tribal solidarity was so strong that it was impossible to conceive of the family as a unit independent of the tribal organization. It was a unit within the tribe; without tribal connotation, it had no meaning at all. People who belonged to two different tribal groups could not be blood relatives. We can imagine a primitive brother and sister, or father and daughter, belonging to two different tribal units. Then they had no family kinship to each other.

For various reasons, kinship on the maternal side was considered by the ancient Hebrews as by most primitive orientals closer than paternal relationship. Maternal kinship is "natural" while paternal is "legal." A mother is a mother with or without marriage, with or without legal sanction, while a father needs marriage or legal presumptions to be declared the father of his children. Taking into consideration the looser structure of the family in more remote antiquity, whether through partial promiscuity or exchange of wives or temporary unions or polyandry, it was natural that mother kinship should be given priority.[2] Second, the

[2] Talmudic law has remnants of the principle of priority of the natural over the legal in respect to kinship among non-Jews. Legal kinship, the talmudists conceive, is a fiat of the revealed law and has its application to the Jews, for whom Revelation was meant. Noahides and proselytes count kinship on their mothers' side primarily. They are permitted to marry daughters, paternal half-sisters, and paternal aunts. An exception to this metronymic rule is the law that the Noahide is prohibited to marry his stepmother, but the exception seems to be artificially derived by exegetical interpretation of a biblical verse out of its context, and in the case of the proselyte even this exception does not exist. See San. 57b–58b; Yeb. 97b; Yad, Issure Bi'ah 14,10–13. However, where legality is the main question, such as inheritance or tribal alliance, the paternal line is the dominating factor. See Ḳid. 17b and 67b.

condition of polygamy which the ancient Hebrew law permitted brought about a closer sense of kinship among the children of the same mother than among those of the same father. Finally, it is believed that the ancient Hebrews had a matriarchal system of family organization. In the biblical period, the patriarchal dominated; nevertheless, remnants of matriarchy, as to sentiment, as to habits of thought, and partially even as to the structure of the family, lingered for a considerable time through the biblical era.[3] These survivals of matriarchy were reflected in the popular feeling that relatives on the maternal side were closer than paternal kin.

Students of primitive tribal organization find among early Semites a concept that parenthood belongs to him who owns the mother of the child.[4] In other words, kinship is based upon ownership. In the sense stated above, that kinship was "tribal" and that the family was what the tribal form of organization declared it to be, this rule also applied to the ancient Hebrews. But it is not true that the ancient Hebrews recognized any sense of kinship between people not united by blood ties. To them kinship was "natural" and not the result of a "legal" fiat. Legal ties played a prominent part in later Jewish law, but in our pre-deuteronomic stage that concept had no meaning at all. Adoption was not recognized; at least it had no bearing on kinship. A woman who married into a family retained membership in her parental group and did not become part of her husband's family. In other words, she was not a relative to her husband's kin, which means to say that kinship on the basis of affinity (as against consanguinity) was not known to pre-deuteronomic Hebrew jurists.

Because of these fundamental characteristics of the legal mind of that early age, the pre-deuteronomic law prohibited only MOTHER and MATERNAL SISTER as first grade incest

[3] Evidences for the existence of a matriarchal order in pre-biblical times are offered by W. Robertson Smith in *Kinship and Marriage in Early Arabia* and by a host of other scholars. Cf. V. Aptowitzer, "Spuren des Matriarchats im jüdischen Schriftthum," in the *Hebrew Union College Annual,* IV, pp. 207–240; J. Morgenstern, "Beena Marriage in Ancient Israel and its Historical Implications," in ZAW, N.S., VI (1929), pp. 91–110; E. B. Cross, *The Hebrew Family,* Chicago, 1927.

[4] Smith and Cross, ibid.

and DAUGHTER as a lower grade of incest. Sex relations between son and mother are not specifically prohibited in the early sections of the Bible, but no other construction can be put upon this omission than that the prohibition was so fundamental that it required no legislative pronouncement and that its violation was altogether unusual. From the very earliest times, the mother was the center of kinship, for this is the essence of the metronymic system. A maternal sister is considered kin to her brother only by their common mother. Therefore it is impossible that the maternal sister be prohibited and the mother be permitted.[5] The prohibition against a maternal half-sister is implied in the statement of Abraham to Abimelek (Gen. 20.12), that Sarai was only a paternal half-sister but no maternal relative, and therefore he was permitted to take her as wife. Evidently, if she had been his maternal sister he could not have married her.[6] In the metronymic tradition mother and maternal sister are considered the closest kin and, to the earliest biblical authors, the primary cases of incest.

The daughter was not so close as either mother or sister. Again going back to the metronymic tradition, the husband is an outsider in his wife's family and a stranger to his children. The patronymic order gave recognition to the kinship between father and daughter, but metronymic habits of thought insisted on that kinship as only of secondary degree. The prohibition of contact with a daughter is implied in the story of Lot and his daughters (Gen. 19), which is apparently recorded in the Bible for the purpose of pointing out the impure origin of Ammon and Moab.[7] That this

[5] C.H. 157 prescribes death by burning for contact with mother. The Bible has no explicit prohibition, as we see it, but the Talmud (San. 58a) finds the prohibition expressed in the verse (Gen. 2.24): "Therefore shall a man leave his father and *mother*. . . ."

[6] Sigismund Rauh, *Hebräisches Familienrecht in vorprophetischer Zeit,* would interpret this biblical verse to mean that any half-sister, maternal or paternal, is permitted. The talmudic interpretation (San. 58b) is similar to ours and has sounder logic. The idea of a half-sister in which both maternal and paternal half-sisters are included is alien to the Bible. It is either a maternal sister or a paternal sister, and they are not equal in quality of kinship.

[7] See Mittlemann, *Der altisraelitische Levirat,* p. 40.

intends a condemnation of such a union cannot be denied, but the condemnation is not too severe. One has the impression that the Bible means to say that such a union would not have occurred except under the great alarm of the daughters at the destruction of Sodom, and the intoxication of the father. Nevertheless, the offspring of that union, Ammon and Moab, bear no reproach and are quite acceptable cousins to the Hebrews.[8] In Code Hammurabi (154), where incest with a mother is punished by burning, contact with a daughter is punished only by expulsion from the city. Probably the Hebrews, too, considered carnal union with a daughter incest of a lower degree.

Contact with a daughter-in-law was probably not approved by the early Hebrews, but it did not constitute incest in any sense. The daughter-in-law is twice removed from kinship with her father-in-law. First, in the metronymic tradition father and son are only secondary relatives. Second, her kinship to the family of her husband is not of blood but of affinity, which the Hebrews of the pre-deuteronomic period hardly recognized at all. No prohibition, therefore, is expressed in the early sections of the Bible against contact with a daughter-in-law. The moral disapproval of such a union, however, is reflected in the Judah-Tamar story (Gen. 38). There we have an indication that in the more remote past it was customary for the father-in-law to take in marriage the wife of his deceased son, in fulfillment of the levirate duty.[9] The Hebrews of the time of that story's writing no longer permitted father-in-law levirate and imposed the duty exclusively upon the brothers of the deceased. But Tamar, under justifiable provocation, manipulated a levirate union with her father-in-law. Judah, the Bible assures us, was innocent in the part he played; Tamar was perhaps justified in her designs; and there was no repetition of the union. The occurrence, the Bible would wish us to believe, was improper and irregular, but no scandal was involved and no

[8] See Deut. 2.9, 19 demanding peaceful relations with Ammon and Moab. The prohibition against intermarriage (Deut. 23.4–7) is based on political friction, not on impurity of origin.

[9] See Mittelmann, pp. 6–8; Koschaker, *Zum Levirat nach hethitischem Recht*, pp. 80, 90. See Assyrian Code, I,33 and Hittite Code 193.

reproach was cast upon either Judah or Tamar.[10] The levirate situation, naturally, had something to do with the sentiments connected with this incident, but the inference still holds good that there was no prohibition of incest against contact with a daughter-in-law, else a levirate act by the father-in-law, when the brother-in-law could and should have performed it, would have been recorded with more emphatic protest. For a long period, down to exilic times, there was a lack of moral revulsion against sex relations between father-in-law and daughter-in-law; and the prophet Ezekiel (22.11) raised an indignant condemnation against such moral laxity.

Logically, the father's wife should be the same kin to the son as the son's wife to the father. In other words, the step-mother should be prohibited to the same degree as the daughter-in-law. However, it is unsafe to base conclusions on this type of reasoning, for we often get the feeling that to the ancients kinship in the ascending and descending lines did not have the same quality. Nevertheless, as much information as we can find in the most ancient records of the Bible gives us the conviction that the step-mother's kinship to the family was approximately the same as that of the daughter-in-law. The difference was one in social position. There were then two kinds of step-mothers, the one who was chief wife of the father, the *gebirah,* and the secondary wife, the concubine. There was no sense of incest attached to either one, as none was attached to the daughter-in-law. But their respective positions in the family determined the admissibility or inadmissibility of marriage by the son and heir after the father's death.

The widowed *gebirah,* if she had sons, always remained the queen mother in her son's household. If she had no sons, she was at liberty to go back to her parental home,[11] or she might choose to remain in her husband's household. Suppose in either case her husband's son by another wife asked her

[10] C.H. 155 prohibits contact with a daughter-in-law, especially if the son has already had intercourse with her, but this applies only while the son lives. The Book of Jubilees partly exonerates Judah for intercourse with Tamar on the ground that the sons had not lain with her, a reflection of the distinction drawn in Code Hammurabi.

[11] See above p. 83 under subject of Levirate.

hand in marriage. She would be free to marry him, since there was no incest involved, but she would not do so, out of respect for her position as *gebirah* to the deceased patriarch. Probably the son would be considered more guilty than the wife, because he had acted disrespectfully to his father's *gebirah*.[12] A prohibition of a kind probably existed against marrying a step-mother, but it was not of the nature of incest.[13]

If the step-mother, however, was a wife of secondary order, a concubine or slave-wife, the situation was different, because her social position was different. She never had the dignity of a free wife, and if she remained in the household was under control of the heir after her husband's death. It appears that generally she went with the estate and was inherited by the deceased patriarch's successor – his oldest son.[14] There was absolutely no prohibition involved in the union between the son and his father's concubine, and Adonijah had no hesitation in asking in marriage the Shunamite girl who had been his father's consort.[15] Of Reuben and Absalom[16] it is reported that they had criminal union with their respective fathers' concubines even while their fathers were alive, and this was considered not incest but rebellion against their fathers. Even as in the case of the daughter-in-law, the sense of incest about a step-mother was not generally recognized among the Hebrews as late as the days of Ezekiel.[17]

Definite and unrestricted permission of marriage with all other members of the family group in this pre-deuteronomic period is to be assumed, and among them some that were later

[12] See C.H. 158. As against the penalty of being driven from the city for contact with a daughter (C.H. 154) an offense with a step-mother is penalized by being "driven away from his father's house." Evidently, the former case is an offense against community morality, while the latter sins against parental dignity.

[13] A form of levirate where the surviving son married the wives of his father (except his own mother) was known in the ancient Orient (Assyrian Code, I,43), but not to the Hebrews, especially since levirate among the Hebrews applied only when the deceased husband left no sons.

[14] See Chapter on Concubinage above, p. 52.

[15] I Kings, 2.17.

[16] Gen. 35.22; 49.34; II Sam. 16.20–22.

[17] Ezek. 22.10.

legislated as clear cases of incest. Thus, the paternal half-sister was permitted, as in the cases of Abraham and Sarah,[18] and Amnon and Tamar;[19] union of two sisters to one husband was permitted, as evident from the marriage of Leah and Rachel to Jacob;[20] and from the marriage of the parents of Moses we learn that a paternal aunt was permitted in union to her nephew.[21]

The law of incest grew into its second stage of development in the legislation of the Book of Deuteronomy. This book is generally dated at about the latter part of the seventh century before the common era, but it also contains some earlier documents. Among these older texts may be counted chapter twenty-seven, verses 11 to 26. This contains a series of twelve moral proclamations made by the Levites, calling down a curse upon those who would violate them, to which the congregation responded with an Amen. This "curse covenant" is of Israelitish rather than Judean origin and belongs, according to what seems to be the best judgment of scholars, to the ninth century B.C.E. Therein we have a series of incestuous prohibitions which were given full recognition by the Kingdom of Israel at the time of their promulgation, but which were slowly and gradually accepted also in Judea at about the end of the seventh and the beginning of the sixth centuries.[22] They represent to us the deuteronomic law of incest.

The concept of kinship in the deuteronomic law is the same as in pre-deuteronomic times, so far as consanguinity is concerned. No persons could be considered blood relatives unless they belonged to the same family. In other words, kinship was still tribal. But the tribal form of family organization underwent a change in deuteronomic time. The patronymic family became so dominant that people began

[18] Gen. 20.12.

[19] II Sam. 13.13.

[20] Gen. 29.27. Permission also implied in Ezek. 23.2. Evidently there was no prohibition until Leviticus.

[21] Ex. 6.20; Num. 26.59.

[22] See discussion of the subject and conclusions by Jacob Mittelmann, *Der altisraelitische Levirat,* pp. 41–45, which I consider logical and feel justified in following.

to recognize relatives on the paternal side as equal to similar kinfolk on the mother's side. This brought about the new legislation in Deuteronomy that a PATERNAL HALF-SISTER was prohibited like a maternal half-sister.[23] On the basis of logic alone, though unsupported by direct evidence, we have reason to believe that by this new principle, equalizing maternal and paternal relatives, the ban against contact with a DAUGHTER, which in the former stage was of a secondary degree, was raised in deuteronomic time to a primary incestuous prohibition. For if maternal and paternal relatives are equal, then the father is to the daughter what the mother is to the son.[24] However, beyond application of this principle, the deuteronomic legislator did not attempt to enlarge this circle of incestuous consanguinity but left it as he had found it, including only parents and children, brothers and sisters.

He did, however, make a revolutionary contribution to the law of incest by opening up a line of kinship based upon marriage, where there was no blood relationship, thus establishing the principle of incestuous degrees of *affinity*. By the previous concept of kinship we knew only of "natural" ties; now we also have "legal" ties. The application of this principle yields the deuteronomic legislator two new cases of incest, MOTHER-IN-LAW and STEP-MOTHER;[25] that is, the par-

[23] Deut. 28.22.

[24] The omission of daughter as a case of incest is constant in the Bible, pre-deuteronomic, deuteronomic, Ezekiel, and Leviticus. In Ezekiel and Leviticus the omission cannot mean that contact with a daughter was not considered incest, for in the former a daughter-in-law is prohibited and in the latter a daughter's daughter (grand-daughter), neither of which prohibitions is thinkable without assumption of prohibition against a daughter. In Deuteronomy we have no such proof, except the logic that if a sister, "the daughter of thy father," is prohibited to the son, she is surely prohibited to the father.

[25] Step-mother is mentioned in Deut. 28.20; mother-in-law in Deut. 28.23. The question we may here raise is, whether the prohibition applies also against the step-mother after the father's death or against the mother-in-law after the wife's death. In case of the step-mother, it seems reasonable to assume that she was prohibited to the son even after the father's death, else it would be a question of adultery, outside of incest. Then, again, we have reason to believe that this prohibition meant to stop the earlier custom of the son inheriting his father's secondary wives; evidently it prohibited the step-mother after the father's death. We are less certain in the case of a mother-in-law in this deuteronomic period. Logic places the two cases in one category.

ent of a spouse and the spouse of a parent, or the natural kin of a legal relative and the legal kin of a natural relative. Apparently, though, this legal-natural or natural-legal combination is very much restricted in its application. It applies only in the ascending line, i.e., father's wife or wife's mother, and even in that single line it takes in only one link and not more than one, for the prohibition does not extend to the grandfather's wife or to the wife's grandmother. In the lateral line it does not apply at all; therefore, a brother's wife or a wife's sister is not prohibited. Nor is the descending line included in this principle of kinship by affinity, and the deuteronomic code does not mention the daughter-in-law or the wife's daughter among incestuous prohibitions. We have seen above that even in pre-deuteronomic days there was a sense of sin about contact with a daughter-in-law, which, however, did not rise to the level of incest. To the deuteronomic legislator this sense must have been sharpened, for he had gone beyond his predecessors with two pertinent principles, the equality of kinship between maternal and paternal relatives and kinship by affinity, both of which make for closer kinship between daughter-in-law and father-in-law. But sinful contact as he may have felt this to be, he still did not consider it incest of the first order, or he failed to tell us so.

In Judea, the new principles and cases of incest introduced by the "curse covenant" were not immediately accepted. The people of the South remained under influence of the metronymic system, or at least of its memory, for a much longer period than the Hebrews of the Northern Kingdom. Down to the time of Ezekiel, two and a half centuries later than the "curse covenant," the people in the tradition of Judea refused to recognize paternal relatives as equal to maternal. They permitted themselves contact with a step-mother, with a daughter-in-law, and with a paternal half-sister, according to the complaint of the prophet.[26] Nevertheless, despite violations, the deuteronomic law of the North gradually became also the law of the South. The prohibition against a step-mother was recognized in Judea toward the end of the

[26] Ezek. 22.10–11.

seventh century.[27] The paternal sister was acknowledged to be an incestuous kin in the early part of the sixth.[28] The mother-in-law is lost in our records of that period, and we do not know whether the Judeans considered her as a case of incest or not.[29] One definite addition to the list was made in Judea soon after the Deportation — the DAUGHTER-IN-LAW.[30] As seen above, a certain social restriction against contact with a daughter-in-law existed even in pre-deuteronomic times; then that restriction was raised to the level of a semi-incestuous prohibition in earlier deuteronomic legislation; finally, by the time of Ezekiel, it was recognized as a primary case of incest.

The fullest list of incestuous prohibitions and the final one for the biblical period is formulated in the levitical code. In implicit or explicit form, it ratifies the incestuous prohibitions of earlier legislation, namely, mother,[31] maternal or paternal sister,[32] step-mother,[33] mother-in-law,[34] daughter,[35] and daughter-in-law.[36] It adds a number of others, not known before, based upon new legal principles.

One of these is simply the direct extension of the family circle, thus giving the basis of incestuous kinship a wider application. The levitical legislator rules that not only parents and children but also grandparents and grandchildren are included in the circle of kinship; and not only brothers and sisters but also aunts and nephews. Another principle

[27] Deut. 23.1.

[28] Ezek. 22.11.

[29] Ezekiel does not mention the mother-in-law among the incestuous cases, but this proves nothing. I have a suspicion, however, that the word *zimmah* in the last part of verse 9 specifically denotes or at least includes mother-in-law. Cf. Lev. 18.17 and 20.14.

[30] Ezek. ibid.

[31] Lev. 18.7.

[32] Lev. 18.9.

[33] Lev. 18.8 and 20.11.

[34] Lev. 18.18 and 20.14.

[35] There is no specific prohibition in Leviticus against a daughter but the prohibition is not to be doubted, since a daughter's daughter is specifically prohibited, Lev. 18.17. Interesting is the view of R. Ile'a (San. 76a) that the prohibition of a daughter is expressed in Lev. 19.29 — "Profane not thy daughter to make her a harlot."

[36] Lev. 18.15 and 20.12.

is that by virtue of close kinship existing between two males, such as brother and brother or uncle and nephew, one of the males and the wife of the other are considered as belonging to the circle of prohibited degrees. That is, since male and male cannot be said to be prohibited to each other on the basis of incest, that prohibition goes over to the wife of either one. And a third principle evident in the levitical code is a definition of kinship based upon blood relationship that is entirely independent of family organization in the tribal sense. Whether that kinship be of the strictly natural or the strictly legal or the combination of legal-natural, the tribal concept of kinship has only the slightest bearing on the law of incest. The reality of "flesh kinship" cannot be disturbed by tribal lines of family organization. To these three principles, legal in nature and forming the basis of the levitical extension of the rule of incest, we may add two sociological principles that belong to the mental equipment of that age, and which influenced the legislator's thinking on the subject. First, in the time of Leviticus the patronymic system had already long superseded the older metronymic family organization; hence the legislator tends to count kinship closer on the paternal than on the maternal side. Second, kinship in the descending line was considered closer than in the ascending. One is closer to one's son than to one's father. Proof is that the son is heir prior to the father. The lateral line is the weakest of all. The order of succession proves this too. Our levitical legislator had these distinctions in mind in formulating the code of incest, accounting the descending line first, the ascending line next, and the lateral line last in the order of proximity of kinship. By a combination of these legal and sociological principles, he arrived at a number of new cases of incest, which we shall now consider in detail.

By extending the circle of incestuous kinship, he added to the list of prohibitions the GRANDDAUGHTER,[87] as extension of prohibition of the daughter. By another process of logic – which we shall examine later – he arrived at prohibition of a Step-daughter; and as extension of that prohibition he de-

[87] Lev. 18.10.

clared the STEP-GRANDDAUGHTER also prohibited under the law of incest.[38] The legislator, apparently, did not wish to be too radical in employing this new device of extension, and therefore applied it only in the highest direction of kinship, the descending line, and not in the ascending nor lateral directions. Therefore the grandmother is not prohibited even though the mother is, and the wife's grandmother is not prohibited even though the wife's mother is. The lateral line ends with the sister and brother and there is no extension to their children.

The second principle of the levitical legislator may be considered as an exegetical derivation from a certain phrase of the deuteronomic code. There we have this prohibition of a step-mother: "Cursed be he who lies with his father's wife, for he hath uncovered the skirt of his father."[39] Our levitical author understood that lying with a father's wife was a violation of the father's sexual privacy; almost as if he were lying with the father. That is to say, since the father is within the circle of incestuous kinship, and is male, the incestuous prohibition goes over to his wife. This principle the levitical legislator generalized for all cases where the male is within the degree of incestuous kinship. He believes that prohibition of a daughter-in-law is due to the same principle, that contact with the son's wife is almost equal to contact with the son.[40] On that basis he prohibits contact with the BROTHER'S WIFE,[41] since the brother is within the incestuous degree of kinship. By the third rule, which we shall consider presently, he added the prohibition of father's sister. This means that father's brother is within the range of incestuous kinship. Hence it follows that FATHER'S BROTHER'S WIFE[42] be prohibited under the rule of incest. The same logic may well apply to mother's brother's wife, yet

[38] Lev. 18.17.

[39] Deut. 28.20. Lev. 18.8 retains the same moral motive by the phrase "It is thy father's nakedness." See Lev. 20.11.

[40] Lev. 18.15.

[41] Lev. 18.16 and 20.21 — "He has uncovered the nakedness of his brother."

[42] Lev. 18.14; 20.20. — "He has uncovered the nakedness of his uncle." A beraita (San. 54a) teaches that contact between son and father or nephew and uncle is not only a case of sodomy but also of incest. This view bears out our thesis.

she is not proscribed by the levitical code, because the legislator thinks of paternal relatives as closer than maternal kin, according to the patronymic system dominant in his day, and therefore thus limits application of his new principle.[43]

Further additions to the list are introduced on the basis of a third principle. Whereas blood ties were secondary to tribal concepts of kinship in the earlier days, our author declares "flesh kinship" (*she'er basar*) to be primary in the whole concept of incest and independent of family organization. He considers this legal principle so important that he heads his code with the words: "No one shall approach unto any that be a kin of flesh to him." [44] In reaffirming the prohibition of a half-sister, maternal or paternal, he adds the emphatic expression, "whether born at home or born abroad"; [45] as though to say that the system of family organization is of no ultimate importance. And yet he goes on to emphasize this point further in the next verse, which reads: "The nakedness of the daughter of thy father's wife born of thy father, she is thy sister; thou shalt not uncover her nakedness." [46] We wonder why another verse to prohibit a half-sister, and why is she called "the daughter of thy father's wife born of thy father?" Our answer is that here the legislator finds a case of a half-sister who distinctly belongs to an-

[43] Further on this subject on p. 236 and note 50.

[44] Lev. 18.6. The term *she'er* for kinship is not found in earlier texts. In post-exilic Hebrew it means kin not necessarily in the family circle. When in the family circle, he is called *she'ero mimishpaḥto* or *she'er besaro mimishpaḥto* (Lev. 25.49). Next of kin who is also of the same family circle is described as *she'ero ha-ḳarob elav mimishpaḥto* (Num. 27.11).

[45] Lev. 18.9. "Born abroad" definitely means born outside the family (see Judg. 12.9 and Deut. 25.5); "born at home" means born in the family (see Gen. 17.27, etc.). According to some exegetical commentators, the maternal sister is called "born abroad" and the paternal sister "born at home" (see *Keter Torah* a.l.c.). Naḥmanides (a.l.c.) takes born abroad or born at home to refer to the maternal sister, and to mean born in wedlock or out of wedlock. I find Ibn Ezra's interpretation more acceptable, that it refers to either maternal sister or paternal sister and the expression born abroad or born at home (like Naḥmanides' interpretation) means born in wedlock or out of wedlock. It refers, in other words, to a sister who may be normally in the family or to a sister that claims the paternity of her father by legal rules or blood ties but has not been counted in the family.

[46] Lev. 18.11.

other family group, yet is a sister by the principle of "flesh kinship." She is not merely "born abroad" and admitted into the family, as may be the status of a girl born out of wedlock. She is the child of a metronymic marriage; her mother is the wife of her father; yet she is not her father's daughter, according to the system of family organization. She is technically "the daughter of thy father's wife born of thy father," belonging to her mother and counting in her mother's family. But by the rule of "flesh kinship" she is also prohibited as a sister.[47]

This principle of "flesh kinship" extends the line of proscribed marriages to persons outside the immediate family circle who are next of kin to members of the immediate family. FATHER'S SISTER and MOTHER'S SISTER are therefore prohibited, since they are next of kin to father or mother respectively.[48] And by a slight peripheral extension of the same principle, and assuming that the kinship of affinity between husband and wife is real, the code adds WIFE'S DAUGHTER and WIFE'S SISTER together with the wife's mother (previously prohibited), because they are next of kin to the wife.[49]

To summarize the proscribed marriages contained in the levitical code, some of which are older and some newer legislation:

I. In the ascending line, through the mother:
1. Mother and (laterally) 2. Mother's sister.

II. In the ascending line, through the father:
3. Father's wife and (laterally) 4. Father's sister

[47] Of course, one may argue that even so nothing new is added by this verse that was not known from the previous verse, for certainly maternal brother and sister belong to two different families in a patronymic system, yet they are prohibited. But to my mind this verse adds the case of paternal brother and sister belonging to two different families. One cannot be inferred from the other, because paternal kinship depends more on legal concepts than maternal kinship.

[48] Lev. 18.12, 13; designated as *she'er* of father or mother, and therein is the source of the prohibition.

[49] Wife's daughter and wife's mother, Lev. 18.17; wife's sister, Lev. 18.18. Mother and daughter are designated as *she'er* to wife; no such designation is given for the sister. The prohibition of a wife's sister is the only explicit exception in the list of incestuous cases in that she is prohibited only during the wife's lifetime, not after her death.

and (laterally by marriage) 5. Father's sister-in-law, i.e., father's brother's wife.

III. In the descending line, through the daughter:
6. Daughter, 7. Daughter's daughter.

IV. In the descending line, through the son:
8. Son's wife, 9. Son's daughter.

V. In the lateral line, through the sister:
10. Sister or half-sister.

VI. In the lateral line, through the brother:
11. Brother's wife (without levirate duty).

VII. In the line of affinity, through the wife:
12. Wife's mother, 13. Wife's daughter, 14. Wife's sister (during lifetime of the wife), 15. Wife's granddaughter.

A graphic summary of the levitical code of incest may be formulated in this wise. Proscribed degrees of kinship are: in the ascending line one step upward (mother and father's wife) and one step horizontally (maternal and paternal aunts and paternal aunt-by-marriage); in the descending line two steps downward (daughter and granddaughter); in the lateral line one step horizontally (sister and brother's wife); through the wife one step upward (wife's mother), two steps downward (wife's daughter or granddaughter), and one step horizontally (wife's sister).

The prohibition is imposed on the man. Not that the woman is free of guilt in an incestuous contact, but that the Torah addresses itself to the man, especially in matters of marriage, for it is the man who marries the woman. The direction of the prohibited degrees of kinship, therefore, always starts with the man. An uncle is to his niece what an aunt is to her nephew, but since we count from the man the directions are different. The uncle counts in a lateral direction, for his niece is next of kin to his brother or sister, and the lateral direction is weakest. But the nephew counts in the upward direction, his aunt being next of kin to his father or mother, and the ascending direction is stronger. Hence an aunt is prohibited but a niece is not. Likewise, a grandfather is to his granddaughter what the grandmother is to her grandson. However, counting from the male, the grandfather counts in the descending line of kinship while the grandson counts in the ascending direction; and we have already mentioned that relatives in the descending line are closer than those in the ascending line. Hence granddaughter is prohibited but grandmother is permitted. The same is true of the wife's relatives. Wife's granddaughter, who is in the descending line, is prohibited; but wife's grandmother, who belongs to the ascending line, is permitted.

Maternal relatives and paternal relatives are treated by the levitical legislator as equal in the matter of incestuous prohibitions. There is only one exception, that of an aunt by marriage; the wife of the father's brother is prohibited, while the wife of the mother's brother is permitted. Here the patronymic bias of the legislator comes to the surface. He could not rule out maternal relatives from the circle of incestuous degrees of kinship, but this case, the aunt by marriage, was most distantly removed from the center of the circle. There are three weaknesses in her kinship to her nephew: she is a kin only by marriage; her nearest relative, her husband, belongs to the weakest line of kinship, the lateral line; he in turn is next of kin to the father or to the mother, who belongs to the next of the weakest line, the ascending line of kinship. To have prohibited an aunt by marriage at all was an innovation of the levitical legislator and was based definitely on the well rooted tradition of the patronymic family that the *dod*, paternal uncle, was regarded as the "elder" of the family, vested with great authority and held in affectionate esteem. He was known as *dod* because he was the "beloved" *per se*.[50] It is therefore because of the distinctive position of the *dod* that the incestuous pro-

[50] In later Hebrew any uncle is a *dod*, but in the technical language of Leviticus it means only a paternal uncle, and his wife alone is *dodah*. He had special rights in the family, such as in the matter of succession (Num. 27.9–10) or as "redeemer" (Lev. 25.49). His son, designated as *ben dod* is the first claimant to the hand of the niece, and for this reason so many cousin marriages are recorded in the Bible (Gen. 28.9; Num. 36.11; Josh. 15.17). From Jubilees (4.15; 19.24) and Tobit (4.15) we learn that such marriages were considered highly desirable. This position of the paternal uncle in a patronymic system is held by the maternal uncle in a metronymic system; he is the "*wali*" of the Arabs, with unusual authority in the family.

hibition was extended to his wife. In a patronymic family, which was the average family in the time of Leviticus, the maternal uncle held no such position; therefore the maternal uncle's wife was not prohibited.

The biblical law of incest as we have presented it here leaves a few questions in our mind for which we should seek authoritative answers. In the case of a sister, the Bible specifies that the prohibition applies also to a half-sister, maternal or paternal. Can it be said also that the wife of a half-brother, maternal or paternal, is prohibited like the wife of a full brother? Is that true also of an aunt by marriage who is the wife of father's half-brother, or of an aunt who is father's or mother's half-sister? We can go into deeper questions. Does a mother count as mother to the child born out of wedlock; does the father count as a father; how do we rate brothers and sisters and uncles and aunts in such cases? When we consider the category of incest based on marriage, we have more questions. Does the prohibition continue even after the marriage is dissolved? That question may be raised in connection with a mother-in-law, a step-daughter, a step-granddaughter, a wife's sister, a brother's wife, a father's wife, a paternal uncle's wife. Then again, we may ask what constitutes marriage in the calculation of incestuous kinship; is it the biblical betrothal or actual living together as husband and wife? We should also wish to know the penalty for various cases of incest. The Bible indicates the punishment of some and not of others. Finally, it interests us to learn the status of a child born of an incestuous union.

For our answers we shall have to draw upon post-biblical sources. These, it is true, will not tell us what the biblical authors themselves had in mind, but they will offer enlightenment on how later authoritative teachers understood the biblical law of incest.

There seems to be no doubt that prohibition of a mother includes the case where the child is born out of wedlock or in adultery, and as far as we know no one ever doubted it. The Bible itself offers proof, for if a mother was prohibited only when married to the father, she would be prohibited not only as mother but also as father's wife.[51] From this argument follows also the conclusion that a mother is prohibited after the death of the father as during his life; else there would be a prohibition of adultery even were it not incest.[52] The penalty for criminal contact with a mother is not given in any specific manner in the Bible itself. The levitical code makes the general statement for all incestuous prohibitions: "For whosoever shall do any of these abominations, even the souls that do them shall be cut off from among their people." [53] To the legislator this meant ostracism from the community, and the inference would, therefore, be that no severer penalty was contemplated. But this conclusion seems to be faulty. We must assume with the rabbis [54] that in the list of incestuous prohibitions some were meant to be penalized by death, as step-mother, mother-in-law, and daughter-in-law, for which the capital penalty is prescribed in the twentieth chapter of Leviticus. Therefore we reason that the levitical legislator did have in mind a death penalty for offence with a mother, even though he did not state it explicitly; for it is illogical to assume that he would consider contact with a step-mother a capital crime and treat incest with a mother as a lesser crime. Nevertheless, the kind of capital punishment for incestuous relations with a mother cannot be inferred from the Bible itself. The rabbis, however, by their hermeneutic method, infer from verbal indications in the Bible that the death penalty is stoning.[55]

That a mother counts as mother under all circumstances can be said with greater certainty than that a daughter

[51] Sifra, ed. Weiss 92a–b; M. San. 53a; Gemara ibid. 53b–54a. The decision of the law is that contact with a mother who is also the wife of the father entails a double crime of incest. Yad, Issure Bi'ah 2,2.

[52] See *Leḥem Mishneh* ad Yad, ibid.

[53] Lev. 18.27.

[54] To the rabbis the penalty of *karet* is basic in all incestuous prohibitions. Where there is no death penalty, *karet* alone is applied. We shall see the operation of this rule in such instances in connection with prohibition of a sister. Where there is a death penalty, *karet* applies, if for technical reasons court action cannot be taken against the offender. M. Ker. 2a; Yad, Issure Bi'ah 1,1–2.

[55] Sifra 92b; San. 53–54.

is a daughter in respect to incest no matter what be the condition of her birth or her status in the family. Possibly a natural child counted as a stranger to the father, because the child was not reckoned in the father's family. The Bible itself gives us no information on this subject, and in fact altogether omits mention of the prohibition of a daughter. We may argue, though, that since the Bible states specifically that a sister is prohibited regardless of her legal status in the family, the daughter too is prohibited "whether born at home or born abroad." This is the view of the talmudists; [56] although they do indicate that there was a sectarian teaching which declared a daughter born out of wedlock as not prohibited to her father under the head of incest.[57] However, rabbinic law admits that a daughter born of a gentile or slave mother by a Jewish father, being accounted gentile or slave according to the status of her mother, is not at all recognized by the law as her father's daughter, and the law of incest does not apply to her.[58] But even this legal artificiality was somewhat amended, for later authorities declared contact between a father and his daughter by a gentile or slave woman rabbinically prohibited, even though it was not biblical incest.[59]

The penalty for incest with a daughter is not given in the Bible, since the prohibition itself is not explicitly stated. Code Hammurabi (154) commands expulsion of the father; the Hittite code (189) demands capital punishment. The Book of Jubilees (16.9) interprets the utter destruction of the family of Lot as divine retribution for the sin committed by Lot in lying with his daughters. The rabbis rule, as a result of their hermeneutics, that incest with a daughter is punishable by burning both offenders to death.[60] Let us add that incest with a granddaughter has the same legal char-

[56] San. 76a; Yeb. 97a. In case of a legitimate daughter, there are two violations, as daughter and as wife's daughter. See Yad, Issure Bi'ah 2,6.

[57] San. 87b. See Samuel Bialoblocki, *Materialien zum islamischen und jüdischen Eherecht,* p. 38; see also note 42 in the chapter on Levirate.

[58] M. Yeb. 22a; Gemara, ibid. 22b–23a.

[59] See note of Isserles ad E.H. 15,10. The note deals with a sister but applies equally to a daughter.

[60] M. San. 75a; Gemara, ibid. 76a.

acter as offence with a daughter, both as to the nature of the crime and the penalty required; for not only are both crimes logically equal but, as a matter of fact, it is the crime of incest with a granddaughter that is specifically stated in the Bible and the case of a daughter is merely implied by inference.

The sister is equal to the daughter in respect to the legal definition of the crime. That the prohibition against contact with a sister exists whether the sister belongs to the family or not is sufficiently emphasized in the Bible itself. Yet it may be assumed that the same sectarians who permitted contact with a natural daughter also considered a sister as not incestuously prohibited, if she was born out of wedlock and was only a paternal half-sister.[61] The rabbis noted that Leviticus has two verses prohibiting a sister, even a half-sister, one (v. 9) calling her "father's daughter," the other (v. 11) designating her as "the daughter of thy father's wife born of thy father." They believe, therefore, that the former verse means to specify a sister born out of wedlock, while the second refers distinctly to one whose mother is "thy father's wife," that is, legally married to him.[62] Thus they assume definite biblical proof that a sister born out of wedlock counts as a full legal sister in respect to incest. However, here as in the case of a daughter the rabbis agree that a sister, born of the father by a gentile or slave woman, is legally not a sister, and contact with her is not incest but bears a rabbinic prohibition.[63]

The penalty for incest with a sister is given in Leviticus (20.17) in the following verse: ". . . they shall be cut off in

[61] There seems to be no possibility of permitting a maternal half-sister, no matter what the circumstance of her birth. But in respect to a paternal half-sister these sectaries may have considered her permissible, assuming that the phrase "born at home or born abroad" means only to indicate whether maternal or paternal, but in either case only if there was legitimate marriage, and the sister is legitimately either a maternal or paternal sister.

[62] Yeb. 22b. A legitimate sister who is both a "sister" and the "daughter of the father's wife" bears a double prohibition, according to the sages, but only one prohibition according to R. Jose b. Judah. The significance of a double prohibition consists in the fact that if violated unknowingly two sacrifices must be offered to atone for the two transgressions.

[63] E.H. 15,10.

the sight of the children of their people," which the rabbis call the penalty of *karet*. The literal statement in the Bible creates the impression that it proposes a public ceremony of ostracism from the family estate or from the community. To the rabbis, *karet* means something else, something vaguely technical in which there is a combination of divine vengeance and human penalty. In severity it belongs to the capital crimes and is distinguished from the ordinary death penalty merely by the contrast that one is "execution by man," the other "execution by Heaven." And Heaven carries out its judgment by dooming the offender to childlessness, to sudden death, or to premature death, say at the age of fifty.[64] The human court only imposes the penalty of flagellation, if the crime was committed knowingly, or the duty of offering a sin-offering on the altar, if committed unwittingly.[65]

The levitical prohibition against a father's or mother's sister is not stated in the Bible in such a way as to permit the conclusion that even a father's or mother's half-sister is also prohibited.[66] But the rabbis maintain that even if she be half-sister, maternal or paternal, to father or mother she is included in the prohibition of an aunt. However, an aunt by marriage, that is, the wife of an uncle, is prohibited only if she is the wife of father's paternal brother; mother's brother or father's maternal half-brother is an uncle of a more distant grade, and while his wife is prohibited by later rabbinic enactment, she is not biblically prohibited as incest.[67] The penalty for contact with an aunt, where there is a biblical incestuous prohibition, is stated in the Bible in moral rather than in legal terms: "they shall bear their guilt, they shall die childless." The rabbis understood by this expression the penalty of *karet*, and so far as jurisdiction of the human court is concerned it means only the penalty of flagellation.[68]

In respect to the incestuous prohibitions based not on consanguinity but on affinity, we have before us the first question: Is kinship established by betrothal alone or only by

64 M. Ḳ. 28a; Yer. Bik. 64c.
65 M. Ker. 2a; Mak. 13b.
66 Yeb. 54b.
67 Yeb. ibid.
68 M. Mak. 13a.

betrothal plus nuptials? This query arises in cases where kinship is based on one's own marriage, as in wife's mother, sister, daughter, or granddaughter, as well as in cases where the marriage of a relative is the basis for the extension of kinship, such as a father's wife, son's wife, brother's wife, paternal uncle's wife. Our inclination would be to say that since the Bible calls the betrothed a "wife" and declares her capable of "adultery,"[69] the betrothed is also equal to the wedded wife in respect to the law of incest. But on closer examination such a conclusion is not warranted, for there is a fundamental difference between adultery and incest. Adultery is based on the violation of marriage vows, similar in character to theft of private property; and marriage vows or property rights have their source in the marriage contract, — in other words, betrothal. Incest is rooted in the sense of revulsion to sex relations among kin, and the Bible refers to the sense of privacy and shame in the words "uncovering the nakedness"; hence it is not illogical to suppose that unless the kinship of affinity is established by actual sex relations, not by mere contract, there is no incest.

In pre-biblical times Hammurabi drew that distinction when he ruled in his Code (155–6) that a father-in-law lying with his daughter-in-law commits a capital offense only if the son has known her before; otherwise his offense is minor. This exact sentiment is again expressed in the Book of Jubilees (41.27) wherein the act of Judah in lying with his daughter-in-law, Tamar, is partly exonerated because his sons had not previously had marital relations with her. Also the Samaritans, probably at about the first century of the common era, seemed to have conceived the idea that betrothal was not sufficient to establish a basis for incestuous prohibition. For, as previously mentioned, this was the basis

[69] Deut. 22.24. Dr. Samuel Belkin, *Philo and the Oral Law*, pp. 244 f, believes that even in respect to adultery the Alexandrian Jews did not recognize betrothal as equal to nuptials, because this was the sentiment of the people under the influence of Greek and Roman law. This would be rather surprising, since it is directly contrary to the Bible. The insertion into the Alexandrian ketubah of the phrase "when thou comest into my house shalt thou be my wife according to the law of Moses and Israel" (Tos. Ket. 4,9) was not meant to justify unfaithfulness after betrothal, as Belkin believes, but to shift the ketubah obligations from betrothal to nuptials. See JMC, p. 15.

for their ruling that levirate marriage applied only to the betrothed, not to the wedded.[70] This distinction between betrothed and wedded in respect to incest was also maintained by Roman and Greek law, featured in the law of the early Arabs, and accepted into the law of the early Karaites.[71]

As the pharisaic teachers contested the Samaritan distinction between the betrothed and the wedded in respect to levirate, they established the principle that the betrothed and wedded are alike in respect to all laws of incest.[72] Therefore step-mother, sister-in-law, daughter-in-law, and aunt by marriage are incestuously prohibited from the moment they are *betrothed* to father, brother, son, or uncle respectively; likewise, mother-in-law, sister-in-law, step-daughter, and step-granddaughter become prohibited as incestuous from the moment a person has betrothed his wife, even though nuptials have not been solemnized.[73] It cannot be said that the rabbis were wholly consistent in that position, for there are still some survivals even in talmudic law of a distinction between the betrothed and the wedded as regards questions of incest. But the rabbis considered these instances as exceptions, that is, *gezerot* made necessary for the sake of avoiding errors or misinterpretations.[74] The general rule remained firm and fixed that the betrothed and the wedded were alike in the

[70] See the chapter on Levirate, above, pp. 91–92 and notes.

[71] See notes 40 and 241 on Levirate, above.

[72] M. San. 53a.

[73] See Yad, Issure Bi'ah 2,1, 7.

[74] If the levirate widow is a sister to the levir's wedded wife there is no levirate situation at all because she is incestuously prohibited to the levir. But if she is a sister to the levir's *betrothed* wife, before nuptials, the law, according to the Hillelites, requires ḥaliẓah for the widow. M. Yeb. 29a, 41a. We find a similar distinction in the following case. If the husband marry the sister of his wedded wife, the marriage is not valid because it is incestuously prohibited. But if he marries the sister of his betrothed wife, before nuptials, it is valid to the extent of requiring a divorce, according to amoraic interpretation of the view of R. Akiba. See Yeb. 94b and Yad, Gerushin 10,10. Also the Tosafists (Yeb. 97a, s.v. *'Arayot* and Yeb. 3a, top) sometimes seem to fall back upon this old distinction between nuptials and betrothal in the law of incest and seek special proof for the law of incest in the case of the betrothed. *Sha'ar ha-Melek* (*Ḥuppat Ḥatanim*), Ishut 10,5 infers from Tosafot above that the groom, after betrothal to his bride, commits no incest, if he has sex relations with the mother or daughter of his betrothed. The inference, however, is faulty, as is correctly analyzed by *Pitḥe Teshubah,* E.H. 15.5.

matter of incest. The law, however, makes it clear that only legal marriage establishes kinship of affinity, but that there is no kinship between a man and a woman who have marital relations without legal marriage. A father and a son, therefore, who visit the same prostitute do not violate any law of incest.[75] Likewise, there is no incestuous prohibition against marrying a sister of a woman with whom one has had sex relations without marriage, although the law considers it contrary to public policy and prohibits it rabbinically.

We must answer another question in regard to these incestuous prohibitions based on marriage. Does the prohibition continue when the marriage is dissolved? In respect to prohibitions based on the marriage of a kin, father, brother, son, or paternal uncle, we should judge on the evidence from the Bible itself that the prohibition extended to their wives even after their death or even after the marriage was dissolved by divorce, for in their married state the prohibition is one of adultery outside of incest.[76] Thus was the biblical law understood by non-rabbinical teachers[77] as well as by the rabbis of the Talmud.[78]

[75] Amos 2.7 condemns such practice but it was not accepted in the halakah; nor was the view of R. Judah accepted, prohibiting to the son the unmarried consort of his father. See Yeb. 97a.

[76] See note 25 above. We should recall also that the prohibition against step-mother and daughter-in-law came as a reaction to the older practice of levirate by the father or by the son of the deceased, which means that the prohibition continued after death of the husband. More direct evidence is the sentiment of Judah in putting away Tamar after discovering her identity.

[77] For step-mother see Jubilees 33.15. Albeck, *Das Buch der Jubiläen und die Halacha*, p. 29, derives from this verse that the author did not consider the step-mother, after the father's death, a case of incest. The text, however, does not warrant that inference. Philo, *Spec. Leg.* III, 3,20, states definitely that a step-mother is prohibited by the Bible even after the father's death.

For daughter-in-law the inference is clear from the Bible itself that she is prohibited even after the son's death, and Jubilees 41.23 takes this inference for granted. Philo, *Spec. Leg.* III, 5,26, speaks of any woman "who *has been* the wife to an uncle or son or brother." (Cohn's translation reads: "*mit der ehemaligen Gattin.*"). He teaches, therefore, that in the cases of incest here considered the prohibition continues even after the marriage is dissolved.

[78] M. San. 53a; Derek Ereẓ, 1. That this is an early rabbinic interpretation may be inferred from the fact that the discussion between the Shammaites and the Hillelites on the question of *ẓarat ha-bat* is based on the concept that the widowed sister-in-law, where there is no levirate duty, is incestuously prohibited to the surviving brother-in-law. See Yad, Issure Bi'ah 2,1.

In the group of cases of incest based on one's own marriage, mother-in-law, step-daughter, step-granddaughter, and wife's sister, we are less certain from internal biblical evidence that the prohibition continues even after the marriage to his wife is dissolved by divorce or by her death. The Bible itself states in the prohibition of a wife's sister that it continues only as long as the wife is alive. This particular ruling only in one case would lead us to the inference that the other incestuous prohibitions continue even after the wife's death. Philo confirms this inference;[79] so does the Talmud.[80] The halakah, thus, concludes that all the relatives of a wife within the proscribed degree of kinship are prohibited even after the wife's death or even after divorce except the wife's sister, who is incestuously prohibited as long as the wife is alive, even if she be divorced, but is permitted after the wife's death.[81]

In the "affinity" group of incest, we have three cases, father's brother's wife, brother's wife, and wife's sister, concerning which we must determine whether the term brother or sister implies full brother or full sister, or whether it includes also half-brother and half-sister, maternal or paternal. We have seen that in all consanguineous kinships a half-brother or half-sister is equal to a full brother or a full sister in respect to incest. The rabbis of the Talmud consistently carry over this principle to those cases of incest that are based on affinity. In other words, a half-brother's wife or a wife's

[79] Philo, l.c.

[80] Derek Ereẓ, 1.

[81] San. 76b; Yeb. 94b cite the view of R. Akiba that after the wife's death contact with a mother-in-law has not the same severity as incest with a mother-in-law while the wife is alive. According to some, R. Akiba means to teach that after the wife's death, the mother-in-law is not prohibited as incest but as a general biblical prohibition; according to others it is incest not punishable by burning but by *karet*. Furthermore, the majority of scholars maintain that R. Akiba drew that distinction only in the case of the mother-in-law, not of the wife's daughter or granddaughter. Maimonides believes that R. Akiba ruled the same for all kin of the wife, that after the wife's death the severity of the incestuous prohibition was reduced and punishable only by *karet*. See Yad, Issure Bi'ah 2,7–8, and *Maggid* thereto. However, the reliability of the tradition concerning the view of R. Akiba may be seriously doubted, as, indeed, the amoraim themselves are not unanimous about it. The final halakah on this matter has also remained uncertain.

half-sister is also prohibited as incest.[82] There is only one exception to this rule, the aunt by marriage. The wife of father's brother is biblically prohibited only if he is a full brother or at least a paternal half-brother of the father, but not if he is only a maternal half-brother of the father, as we have already stated.[83]

The penalties which the rabbis thought the Bible meant to prescribe for violation of these incestuous laws are as follows. For contact with a step-mother or with a daughter-in-law, the punishment is according to the Mishnah stoning to death.[84] Incest with a brother's wife or a paternal uncle's wife is penalized, according to the rabbis, with *karet* and flagellation.[85] The penalty for incest with the wife's kin, with one exception, is death by burning. The Bible itself prescribes this sentence for incest with a mother-in-law,[86] and the rabbis follow out a hermeneutic chain of argument to prove that the same penalty applies to step-daughter and step-granddaughter.[87] The one exception is the wife's sister, where the penalty is *karet* and flagellation but no execution by human decree.[88] The rabbis may have had in mind another penalty for incestuous relations with the wife's kin after the wife's death, for we have seen that distinction drawn by R. Akiba. Indeed, it is so maintained by Maimonides, that the punishment for contact with wife's mother, daughter, or granddaughter after the wife's death is not capital, but *karet* and flagellation. Other scholars oppose this view, and the halakah leaves the matter unsettled.[89]

From the tannaim of the second century we have the formulation of what was probably an older principle, that all marriages of a biblical incestuous prohibition are totally void and require no divorce for their dissolution.[90] Here

[82] Yeb. 55a.
[83] Yeb. 54b.
[84] M. San. 53a. The Book of Jubilees prescribes stoning for step-mother (33.13) but burning for daughter-in-law (41.25–26).
[85] M. Mak. 13a.
[86] Lev. 20.14; so also Jubilees 41.25–26.
[87] M. San. 75a.
[88] M. Mak., ibid.
[89] Yad, Issure Bi'ah 2,7–8 and commentators. See note 81 above.
[90] Yeb. 94b; M. Yeb. 13a.

too Rabbi Akiba proposes two exceptions, wife's sister and brother's wife. We must understand R. Akiba's view, however, not as giving such marriages full validity but as requiring a divorce as a matter of public policy.[91] As to the offspring born of an incestuous union, we have three views. One, only where capital punishment is prescribed is the offspring a mamzer; two, even where the union is prohibited on penalty of *karet,* the offspring is a mamzer; three, the offspring is a mamzer if born of any union biblically prohibited on the basis of consanguinity or affinity.[92] The middle view prevails in the halakah.

Before we are done with biblical incest as seen through the eyes of the rabbis, we should notice another angle of the law, the rabbinic concept of what constitutes valid and authoritative rules of incest for gentiles. It goes without saying that later rabbinic enactments in the matter of incest do not apply to gentiles. It may be further said that any law of incest based on Revelation also does not apply to gentiles, for Revelation yields a Jewish Torah, not a universal code of conduct. However, the sons of Noah, before Revelation, also had some code of morality; parts of that code are referred to in the Bible and evidently given some sanction. That code is binding upon gentiles and constitutes the code of Noahide laws which is the foundation of all laws considered by Judaism as applicable to gentiles.

[91] Yeb. 94b. The Talmud itself cites a view that only if the wife was betrothed but not wedded does her sister require a divorce, and likewise, if the brother's wife had been only betrothed but not wedded to the brother, she would need a divorce if taken in marriage by another brother. The matter of public policy consists in the fact that a betrothal is sometimes conditional, and if the conditions are not fulfilled the betrothal comes to naught; people, therefore, seeing this incestuous marriage, would conclude that the betrothal had been nullified because of a condition, and thus thinking the marriage of the second brother fully valid would be scandalized to see it dissolved without divorce. See Yad, Gerushin 10.10. Another view is that even after nuptials R. Akiba's rule holds good, that an incestuous marriage with a sister-in-law requires a divorce for its dissolution. The point of public policy is thus explained: A wife's sister loses her incestuous status with the wife's death, and a brother's wife loses her prohibited status in a levirate situation. People seeing the incestuous marriage will assume that the woman's status has changed, and, believing therefore the marriage to be wholly valid, will be scandalized if it is dissolved without divorce. See Lewin, *Oẓar,* Yeb. p. 188.

[92] M. Yeb. 49a.

The Noahides, say the rabbis, recognized only the most elemental and the closest degrees of kinship, and prohibited as incest only mother, maternal sister, and step-mother.[93] The selection is rather strange and the hermeneutic derivations do not help the matter. Yet it has its basis in the nature of the Noahide family. Mother is, of course, center and source of kinship in the old metronymic family. Brother and sister are the closest relatives. It is the brother who approves or disapproves a marriage proposal for his sister [94] and it is he who defends her honor.[95] Naturally, in a metronymic family only a maternal brother counts as a brother. The father's wife is prohibited not so much on the basis of close kinship as on that of respect for a parent; and this prohibition grew in intensity and changed in character as the patronymic order gradually became dominant in the ancient family, when the father became the patriarch and his wife assumed the forbidding dignity of the matron. The daughter is not prohibited,[96] nor is the brother's wife,[97] nor any of the wife's kin.[98]

A proselyte cuts himself off completely from his heathen family by entrance into the Jewish community. He is treated as if at the time of proselytization he were a new-born child. He should, according to the legal logic of the rabbis, have no incestuous prohibitions whatever in respect to his heathen relatives, even if they, too, have been proselytized. But by rabbinic enactment the law imposed upon the proselyte the

[93] San. 58. This is the view of R. Akiba. R. Me'ir submits a tradition, supposedly in the name of R. Eliezer, that a step-mother is not prohibited to a Noahide. According to the talmudic discussion there, R. Me'ir generalizes R. Akiba's view under the principle, "A Noahide is prohibited against every incest for which Jewish law prescribes capital punishment." This would mean that also daughter, granddaughter, and daughter-in-law are prohibited to the Noahide. Maimonides rejects this tradition and Karo cannot understand why. See Yad, Melakim 9,5, and *Kesef Mishneh* thereto. Maimonides rejects the tradition because an amora, Rab Huna (ibid. 58b), rules that a gentile may marry his daughter, and, *a fortiori*, granddaughter and daughter-in-law.

[94] Gen. 24.55, etc. And that is why Abraham poses as Sarai's brother, Gen. 12.13.

[95] Gen. 34.31; II Sam. 13.20.

[96] San. 58b.

[97] San. 58a; Yeb. 98a.

[98] San. ibid. See Rashi, s.v. *wesha'ar*.

laws of incest that apply to the Noahide, lest he think that as a Jew he had lower standards of morality than those he had as a heathen.[99] He is therefore prohibited to marry his mother or his maternal half-sister. He is permitted, however, to marry his step-mother, because so long as she herself is no kin to him he will recognize that by his entrance into the Jewish community even his father's kinship to him has lost legality, and so much more that of his father's wife.[100] Should he have his mother or his maternal sister as a wife at the time of his conversion, he must put her away, because this was wrong for him even as a heathen. Beyond the prohibitions of a Noahide, the rabbis imposed on the proselyte a prohibition against marrying any of his maternal relatives within the incestuous degree of kinship, namely, mother's maternal sister or mother's maternal brother's wife. However, if at the time of conversion he was married to such an aunt and the aunt was converted with him, he was not required to put her away, because he had violated no heathen law in marrying her when he was in his heathen state.[101] Paternal relatives of all kinds and the heathen relatives of his wife are not prohibited to him at all. He may thus marry his heathen daughter, granddaughter, paternal half-sister, paternal aunt, mother-in-law, step-daughter, or step-granddaughter.[102] A slave is a half convert; he is neither a fully proselytized Jew nor a full gentile; therefore he is free from all incestuous restrictions, either Jewish or heathen, so that he may marry even his own mother.[103]

With this we conclude our investigation into the incestuous prohibitions of the Bible on the basis of certain evidences from the Bible itself, and more especially on interpretations of post-biblical teachers as to the definition of kinship within

[99] Yeb. 22a.

[100] San. ibid.; Tosafot, ibid. s.v. *nasa;* Yad, Issure Bi'ah 14,13; Elijah Wilna note 3 ad Yoreh De'ah, 269,2.

[101] Yad, ibid. See Yer. Yeb. 12a.

[102] With reference to his wife's relatives, he may marry them after the marriage to his wife is dissolved. However, he may not have two wives one of whom is mother, daughter, or maternal sister of the other. San. ibid.; Yad, Issure Bi'ah 14,15. Obviously, all kinships established by the proselyte after proselytization are valid bases for all kinds of incest that apply to native Jews.

[103] San. 58b; Yad, Issure Bi'ah 14,17.

the proscribed area, as to the conditions under which the prohibitions continue forever or terminate at a certain time, as to the penalties intended by Scripture for violation of these injunctions, and as to the legitimacy of the children born of incestuous unions. We must now turn our attention to the activities of the post-biblical teachers and legislators in their effort to extend the law of incest beyond the limits set down in the Bible.

II

We shall consider first an attempt at extension of the law of incest made by the Zadokite sect at the beginning of the first century before the common era. They apparently did not arrogate to themselves the right to add to the biblical law of incest by any legislative power of their own, but evolved a new principle of interpretation which yielded them additional prohibitions. They charge the Pharisees with countenancing unlawful unions in the following verses: "And they marry their brothers' daughter and their sisters' daughter. Now, Moses said, thou shalt not approach thy mother's sister, she is thy mother's near kin. Thus is the law of incest written for men, and the same law applies to women. Therefore, if the brother's daughter uncovers the nakedness of her father's brother, it is a union of kin." [104] This form of deduction is known as the "principle of analogy," which was later employed by the Karaites to a much wider extent than was intended by the Zadokites. The Zadokites do not argue from direction to direction, that is, from the ascending to the descending line, to prove that a niece is as close a relative as an aunt. They grant that kinship may be closer in one direction than in another. But they argue against the basic assumption of the Pharisees that the direction of kinship starts with the man and not with the woman. Though the Torah, in its laws of incest as in other laws, addresses itself to the man, it has the woman in mind fully as much as the man, say the Zadokites. Kinship may be reckoned, therefore, from the woman just as from the

[104] Fragments of a Zadokite Work, ed. Schechter, 5.7; in Charles' edition, 7.9.

man. Hence, as the law prohibits a man marrying his aunt, so does it prohibit a woman marrying her uncle; or in other words, the union of uncle and niece is incest.

Their teaching, to my mind, was not altogether without basis in Jewish sentiment and tradition, even though the Bible does not count the niece among the incestuous prohibitions. We have good ground to suspect that the Hebrews of biblical time avoided marrying nieces, for not a single marriage of a niece is recorded in the Scriptures, where the tendency is definitely endogamous.[105] Whether it was an old halakah of pre-Zadokite time which the Pharisees rejected, as some scholars maintain,[106] or not, certain it seems to be that popular sentiment was averse to unions between uncles and nieces. Such sentiment is recorded even in pharisaic writings.[107] Along with the Zadokites, Samaritans and Falashas and Karaites maintained the prohibition against marrying a niece.[108] Nor can we ignore the sentiment of the non-Jewish neighbors who taught likewise, such as the Romans and early Arabs,[109] especially in regard to a sister's daughter; and indeed the Pharisees did charge the sectaries directly with the offense of following foreign laws.[110]

Against all this weight of public sentiment in favor of the Zadokite ruling, the Pharisees taught that marrying a niece was permitted, and not only permitted but meritorious. They opposed the very basis upon which the new law of the Zadokites was founded. First, the Pharisees opposed ex-

[105] The endogamous tendency in the Bible goes as far as cousin marriages, and many such marriages are recorded, Num. 36.11, etc. See also Tobit 4.15, etc. If niece marriages are not recorded it is not simply an omission but an indication that such unions were considered too close to the proscribed line. The marriage of Athniel with the daughter of Kaleb — Josh. 15.17 — cannot be taken as a marriage of niece and uncle, because the chronological tables prove them to be more distantly related. See Ḳimḥi ad Jos. ibid.

[106] Krauss, "Die Ehe zwischen Onkel und Nichte," in *Jewish Literature in Honor of Kaufmann Kohler*, Berlin, 1913, pp. 168, 171; Louis Ginzberg, *Sekte*, p. 31.

[107] M. Ned. 63b; 66a below; Krauss, ibid. p. 171.

[108] Krauss, ibid. pp. 167–8; Ginzberg, ibid. p. 31 and notes.

[109] *Kaftor wa-Feraḥ*, ch. V at end; Zunz, *Gesammelte Schriften*, II, p. 303; Krauss, ibid., pp. 168, 174.

[110] Megilat Ta'anit, chapter 5, "Under hellenic rule they used to judge according to gentile laws," may refer to rules of incest, among others.

tension of the laws of incest by the method of interpretation; direct and authoritative legislation was the only method they permitted.[111] They rejected interpretation because they felt that logic was inadequate to make comparisons between degrees of kinship. More probably, they were afraid that logic might go to extremes and impose upon the people new marriage prohibitions that would have no basis in the moral sense of the people, as indeed the Karaites have done. Second, they did not grant the basis of Zadokite logic, that you can count kinship from the woman as from the man, but stood by the original biblical view reckoning kinship from the man only. Foreign standards did not intrigue or daunt them; popular sentiment among the Jews, they felt, was inspired by non-Jewish standards. They therefore took a militant attitude of antagonism to the Zadokite prohibition against marrying a niece, and preached the doctrine that such a union was looked upon by the Almighty with special favor, especially union with a sister's daughter. The Pharisees must have scored an early victory over the sects on that point, for numerous instances come to light of marriages in Temple days between uncles and nieces with no implication of reticence. Thus John the Baptist protests Herod's marrying his brother's wife,[112] completely ignoring, however, the fact that she was also his niece. In Herod's family we have two instances of marriage between uncle and niece, Joseph, Herod's uncle, and Philippus, Herod's son by Cleopatra.[113] The Shammaites and Hillelites carried on a lively controversy on the status of the co-wife of one's daughter in a levirate situation, which means that the deceased brother had married his niece.[114] Among the tannaim, we find three niece marriages on record, that of R. Elazar,[115] Abba, brother of Rabban Gamaliel,[116] and R. Jose of Galilee.[117] In amoraic times marriage of uncle and niece

[111] Sifra, Lev. 18.16: *En mebi'in 'arayot min ha-din,* or in later terminology: *En maḳishin ba'arayot.*

[112] Mark 6.18; see J. E. s.v. "Herodias."

[113] See Krauss, o.c., p. 170 and note 3.

[114] Yeb. 15b–16b: *Ẓarat ha-bat.*

[115] Ab. R. N. chapter 16.

[116] Yeb. 15a.

[117] Gen. R. 17,3.

must have been a common occurrence, for the amoraim thought that the date was inserted in the bill of divorcement in order to make forgery impossible in a case where an uncle married his niece.[118]

Emphasis was placed by the rabbis, as mentioned in passing, on the special merit of marrying a sister's daughter.[119] The need for such emphasis can be understood in the light of the feeling existing then among their non-Jewish neighbors that a sister's daughter is an especially close relative.[120] It is possible, then, that the Jews yielding to rabbinic teaching that there is no incest in marrying a brother's daughter refused to yield in respect to a sister's daughter. Though the Zadokites charge the Pharisees with incest in marrying a brother's daughter or a sister's daughter, they seek to prove the prohibition of the former only. Apparently they did not think it necessary to prove that a sister's daughter was prohibited, because that was taken for granted by the people. Also when the Mishnah speaks of "resistance" to marriage of a niece,[121] it refers specifically to a sister's daughter. Likewise, we have polemical writings of Mohammedans who charge Jews with the offence of marrying a brother's daughter; but they do not accuse them as readily of marrying a sister's daughter.[122] Apparently the popular feeling against marriage with a sister's daughter was so deep-rooted and so long remembered that in order to cope with such popular antipathy the rabbis had to exert special pressure and emphasis. The rabbis won out ultimately; the halakaic tradition has been consistently in favor of niece marriage,[123] and

[118] Giṭ. 17a; Yeb. 31b, statement of R. Johanan.

[119] San. 76b; Yeb. 26b; Tos. Ḳid. 1,4. Rashi (Yeb. ibid. at bottom) and Tosafot (Yeb. ibid., s.v. *wehanose;* Yeb. 99a, s.v. *Safeḳ*) discuss whether there really is more merit in marrying a sister's daughter and why.

[120] The metronymic tradition of early Arabs is sufficiently described by W. Robertson Smith in *Kinship and Marriage in Early Arabia,* and according to that tradition the mother's brother, the *wali,* is closest of kin. In Rome we know of legislation in the middle of the first century permitting marriage of a brother's daughter but not of a sister's daughter, as recorded by Tacitus and cited by Krauss, o.c., p. 174.

[121] See note 107 above.

[122] Steinschneider, *Polemische Literatur,* p. 398; ZDMG, Vol. 42, p. 597, cited by Krauss, ibid. p. 168.

[123] Yad, Issure Bi'ah 2,14.

in practice down to our own day, marriage of uncle and niece among Jews is not a too rare occurrence.[124] Among the many strange recurrences in history is that of R. Judah ha-Ḥasid taking up the question again at the end of the twelfth century and counseling against marrying a niece,[125] but the halakah ignored his view completely.

Returning to the Zadokite principle of analogy and applying it in its most restricted sense, are there any other prohibitions that the Zadokites added, we may ask, even though they did not specify them in their code? On the basis of their principle, women being prohibited to marry their kin in the same manner as men, we should be inclined to believe that the Zadokites also added the following prohibitions. (1) A man is not permitted to marry his father's brother's wife; therefore, a woman may not marry her father's sister's husband. (2) A man may not marry his brother's wife even after the brother's death; likewise a woman may not marry her sister's husband even after the sister's death. This point seems contrary to the explicit statement in the Bible, but perhaps by a method of interpretation of their own they circumvented the difficulty.[126] (3) A man may not marry his wife's granddaughter; therefore a woman may not marry her husband's grandson. (4) A man may not marry his own granddaughter; conclude from this also that a woman may not marry her own grandson.

None of these prohibitions are found in the Bible, and if the Pharisees did not recognize them we face the problem: Why did the Zadokites limit their attack on the Pharisees

[124] In the state of Rhode Island, marriage of a niece is prohibited as incest, but permitted for Jewish citizens in accordance with the teachings of their own faith. Apparently such marriages were not uncommon even on the American continent.

[125] *Sefer Ḥasidim*, p. 282, and Testament. In the Testament he adds the prohibition of marrying a brother's daughter.

[126] This circumvention is possible according to Zadokite exegesis, for they interpret Lev. 18.18 as teaching not a prohibition of marrying a wife's sister but a general prohibition of polygamy. The word *beḥayeha* only indicates that after the death of one wife the husband may marry another, or, according to Dr. Ginzberg, also after the first wife is divorced. Professor Ginzberg (*Sekte*, pp. 24–25, 183 f) takes this derivation seriously and argues that the Zadokites prohibited a wife's sister even after the wife's death. Our refutation of this logic seems to break down his conclusions.

to the case of the marriage of a niece, and fail to accuse them of these other instances of incest which the Pharisees permitted and they prohibited? This must convince us that our logic is faulty, and here lies the weakness of our reasoning. The Zadokites could apply the principle of analogy only in cases of kinship based on consanguinity, not in cases where the kinship was based on affinity. Where marriage is the basis of kinship, it cannot be said that the husband's relatives are to the wife what the wife's relatives are to the husband, for the simple reason that the wife comes into the husband's family but the husband does not come into the wife's family group. Hence an aunt's husband is not as close to the nephew as an uncle's wife. Nor is a sister's husband as close as a brother's wife. Nor is a husband's grandson as close as a wife's granddaughter.[127] This disposes of any argument that the Zadokites prohibited the three first cases enumerated. The fourth case is the only one where the logic holds good. Here we have a case of consanguinity, and the logic is irrefutable that as the man may not marry his granddaughter, the woman may not marry her grandson. If the Zadokites' reasoning is to be taken seriously, there is no escape from the conclusion that they prohibited the marriage of a grandmother and her grandson; and this is a new prohibition, not recorded in the Bible. But the fact that the Zadokites did not charge the Pharisees with incest for permitting grandmother and grandson to be married forces upon us the second conclusion that marriage of a grandmother, included in the Talmud in the list of "secondary incest" cases, was at the time of the Zadokite controversy already prohibited by the Pharisees. On what ground and by what method did the Pharisees arrive at this new prohibition? Evidently not by a hermeneutic, interpretive principle,

[127] I cannot be quite as sanguine here, as in previous cases, in pointing out the logical difference between a husband's grandson and a wife's granddaughter. The distinction is not quite so sharp. If we are to assume that the Zadokites actually prohibited a husband's grandson (i.e. a step-grandmother), then we shall have to conclude here too that a step-grandmother had already been prohibited by the Pharisees as "secondary incest" at the time of the Zadokites, and that is not impossible. It is not unlikely that the same court legislated the prohibition of a grandmother and a step-grandmother at the same time.

which they opposed in the Zadokites, but by a legislative act of the court; and this was not an isolated instance of new legislation by the Pharisees which gave considerable extension to the circle of proscribed degrees of kinship.

III

But before we go over to the legislative activities of the Pharisees and their successors, the rabbis, we must record one addition to the list of biblically prohibited marriages made by them, the (16) WIFE'S GRANDMOTHER, maternal or paternal. This addition is made not as a matter of legislation but on the basis of their biblical exegesis. Though opposed to extension of the law of incest by hermeneutic derivation, they felt that the wife's grandmother was actually included in the levitical law in veiled or implied form. Leviticus does not speak of mother-in-law, as does Deuteronomy, but of "woman and daughter" (Lev. 18.17) or "woman and mother" (Lev. 20.14). In both instances, the levitical legislator makes the moral appeal; "it is *zimmah*," wickedness. Apparently Leviticus does not wish merely to state a prohibition against marrying a mother-in-law, but wishes to develop a *zimmah* principle in the law of incest. Three generations are included in this *zimmah* category — mother, daughter, and granddaughter. Hence, the rabbis argue, it should make no difference which is the wife; all three generations should be prohibited. If mother is the wife, the prohibition reaches down to granddaughter, and if granddaughter is the wife, the prohibition reaches up to grandmother. By this logic they believed that the wife's grandmother was biblically prohibited as if the law were explicitly stated in the text.[128] As a biblically prohibited case of incest, marriage with wife's grandmother is not valid and the offspring are accounted mamzerim; the penalty consists in execution by burning, and the prohibition continues even after the wife's death.[129]

[128] Mishnah and Gemara San. 75a–b; M. Yeb. 2a.

[129] It must be understood that the discussion of R. Ishmael and R. Akiba as to the nature of the prohibition of a mother-in-law after the wife's death (San. 76b) applies equally to a grandmother-in-law.

By acts of legislation, the rabbis added quite a number of new incestuous prohibitions, keeping in mind always, however, that the new additions had only rabbinic authority and were quite different in character from biblical incest. As a matter of fact, they are not incest at all; they are rabbinic marriage prohibitions built up on the foundation of the biblical law of incest. In their new legislation, the rabbis were inspired by a motto inherited from the Men of the Great Synagogue: "Make a fence around the Law." Thus they prohibited that which approximates biblical incest, that which resembles biblical incest, or even that which sounds like biblical incest.[130] These are represented as belonging to one group designated as *sheniyyot,* "secondary incest." They are sometimes grouped together under the title of *"issur miẓwah,"* that is, prohibitions based on the legislative authority of the rabbis; sometimes they are called *"issur ḳedushah,"* prohibitions motivated by self-discipline as a means of attaining holiness. These different appellations come to us from the time of the middle of the second century of the common era,[131] but the impression conveyed is that they are old terms and the legislation is ascribed to the soferim, "scribes." Some people take these indications seriously and believe that "secondary incest" is really an enactment of the Men of the Great Synagogue, for whom the term "scribes" is generally employed.[132] This theory is not impossible and yet by no means certain, for the term may be here used in the technical sense of "rabbinical" as opposed to biblical. It is more logical to believe that the secondary prohibitions do not represent a unit enacted at one par-

[130] Yeb. 20a–21b.

[131] R. Me'ir, R. Judah and a younger scholar, R. Elazar b. R. Simeon, are mentioned in connection with legal interpretations of what we call secondary incest (Tos. Yeb. 2,4; Yeb. 20a). The term was not coined by them and the manner in which they use it indicates that it was well known in their day. Yet no authority before them used that term. The Mishnah (Yeb. 20a) seeks to identify secondary incest with *issur miẓwah.* R. Judah identifies it with *issur ḳedushah.* This effort, too, belongs to their own time, and prior to that probably *issur miẓwah* included only *Nathin* and mamzer and *issur ḳedushah* included only the marriage prohibitions of priests.

[132] N. Krochmal, *Moreh Nebuke ha-Zeman,* Lemberg, 1863, p. 155a; Z. Frankel *Darke ha-Mishnah,* Leipzig, 1859, p. 3.

ticular time, but are an accumulation of prohibitions added gradually one after another during the Second Commonwealth and some even after the fall of the Jewish state.

We have reason to believe that the prohibition against a grandmother, one of the group of secondary incest, was known in Maccabean times.[133] Perhaps the prohibition against a step-grandmother goes back to the same period.[134] The prohibition against wife of a maternal uncle seems also to belong to an early date, at least prior to destruction of the Temple, for Philo mentions the prohibition of an aunt-by-marriage and uses the term Θεῖος in that connection, which includes the wife of a maternal as well as a paternal uncle.[135] It is also not unlikely that the prohibition against wife of father's maternal half-brother was known to Philo and was included by him in the same term.[136] Indeed, though we are not certain as to the exact age of these new rabbinic prohibitions, we cannot doubt the general conclusion that most of the older secondary prohibitions go back to a considerable antiquity.

The older group of secondary incest is recorded in tannaitic sources and includes eight new prohibitions, as follows: (17) Mother's Mother, (18) Father's Mother, (19) Wife of Father's Father, (20) Wife of Mother's Father, (21) Wife of Father's Maternal Half-Brother, (22) Wife of Mother's Paternal Half-Brother, (23) Wife of Son's Son, (24) Wife of Daughter's Son.[137] This group contains no extensions on the side of a wife's relatives.

Rab and R. Ḥanin, among the earliest amoraim and pupils of Rabbi Judah the Nasi, and Ze'era, a later amora, submit a tradition that the cases in this original group, with some exceptions, are interminable and continue ad infinitum.

133 We have inferred it from the Zadokite controversy, as given above on p. 255.

134 See note 127 above.

135 Philo, *Spec. Leg.*, III, 5, 26.

136 According to Raba (Yeb. 21b) prohibition of the wife of a father's maternal half-brother came ahead of prohibition of the wife of mother's brother.

137 Yeb. 21a; Yer. Yeb. 3d; Derek Erez, ch. 1.

R. Ḥanin records only one exception, (20) wife of mother's father; that is to say, wife of mother's grandfather is permitted,[138] but all the other seven new prohibitions are interminable. Rab cites three exceptions, (21) wife of father's maternal half-brother, (22) wife of mother's paternal half-brother, and (24) wife of daughter's son. These three, according to Rab, end the line of prohibition, but the other five are interminable. Ze'era reports a combination of the exceptions cited by Rab and R. Ḥanin, thus making four terminable and four interminable as follows: (25) MOTHER'S MOTHER'S MOTHER, ad infinitum, (26) FATHER'S MOTHER'S MOTHER, ad infinitum, (27) WIFE OF FATHER'S FATHER'S FATHER, ad infinitum, and (28) WIFE OF SON'S SON'S SON, ad infinitum. This view is followed by the halakah.[139] Bar Ḳappara, another pupil of Rabbi Judah the Nasi, makes two more additions to the list, whose prohibition, however, is terminable — (29) MOTHER'S FATHER'S MOTHER, and (30) FATHER'S FATHER'S MOTHER.[140]

The largest and most important additions to the list of secondary incest were made by R. Ḥiyya, another pupil of Rabbi Judah the Nasi. The group added by him is treated in the halakah as a unit, and is called "the secondary prohibitions of R. Ḥiyya." These include: (31) SON'S SON'S DAUGHTER, (32) SON'S DAUGHTER'S DAUGHTER, (33) DAUGHTER'S SON'S DAUGHTER, and (34) DAUGHTER'S DAUGHTER'S DAUGHTER — in other words, all great-granddaughters. On the wife's side there are: (35) WIFE'S SON'S SON'S DAUGHTER, (36) WIFE'S SON'S DAUGHTER'S DAUGHTER, (37) WIFE'S

[138] Yer. Yeb. ibid.; REBJH decides against R. Ḥanin and Ze'era and prohibits (a) *the wife of mother's mother's father, ad infinitum.* See next note.

[139] Yad, Ishut 1, 6; *Ṭur* E.H. 15; E.H. 15, 2, 4, 6, 19. REBJH decides against Ze'era and R. Ḥanin, declaring that the wife of mother's father is also an interminable prohibition, so that the wife of mother's mother's father, etc. is also prohibited. The codes do not accept the views of REBJH. See *Hagahot Maimoniyot* ad Yad, ibid. and *Bet Joseph* ad *Ṭur*, ibid.

R. Israel Isserlein in *Terumat ha-Deshen*, 214, rules that (b) *the wife of father's mother's father* is also prohibited, and this ruling is accepted by R. Moses Isserles, note ad E.H. 15,7.

[140] Yer. Yeb. ibid.; D.E. ibid. R. Solomon Luria, quoted in *Pitḥe Teshubah*, E.H. 15,3, maintains that one additional generation should be added to the prohibitions of Bar Ḳappara, thus prohibiting (c) *mother's father's mother's mother* and (d) *father's father's mother's mother.*

DAUGHTER'S SON'S DAUGHTER, (38) WIFE'S DAUGHTER'S DAUGHTER'S DAUGHTER – that is, all step-great-granddaughters; and finally (39) WIFE'S MOTHER'S MOTHER'S MOTHER, (40) WIFE'S MOTHER'S FATHER'S MOTHER, (41) WIFE'S FATHER'S FATHER'S MOTHER, and (42) WIFE'S FATHER'S MOTHER'S MOTHER – which means all the wife's great-grandmothers.[141]

Concerning these cases of secondary incest introduced by R. Ḥiyya, the Talmud raises the question whether they are interminable or not and comes to no conclusion. Maimonides, therefore, rules that all of them terminate just there; [142] Naḥmanides rules that the first four are interminable, being in the direct line of descent.[143] Support for the Naḥmanidean view is found in a Palestinian tradition submitted in the name of Rab, to the effect that Father Abraham and Mother Sarah, if alive today, could not marry a single Jew or Jewess, which tradition, however, is not known to the Babylonian Talmud. Other authorities, among them R. Eliezer of Metz, R. Asher b. Yehiel, and his son R. Jacob, as well as R. Joseph Karo, decide that all of R. Ḥiyya's secondary prohibitions are interminable.[144]

Further additions to our list come from the last amoraim. The Talmud asks whether the prohibition enacted by the tannaim against the wife of (22) mother's paternal half-brother should also apply equally to the wife of mother's maternal half-brother. The decision is to prohibit (43) WIFE OF MOTHER'S MATERNAL HALF-BROTHER,[145] in the same manner as the wife of her paternal half-brother. Another question raised by the amoraim concerns marrying paternal grandfather's sister or his sister-in-law (brother's wife). Amemar, a Babylonian amora, permits both, but the tosafist, R. Isaac of Dampierre, on talmudic evidences, rules against Amemar, adding these two new prohibitions, (44) WIFE OF

[141] Yeb. 22a.
[142] Yad, Ishut 1,6.
[143] RSBA and Yeb. 22; *Maggid* ad Yad, ibid.; *Bet Joseph* ad *Ṭur*, E.H. 15.
[144] *Sefer Yere'im*, 219; *Ṭur*, ibid.; E.H. 15,12, 14, 15.
[145] Yeb. 21b.

FATHER'S FATHER'S PATERNAL BROTHER and (45) PATERNAL SISTER OF FATHER'S FATHER.[146] Finally, the tosafists assume that mother's mother's sister is the same in status as father's father's sister; [147] hence by authority of the same R. Isaac of Dampierre another prohibition is added, (46) MOTHER'S MOTHER'S SISTER. The leading codes accept these three additional rulings by authority of R. Isaac.[147a]

It will be helpful now to summarize in outline the list of secondary incest introduced by the rabbis as our final halakah has it:

I. The Bible prohibits mother; the rabbis add:
  1. Grandmother and,
  2. Grandmother's mother, ad infinitum,
  3. Grandfather's mother, and according to Luria even
  4. Grandfather's mother's mother.

II. The Bible prohibits step-mother; the rabbis add:
  1. Father's step-mother, ad infinitum,
  2. Mother's step-mother,
  3. Maternal grandmother's step-mother (according to REBJH).
  4. Paternal grandmother's step-mother (according to Isserlein).

III. The Bible prohibits sister, father's sister, mother's sister; the rabbis include also:
  1. Paternal grandfather's sister,
  2. Maternal grandmother's sister.

IV. The Bible prohibits brother's wife and father's paternal brother's wife; the rabbis add:
  1. Father's maternal brother's wife,
  2. Mother's paternal or maternal brother's wife,

146 Tosafot Yeb. 21b, s.v. *Amemar*. Maimonides rules with Amemar and permits 44–45. R. Asher prohibits also (e) *the wife of mother's mother's paternal brother*, but Karo permits it. See *Bet Joseph* ad *Tur*, ibid.

147 Tosafot Yeb. 21b, s.v. *Eshet; Tur*, ibid.; E.H. 15, 18.

147a *Halakot Gedolot*, 'Arayot, prohibits also step-mother's mother and mother of paternal uncle's wife, but there are contradictions, and it is assumed that the readings in the text are not reliable. See Lewin, *Oẓar*, Yeb. 21.

3. Paternal grandfather's paternal brother's wife,
4. Maternal grandmother's paternal brother's wife (according to R. Asher).

V. The Bible prohibits daughter and granddaughter; the rabbis add:
1. Great granddaughter, ad infinitum.

VI. The Bible prohibits son's wife; the rabbis add:
1. Grandson's wife,
2. Great grandson's wife, ad infinitum, i.e., only if it be the wife of son's son's son, etc.

VII. The Bible prohibits wife's mother and (by rabbinic inference) grandmother; the rabbis add:
1. Wife's great grandmother, ad infinitum.

VIII. The Bible prohibits wife's daughter and granddaughter; the rabbis add:
1. Wife's great granddaughter, ad infinitum.

IX. The Bible prohibits wife's sister, to which the rabbis offer no secondary prohibitions.

It will be noticed that rabbinic law has applied itself mainly to extensions in the ascending and descending lines. Some brothers and sisters of parents and grandparents are within the range of rabbinic incest, some are not; but all brothers and sisters of great-grandparents are beyond the range. There are no prohibitions of brothers and sisters in the descending line nor in the wife's kin, except the biblical prohibition of wife's sister.

A Palestinian tradition prohibits a wife's step-mother, "because of appearance"; the Babylonian Talmud permits it.[148] Although R. Jacob Tam is inclined to follow the Palestinian tradition in this instance, our halakah follows the Babylonian ruling.[149] The Palestinian Talmud also prohibits marrying a step-sister, where there is no blood kinship at all, "because of appearance." The Karaites consider this a case of real biblical incest.[150] But the Babylonian Talmud permits it and we follow this practice.[151] Both Palestinian and Babylo-

[148] Yer. Yeb. ibid.; Derek Ereẓ, ch. 1; Yeb. 21a–b.

[149] Tosafot Yeb. 21a, s.v. *umuttar;* E.H. 15,24.

[150] *Aderet Elijahu,* 'Arayot, ch. 3.

[151] Sotah 43b; E.H. 15.23. R. Judah ha-Ḥasid, *Sefer Ḥasidim,* 1116, discourages it as an unlucky marriage.

DIAGRAM OF PROHIBITED MARRIAGES BASED ON KINSHIP

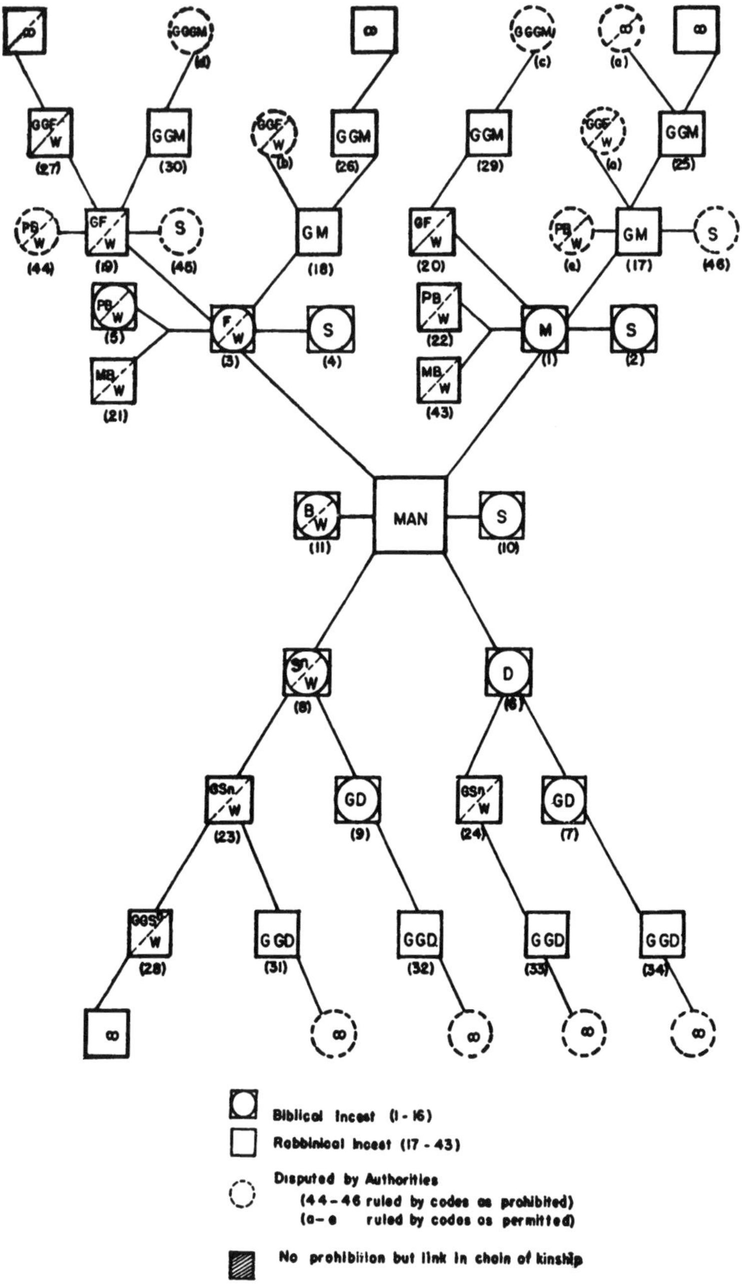

MAN
F W (3)
S (4)
M (1)
S (2)
B W (11)
S (10)
PB W (5)
MB W (21)
PB W (22)
MB W (43)
GF W (19)
PB W (44)
S (45)
GM (18)
GF W (20)
PB W (e)
GM (17)
S (46)
GGF W (27)
GGM (30)
GGF W (b)
GGM (26)
GGM (29)
GGF W (a)
GGM (25)
GGGM (d)
GGGM (c)
∞
Sn W (8)
D (6)
GSn W (23)
GD (9)
GSn W (24)
GD (7)
GGS W (28)
GGD (31)
GGD (32)
GGD (33)
GGD (34)
Biblical incest (1 - 16)
Rabbinical incest (17 - 43)
Disputed by Authorities
(44 - 46 ruled by codes as prohibited)
(a - e ruled by codes as permitted)
No prohibition but link in chain of kinship

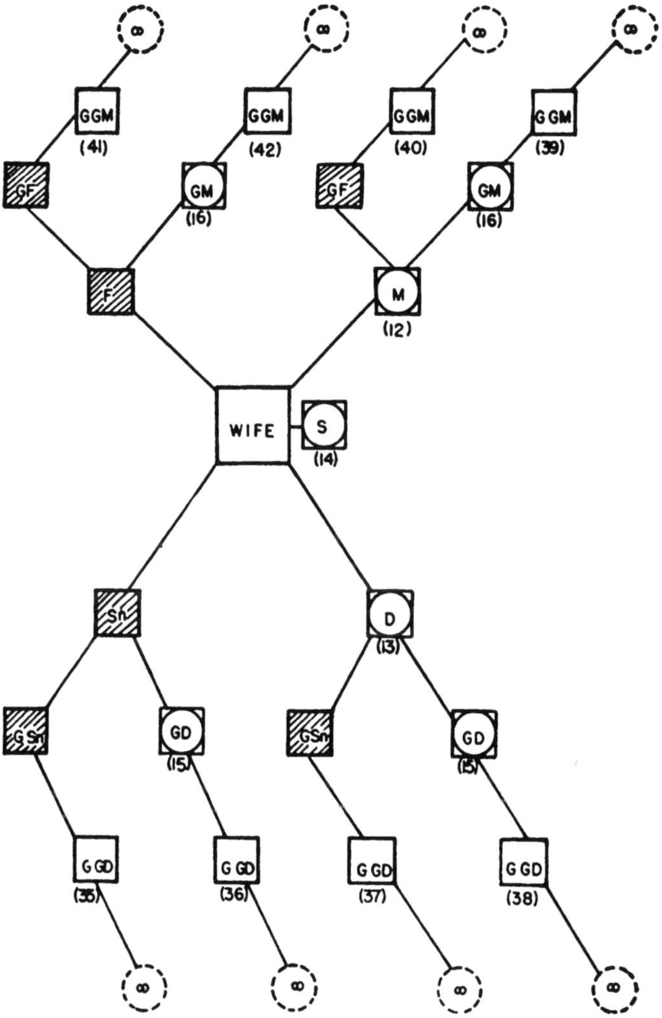

M	Mother	Sn	Son
F	Father	D	Daughter
S	Paternal or maternal sister	PB	Paternal brother
G__	Grand______	MB	Maternal brother
GG__	Great grand______	W	Wife of
GGG__	Great greatgrand__	∞	ad infinitum

nian sources permit marriage of a step-son's wife, a step-father's wife, a son-in-law's wife, and a nephew's wife.[152]

We have mentioned in passing that it was a fundamental principle with the rabbis to keep biblical incest and rabbinical incest on distinctly different levels. A biblical incestuous prohibition invalidates a marriage; a rabbinical prohibition does not in any way challenge the validity of the marriage, nor the legitimacy of the offspring, nor even the fitness of parents or offspring for priestly privileges.[153] Perhaps because of this leniency, the law imposed on the woman entering such a union greater penalties than if she entered a biblically prohibited marriage. She loses all her standard ketubah provisions. She forfeits the right to support during the husband's lifetime or alimony if she be widowed. The ketubah clauses of ransom, burial, and support of minor children are canceled. She can sue for payment of the gifts promised her by her husband at the time of the marriage (*mattan*), but she cannot collect for any losses in the value of her dowry or private property used by the husband. She gets nothing of the *mohar*, which is the two hundred *zuzim* of the "marriage price," but she takes only what she finds of her dowry, trousseau, and personal property, and is sent off with a divorce. Divorce is compulsory, enforced by flagellation or imprisonment.[154]

IV

Our investigation into the rabbinic law of incest comes to an end at this point, but we still have before us the task of examining the karaitic teaching. We may notice now in retrospect, from what has been said in previous pages, that the rabbinic law of incest was practically completed with the close of the Talmud, over two centuries before Karaism came into being. What little contribution was made by post-talmudic rabbis to this section of the law was in the form of comments upon or interpretations of talmudic texts. Hence

152 Derek Erez, l.c.

153 M. Yeb. 84a; Yeb. 85a–b.

154 M. Ket. 100b; Yad, Ishut 24,2; and see a fuller treatment of the penalties in JMC pp. 228–9 and notes.

it will be evident that the rabbinic law of incest owes nothing to the Karaites. On the other hand the Karaites owe to rabbinic law much more than they are willing to admit. Yet by no means can the karaitic law of incest be considered a direct development of rabbinic law. Essentially the Karaites conceived of their teaching as in direct opposition to that of the rabbis. Far from permitting themselves conscious adoptions from the rabbinic legal system, they aimed on the contrary to make wholly independent investigations into the source of the law, the Bible, and to build their entire law on foundations distinctly their own. Surely their law of incest is a creation of their own, for in few sections of the law are the Karaites and the Rabbanites at such a distance from each other as they are in the matter of marriage prohibitions.

In their definition of consanguinity, the Karaites are closer to nature than the Rabbanites. To them maternal and paternal relatives have the same quality of consanguinity in respect to incest.[155] Wherefore maternal half-brothers or half-sisters count in every respect like full brothers and full sisters.[156] They also treat natural brothers and sisters, even where one of the parents has been a slave or gentile, as equal to fully legitimate brothers and sisters as regards incest.[157] Likewise, proselytes carry over their natural kinships into their Jewish state, and to them as to native Jews apply all the incestuous prohibitions.[158] Their definition of kinship by affinity is not radically different from that of the Rabbanites. While the earlier Karaites, as mentioned,[159] taught that betrothal without nuptials does not establish affinity for the

155 Hence to them the wife of mother's brother is prohibited to the exact degree as the wife of father's brother. See *Aderet Elijahu*, 'Arayot, 5, p. 149a.

156 'Anan himself did draw a distinction between maternal and paternal kinship in his treatment of the biblical prohibition of an aunt (*Sefer ha-Mizwot*, Nashim 7,8,9,10), but drew no such distinction in other cases of incest. See ibid. 17. However, later authorities deny any distinction whatever in any case of incest. The challenge to this differentiation between maternal and paternal kin is taken up by Joshua b. Judah, *Sefer ha-Yashar*, ed. Markon, pp. 111–2, and followed by the codes. See *Aderet Elijahu*, p. 146b.

157 *Sefer ha-Mizwot*, Nashim 3,12,23; *Sefer ha-Yashar* pp. 106–7.

158 *Aderet Elijahu*, p. 144d.

159 See p. 243 above and note 71.

purpose of any incestuous prohibition, the final karaitic halakah makes the betrothed, even before nuptials, fully the wife of her husband and therefore prohibited to his kin.[160] Unmarried sex contact does not establish affinity either to the Karaites or the Rabbanites, but the Karaites have somehow discovered a new basis for drawing the unmarried consort of a kin into the vortex of incestuous prohibitions and they call this incest by *hagbarah*,[161] i.e., arising from a severe interpretation of the Law.

The major deviations of the Karaites from rabbinic tradition rest upon three principles which the Rabbanites rejected but which the Karaites accepted as fundamental in their interpretations. They revived the old Zadokite teaching that the law of incest was directed to woman just as much as to man, and that therefore kinship can be reckoned from the woman to the man with the same legal force as from the man to the woman.[162] The effect of this principle is not only to prohibit a niece, as did the Zadokites by the same reasoning, but to open up the way to many other new prohibitions, as we shall soon attempt to follow. In the second place, the Karaites take the verse: "Thou shalt not uncover the nakedness of the daughter of thy father's wife . . . she is thy sister" (Lev. 18.11) to refer to a step-sister who is no blood relative at all. By this interpretation, they build up a new type of kinship; "step-kinship" it may be called. Some karaitic schools consider step-kinship equal to consanguinity, others rate it lower in quality. But all Karaites consider this type of relationship an additional link in the

[160] *Aderet Elijahu*, p. 157c. 'Anan, *Sefer ha-Miẓwot*, Nashim 5,6,24, rules that while a father's wife or a son's wife is prohibited under all circumstances, her kin, e.g., daughter or sister, is not prohibited unless she has borne a child to father or son respectively. Joshua b. Judah, *Sefer ha-Yashar*, p. 107–8, contests this ruling, and his contrary opinion is accepted by karaitic halakah.

[161] *Aderet Elijahu*, pp. 146a; 150a. Likewise, to the Karaites, a man may not marry his own unmarried consort, if in the meantime she has been married to and divorced from another man. But the prohibition is only secondary, or as we may say, rabbinical in character. See *Gan 'Edan*, p. 134d.

[162] *Aderet Elijahu*, p. 149c. Joseph ha-Ro'eh is recorded as limiting application of this principle, considering the prohibition applied to woman to be *derived* from the corresponding prohibition to man. The codifiers, however, consider the prohibition intended by the Bible directly for woman as for man.

chain of incestuous prohibitions.[168] In the third place, to the Karaites an injunction in the levitical code does not merely represent a single, specific prohibition, but a general legal principle from which may be inferred any number of new prohibitions by the application of certain logical methods.

The rabbis, as mentioned above, were opposed to the use of logical derivations in any form whatever for the extension of incestuous prohibitions. The Karaites ridiculed this position, and agreed without exception to the full and free authority to employ logical methods in formulation of their code of incest. The question was how much logic and what particular method was proper. There was a school of maximum logic and one of minimum logic. The proponents of maximum logic were called *Ba'ale ha-Rikkub*, i.e., those employing the "grafting" method; their antagonists, who limited themselves to the method of "analogy," were called *"Ba'ale ha-Heḳesh."* The first generations of Karaites, from the eighth to the eleventh century, were radicals in the employment of logical reasoning in the formulation of the law of incest. They used every available method of logic and used it without restraint. Later generations of Karaites, beginning with the eleventh century, revolted against their predecessors, whose incestuous prohibitions extended so far that they became unbearable. They were led by Joshua b. Judah (Abu al-Faraj Fukan) and his teacher Joseph ha-Ro'eh (Yusuf al-Basir), both of the eleventh century. They rejected the *rikkub* method altogether, took issue with the earlier authorities on a number of other premises posited by them, opposed the extravagant and unbridled use of logical inference, but applied themselves to the development and employment of the one logical method, "analogy." Their views prevailed in the final karaitic codes.

The *rikkub* principle featured in the logical system of the *Ba'ale ha-Rikkub* and from this they derived their name. According to this principle, a man and his wife are one person, as may be proven from many biblical expressions and indica-

[168] *Aderet Elijahu*, p. 146c–d.

tions.[164] Hence to a man his wife's relatives are like his own, and likewise, to a woman her husband's relatives are like her own kin. Furthermore, whenever the Bible prohibits a certain female kin, her husband is included in the prohibition, and by the husband we mean not himself, for he is male, but his other wives. Hence, to take only one example out of the many complicated combinations, a man is prohibited to marry his father's wife's husband's wife, and a woman, likewise, is prohibited to marry her father's wife's husband or her mother's husband's wife's husband. Evidently, this process of reasoning might go on endlessly, but, by what seemed to later authorities an arbitrary rule, they allowed the process to be carried only four steps and beyond that recognized no incestuous kinship.[165]

Two more rules of logic are included in the system of the *Ba'ale ha-Rikkub,* one called "nominalism," the other "inversion." By the first rule, a step-sister, being called by the Bible a "sister," has the status of a real sister, and all prohibitions applying to the kin of a sister apply also to kin of a step-sister. By the second rule, if a step-sister is like a real sister, then a step-brother is like a real brother, step-son like a real son, and step-daughter like a real daughter.[166]

[164] Summarized by *Aderet Elijahu* at the beginning of 'Arayot, 5, p. 148c–d.

[165] *Gan 'Eden,* p. 130b; *Aderet Elijahu,* p. 148c.

[166] The *Ba'ale ha-Hekesh* permit themselves to infer only that as daughter of father's wife is prohibited so is daughter of mother's husband (*Gan 'Eden,* 'Arayot, end of ch. 2). Beyond that they permit no extension of the step-kinship principle. The *Ba'ale ha-Rikkub,* however, generalize the step-kinship and say that not only are a woman and her daughter prohibited to one man but also a woman and her step-daughter, that is, her husband's daughter, and even her husband's step-daughter; and the woman is prohibited to marry her husband's son or step-son.

The logical implications of the *Ba'ale ha-Rikkub* are too extensive and too complicated to be enumerated here. But some of their prohibitions may be mentioned here as illustrations of their extravagances.

'Anan, founder of the sect, gives the following prohibitions beyond those mentioned in the Bible:

Mother's husband's wife (= mother's rival) and her rival's rival; mother's husband's daughter or daughter-in-law, sister or sister-in-law; mother's brother's wife, and the latter's sister; mother's sister's husband's wife and the latter's sister.

Father's wife's husband's wife (step-mother's rival), her sister or sister-in-law, daughter or daughter-in-law; father's brother's wife's (aunt's) sister; father's sister's husband's wife (aunt's rival) or the latter's sister. Brother's

The *Ba'ale ha-Hekesh* opposed this entire system, terming it an endless process leading to grafting on top of grafting and to analogy on top of analogy. Yet there are a few assumptions, which were acceptable to them and which they put to proper use in their own process of reasoning. (1) The wife, they said, is like the husband only to the extent that whenever Scripture or logic indicates a prohibition of the male to the male, this means the wife of one male to the other; and conversely, a prohibition of female to female

---

wife's husband's wife (sister-in-law's rival). Sister's husband's wife (sister's rival) and the latter's rival.

Son's wife's daughter or son's wife's son's wife (daughter-in-law's daughter-in-law).

Daughter's husband's daughter or daughter's husband's son's wife (son-in-law's daughter-in-law).

Wife's granddaughter's sister (who is not wife's granddaughter), and wife's grandson's wife and the latter's sister.

These prohibitions for men have corresponding prohibitions for women in respect to males of the same kinship status.

The successors of 'Anan have gone further in extension of incestuous prohibitions under the logical system of the *Ba'ale ha-Rikkub*. A few examples may suffice. They give the following five (or six) persons the name of father and prohibit their kin as if they were father's kin. (1) Father, (2) Step-father (mother's husband), (3) Step-step-father (step-mother's husband), (4) Step-father's rival (step-father's wife's husband), (5) Step-father's rival's rival (step-father's wife's husband's wife's husband) or step-mother's rival's husband (father's wife's husband's wife's husband). Likewise, there are five sons. Son, step-son, wife's step-son, wife's husband's step-son, wife's husband's wife's husband's step-son. There are also five (or six) fathers-in-law: Wife's father, wife's step-father, wife's step-father's rival, wife's step-mother's rival's husband, wife's step-father's rival's rival (wife's mother's husband's wife's husband's wife's husband) or wife's step-mother's rival's rival's husband (father's wife's husband's wife's husband's wife's husband). Of course, there are corresponding mothers and daughters and mothers-in-law and for every prohibition for men there is a corresponding prohibition for women.

The extension of prohibitions to "rivals" is perhaps the most prominent feature of the *Ba'ale ha-Rikkub*, for this is basically their principle, that husband and wife are one; wherefore, two wives of the same husband have a real kinship between them, and similar kinship exists between two husbands (successively) of the same wife. Prohibitions of "rivals" may be here enumerated as follows: Mother's or step-mother's rival and rival's rival; daughter's or daughter-in-law's rival and rival's rival; sister's and sister-in-law's rival and rival's rival; aunt's or niece's (real or by marriage) rival; the rivals of similar relatives of the wife. Of course, not alone the rivals but also the mothers, step-mothers, daughters, sisters of these relatives or of similar relatives of the wife are prohibited as incest. Cf. *Sefer ha-Miẓwot* of 'Anan under the laws of *Nashim we'Arayot* and *Sefer ha-Yashar* of Joshua b. Judah, especially pp. 58, 63–4, 67, and 75 in Markon's edition.

means the husband of one to the other.[167] (2) They admit that a step-sister is like a real sister in respect to her own kinship to members of the family; but her kinship does not extend to her relatives where she herself is not involved in the combination. (3) They generally grant also that incestuous kinship can be counted from the woman as from the man and that, therefore, any of the biblical prohibitions for the man implies a corresponding prohibition for the woman.

On the other hand, they set forth the following restricted program of reasoning. (1) The levitical code lays down a general principle as the foundation of incestuous prohibitions, the kinship (*she'er*) of the male and female involved; and then, in a series of injunctions, dealing with specific cases, illustrates and defines the term kinship. (2) Given this biblical definition of kinship, we discover new prohibitions by application of the logic of "analogy," that is, by finding that our new cases are similar to actual cases of the Bible or fall logically within the biblical definition of kinship. (3) Analogy must be made with biblical cases or biblical definitions, not with such as are themselves derived by the process of analogy. (4) The Bible indicates that only kin and kin's kin are within the prohibited degree, but not kin's kin's kin. Except in the *direct* ascending and descending lines, where, by special biblical indication, the distance of generations does not matter, no incestuous prohibition

[167] This is the view of the dominant school among the Karaites, called *Ba'ale ha-Ẓe'idah,* who permit the argument that the prohibition of a female to another female must be taken as a prohibition of a female to the husband of another female. They say that when the Bible prohibits marrying a father's sister, the prohibition is directed to a woman as well as to a man. But a woman cannot marry a woman; therefore, by the rule of logic, it means that a woman is not permitted to marry her aunt's husband. Joseph ha-Ro'eh and his followers constitute the school that oppose the *ẓe'idah* method. They say, when the Bible prohibits a father's sister, the prohibition is for men only. To derive a prohibition for the woman to marry her aunt's husband, two steps are necessary. First we must infer that she may not marry her father's sister (which prohibition is limited in the Bible to men), then we must infer that the prohibition is to be "transferred" to the aunt's husband. This would mean an inference based upon an inference, which is contrary to the limits of logical processes permitted by the whole school of *Ba'ale ha-Hekesh.* A full discussion of the position of the opponents of the principle of *ẓe'idah* is given in *Sha'ar Yehudah,* by the Karaite, Judah Poki Tchelebi.

can be imposed where there is not in the complex a consideration of at least the second degree of kinship. Finally (5) a "nominal" kin is by special biblical fiat declared a kin but beyond the realm of logic; therefore the "nominal" kin cannot be made the basis for logical extension of prohibitions by means of analogy.

Now, an analysis of the levitical code shows us six categories of prohibited kinship or prohibited combinations of kinship.

I. In the first we have a prohibition of all primary kin, six in number, viz., father, mother, brother, sister, son, daughter. These prohibitions are interminable; the females and the wives of the males are interminably prohibited to the men, and the males and the husbands of the females are interminably prohibited to the women.[168]

II. In the second category we have a prohibition of all secondary kin, i.e., kin of kin, grandparents, grandchildren, uncles and aunts, nieces and nephews. In the case of grandparents and grandchildren the prohibition is interminable, by the rule stated in the first category, but in the cases of uncles, aunts, nephews, and nieces, the prohibition continues no further. And here, too, the females and the wives of the males are prohibited to men, and the males and the husbands of the females are prohibited to women.[169]

III. The third category is derived from the levitical injunction prohibiting a man to marry mother and daughter. Generalized into a rule of law, this injunction teaches that a man may not have two wives (even successively) who are first degree kin to each other, nor may a woman have two husbands who are first degree kin to each other.[170]

[168] *Aderet Elijahu*, 'Arayot, first part of ch. 6; *Gan 'Eden*, 'Arayot, ch. 9, sec. 1. We follow both of these works, which constitute the authoritative karaitic codes, in our presentation of their law of incest.

[169] This category includes grandmother and grandfather's wife; aunts and aunts-by-marriage; nieces or nieces-by-marriage; granddaughters and granddaughters-in-law.

[170] This category offers three patterns of prohibitions, for each of which we shall give the formula and single examples.

(1) It is prohibited to marry the spouse of a kin. Example: One may not marry a daughter's husband. Even to a man this prohibition applies; but by

IV. The fourth category is derived from the biblical law prohibiting a man to marry a woman and her granddaughter, which can be reduced to the principle that a man may not marry (even successively) two women who are second degree kin to each other, and likewise a woman may not marry two men who are second degree kin to each other.[171]

V. The fifth category rests upon the karaitic teaching that a man may not marry his step-sister, who is, according to their interpretation, "the daughter of thy father's wife . . . she is thy sister." They generalize this injunction into the rule that two persons who are first degree kin cannot marry two other persons who are also first degree kin to each other. It is for this reason, they say, that one may not marry his step-sister, for then he and his father would be married to woman and daughter. Likewise it is prohibited for two brothers to marry two sisters.[172]

---

prohibition of the daughter's husband, we mean his wife. Hence a daughter's rival is prohibited.

(2) One may not marry the kin of a spouse. Example: One may not marry the wife's son. To a man, the prohibition is to be understood to mean that he may not marry his wife's son's wife, or his wife's daughter-in-law.

(3) One may not marry the kin of his spouse's spouse. Example: One may not marry his wife's step-daughter. For father and daughter are first degree kin, and since the father would thus be prohibited to him, the father's wife (who is now his wife) would likewise be prohibited to him.

171 This category, too, falls into three patterns which we shall present with leading examples as follows.

(1) One may not marry the spouse of kin's kin. Example: It is prohibited to marry a niece's husband. For men, the prohibition extends to the niece's husband's wife.

(2) One may not marry his spouse's kin's kin. Example: The wife's grandson's wife (wife's granddaughter-in-law) is prohibited, like the wife's granddaughter.

(3) One may not marry his spouse's spouse's second degree kin. Example: One may not marry his wife's husband's aunt. The husband and his aunt are secondary degree kin to each other. Marrying both is therefore prohibited. But there can be no prohibition of man marrying man; therefore, the prohibition extends to the wife (who is now his wife).

172 The prohibitions in this category also fall into three patterns which may be given here with single examples of each.

(1) One may not marry his kin's spouse's kin. Example: A woman may not marry her daughter's husband's son, for then father and son would be married to mother and daughter. Translated for man, a man may not marry his daughter's husband's son's wife, i.e., his son-in-law's daughter-in-law.

(2) It is prohibited for one to marry his kin's spouse's spouse's kin. Ex-

VI. The sixth category moves directly one step beyond the fifth. It prohibits the marriage of two persons who are second degree kin to two other persons who are first degree kin to each other. This is an extension of the biblical law which prohibits marrying father's brother's wife and extends the prohibition even to father's step-brother's wife. This category is treated in karaitic law as doubtful incest, because it is an innovation of Joshua b. Judah which was not recognized by his predecessors and even directly contested by his teacher Joseph ha-Ro'eh.[178]

---

ample: One may not marry his sister's husband's wife's daughter. It should be understood in this light. The man and his sister cannot be married to mother and daughter, and here the mother's husband takes the place of the mother; therefore he is prohibited as husband of the sister whom he had already married.

(3) A man is prohibited to marry his spouse's kin's spouse's kin. Example: One may not marry his wife's brother's wife's mother, i.e., his brother-in-law's mother-in-law. Wife and brother-in-law are kin; brother-in-law's wife and mother-in-law are kin. The combination would make two kin married to two kin (the man reckoning as substitute for his wife).

[178] The prohibition of marrying father's step-brother's wife properly formulated means that one is prohibited to marry grandfather's step-son's wife (for grandfather's step-son is father's step-brother). This means that man and grandfather cannot be married to mother and son (i.e., son's wife). Hence formulation of the principle of this category. It should also be noted that the rule must read, man and grandfather, or man and grandson cannot be married to two first degree kin, but man and nephew or man and uncle may. In other words the prohibition is meant only for two second degree kin in the ascending or descending line, not for second degree kin in the lateral line.

This category falls into six patterns, as follows:

(1) One may not marry his kin's kin's wife's kin. Example: Father's father's wife's father's wife, i.e., grandfather's step-mother-in-law.

(2) One may not marry his kin's kin's spouse's spouse's kin. Example: One may not marry his daughter's son's wife's husband's mother, i.e., his granddaughter-in-law's mother-in-law.

(3) One may not marry his kin's spouse's kin's kin. Example: One may not marry his step-mother's grandmother or step-grandmother (father's wife's father's mother or step-mother).

(4) One may not marry his kin's spouse's spouse's kin's kin. Example: One may not marry his step-mother's husband's grandmother (father's wife's husband's mother's mother).

(5) One may not marry his spouse's kin's spouse's kin's kin. Example: One may not marry his father-in-law's wife's grandmother (wife's father's wife's mother's mother).

(6) One may not marry his spouse's kin's kin's spouse's kin. Example: One may not marry his father-in-law's step-sister (wife's father's father's wife's daughter).

To the Karaites, like the Rabbanites, incestuous marriages are not valid and no divorce is necessary for their dissolution. The children born of such marriages are mamzerim. However, there are two principles on which Joshua b. Judah and Joseph ha-Ro'eh do not agree, and karaitic halakah made no decision as to which view to follow. They are (1) the sixth category, as mentioned above, which R. Joseph denies, and (2) the principle that you may count kinship from the woman as from the man, which R. Joseph also denies. All cases of incest, therefore, that fall within scope of this double controversy between these karaitic sages, are doubtful in their law, and require a divorce for dissolution of such marriages.[174]

V

We may conclude our chapter on incest by recording briefly the attitude of Reform Judaism to the law of incest. Attitude alone it may be called, not a code, for to my knowledge there has been no final formulation of the Reform law of incest either in Europe or in America. A commission to deal with the marriage and divorce laws of Reform Judaism was appointed by the Central Conference of American Rabbis, re-appointed and recast from time to time during the second and third decades of the present century. From its reports, papers, and discussions one gathers the following impressions.

The levitical code of incest was never seriously challenged by Reform Jews. In fact, they maintain an attitude of great reverence to these laws because of the emphasis that the Bible itself puts upon them and because of the deep roots that they sank into the Jewish conscience. Only one incestuous prohibition was challenged by them, that against marrying a deceased brother's wife. The Bible permits such a union under the requirement of levirate, when the deceased brother has left no issue; otherwise it is declared incestuous by levitical law. Reform Jews have abrogated

[174] Another type of incest should be added which requires a divorce: marrying father's or brother's or son's unmarried consort, because that incest has no biblical authority. See *Gan 'Eden* p. 135a and note 161 above.

the requirement of levirate. Therefore it is the same to them whether a levirate situation exists or not. Logic, then, compels a decision either that the brother's widow be always permitted or always prohibited. Kohler and Simon argued at the Conference of 1915 for permission of such a union, since marriage of a deceased wife's sister is permitted. The tendency in the 1925 Conference was to prohibit such a union.

Greater severities in the law of incest have been more frequently demanded from the Reform platform than leniencies. In response to the tendency to recognize the biblical prohibition of a brother's widow, Philipson demanded that a wife's sister be likewise prohibited. Evidently, this plea fell on deaf ears, because there is no precedent for it in Jewish law, and such a prohibition is not generally recognized in the laws of the states of the Union. Other severities, however, were urged by the commission in their 1915 report, which have received great attention, because they were in keeping with generally accepted standards of marriage prohibitions in many states. Marriage of niece and cousin marriages were proposed for prohibition by the Central Conference. To my knowledge, prohibition of such marriages was not officially pronounced, but it has been the policy of the Reform Jewish clergy to consider both the levitical code and the code of the particular state where the question arises as religiously binding.[175]

[175] Cf. *Yearbook of Central Conference of American Rabbis*, Vol. 25, pp. 370 f, 383–88, and Vol. 35, pp. 364 ff. See also Union American Hebrew Congregations, *Tract on Judaism and Marriage*.

CHAPTER VI

OTHER MARRIAGE PROHIBITIONS

I

THERE are many marriage prohibitions in the Bible and the Talmud that are not based upon the sense of incest, which we propose to discuss in the present chapter. Some apply to all Israelites, some to certain groups of Israelites only; some are permanent prohibitions, others apply only for a time; some are standard legal prohibitions, others mere folk customs or superstitions. We shall preserve these groupings in our treatment, and in each group present the specific prohibitions in the order of their antiquity. However, we are compelled at the outset to deviate from the rule of historical sequence and give priority to one prohibition which is of a later date, because it logically links up with the two previous chapters, that on Levirate and the one on Incest. We have referred to it previously as "ziḳah-incest."

Ziḳah, we recall, is the bond that ties the childless widow to the surviving brothers of her deceased husband. Until the levirate marriage takes place or until the widow is released by ḥaliẓah, she remains in a state of ziḳah, which is not dissimilar to that of betrothal. It suggests itself immediately that, if betrothal creates kinship of affinity so that the groom may not marry any of the kin of his betrothed bride, possibly ziḳah creates a similar state of kinship; and the levir, therefore, may be prohibited from marrying any of the kin of the childless widow. The general principle, whether ziḳah is like betrothal or not, was a subject of controversy in the days of Shammai as in the time of Samuel.[1] Without deciding the principle, the Talmud from early tannaitic days maintains the tradition that the levir is prohibited to marry all primary kin of the widow, so long as she retains the bond of ziḳah.[2]

[1] See chapter on Levirate, pp. 104–107 above.

[2] Yeb. 17b–18a cites a number of tannaitic texts to the effect that the levir

This prohibition, however, is not biblical in nature nor incestuous in severity, but has the character and legal force of a rabbinical ordinance.[3] Since as many widows as may remain are all under bond of ziḳah to all the surviving brothers, none of the brothers may marry any of the primary kin of any of the widows. We have no ruling in the Talmud whether this prohibition extends also to those kin who belong to the category of "secondary incest." Nor does talmudic law prescribe penalties for the violation of ziḳah-incest. But the tosafists rule that if the levir has married the widow's kin in violation of the law, he is compelled to divorce her.[4]

Ziḳah is dissolved when one of the brothers marries one of the widows or releases one of them by ḥaliẓah. After dissolution of ziḳah, the widows themselves still remain prohibited to all the brothers under biblical law as interpreted by the rabbis, although the prohibition does not fall under the biblical rule of incest.[5] There is no prohibition, however,

---

is prohibited to marry the kin of the widow. From M. Yeb. 29a it is evident that even the Hillelites knew of the concept of ziḳah-incest or ḥaliẓah-incest. The question that interests the amoraim is whether the prohibition continues after the death of the levirate woman, when her demise, so to speak, has dissolved the ziḳah. See Yer. Yeb. 3c.

Of course, even those who maintain that there is no ziḳah-kinship, cannot deny the prohibition of marrying the widow's kin which has the authority of the oldest amoraim, but they give another reason for the prohibition. They say that by marrying a kin the possibility of ever taking the levirate widow in marriage is eliminated (*asur lebaṭṭel miẓwat yebamin*). This reason is highly artificial, for according to it one should never be permitted to marry his sister-in-law's sister or mother under any circumstances, so long as the brother is childless.

[3] Yeb. 27b, etc.; Yad, Yibbum 1,14.

[4] See Tosafot Yeb. 18b and 23b, both at the head of the page. Tosafot might have proven this point by M. Yeb. 26a and 29a. Because it is possible for ziḳah to be dissolved by another brother and another widow, the Mishnah (Yeb. 41a) permits the brother who has betrothed the widow's sister to retain her until the ziḳah is dissolved. Where, therefore, there is no possibility of such ultimate dissolution of ziḳah, he is not permitted to retain the sister of the ziḳah woman.

[5] There are various views on the subject. Resh Lakish agrees that for the levir who has performed the ḥaliẓah there is only a biblical non-incestuous prohibition, but for the other brothers and the other widows, the prohibition is biblical and incestuous, like the wife of a brother when there is no ziḳah situation. R. Johanan holds the view here recorded, that for every surviving brother and every widow there is only a biblical non-incestuous prohibition (Yeb. 10b). If the widow has been freed by ḥaliẓah, the prohibition, in legal

against any of the brothers marrying any kin of the widows, for once the ziḳah is terminated, there is no kinship whatever between brothers and widows. To remove ziḳah, however, one brother and one widow must be involved either in the levirate marriage or in ḥaliẓah, and this establishes a new form of kinship. Levirate marriage, of course, establishes the kinship of marriage with all its implications in the same manner as the regular marriage. Ḥaliẓah establishes a kind of ḥaliẓah-kinship between the one levir and the one widow involved in the ḥaliẓah ceremony, without any effect whatever on the other brothers or the other widows. The law looks upon ḥaliẓah as similar to divorce, and to the extent to which a husband may not marry the kin of his divorced wife, a levir cannot marry the kin of his ḥaliẓah-freed sister-in-law under the rule of ḥaliẓah-incest. Though, like ziḳah-incest, the prohibition is only of rabbinical authority,[6] the rabbis take ḥaliẓah-incest more seriously, because, while ziḳah can be dissolved, ḥaliẓah-kinship endures forever. Therefore not only the primary kin of the widow but also those in the category of "secondary incest" are prohibited to the levir who has performed the ḥaliẓah rite.[7] If in violation of the law the levir has taken any of them in marriage, he is compelled to divorce her.[8] Not only this, but even the "rivals" of the primary kin of a ḥaliẓah-freed widow are prohibited to the levir.[9] However, none of these prohibitions arising from ziḳah-kinship or ḥaliẓah-kinship are severe

---

technical terms, is a negative one, based upon the rule that "Once he has refused to build his brother's house (levirate marriage), he cannot build any more." But, if the widow has been taken in levirate marriage, the prohibition against marriage with the other widows is positive in nature and expressed in the legal formula, "He can build only one house but cannot build two houses" (Yeb. 11a). Maimonides has a theory that if the ziḳah is dissolved by ḥaliẓah, the prohibition against marrying any of the widows is only rabbinical and not biblical, but *Maggid* corrects him on this point. See Yad, Yibbum 1,12, and *Maggid* thereto.

[6] Yeb. 24a; 41a; 44a–b. According to certain views in the Talmud (44a), R. Akiba declares this to be a biblical prohibition.

[7] M. Yeb. 40a; Yeb. 40b.

[8] M. Yeb. 29a; see note 2 above; see also M. Yeb. 44a and 44b. Interesting in this connection is the first responsum of R. Isaac De Latas, ed. Friedlander, especially p. 10.

[9] M. Yeb. 40b at the end; Yeb. 41a on top.

enough to render a marriage invalid or to make the child born of such a marriage a mamzer, because there has been no real incest in the union and especially because the prohibitions are not biblical but rabbinical.[10]

Ziḳah-kinship and ḥaliẓah-kinship bring to mind a similar type of relation based on a rabbinical marriage. A minor orphan girl, it is well known, cannot contract a biblical marriage, because she is a minor and her father, who is her biblical guardian, is dead. But to protect her against dishonor and to provide the care of a husband, the rabbis by decree permitted her mother and brother to give her in marriage and declared such a marriage rabbinically valid. Similar provision has been made for deaf-mutes, who are incapable by law to contract a legally valid marriage. No divorce is necessary to dissolve such a marriage, but a declaration or indication by the minor orphan girl of her intent to be released from the marriage bond. Now this rabbinical marriage is less than ziḳah. So long as the marriage was dissolved without a formal instrument of divorce but by a mere "rejection" (*mi'un*), the husband may marry his wife's kin and the wife may marry the husband's kin. Furthermore, if after "rejection" the wife has married another and has been divorced from him, she may return to her first husband. However, if she was released by her husband with the regular divorce, even though that was not necessary, the divorce has some legal effect and, therefore, she is prohibited marrying his primary kin and he is prohibited marrying her primary kin, because she is treated as his divorced wife. The prohibition, then, is only rabbinical.[11]

10 Yeb. 44a, etc.; Yad, Yibbum 1,13.

11 Yeb. 108a-b. However, in one instance, the minor girl is prohibited to one of her husband's relatives only, even though she has only "rejected" her husband but received no divorce. The one case (Yeb. 12a) is that where the minor girl was taken into levirate marriage after her husband died and then "rejected" the levir. For through the levirate marriage she was accepted by people as a real daughter-in-law. See E.H. 173,14.

The case of the deaf-mute is similar in principle to that of the minor girl, except that the law prescribes no "rejection" ceremony in place of divorce. Therefore the kinship continues after the marriage is dissolved and the prohibition against marrying any of the spouse's relatives is only rabbinical. The case, however, is not altogether similar to that of the minor girl in respect

II

Of biblical marriage prohibitions, the three already discussed under the heads of levirate, intermarriage, and incest, have their roots in pre-deuteronomic legislation. Those we are to discuss here go no further than the deuteronomic law, for no knowledge of such prohibitions is found in pre-deuteronomic records. These prohibitions have wider implications than indicated by the literal biblical text. The rabbis made full use of these implications in expansion of these laws. The prohibitions are three in number: the mamzer is prohibited to "enter the congregation of the Lord"; [12] the castrated male is prohibited to marry a Jewish woman; [13] the divorced wife cannot return to her husband after having been married to another man.[14]

What is a mamzer? We have partly answered that question in a previous chapter.[15] We have seen that to the biblical author the mamzer was simply a child coming from a certain foreign group that could not be indentified in post-biblical times, probably a group that was despised by the Jewish people for sex irregularities, promiscuity or incest. We have also mentioned that in early tannaitic times the term mamzer was applied as well to the child born of a mixed marriage. Let us add that prior to the common era it was understood that the mamzer was the child born of a harlot, for the term is thus rendered by the Septuagint and by Philo.[16] The latter makes the concept clearer by explaining it as the child that does not know who its father is. Philo's definition, based as it is on Septuagint, is not untrue to the law of his day, but not wholly correct in technical terminology. His weakness, however, lies not in his defini-

to permitting the husband to remarry her after she has married another. Maimonides and RABD discuss this matter on the basis of two readings in a Yerushalmi text. See Yad, Gerushin 11,15, RABD and *Maggid* thereto.

[12] Deut. 23.3.

[13] Deut. 23.2.

[14] Deut. 24.4.

[15] See chapter on Intermarriage, pp. 160, 184, 194–7 and notes 55, 121, 142–152.

[16] Sept. Deut. 23.3; Philo, *Spec. Leg.* I, 60, 326; indicated also in Josephus, *Ant.* 4,8,23. This tradition continues in *Targum Jonathan*, Deut. ibid. See also *Keter Torah* by Aaron the Karaite, Deut. ibid.

tion of mamzer but in his indiscriminate use of the term harlot (*zonah*). The Hebrew *zonah* may be an adulterous wife, a licentious woman, or a professional prostitute. For the purpose of a popular presentation and unwilling to burden his subject with legal niceties, Philo was correct in grouping all these together and calling the child born of any of these a mamzer. Rabbinic writers often take this liberty.[17] But Hillel was more accurate in his definition of mamzer, applying the term only to the child born of adultery. When he was called upon to clear up a matter of Jewish law to the people of Alexandria in connection with a practice that seemed to be adultery and threatened to result in the stain of mamzer upon the offspring, he declared that there was no adultery, and therefore no mamzerut.[18] When he recorded the classification of castes among the Jews, he divided the group mentioned by Philo, those born of harlots, all of whom, it is true, have the stain of mamzer, into three. Those born of adultery are the only ones he designates as mamzer; those of promiscuity he calls "hush-child"; and those of professional prostitution he terms foundling.[19] The child born of adultery is a mamzer even if both father and mother are known; the hush-child's stain consists in the fact that its father is not known; and that of the foundling in the fact that neither father nor mother are known. Technically, therefore, the term mamzer applies only to the child born of adultery. Supporting this conclusion is a family register of Temple days brought to light by R. Simeon b. 'Azzai, wherein is recorded the name of a certain person as mamzer because he was born of adultery.[20]

At about the time of the fall of the Jewish state or perhaps immediately thereafter, the child born of an incestuous union was included in the mamzer concept. This new definition is recorded in the terminology of the schools of

[17] A series of tannaitic texts specify mamzer but mean to include also the hush-child and the foundling, e.g., Tos. Ber. 5,12; Tos. R. H. 4,1; Tos. Meg. 2,7; Tos. Men. 10,13; Tos. Hor. 2,10.

[18] Tos. Ket. 4,9; B. M. 104a.

[19] M. Ḳid. 69a. See Ḳid. 75a, ascribing this mishnah to Hillel.

[20] M. Yeb. 49a. See Büchler, "Familienreinheit und Familienmakel in Jerusalem," *Festschrift Adolf Schwartz*, p. 145 and note 1.

Hillel and Shammai and other teachers of approximately that period.[21] The matter was further discussed in the school of Jabneh, where some of the scholars, taking the older tradition as their basis, that the mamzer is the child of an adulterous union, broadened the definition to include offspring of any union which is in itself a capital crime. Others of the teachers took the newer tradition as their basis, that the child born of incest is a mamzer, and formulated the principle that a mamzer is a child born of a union for which the Bible prescribes the penalty of *karet*. R. Akiba formulated it otherwise, and in a manner not fully covering the concept of mamzer as R. Akiba himself taught it. He designated as mamzer the child of any union biblically prohibited under the head of incest.[22]

This statement of R. Akiba would seem to teach that the penalty of *karet* is not the basis of judgment, but that every incestuous union, even where there is no *karet* – so long as it is incestuous – produces the legal mamzer. But this does not agree with other statements of R. Akiba, for he teaches also that a child born of a union in violation of the law prohibiting a husband to remarry his wife after her marriage to another,[23] or in violation of the law requiring release of the childless widow from her bond of ziḳah before she may marry another, is a mamzer.[24] For this reason, two later tannaim sought to formulate the view of R. Akiba differently. R. Simai declares that according to R. Akiba a child born of any union prohibited by a biblical negative command is a mamzer; while R. Yeshebab believes that any biblically pro-

[21] Tos. Yeb. 1, 9. So does R. Elazar report (ibid., 10), that both schools agree that a mamzer is one born of an incestuous union. This tradition does not seem certain to me because the Mishnah (Yeb. 13a-b) does not raise the problem of mamzerut in the differences between Shammaites and Hillelites, but speaks only of priestly disqualification. However, we have a statement by R. Elazar b. Jacob the first, a contemporary of the Shammaites and the Hillelites, wherein he uses the term mamzer to designate the child born of incest. He prohibits a man taking two wives in different parts of the world lest brother marry sister, not knowing their kinship to each other, and thus beget offspring who shall be mamzerim. Tos. Ḳid. I, 4; Yeb. 37b. See Büchler's article, ibid., p. 145 and note 2.

[22] Yeb. 49a.

[23] Yeb. 44a.

[24] Tos. Yeb. 11, 5–8; Yeb. 92a.

hibited union, whether under a positive or negative command, gives the offspring the legal status of mamzer.[25] The former scholar conceded that R. Akiba would not call mamzer one born of a union prohibited for priests only; the latter teacher, agreeing that R. Akiba had made certain exceptions to his rule,[26] denied making any exception in the case of priestly prohibitions.[27] The amoraim took the severest interpretation of R. Akiba's view as the correct one, but ruled definitely against him. Thus the final halakah recognizes as mamzer only one born of incest or adultery, but not of any other biblically prohibited union.[28]

As to the child of a mixed marriage, we have seen that though the older tradition declared him a mamzer and that there was considerable support for that view among the later teachers, the final halakah declared him to be either Jew or gentile, but not a mamzer.[29]

Now that we have the rabbinical definition of mamzer, we know what the rabbis understood by the deuteronomic law prohibiting a mamzer to "enter the congregation of the Lord even unto the tenth generation." Both males and females born of an incestuous or adulterous union may not marry a Jew or Jewess. The phrase, "even unto the tenth generation" means to the rabbis that the prohibition is perpetual, so that the descendants of a mamzer for all time, so long as one parent has a mamzer strain, counts as a mamzer in the eyes of the law and is prohibited marriage with Jews.[30]

[25] Yeb. 49a; Ket. 29b; Ḳid. 68a. The Talmud suggests that two interpretations are possible in R. Yeshebab's statement; that according to one he would concede that R. Akiba does not count the child born of a union prohibited by a positive command a mamzer; that all he adds in interpretation of R. Akiba is the child born of a priestly prohibition.

[26] One exception is definite, according to amoraic interpretation:—the prohibited union between a high priest and a non-virgin who is neither divorced nor widowed — Ket. 30a — because it is a priestly prohibition of a positive nature. Other exceptions are recorded, such as a child born of contact between husband and wife during her menstruation or of a union between husband and wife after he has learned of her unfaithfulness. The case of a levirate widow who has married an outsider without release is a subject of two contradicting traditions. See Yeb. 92a at bottom. See also Yeb. 49b and Tos. Yeb. 11, 5–8. See also Tosafot Yeb. 49a, s. v. *Hakkol*.

[27] Ket. 49a, etc. See Tos. Yeb. 6, 9.

[28] Yad, Issure Bi'ah 15,1.

[29] See chapter on Intermarriage, p. 196.

[30] M. Yeb. 78b.

A perpetual taint of blood must cause a terrific problem to a people as generation links into generation. The only way by which one can be sure he is free from any such taint is by keeping a family register tracing every link in his genealogy with authentic certification that every member of his family tree is of pure origin. Thus we understand the important role which family records played in the life of the Jews during the Second Commonwealth and for some time thereafter. The priests had more reason to be cautious about family purity because they were more restricted in their marriages by law and tradition than the Israelites. But the Israelites, too, had plenty of reason to scrutinize the genealogical trees of the families into which they married, if only to guard against the taint of mamzer. They had all the more reason to do so, if they sought acceptance in marriage alliances with the priests.

Yet a system of this kind could hardly be satisfactory on a national scale. It was not to be expected that a whole people would perpetually record the origin of every one of its members. At best only the few, select, aristocratic families could maintain their genealogical tables for a certain length of time. And for how long could even these few keep their records and prove their authenticity? With revolts internally, with wars from without, with deportation and exile, the record system was of necessity discredited. A practical, common-sense standard of *approximate* purity of blood took the place of the old time record system. The rabbis employed the traditional term *yuḥasin,* which no longer meant documentary proof of purity of blood but reasonable legal evidence of normal purity. Murmur of ill repute (*'ir'ur*), unchallenged presumption (*ḥazaḳah*), and investigation (*bediḳah*) were accounted legal elements in judging a family's fitness to marry priests or Israelites. Such a standard, as can well be imagined, was quite flexible, and could be applied with greater severity or with more leniency as the tendency of the particular court or the specific country or any definite period in history indicated. Generally, courts under influence of the priesthood were more severe. It may also be said that the further we go back in history the severer is the application of this standard. As for countries, the application of standards varied from land to land. Much laxity existed in many places. Rab, reporting for the Jewish communities around Babylonia, says picturesquely: "Meshan is dead, Media is sick, and Elam is dying," i.e., there is much hope for some, little for others, and none for still others.[81] It is to be expected that Palestine held the banner of high standards of purity, but evidently Babylonia outdistanced it to the point where Babylonians hesitated to marry Palestinian girls.[82]

The progress of the more pliable standard, and therefore the more reasonable attitude to the mamzer strain, can be followed out in the halakah itself. The mamzer could hardly hide his identity for long from public knowledge, and people's memories in those days were retentive. To a reasonable extent, therefore, it was true that "Israel knew the mamzerim in their midst." [83] If a mamzer was lost in the shuffle and his identity no longer known, the Pharisees of olden days were willing to close their eyes and forget it. "When Elijah comes," they said, "he will not bring close those who are far nor hold afar those who are near." [84] The later rabbis followed in the same tradition, teaching that no undue investigation was to be made into families to uncover prohibited strains; once the mixture has occurred, leave it alone.[85] Practical life made this attitude necessary, for a too thorough investigation might bring skeletons out of the closets of some of the most influential families.[86] Legally they formulated a principle that "the certain mamzer may not enter the congregation of the Lord, but the doubtful mamzer may." [87] The Korduans and Tadmoreans had been long regarded undesirable as converts because of the blemish of mamzer, but in the last days of the Commonwealth they were declared acceptable.[88] To many other communities held under suspicion there developed a more tolerant attitude, in accordance with a tradition that "the presumption

[81] Ḳid. 71b.
[82] Ḳid. 71–2.
[83] Ket. 14b.
[84] Eduy. 8,7.
[85] Ḳid. 71a; Yer. Yeb. 9d.
[86] Ḳid. 71a.
[87] Ḳid. 73a.
[88] Yeb. 16a–b.

in law is that all communities are free from any stain that may be a hindrance to marriage." [39]

Even as in the stain of foreign blood, so in the case of suspicion of mamzerut, people were more careful than the law required. Scholars, too, were often more severe than the letter of the law dictated. Sometimes they were much disturbed over the laxity prevailing in certain communities and did not hesitate to make their suspicions known.[40] Where facts warranted, of course, they made public announcement that marriage with certain families should be avoided.[41] Even where such proclamation was not deemed advisable, the almost certain stain of given families was revealed in the academies by word of mouth. [42] In the best of circles suspicions of impurity could not be easily eliminated. Ze'eri refused to marry the daughter of his teacher R. Johanan out of fear of impurity, and the latter complained, "Our Torah is kosher, and our daughters are not?" [43] The illustrious amora R. Isaac, son of an equally illustrious father, R. Judah, attained the dangerous age of "bachelorhood," finding it difficult to discover a bride of whose good stock he could be sure.[44] People were especially suspicious of loud-mouthed, quarrelsome families, believing these signs of an unholy strain.[45]

Halakah and Agadah speculate whether there is a possibility or hope of interrupting the endlessness of the mamzer strain. By planned mating, says R. Tarfon, the strain can be brought to an end. Let the mamzer marry a female slave; the child will then be a slave, following his mother. Then the slave-child can be freed or ransomed. R. Elazar protests, that will prove of no avail, because the child will be both mamzer and slave.[46] The halakah, however, recognized the view of R. Tarfon; and thus mamzerut theoretically can be interrupted.[47] There are two tannaitic traditions in the Talmud; according to one the eleventh generation mamzer, male or female, is permitted to marry a Jew; according to the other only females of the eleventh generation are permitted

[39] Ḳid. 72b; 76b.
[40] Ḳid. 70b; 72a.
[41] Ḳid. 70b; Yeb. 78b.
[42] Ḳid. 71a.
[43] Ḳid. 71b.
[44] Ḳid. ibid.
[45] Ḳid. ibid.
[46] M. Ḳid. 69a.
[47] Yad, Issure Bi'ah 15,3.

to marry, but not males.[48] The law, however, did not deviate from the principle that mamzerut is a perpetual stain.[49] On the other hand, it was believed that by a natural process of selection the Almighty kills off the mamzerim so that the strain is ultimately lost; [50] more, the agadic mind played with the hope that in messianic days the mamzerim would be purged of their inherited impurity and made fit to marry into the congregation of the Lord.[51]

The hush-child and the foundling belong to the mamzer class. The hush-child, called in Hebrew *shtuḳi,* is defined as one who knows his mother but does not know his father; the foundling, called *asufi,* is one who knows neither father nor mother. In the original Hillel tradition, the *shtuḳi* and the *asufi* seem to be the lowest of the castes enumerated, their stain, apparently, worse than that of mamzer or Nathin.[52] Going back to the background of Hillel's classification, we can understand the reason. The child of a harlot, in Philo's terminology, is the mamzer; the adulteress is a criminal harlot but a harlot merely in the sense of being unfaithful; the licentious woman is perhaps less criminal but more a harlot; the professional prostitute is the morally degraded and socially outcast harlot. Therefore, the child who knows his father and mother, though born of criminal contact, is less of an outcast than the child who does not know his father, who in turn is less of an outcast than the child who knows

[48] Yer. Ḳid. 65c; Yeb. 78b. The question was put to R. Eliezer, who gave an evasive answer, as if to say "I have never seen a tenth generation mamzer." He may have meant that by that time the taint was lost in the assimilative process. But the Talmud takes it that he dies off in the natural process.

[49] Yad, Issure Bi'ah 15,1.

[50] Yeb. 78b. The amoraim believed that the mamzer whose identity is known can live; one whose identity is not known dies; one who is the object of suspicion lives only three generations. The Palestinian tradition gives the unidentified mamzer only thirty days to live. Again, the Palestinian teachers believed that once in every sixty or seventy years a plague comes upon the world in order to kill off the mamzerim. Yer. Ḳid. 65c.

[51] Ḳid. 72b.

[52] M. Ḳid. 4,1 and M. Hor. 3,8. I take the former mishnah as giving the castes in exact depreciating order. The latter mishnah varies the order, but the intent of this mishnah is to give the order of religious priority, not the extent of impurity of birth.

neither father nor mother but has been abandoned to the street. In that sense, therefore, the *shtuḳi* and the *asufi* are in the older tradition mamzerim of a worse calibre.

However, as the legal definition of mamzer became more exact, a child born either of adultery or incest, the *shtuḳi* and *asufi* could at the worst be considered doubtful mamzerim. As such, their position was more favorable than that of the mamzer. Furthermore, we have mentioned that a doubtful mamzer is by the later halakah not forbidden entrance into the congregation of the Lord. Hence from the point of view of the later rabbis, the prohibition against marrying a *shtuḳi* or *asufi* cannot be considered biblical, but a rabbinical ordinance in the interest of family purity.[53] The exact legal status of the *shtuḳi* or *asufi* is like that of the child born of an adulterous union where the marriage of the woman to her husband is of doubtful legal validity. He is a doubtful mamzer, and by rabbinic law prohibited to marry into a Jewish family.

So long as the status of the child is based on doubt as to his origin, the law must deal with the admissibility of evidence to clear up this doubt. To what extent can the word of a man be taken who claims to be the child's father? To what extent is the mother's testimony accepted as to the paternity of the child? How far are circumstantial evidences admissible?

By a biblical statute, as the rabbis understood it, a father's testimony concerning the origin of his child, in the absence of positive proof to the contrary, is accepted by the law as final. So long as his fatherhood is not doubted prior to his testimony, he can declare the child a mamzer or otherwise of impure birth.[54] This law probably goes back to the older patriarchal authority of the father over the child, but it has been accepted as valid even in the final halakah.[55] The later authorities, however, confined this paternal authority to testimony affecting, for the moment, the child only; there-

[53] Ḳid. 73a.
[54] Ḳid. 78b, etc.
[55] Yad, Issure Bi'ah, 15,15.

fore, if the child has children of his own, his father's testimony is not admissible.[56] The mother has not the same power of testimony regarding the legitimacy or illegitimacy of her children. Her testimony is never valid against that of the father. In normal married life, even without contradictory testimony from the father and even if the woman's reputation and conduct raise suspicions, the woman may not testify that any of her children is illegitimate, because the law assumes to the contrary.[57] In the case of a betrothed pair, who are not supposed to have had sex relations prior to nuptials, the law assumes the child born to the unwedded bride to be a doubtful mamzer, but the mother's testimony is reliable as to the legitimacy of the child. The same right of testimony is given to the unmarried mother to declare that the child is without blemish of illegitimacy.[58]

In the case of the hush-child, therefore, the mother can testify to the child's purity of birth, or she can even identify the person who is father of the child. Her testimony is valid in respect to the status of the child, but in respect to the man identified as the father it has no validity whatever.[59] The father's acknowledgment, of course, establishes the child's full legal paternity.[60] In the case of a foundling, any man and any woman can claim him as his or hers, so long as he has not been branded as a foundling. Likewise, a midwife can testify to the pure birth of the child before his legal status as *asufi* has been established. Once the child's status has been made clear, definite proof is necessary to alter his record. The law, however, accepts the testimony of a man and a woman who claim to be father and mother, even after the child's status has been declared, if the particular territory is going through a famine — which may explain the

[56] Yeb. 47a. See Tosafot, ibid., s.v. *ve-en,* and Yad, Issure Bi'ah 15,16, wherein the teaching is expounded that where the grandchildren are affected, the father's testimony is not valid even for his children.

[57] Yad, Issure Bi'ah 15,19.

[58] Yeb. 69b, in accordance with the view of Samuel. Ket. 13a, the view of R. Gamaliel and R. Eliezer. See Yad, Issure Bi'ah 15,18.

[59] Yad, Issure Bi'ah 15,14.

[60] Yad, Issure Bi'ah 15,30, based upon Ḳid. 73b, applicable to *asufi* but applying with equal logic to *shtuḳi.*

abandonment of the child and the prolonged silence of the parents.[61]

If the child is found in a city inhabited by Jews and gentiles he is a doubtful gentile in addition to being a doubtful mamzer, and therefore must go through ritual conversion.[62] On the other hand, if the child is found circumcised or with definite evidences of parental care, e.g., oiled, salted, wrapped, put in a place of safety, or placed in front of a synagogue to attract attention of Jews, he is not rated as a foundling at all but as a parentless child.[63]

In addition to the mamzer and the *shtuḳi* and *asufi,* the tannaim had a category of blemish of birth which they called "rabbinical mamzer." This category was introduced by the rabbis as a matter of discipline. If a woman, for instance, on unauthenticated and unproven report of the death of her husband, rushes into another marriage, she must give up both husbands when the report is proven false. Going back to her first husband is prohibited rabbinically, on the threat that the children who may be begotten thenceforth will be rabbinical mamzerim.[64]

The certain mamzer, the doubtful mamzer, and the rabbinical mamzer, of either sex, may not be married to Jews. Whom then shall they marry? Of course, they are Jews themselves and must be bound by Jewish marriage laws, but because of their marriage difficulties certain minimum suspensions of the marriage laws are made in their behalf. Originally the mamzer could marry a proselyte, a freed slave, a Nathin, a *shtuḳi,* or an *asufi.*[65] There was a certain tannaitic challenge to the law permitting a mamzer to marry a proselyte or a freed slave, who also has the status of a proselyte. The objection was on the part of the proselyte, for he is bound by Jewish law, which prohibits marrying a mamzer. That objection was ignored by the halakah on the principle that the mamzer cannot marry into the *congregation* of the Lord, but

[61] Ḳid. 73b.
[62] Ket. 15b; Yad, Issure Bi'ah 15,25–6.
[63] Ḳid. 73a–b.
[64] M. Yeb. 87b; Yeb. 89b.
[65] M. Ḳid. 69a.

proselytes are not included in the *congregation*.[66] Hence, the first marriage possibility for the mamzer, male or female, and one which would be within his social sphere, is the proselyte. A mamzer of any calibre, therefore, may marry a convert. The next tannaitic challenge was against the law permitting the mamzer to marry the hush-child or the foundling, who are doubtful mamzerim. Furthermore, a doubtful mamzer should not marry another doubtful mamzer, said some of the tannaim, for one of the pair might be a mamzer and the other of full legitimate origin, and their union would then be a violation of the law.[67] This last stricture was accepted by the final halakah, which ruled that the certain mamzer may marry, next to the proselyte, only another certain mamzer; the doubtful mamzer may take only a proselyte but neither a certain mamzer nor a doubtful mamzer; a rabbinical mamzer may marry a proselyte and another rabbinical mamzer but neither a certain nor doubtful mamzer.[68]

Finally, another marriage possibility was opened for male mamzerim of any calibre (except probably rabbinical mamzerim) by tannaitic law, permitting them to marry female slaves, which amounts actually to intermarriage and is severely prohibited to other Israelites. This permission was inspired by the desire on the part of legal authorities to find a way of purging the offspring of the mamzer of the perpetual stain; and marrying a female slave, as mentioned, was the only way of attaining that goal. But a female mamzer can never escape the perpetuity of the mamzer stain, and therefore she was not permitted to marry a slave. With little discussion, this special grant of the law to the male mamzerim was accepted by the final halakah.[69]

Deuteronomy prohibits a eunuch marrying a Jewish woman, with the injunction: "He that is crushed or maimed in his privy parts shall not enter into the congregation of the

[66] See p. 200 in chapter on Intermarriage and notes 158–60.

[67] M.Ḳ. 74a.

[68] Yad, Issure Bi'ah 15,21–24.

[69] Ḳid. 69a. The amoraic interpretation of the mishnah, that it teaches an outright permission for union between mamzer and female slave, is probably correct. Yad, Issure Bi'ah 15,4.

Lord."[70] The prohibition is not intended to eliminate sterile males from marriage because of consequent childlessness; for there is no indication in the Bible that sterility is a bar to marriage either for the male or the female. Certainly the woman's duty to beget children is not in any way indicated in the Bible, and even the halakah does not recognize any such duty. The objection to a eunuch's marrying a daughter of Israel is based on the revulsion of the Jews to the practice of castration, prevalent among their neighbors in biblical times. This is reflected in a verse in Leviticus (22.24), which reads: "That which hath its stones bruised or crushed or torn or cut ye shall not offer unto the Lord; neither shall you do thus in your land." It may be assumed, therefore, that in prohibiting the eunuch, the deuteronomic legislator had in mind one castrated by human hands. Samuel, among the earliest Babylonian amoraim, sets it down as the rule of law that only he is prohibited to marry a Jewess who is castrated by the "hand of man," not by the "hand of Heaven."[71] By "hand of man" we understand both intentional castration and castration by accident, and by "hand of Heaven" we understand castration by illness or congenital injury to genitals, except that certain authorities consider any injury due to illness as of the "hand of man" category.[72] The eunuch, like the mamzer, is permitted to marry a woman of the lower castes, proselyte, freed slave, Nathin, *shtuki,* or *asufi;* and the limitations of later law against the mamzer were not set against the eunuch.[73] Whether the eunuch can marry a mamzeret is a matter of controversy among post-talmudic scholars.[74]

Akin in physical defect to the eunuch is the hermaphrodite. There is no biblical or rabbinical prohibition against a hermaphrodite marrying, and there could not be, for his condition is congenital and not by the "hand of man." The

[70] Deut. 23.2.

[71] Yeb. 75b.

[72] E.H. 5,10.

[73] Yeb. 76a; Yad, Issure Bi'ah 16,1–2; E.H. 5,1.

[74] Yad, ibid.; E.H. ibid. Maimonides prohibits, RABD permits. All agree, however, that he is permitted in marriage all the categories of doubtful mamzer.

rabbis treat of two kinds of hermaphrodites, *ṭumṭum* and *androgynus,* the former having undeveloped genitals so that it cannot be determined whether he is male or female, the latter having both male and female organs. The former is accepted, by legal principle, as a doubtful male or female.[75] Concerning the latter there are various tannaitic traditions; in the earlier tradition he is treated as a male, in the later he is declared to be of a special gender, a male-female combination. The latter tradition has been accepted by the halakah. Therefore, the marriage of a *ṭumṭum* either to a husband or to a wife is of doubtful validity and requires a divorce because of the doubt. The *androgynus* is classed with males, the male element being recognized as predominant in the combination, and he is allowed, therefore, to marry only a female. But his marriage to a female, nevertheless, has only doubtful validity.[76]

The closest approach to such defects of the generative organs in the female is the *ailonit,* the man-woman, the female with masculine features. Her characteristics are no pubic hair, no breasts, no *mons veneris,* pain in copulation, and male voice.[77] These characteristics are often not noticeable in a very young girl, and when girls were given in marriage at a tender age it was not infrequent that action was brought by the husband long after marriage to have it annulled. The law, as interpreted by the tosafists, considers such a marriage void, but other authorities contend that a divorce is rabbinically required.[78] But this does not mean that an *ailonit* may not be married. If at the time of the mar-

[75] Yeb. 72a; Bek. 42b.

[76] The older conception of *Androgynus* is quoted in M. Yeb. 81a, the later view is cited as a beraita, Yeb. 83a. See Yad, Ishut, 4,11. RABD maintains that if the *Androgynus* has married a woman no divorce is necessary. See also E.H. 44,5.

[77] Yeb. 80b.

[78] Tosafot Giṭ. 46b, s.v. *Ha-moẓi.* The proof that Tosafot offers from M. Yeb. 2a is not conclusive, because the Talmud (Yeb. 12b top) is even willing to read into the mishnah the case of the *ailonit* whose defect was known to her husband, in which case it is agreed that the marriage is valid. See E.H. 44.4. *Bet Shemuel* (E.H. ibid.) cites *Nimmuke Joseph,* deciding on the authority of R. Tam that a divorce is rabbinically required.

riage the husband has known of her physical defect, the marriage is fully valid.[79] In such a case, however, the problem arises whether the marriage is prohibited or not because the *ailonit* is incapable of child-bearing.

Is a sterile woman prohibited in marriage to a Jew? The question refers not only to the *ailonit* but also to the normally barren woman who by previous marriages has proven herself sterile, to the woman who through medication or operation has become barren, to the woman who has passed the child-bearing age, and even to one who is too young for conception. There is no biblical derivation for such a prohibition, and it is admitted that the whole question is on the level of rabbinical law.[80] Philo considers the marriage of a sterile woman prohibited, arguing that such unions are for lust and contrary to piety.[81] There is no parallel to this prohibition in rabbinic law, and yet in many tannaitic texts there is an assumption that such a marriage was prohibited by the rabbis.[82] In the final development of tannaitic halakah, the sentiment expressed by Philo that such a marriage is a lustful waste of powers is wholly lost sight of, and the whole question hinges on the duty of procreation. Man is duty bound by biblical injunction to beget children and children's children. According to the Shammaites one must have a minimum of two sons; to the Hillelites, one son and one daughter. Before he has fulfilled this obligation, he may not be unmarried[83] and he may not marry a barren wife; after he has fulfilled the duty of procreation, he is ethically bound to be married and to marry a woman who will bear him

[79] M. Ket. 100b; Yad, Ishut 4,10.

[80] Ket. 77b at bottom. See Rashi, ibid., s.v. *litani,* where he points out that the biblical command to "multiply" can be fulfilled by a polygamous marriage; therefore the prohibition against marrying a barren wife, in and for itself, is no more than rabbinical.

[81] Philo, *Spec. Leg.* III, 6,36.

[82] E.g., M. Soṭah 24a; M. Yeb. 64a; Tos. Yeb. 8,4; Ber. Yeb. 62b. On the presupposition that polygamy is permitted, it is curious that fruitless marriages are prohibited in these texts without specifying that such prohibition applies only in the event of the husband's utter childlessness in any other marriage.

[83] M. Yeb. 61b; Yeb. 61a at bottom; Tos. Yeb. 8,4 at the end.

children, but legally he may remain unmarried or may take a barren woman.[84] However, the difference between the ethical and the legal in Jewish law is exceedingly thin; hence in the final halakah some teachers are more severe and some more lenient in restricting a man who has children against marrying a barren woman.[85]

The third marriage prohibition legislated in Deuteronomy concerns remarriage of a divorced wife after she has been married to another. The biblical verses read: "When a man taketh a wife and marrieth her, then it cometh to pass, if she find no favor in his eyes . . . that he writeth her a bill of divorcement . . . and sendeth her out of his house; and she departeth out of his house and goeth and becometh another man's wife; and the latter husband hateth her and writeth her a bill of divorcement . . . or if the latter husband die . . . her former husband who sent her away may not take her again to his wife after that she is defiled, for that is abomination before the Lord; and thou shalt not cause the land to sin . . ." [86] Jeremiah refers to this law with great vehemence, as something very shocking to the people: "If a man put away his wife and she go from him and become another man's, may he return to her again? Will not the land be greatly polluted? " [87] The reference both in Deuteronomy and Jeremiah to the pollution of the land reveals the Jewish conscience on the subject. Such an act seemed akin to promiscuity. Philo records this law with no addition to the Bible's words, but his reason for the prohibition is that such a union displays lack of courage and manliness in the husband.[88]

Rabbinic halakah does not go into motives, but seeks to establish the exact operation of this law. It rules that the

[84] M. Yeb. ibid.; M. Ket. 100b; M. Soṭah 24a; M. Giṭ. 46b. The ethical duty is emphasized in Yeb. 62b and 63b. Extenuating circumstances sometimes remove this ethical duty and even the biblical duty of procreation.

[85] Yad, Ishut 15,7,16. Maimonides puts this on an ethical basis, but R. Moses ha-Kohen (cited in *Maggid*, Ishut 15,7) puts it on the level of a rabbinical law, prohibiting any man marrying a barren woman.

[86] Deut. 24.1–4.

[87] Jer. 3.1.

[88] Philo, *Spec. Leg.* III, 5,30–31. Philo says that a death penalty is prescribed for violation of this law.

law applies only when there have been two marriages, to the first and to the second husbands. If she has lived with the first husband in a state of concubinage, or with the second in harlotry or concubinage, she is not prohibited to return to her first husband. On the other hand, if she has had no sex contact with either, has merely been betrothed to the first or to the second husband, she may not return to her first husband. In case she is a fatherless minor and her marriage to the first or second husband is only of rabbinical validity, she may return to her first husband, if released from him by *mi'un,* which is the process of "rejection" referred to above. But if released from her first husband by a bill of divorcement, though it was superfluous, he may not remarry her after she has been married to another. The prohibition in this case is rabbinical in character, as something that in the minds of the uncultivated populace resembles the biblical prohibition. As a matter of fact, the rabbis have put the same restriction on any man caught in a situation where he must write a bill of divorcement for a woman, because of rumors or other legal complications; after the woman's marriage to another man, he may never marry her, because it will look as though she is "returning" to him.[89]

Though inarticulate, the rabbis recognized the original biblical motive for this prohibition, and from this they inferred another and much similar prohibition. An unfaithful wife is certainly an "abomination" to the Lord and a defilement of the land. Hence a man may not continue to live with a wife proven to have committed adultery or whom the husband charges with adultery. And from this follows the prohibition to remarry a faithless wife once divorced.

[89] The law in the ordinary case is given in Yeb. 11b, Yer. Yeb. 11a, where R. Jose b. Kippar declares that only after she has been married to another is she prohibited to return to her first husband. But the majority scholars ruled against him, declaring that if only betrothed to another she is prohibited to her first husband. Ordinary promiscuity without marriage does not prohibit her returning to her husband (if occurring after her divorce) according to the ruling of all legal teachers. See Rashi, Soṭah 18b, s.v. *Weniṭma'at;* Yad, Gerushin 11,12–13 and *Hagahot Maimoniyot,* ibid.

The case of the minor orphan girl is given in Yeb. 108b; Yad, Gerushin 11, 16. The prohibition in case she was divorced because of a rumor of marriage is based upon Giṭṭin 89b. See Yad, Ishut, 9,26; E.H. 10,1; 46,5.

The Bible knows of no such prohibition, but by application of hermeneutic logic the rabbis inferred it from the biblical use of certain terms and phrases, and thus set it on the level of a biblical law.[90]

III

We approach our investigation into a series of marriage prohibitions that are distinctly rabbinical ordinances, by which no claim is made of biblical sanction or derivation. They are intended to govern Jewish life in accordance with certain beliefs and concepts prevalent in rabbinic times and more especially in accord with a scrupulous conscience in the matter of public morality. The first of the rabbinic ordinances under this head is the prohibition against marrying a woman who has been widowed several times. The tannaim had an eye for the problem of health in relation to marriage, but advanced as they were for their time in medical knowledge, they may be pardoned for accepting certain recurring disasters as a token of disease even where no disease could be traced medically. They argued that there must be something of an unaccountable, dangerous disease, or if you will, of ill omen, in a woman who had been widowed several times. She ought to be considered dangerous and ought not to be permitted to remarry; she is a *ḳaṭlanit,* a "killer."

It was not an alien principle in rabbinic law that an event occurring several times under the same conditions established a presumption that it would occur again under the same conditions. This principle is invoked to prohibit circumcision of a child if several of his brothers before him have died after circumcision. The law declares a woman barren, if she has remained childless with several husbands. The law establishes a menstrual period for a woman after regularity of several months. Other matters of law hinge upon this principle, too many to enumerate. The same mathematical

[90] Soṭah 27b–28a; Yeb. 11a–b; 49b, and Tosafot, ibid. s.v. *Soṭah;* Yad, Gerushin, 11,14. Maimonides teaches that in the case of proven adultery the prohibition is biblical but in adultery charges it is only rabbinical. Adret teaches that the prohibition is biblical in both cases. See *Maggid,* ibid.

legal formula is invoked by the rabbis in warning that if several husbands of the same woman have died, the chances are poor for the next husband. To establish this presumption in law, repetition of the event twice is enough, according to Rabbi Judah the Nasi; according to R. Simeon b. Gamaliel it must occur at least three times. To the former, therefore, a woman widowed twice cannot be married to a third husband; to the latter, if widowed three times, she cannot marry a fourth husband.[91] The halakah accepted the former view and prohibits the widow entering a third marriage.[92] No penalty, however, is prescribed for violation of this prohibition.[93]

The Talmud nowhere refers to any prohibition against a man remarrying after being twice widowed, and from this post-talmudic teachers infer that no such interdiction was contemplated.[94] The reason for this distinction is partly that the rabbis did not want to interfere with the man's right of marriage, to whom procreation is a biblical command. Another reason probably is that their medical sense prompted them to fear danger from infection carried by women more than by men. In the hands of the amoraim, this law assumed two interpretations, one interpreting the law on the basis of infection, another basing it on the woman's bad luck. According to the former view, if the woman was widowed during betrothal, before nuptials, that widowhood does not count, because she had had no contact with her husband. According to the latter view even this kind of widowhood counts. Likewise, the case is disputed when the husband has died of an accident, which may be a matter of bad luck but not of infection.[95] The final halakah makes no decision in this amoraic controversy, but is inclined to advise caution even in cases of widowhood arising from accidents or before

[91] Tos. Sab. 15,8; Yeb. 64b.

[92] Yad, Issure Bi'ah 21,31; E.H. 9,1.

[93] According to Asheri, quoted in *Ṭur* E.H. 9, divorce is compulsory, and if the husband did not know that her former two husbands had died while married to her she loses her ketubah.

[94] See *Bet Joseph* ad *Ṭur*, ibid. However, *Ḥelḳat Meḥoḳeḳ* ad E.H. ibid. advises caution even in the case of the man widowed twice before.

[95] Yeb. ibid.

nuptials.[96] Among post-talmudic authorities, there are some who teach that even a divorcee from two husbands may not marry a third, but the halakah takes the opposite view, seeing no danger in marrying a divorcee no matter how many times divorced.[97] On the other hand, there is a bit of good modern eugenics when the amoraim teach that one shall not marry a woman in whose family there is a history of leprosy or epilepsy, where three cases of such disease are known to have occurred; and the final halakah stands fully by this prohibition.[98]

To stabilize family life, the rabbis enacted an ordinance prohibiting marriage between a man and a divorced woman if the man was named as co-respondent in the divorce proceedings. The prohibition applies generally to all cases where the man's intimacies with the woman were the cause of the divorce, but the boldness of the intimacies tempers the severity of the prohibition. The worst case is where there is definite testimony by witnesses that he cohabited with the woman while she was still married to the former husband. Then his marriage is considered biblically prohibited, and divorce is compulsory even if she already has had children by him. The next and similar case is that of *soṭah,* where the husband, suspicious of his wife's relations with the co-respondent, commands her before witness not to meet him in private, and where thereafter, in violation of her husband's command, witnesses testify to have found them in intimate privacy together. Though there is no testimony of actual adultery, so long as she has violated the command of jealousy, the husband is in duty bound to divorce her (or to put her through the ordeal of bitter waters prescribed in Numbers). The co-respondent, then, is biblically prohibited to marry her, and if he does he is compelled to divorce her, even if she has had children by him. Lower in severity is the case where a jealous husband presents witnesses to the court that his wife and the co-respondent have been seen in compromising positions and that their intimacies have been

[96] See note of Isserles ad E.H. ibid.
[97] Isserles, ibid.
[98] Yeb. ibid.; Yad, Issure Bi'ah 21,30.

rumored about town as adulterous unions, but there is no legally valid testimony to prove adultery. In that case, marriage is only rabbinically prohibited; divorce is compulsory if the co-respondent has married her in violation of the prohibition, provided, however, that she has no children by this new husband. If there are children by this marriage, the case is dropped, for protection of the children's reputation. Finally, there is a fourth case, lowest in severity, where rumors of adultery are lacking or evoke counter rumors, but definite testimony is presented that the wife and the co-respondent have been seen in a compromising position. Here, too, the co-respondent may not marry the wife after she is divorced by her husband, but if he has married her in defiance of the law, even if they have no children, the case is dropped and he may retain her as wife.[99]

Not only adultery but also other prohibited relations between a man and woman establish a rabbinical prohibition against their marriage thereafter. Thus, if there have been sex relations between a Jew and a gentile woman or female slave, or between a gentile or slave and a Jewish woman, they may not marry even when the slave is freed or the gentile converted. Apparently the rabbis did not want to sanction by the marriage rite marital relations begun in sin. However, if in defiance of the rabbinic prohibition the marriage has taken place, no measures are taken by the court to separate them, even if they have had no children.[100] Unmarried relations between a Jewish man and a Jewish girl, so long as marriage between them is possible, is not considered in the Jewish law as "sin" but as improper. Therefore, should they wish to marry afterwards, the law does not in any way object. On the contrary, it is the proper thing to do according to biblical prescription.[101] In that case, however, a new set of prohibitions were enacted by the rabbis. The man may not marry the girl's sister or mother or daughter. One is inclined to say that this law meant to spare the girl's feelings, she having been seduced and jilted, not to have

[99] Soṭah 27b–28a; Yeb. 11a–b; 24b–25a; Yad, Soṭah, 2,12–16.
[100] M. Yeb. 24b; Tos. Yeb. 4,6; Yer. Yeb. 4a.
[101] Ex. 22.15; Deut. 22.29.

her own nearest kin the victorious rivals. But this is not in the mind of the rabbis. They have a moral consideration. After marrying the girl's sister or mother or daughter, she will be a frequent visitor in his home and a constant temptation to him to continue the intimacies of former days, now being incestuously prohibited to him. This prohibition is not enforced by penalties, so that if the marriage has taken place in disregard of the law they are not compelled to divorce.[102] Should the husband continue immoral and incestuous relations with this girl who was his consort before his marriage, he would be punished in accordance with the law of incest, but that would not affect his marriage in the least.[103]

The high moral sense of the rabbis accounts for other enactments in regard to marriage restrictions. They ruled that the agent of the husband who delivers a bill of divorcement to the wife and certifies that the bill was written under authority of the husband and especially intended for the wife named therein, may not marry that woman. Likewise a judge who has ruled in a case of annulment of vows in a manner making it necessary for a husband therefore to divorce his wife, may not marry the woman. Also a witness who testifies in the disappearance of a husband that he has seen him murdered or that he otherwise knows for certain that he has died, being the only witness and carrying the responsibility for declaring the woman a widow, may not marry her.[104] In all these cases the motive of the prohibition is evident, that there be no suspicion that that agent or judge or witness has acted under the bias of hoping to marry the

[102] Tos. Yeb. 4,5; Yeb. 26a. Yeb. 97a states that after the girl's death the entire prohibition vanishes. See Yad, Issure Bi'ah, 2,11.

[103] Yeb. 95a; Yad, Issure Bi'ah 2,10, and see RABD note thereto.

[104] M. Yeb. 2,9–10; Tos. Yeb. 4,5. This does not mean that any witness or judge in a case has restrictions against marrying the litigant who has been released by action of the court or testimony of the witness. The prohibition here, as the Talmud (Yeb. 25b) explains it, is due to the fact that the action of one judge, one witness, or one agent is sufficient to determine the woman's freedom to remarry. Tosephta implies, however, that higher moral considerations should deter judge or agent or witness from marrying any woman who has benefited by his action on the principle, "Keep at a distance from that which is ugly and also from that which resembles the ugly."

woman involved. If the woman has in the mean time married another and thereafter been divorced from him, any of the men in the above categories may marry her. Also, if the agent or judge or witness was married at the time the woman was released from her husband, and then was widowed or divorced without provocation on his part, he may then marry her. The law does not call for enforcement of this prohibition, so that if the marriage has taken place in violation, no attempt is made to separate the pair.[105]

A few more marriage prohibitions were enacted by the rabbis out of consideration for "general public welfare." Thus they ruled that a man may not remarry his wife if he has divorced her for one of the following reasons: because she has proved to be an *ailonit* and therefore barren;[106] because she has no regular menstrual periods;[107] because her loose conduct has cast on her a suspicion of unfaithfulness; [108] because of certain vows leading to divorce.[109] Two reasons are given by the tannaim for these prohibitions. The first, applicable to all cases, is that these causes for divorce are likely to be eliminated in time; the *ailonit* may be discovered to be no *ailonit* at all but to have suffered some temporary physical defect; the menstrual period may adjust itself in time; the suspicion of unfaithfulness may be found to have been without foundation; and the vows may be annulled. Should the husband be permitted hope of remarrying her, he might seek an annulment of the divorce and complicate matters for the woman's second husband and her children by him. The second reason applies specifically to divorce on the ground of reputed unfaithfulness or on the ground of vows. According to this second explication,

[105] M. Yeb. 26a and Gemara thereon; Tos. Yeb. 4,6. Tosephta indicates that only if the judge or agent or witness was widowed does the prohibition cease but not if he was divorced, lest the divorce be part of the original plot. Talmud Yeb. 26a allows also for divorce, provided the divorce was initiated by the wife, not by the husband. See Yad, Gerushin 10,14–16.

[106] M. Giṭ. 46b; Ket. 100b. However, if the husband divorced his wife because of childlessness, the cause being other than *ailonit,* he may remarry her. See Tosafot, Yeb. 65a, s.v. *ee.*

[107] Nid. 12b.

[108] Giṭ. 45b; Tos. Giṭ. 3,3; Yad, Ishut, 24,15; Gerushin 10,12.

[109] Giṭ. 45b; Tos. Giṭ. 3,3; Ket. 70a–71a.

the enactment was simply a measure of discipline against a woman loose with her tongue who makes vows thoughtlessly, or loose in her conduct and arousing suspicions of unfaithfulness.[110] Hence, according to this view, the prohibition against remarrying a wife who has been divorced because of vows applies only when it is the wife who offered the vows, but not when the husband has made the vows that led to divorce; the halakah accepts this view.[111]

Rabbinical enactments prohibit marriages under certain temporary conditions; therefore the prohibitions themselves are temporary in nature. They may be more properly called marriage postponements. Aside from certain days in the year when marriage is rabbinically prohibited – which, however, do not come within the scope of our present study – marriage is sometimes banned by the rabbis for a certain duration of time. Thus marriage is prohibited during mourning, both to men and to women, for a period of thirty days, according to talmudic law. However, because of the duty of procreation, men are permitted to marry after the first seven days of mourning, so long as they have not the number of children required by the law. No reduction of the thirty days of mourning is made for women, because women have no duty of procreation in the eyes of the law.[112] This rule, as it applies to mourners for father or mother or brother or sister, should apply equally to those bereaved of husband or wife. Yet greater restrictions against marriage have been put upon the widower and the widow. Evidently delicacy requires that one should not change his or her love too suddenly, and that the memories of a former marriage should not crowd upon the happiness of a new marriage.[113] Therefore the widower is required by law to wait a period of time to include three festivals, according to other teachers two festivals, before he takes another wife. However, this period is reduced to the minimum of seven days in case the husband

[110] Tos. ibid.; Yeb. 46a. Apparently R. Elazar b. R. Jose and R. Jose b. R. Judah (Tos. and M. ibid.) hold the same view, and contrary to the other tannaitic teachers.

[111] M. Giṭ. ibid.; Giṭ. 46a; E.H. 10,7.

[112] M.Ḳ. 23a; Sem. ch. 7; note of Isserles, Y.D. 392,2.

[113] Tosafot M.Ḳ. 23a, s.v. *'ad*.

is childless or he is left with small children who need a woman's care, or if the husband himself finds himself helpless without the personal attentions that a woman can give him. Which means that the law has made the restriction so pliable that a husband can under any pretense nullify it completely and remarry after the first seven days of mourning following his wife's death.[114] For the widow, the period of mourning for her husband is the same as for her father or mother or brother or sister, a minimum of thirty days in which she cannot remarry. No reduction from this period of time is made for her on any condition.[115] But an extension of the period has been made on other grounds, which we shall now consider.

Tannaitic law has it that any married woman, after being divorced or widowed from her husband, may not enter a second marriage for a period of three months (ninety days). One has reason to believe that this prohibition has the same motive as the similar prohibition to men in widowhood, to allow time for the dissolution of former sex experience before new ones are entered upon. In the case of a woman, the moral sentiment against mixing sex associations or even sex memories must have been much stronger than in the case of man. Possibly this prohibition goes back to an older period than the talmudic records indicate and possibly it represented a more general, even non-Jewish, sentiment in the ancient orient. Viewed from this point, we can understand the wide application of the prohibition. It applies, according to tannaitic teaching, to the woman widowed or divorced after betrothal just as after nuptials, to the virgin as to the non-virgin, to one who is too old for child bearing as to one who is too young, even to a barren woman or *ailonit,* even if the woman has been widowed during pregnancy or has had a miscarriage soon after her husband's death. In all these cases, the woman must wait three months after being widowed or divorced before she can remarry, even before she can be betrothed.[116] The prohibition is valid also if immediately

[114] M.Ḳ. ibid.; Sem. ibid.; Yer. Yeb. 6b.
[115] M. Yeb. 41a; Tos. Yeb. 6,6; Yeb. 43b.
[116] M. Yeb. ibid.; Tos. Yeb. ibid.; E.H. 13,1.

prior to his death or prior to granting the divorce the husband has been sick or imprisoned or away from home in a distant land for a considerable uninterrupted length of time. Again, this sociological explanation of the law further explains the exception in the case of a minor orphan girl, who does not have to wait three months for remarriage,[117] because such a marriage has been one only in name, by rabbinical enactment, and is not looked upon as of valid sexual significance.

The law officially, however, has another reason for this period of three months' waiting between marriage and marriage, to make sure whether the child born after the second marriage has the first or second husband as father. Logically this prohibition should apply only where pregnancy was possible either with the first or second husband, but the law would say, error as to the paternity of a child is so important morally that for the sake of avoiding error where it is possible the prohibition has been made so general as to include those cases where it is altogether impossible. Assuming this motive of the law, "to distinguish between the seed of the first and the seed of the second husband," the law teaches that if the woman is to be remarried to her own husband from whom she has been divorced, there is no requirement of any period of waiting.[118] On the other hand, a gentile pair converting to Judaism together and continuing as husband and wife after conversion must be separated for a period of three months from the moment of conversion, before they can be reunited as husband and wife under sanction of Jewish law, in order that it be known as to the first child whether he was conceived of holy or of heathen seed.[119]

If the motive of the prohibition is to make it possible to ascertain the paternity of the child, then the law should demand a period of three months' waiting even for certain *first* marriages, where the girl is known to be non-virgin or has the legal status of a non-virgin. Thus, the leading

[117] Yeb. 34b; Ket. 100b; E.H. 13,6.

[118] A correct post-talmudic inference from the Talmud. See responsa of RIBS, 462, and E.H. 13,4.

[119] Yeb. 42a.

authorities require a pre-marital period of three months' abstinence from male contact for the following: the professional or non-professional prostitute; the girl raped or seduced; and likewise those who have the legal status of a non-virgin, such as the freed captive woman, the liberated female slave, or the female proselyte.[120] But R. Jose, who was generally lenient in this particular case, taught that no prohibition need be applied to any first marriage of a girl even where she is known to have had previous sex contacts.[121] R. Jose's view is perfectly logical, if our conjecture is right that the law originally intended to wear away affections and sex experiences, but from the point of view of the halakah, emphasizing the motive of ascertaining paternity, the view of R. Jose is explained by a general legal assumption that an illegitimate sex union does not produce pregnancy because the woman takes precautionary measures.[122] The final halakah has accepted all severities in enforcing the three months' wait between one marriage and another, but also the leniencies of R. Jose's view, demanding no waiting period for any unmarried woman after pre-marital sex experiences.[123]

Rabbinic law also provides that a pregnant woman shall not be married until she is delivered. Various reasons are offered. Yerushalmi cites a combination of biblical verses: "Remove not the ancient landmarks which they of old have set, and enter not into the fields of the fatherless." [124] Babli suggests that the foetus is endangered by careless intercourse on the part of the new husband who has no interest in the unborn child. Another reason by Babli is that a pregnant woman is prohibited in marriage because nursing will follow and the new husband will not provide properly for the

[120] Tos. Yeb. 6,6; Yeb. 35a; Pesikta of R. Kahana, ed. Buber, p. 106.

[121] Tos. ibid.

[122] Tos. Yeb. 35a. Yer. Yeb. 5a injects the thought that shielding the child's reputation is motive of the law's permission for the girl who has been raped or seduced to marry without waiting.

[123] Yad, Gerushin, 11,22; E.H. 13,6.

[124] Deut. 19.14; Prov. 22.28; 23.10. See Yer. Soṭah 19c; Tos. Nid. 2,7. The word *'Olam* is translated by them as "of tender age" and *ubisede* is rendered by them as "and in the *breasts*," as if it were *ubishede*. See Lewin, *Oẓar*, Yeb. pp. 96–7.

child's care during that period.[125] This would seem to apply to all pregnant women, widowed, divorced, or even unmarried mothers,[126] and it bans not only nuptials but also betrothal.[127] If the pregnant woman has been married contrary to this law, according to one view divorce is mandatory and they may never remarry; according to the milder view, accepted by the halakah, they are separated the required period and then reunited.[128]

A nursing mother, likewise, cannot be taken in marriage until the child has attained the weaning age. By this we understand that she may be neither married nor betrothed, and it does not matter whether she has been widowed or divorced, so long as she has the responsibility of nursing the child, and, for that matter, even if she is an unmarried mother.[129] The weaning age, according to the Shammaites, is when the child is twenty-four months old; according to the Hillelites, eighteen months. The prohibition is intended to protect the child's health, for should the mother be married and become pregnant, after three months of pregnancy her milk would become unfit for the suckling. Having this in view, R. Simeon b. Gamaliel sought to reduce the waiting period, so that three months before the weaning age the woman should be permitted to remarry.[130] However, the

[125] Yeb. 42a–b. Maimonides, Yad, Gerushin, 11,25 accepts the former reason, although the Talmud seems to emphasize the second.

[126] If the prohibition against marrying a pregnant woman is because intercourse is dangerous to the foetus, it stands to reason that there is no difference as to the status of the child. If the question is the nursing of the child after his birth, then the problem of the pregnant woman is the same as that of the nursing mother, which will be treated in a succeeding note.

[127] The provisions for the pregnant woman and for the nursing mother are the same. See E.H. 13,11 and note 129.

[128] M. Soṭah 24a; Soṭah 26a; Yer. Soṭah 19c; Yad, Gerushin, 11, 28; E.H. 13, 12. See next note.

[129] Tos. Nid. 2,2; Ket. 60a–b; Yer. Soṭah 19c. On the question of the unmarried mother a decision is given by Mordecai of Turmasha permitting her marriage (see Mordecai Yeb. 463), but other scholars disagree. *Bet Joseph, Ṭur* E.H. 13 coincides with the view that it be prohibited, and it is so recorded in E.H. 13,1. Whether the divorcee who has a nursing child has to wait two years is a question discussed by the tosafists. Some permit it, because the divorcee has no obligation of nursing her child, who belongs legally to the father. Rashi prohibits it, and it is so accepted by the halakah. See Tosafot Ket. 60b at bottom, Rashi, Soṭah 24a, s.v. *Me'ubberet.*

[130] Tos. Nid. 2,2–5; Ket. 60b; Yer. Soṭah 19c.

amoraim accepted the twenty-four months' period and allowed no reduction, and the final halakah declares a nursing mother may not marry until her child is two years old.[181]

The assumption of this law is that there is no substitute for the mother as nurse for the child. That is quite correct; once the child has begun feeding at his mother's breast and has thus become accustomed to her, there is danger to his health, say the rabbis, if his routine is changed.[182] However, if he has never begun nursing from his mother, a substitute nursing woman might be satisfactory, except for the fact that no woman hired for a fee is wholly reliable in the eyes of the law, and the child may still have to come back to his mother. Therefore the woman is prohibited marriage before her child is two years old, even if a wet nurse has been hired.[183] If the child has been weaned before the two years the woman still cannot marry, because the law will put no temptation in the way of the woman to wean the babe prematurely at the risk of his health.[184] Two distinctly opposing rulings are recorded in regard to the woman's right to marry if the child died before he was two. An amoraic view declares she may not, for if the law should permit her to marry in such a case, she might be tempted to do away with the child in order to gain freedom to remarry. This is the ruling and the practice of the Palestinian authorities.[185] The Babylonian Talmud decides that no such suspicion against a mother is

181 Ket. 60b; Yad, Gerushin 11,26; E.H. 13,11.

182 Tos. Nid. 2,5; Tos. Ket. 5,5.

183 The view of R. Naḥman, Ket. 60b. In the case of a divorcee who has not even begun nursing her child but has given it over to a wet nurse, RSBA permits marriage immediately, because no law can compel the mother, after divorce, to nurse her child unless the child has become accustomed to her. A gaonic ruling permits every nursing mother to remarry, if the child has been cared for by a wet nurse before the death of the husband. Many authorities oppose this ruling but agree that, if because the child was nursed by another person the mother has no more milk, there is no use extending a prohibition uselessly. See Lewin, *Oẓar*, Yeb. pp. 95–6; *Bet Joseph, Ṭur* E.H. 13; E.H. 13,11.

184 Ket. 60b. The gaonic ruling mentioned in the previous note applies also in case the child was weaned before the death of the husband or before the divorce. On authority of Asheri, this ruling has been accepted by *Ṭur* and E.H. ibid.

185 Yer. Soṭah 19d, a statement of Mar'Uḳba. See *Oẓar*, Yeb. p. 94; Miller, *Ḥiluf Minhagim*, No. 3.

logical; therefore, when the child is dead, the restriction is completely removed.[136] Following this ruling, the Babylonian post-talmudic authorities continued the practice of permitting the mother to remarry immediately after the child's death, and this has come down to us as the final decision of our halakah.[137] If in defiance of the law the woman has remarried while having a nursing child, the rule is that in the event the remarriage was only betrothal, she is made to wait for nuptials until the child is two years old; but if a full marriage, including nuptials, she must be divorced and is at liberty to remarry her new husband (if he is not a priest) when the child has attained the age of two.[138]

IV

The law knows of certain restrictions that apply to the marriage of priests, above those here treated which refer commonly to all Jews. While they are biblical, these rules come to us from post-exilic sources. There is nothing in the earlier sources that would set up different standards of marriage for priests from those of lay Israelites. Recognizing, however, that generally new legislation has its roots in older traditions, it is not far-fetched to assume that the levitical laws for priestly marriages existed in pre-exilic times as uncodified priestly traditions.

As a mere conjecture and without explicit proof, we are inclined to believe that either all the levitical tribe or at least some of the more distinguished families among them insisted on marrying only within their tribe. We have already noticed the rule of endogamy among the Jewish people as a whole, which accounted for the prevalence of cousin marriages during the biblical period and which was also the foundation of Jewish resistance to intermarriage with foreign nations. This rule of endogamy was much sharper, probably, in the case of priests, as is usual for people of aristocratic distinctiveness, and led to the standard of

136 Ket. 60b; *Ḥiluf Minhagim,* ibid.

137 Yad, Gerushin 11,27; E.H. 13,11.

138 Soṭah 24a, 26a; Yeb. 24a; Yad, Gerushin 11,28 and *Maggid* thereto; E.H. 13,12.

priests marrying priests. Like the general rule of endogamy, the priestly standard was merely social but not legal, and no penalties were imposed on priests who married outside their tribe. Remnants of this social rule are to be found in legal and social standards of post-exilic times down to the rabbinic period. Thus Ezekiel, requiring priests, the descendants of Zadok, to marry virgins of the seed of Israel, makes one exception in permitting them to marry the widows of priests.[139] Leviticus requires only high priests to marry virgins, but insists that they be of the priestly tribe, according to the Septuagint interpretation.[140] The existence of a group of aristocratic Jews during the Second Commonwealth, "who married their daughters into the priesthood," while it proves definitely that at that time there were alliances between priests and Israelites, tends to show also that the priests maintained a closed circle which was not easily penetrated except by a few Israelitish families of exceptional distinction. Priestly marriages, we are told in the

[139] Ez. 44.22. Ezekiel's priestly laws are different from those of Leviticus. The Talmud (Ḳid. 78b) does not recognize the difference and reinterprets this passage as follows: The high priests shall not take as wives either the widow or the divorcee but only virgins of the seed of the house of Israel; yet, as to the widow, some priests (other than high priests) may take her who is widowed. The Talmud evidently strains the text, and to us it seems that this represents earlier legislation than that of Leviticus. The relation of Ezekiel's law to that of Leviticus may be conceived in either of two ways. Either Ezekiel is generally more restrictive than Leviticus, or Ezekiel accepts the levitical law for ordinary priests but puts greater restrictions upon priests of the house of Zadok who belong to the high priestly family. Conversely, as to Leviticus, either it legislated milder priestly laws in general than those observed in Ezekiel's time, or it wiped away the difference between the priests of the house of Zadok and any other priest.

[140] Lev. 21.14. The term *betulah me'amav* is interpreted by Geiger, *Ḳebuẓat Ma'amarim,* pp. 132 f., in the sense of the Septuagint that a priest may marry only within the priestly tribe. Professor Louis Ginzberg in his *Hosafot* takes issue with Geiger, maintaining Septuagint was mistaken; Philo followed the Septuagint, and therefore Geiger is wrong. I have not been able to find proof of Dr. Ginzberg's conclusions as affecting the time of Leviticus or even the time of the Septuagint. Pharisaic halakah which permits a priest or even a high priest to marry an Israelitish woman is centuries later than both Leviticus and Septuagint. Dr. Geiger, however, is wrong in concluding that even in pharisaic times high priests permitted themselves to marry widows of priests, for I believe that even Ezekiel did not permit high priests to marry widows of any kind; the permission was intended only for the sons of Zadok, who were merely the rank and file of the elite of the priesthood.

Mishnah, had higher standards of ketubah obligations than those usual for other Jewish marriages; and the amoraim believe the reason to have been to discourage intermarriage between priests and Israelites.[141] Also the tradition of priest cities indicates that there was much inbreeding among the priests.[142]

Pharisaic halakah gradually destroyed this closed circle of the priests, and beginnings of this process are seen in the Bible itself. Ezekiel permitted priests to marry Israelitish virgins but only priestly widows. Leviticus permitted them also to marry Israelitish widows. For the high priest Leviticus rules that he may marry only a priestly virgin, and it would not be surprising that until the time of the Septuagint this law was actually enforced in practice; but the Pharisees reinterpreted it to read that a high priest might marry only a virgin from among his people, meaning a Jewess, whether or not of the priestly tribe.[143] The aristocracy of priesthood was not much to the liking of the Pharisees; there were other aristocracies in Israel, that of royalty on the one hand and of learning on the other; in fact, every Jew, according to the Pharisees, is an aristocrat of noble birth. As time went on the monopoly of the priesthood on aristocracy of birth came to an end, and then the law ruled officially that "priests and Levites and Israelites are permitted to marry with one another." [144]

That priests did not marry heathens is, of course, a preexilic tradition, but in this they were not different from Israelites, who also resisted marriage with foreigners. When Ezra excluded proselytes from marriage with native Jews, he ruled both for priests and for Israelites. When, however, he also excluded the children of proselytes from marrying into pure-blooded Jewish families, he legislated for Israelites only, for the requirement that a priest marry only one of Jewish parentage was known before Ezra's time. It was taught by Ezekiel as a formal priestly law, that the priests,

141 Yer. Ḳid. 66a. See JMC pp. 73 f. See also Ber. 44a, showing the prevalence of marriages between priests and priests.

142 See chapter on Intermarriage, p. 149 above.

143 Sifra ad Lev. 21.14; Yer. Ḳid. 66b.

144 M. Ḳid. 69a.

descendants of Zadok, marry only "virgins of the seed of the house of Israel." But once Ezra's ruling was accepted, prohibiting all Israelites to marry women of foreign extraction, there was no need for invoking such a ban especially in the case of priests. Therefore the law for priestly marriages in the levitical code entirely omits the requirement that they marry wives of Hebrew descent, for this was then required of all Israelites.

During the Second Commonwealth, if we recall what we have learned in our chapter on Intermarriage, the influence of the Pharisees was exerted in the direction of completely eliminating the taint of foreign blood. They succeeded more readily with those of the Israelitish castes but not so readily with the priests and those aristocratic Israelitish families that wanted to marry into priestly families. Then the question of foreign descent became entirely a matter of priestly marriage laws. The priests held to the old tradition and were supported by the sadducean courts. They maintained their genealogical records, and, when records became confused and less reliable, they depended to a large extent on memory to trace the ancestry of any family. A certain *ḳeẓaẓah* ceremonial was employed by them to keep fresh in people's minds the memory of a taint of foreign blood. The Talmud describes this rite as follows. "If one of the brothers married a woman of undesirable strain, the members of the family would assemble and bring a barrel full of fruit and break it in the middle of the open street, proclaiming thus: Brothers of the house of Israel, our brother so-and-so took a wife of undesirable strain and we fear lest his children intermarry with our children; come now, therefore, and mark well as a token for generations to come that his seed and ours do not intermarry." [145] When both records and memory failed to give certainty, then court investigations had to be resorted to, and special sessions were dedicated to the task. But with the rise of the pharisaic courts to greater power and influence, the priests gradually yielded some of their restrictions against marriage with women of foreign

[145] Ket. 28b; Yer. Ket. 26d. See Freund in *Schwartz Festschrift*, p. 179 and note 3.

descent. Their first compromise was to investigate no further back than three generations; then they were satisfied to marry one who could trace her Jewish descent for only two generations; they were content, in the next stage, to marry one who had native born Jewish parents; and finally, one native Jewish parent was enough for them. Beyond that they did not go.[146]

Thus the final rabbinic halakah reduces priestly marriage prohibitions based upon foreign blood to a few simple rules. First, a priest may not marry a proselyte woman. The reason, according to later rabbinic interpretation, is not because of her foreign blood but because the law has declared her a statutory *zonah*.[147] R. Simeon b. Yoḥai would permit a priest to marry even a proselyte woman, provided she was converted before she was three years old; but the halakah did not recognize this view and prohibited priests marrying any proselyte no matter when converted.[148] Second, a priest may marry a woman whose father or mother is a native Jew, but not one whose parents are both proselytes. This is a concession to the stubbornness of priestly tradition, for the halakah recognizes the view of R. Jose who maintains that the daughter of two proselytes is fit for marriage into priesthood. Since, therefore, it is a restriction in which the halakah has no conscience, the law takes no action against any priest who violates it. In other words, if a priest marries a woman both of whose parents are proselytes, the law makes no effort to separate them.[149] Third, a priest may not marry a woman whose mother is Jewish and whose father is an (uncon-

[146] See discussion of this subject in chapter on Intermarriage, pp. 192–194 and notes thereto.

[147] See note 134 on Intermarriage. RABD, in note on Yad, Issure Bi'ah 18,3, contests the view that a proselyte woman has the status of a *zonah*. He considers the prohibition based on her foreign blood in accordance with Ezekiel's rule. See *Maggid* thereto.

[148] Ḳid. 78a; Yeb. 60b; Yad, Issure Bi'ah 18,3. The view of R. Simeon b. Yoḥai must be based on the concept that the proselyte woman is prohibited because she is a statutory *zonah* and not because of foreign blood. For in respect to foreign blood the age limit of three years has no meaning, while in respect to *zonah* it is an accepted rule in the halakah that cohabitation with a minor below three has no legal consequences. Hence a *zonah* below the age of three is no *zonah*.

[149] See note 140 on Intermarriage and Yad, Issure Bi'ah, 19,12.

verted) gentile or slave. We recall that according to some views the child of a mixed marriage is a mamzer, but the final halakah accepts the view that the child is not a mamzer. Nevertheless, the child is unfit for marriage into priestly families, according to the leading codes.[150] It is understood, of course, that if the father is Jewish and the mother gentile, the child, following the mother, is gentile and cannot be married to a priest even after conversion.

Here we may pause to consider a disqualification for priestly marriage designated technically as "*'issah.*" The priests, we are told, did not permit marriage with an *'issah* daughter or an *'issah* widow. Our oldest source for this term and for this priestly marriage restriction is the following mishnah. "R. Joshua and R. Judah b. Beteira cited the tradition that the widow of *'issah* is fit to marry into priesthood, for *'issah* is reliable as to testimony regarding purity or fitness for priestly marriage. But Rabban Gamaliel retorted: The tradition you cite is correct but we are powerless to do anything about it, since R. Johanan b. Zakkai ordained that the court should not take up this matter, because the priests will follow a court decision to retain restrictions but not to remove restrictions." [151] The term *'issah* is interpreted to mean dough consisting of fine flour and coarse grain in conglomerate mixture, and it expresses pictorially the concept of a disqualification for priestly marriage due to uncertainty as to purity of a certain person, family, or group of families.[152] Just what impurity is suspected under the designation of *'issah* is a matter of discussion among scholars. The rabbinic tradition applies the term in a loose sense to any disqualification for priestly marriage based upon suspicion,[153] but in a

[150] Yeb. 45a. Maimonides does not seem to take this prohibition seriously; Naḥmanides considers it doubtful; so does Alfasi. But *Tur,* E.H. 4, and Karo, E.H. 4,5, support the prohibition.

[151] M. 'Eduy. 8,3.

[152] See Rashi Ket. 14a, s.v. *tere;* Maimonides Commentary ad M. 'Eduyot, ibid.; Graetz, MGWJ, 1879, pp. 481 ff.; Rosenthal, MGWJ, Vol. 30 (1881) pp. 38 ff. See note 1 on p. 45 and note 1 on p. 48 in Rosenthal's article. See also the contrast pointed out by Rosenthal on pp. 116–17 between the expression *"Solet neḳiah"* and *'issah.*

[153] Ḳid. 71a, where certain lands are considered *'issah* in respect to others; Yer. Ket. 25d, where a girl whose identity was not known was relegated to the *'issah* class.

technical sense and according to tannaitic definition, *'issah* is any family in whose ancestry there is a suspicion of the blemish of ḥalalut, and by this is meant a suspicion that one of the ancestors was wed contrary to priestly marriage laws and begot offspring who were to be excluded from priestly marriage.[154] Two modern scholars, Rosenthal and Büchler, deviate to a certain extent from the rabbinic tradition and believe the *'issah* term to include the blemish of foreign blood.[155]

It is agreed by all, however, and this conclusion cannot be doubted on the basis of the sources, that *'issah* was originally not a legal concept in the abstract but a name given to a certain definite group among the Jews of the Second Commonwealth, and that the concept grew out of this particular name. Our task is therefore first to establish which group was so named and thereafter to follow out the attitude of the law toward the group and creation of the general legal concept of *'issah*. Rosenthal suggests that the *'issah* group is the same as the group of families in Ezra's time who could not produce documentary proof of their Hebrew origin. We take this suggestion as our starting point, for in general it has much merit, but we find ourselves compelled to introduce some novel features in order to overcome certain difficulties. During the latter part of the Second Commonwealth, when the *'issah* question was discussed, the group of Jews who had no documentary proof of Jewish lineage from pre-exilic records constituted practically the bulk of the Jewish people. There was on one side a group with definite traces of impurity, and on the other those who had genealogical records of pure ancestry. The mass of the Jews belonged in the middle, with no record of purity and likewise with no record of definite blemish. It was concerning these people that the law ruled that after investigating four or five generations back they might be married into the priesthood. It is not likely that the bulk of the Jewish people would be called by a special name *'issah,* and would be the subject of a special set of

[154] Ket. 14a–b; Tos. Ḳid. 5,3.

[155] Rosenthal, "Über 'Issah" in MGWJ, Vol. 30 (1881), pp. 38 ff. and Büchler, in *Festschrift Adolf Schwartz,* pp. 157 ff.

regulations. Again, in Rosenthal's suggestion we fail to see how the original *'issah* whose blemish was foreign blood turned into the tannaitic *'issah* whose disqualification is that of ḥalal.

We agree with Rosenthal that the *'issah* group had its beginning in Ezra's time and in the group of doubtful Hebrew ancestry. But there were two elements in that group, certain Israelitish families and certain priestly families. The Israelitish families gradually lost their identity by mingling with the rest of the Jewish population, and became the substance of the general un-aristocratic mass of the Jewish people. But the priestly families who at the time of Ezra could not prove their Jewish ancestry retained their identity throughout the Second Commonwealth. They were identified as priests not permitted to perform priestly functions. Such an identification could not easily be lost. Hillel, reporting the ten classes of Jews that came from Babylon under Ezra, mentions the ḥalal as one of them. Accustomed to the definition of ḥalal given by later tannaim, we have assumed that this is what Hillel also had in mind. This is not quite logical. In the first place, no such class is mentioned in Ezra or Nehemiah to have been set aside as a group because they were born of marriages prohibited for priests. Leviticus speaks of the female ḥalalah but knows of no male ḥalal. The male ḥalal in reality has no special status in the marriage laws of either priests or Israelites; it is only when he begets a daughter that the question comes up; and the daughter does not belong to any class, because by marrying an Israelite she makes an end to the strain of ḥalalut in her. We must understand, therefore, Hillel's use of the term ḥalal to be a designation for that group of priestly families in Ezra's time who were demoted from the priesthood, made profane or secular, for such is the original technical meaning of the word ḥalal in Hebrew.

This group of priestly families, then, referred to in Ezra and Nehemiah [156] as of doubtful Hebrew origin and as a consequence demoted from priesthood, survived up to the time of Hillel, who called them by the technical name

[156] Ezra 2.61–3; Neh. 7.63–5.

"ḥalali," demoted priests. They continued as a group to the end of the tannaitic period, under the name *'issah*.[157] The rabbinic tradition that this group was singled out not because of any blemish of mamzer or Nathin or slave but because of ḥalal,[158] in fact for no hindrance to marriage with Israelites but with priests, is historically quite correct. But whereas the original ḥalal was the one demoted from priesthood because of doubtful Hebrew origin, the ḥalal in the late tannaitic period[159] was a priest unfrocked for any reason whatever, even one born of pure Hebrew priestly ancestry but of a union prohibited for the priesthood.

Now, the attitude of the priests to these ḥalalim or, as they called them, the *'issah* families, was the same as that of the Israelites to the Nethinim or Samaritans. Their doubtful non-Jewish origin condemned them forever, no matter how many generations of Jewish descent they could prove. They yielded to the pressure from the Pharisees and permitted marriage to Israelites and priests who had no genealogical documents, if the latter could prove four or five generations of pure unblemished Hebrew ancestry. But in the case of the *'issah* group a proof of four or five generations of

[157] That the rabbis understood *'issah* to be a priestly family can be inferred from two sources. R. Me'ir says (Yer. Ḳid. 25d) that if there is real suspicion concerning the purity of the *'issah*, an examination should be made of *four* generations back. He evidently refers to M. Ḳid. 76a, and the Talmud confirms that this mishnah belongs to the tradition submitted by R. Me'ir. See Ḳid. 76b on top. But the mishnah demands four generations of purity for priestly families only, while for Israelitish families it demands *five* generations of purity. Again the Talmud is definite that the problem of *'issah* is that of ḥalalut. According to talmudic law, a ḥalalah married to an Israelite ends the ḥalal strain altogether (Ḳid. 77a). If the *'issah* were an Israelitish family, then, there would be no ḥalalut problem.

[158] Tos. Ḳid. 5,2; Ket. 14a–b; Tos. Ḳid. 5.3.

[159] Demotion from priesthood for one born of a union prohibited for priests is an old tradition. The Pharisees wanted to demote Alexander Janaeus (or his father, John Hyrcanus, 175–104 B.C.E.) from the high priesthood because his mother had been rumored to have been made captive (Ḳid. 66a; Josephus, *Antiq.* 13,10,5). See JE "Hyrcanus, John I." Also the tannaim of the first century speak of the demotion of one whose mother was a divorcee or had been released by ḥaliẓah. See M. Terum. 8,1; Ḳid. 66b. However, the term ḥalal is not applied to one so demoted until late tannaitic times. As a matter of fact, the new definition of ḥalal comes to us only from an amoraic (Ḳid. 77a–b) interpretation of a late tannaitic text (Sifra, Lev. 21.7,14, ed. Weiss, pp. 94b, 95a).

Hebrew descent would be of no avail, because they had a tradition of doubtful Hebrew descent in the remote past. R. Johanan b. Zakkai reports the priestly attitude, "to hold no court investigation," [160] because should the court find several generations of pure Jewish ancestry it would do no good. The Pharisees took the attitude that the *'issah* families should be treated like any other priestly family without genealogical record. They should be investigated by the court and if no foreign strain be discovered within four generations, they should be permitted to marry into the priesthood.[161]

However, the ancient ḥalal families who were suspected of foreign blood grew in numbers by the addition of the newer type of ḥalalim, those demoted from the priesthood because born of a union prohibited to priests, although they were of pure Hebrew stock; for it is natural that demoted priests should marry into the families of other demoted priests. To the Pharisees, the new ḥalal who was now part of the *'issah* complex was more seriously disqualified for priestly marriage than the old ḥalal whose foreign ancestry was remote and doubtful, for as regards foreign blood, as we have already noticed, the Pharisees tended to minimize its significance in the priestly marriage laws, while a blemish based upon violation of a marriage law represented a real hindrance to noble marriage. For this reason they did not minimize the blemish of the *'issah* daughter who could be held under suspicion that she was the descendant of an unbroken line of ḥalalim and hence unfit for priestly marriage. But the exclusion of the *'issah* widow from marriage with priests could have no other foundation than tracing the genealogy of her

[160] The expression, *She-lo le-hoshib,* (M. 'Eduy. 8,3) brings to mind *yoshabin u-bodeḳin* (Tos. Hagig 2,9) or *yoshebet we-danah* (M. Tamid 5,4), and refers not to court legislation but to court investigation.

[161] The expression in M. 'Eduyot, *she-ha-'issah kesherah,* means the same as *she-ha-'issah ne-emenet* (Tos 'Eduy. 3,2). The Talmud seems to feel that the woman's own testimony is sufficient (Ket. 14a) but this is not likely in view of the fact that prior to the destruction of the Temple the priests investigated four generations of mothers even in the ordinary, undocumented, priestly family. We believe, therefore, that M. 'Eduyot simply teaches that testimony is accepted according to the rule of the day, contrary to the claim of the priests that testimony is of no avail.

deceased husband to an ancestry of uncertain foreign blood, for at this stage of the halakah the husband's demotion from priesthood for any other reason would not disqualify the widow.[162] Hence the Pharisees directed their attack against the disqualification of the *'issah* widow, but admitted that the *'issah* daughter was a serious problem. Her case should be investigated by the court; she must prove that she is not descended from a male line of ḥalalim; but such proof as she can offer is acceptable.[163]

While during the existence of the Temple the Pharisees could not get the priests to accept their ruling concerning the *'issah* family, neither as to the widow nor as to the effectiveness of evidence for the daughter, the rabbis of a century and a half later had no difficulty in establishing a definite legal principle about the *'issah* family and to impose it upon

[162] That a woman is disqualified for priestly marriage by contact with a ḥalal is an uncertain late tannaitic ruling. Tos. Nid. 6,1 enumerates a number of male contacts that make the woman unfit for priestly marriage. The ḥalal is not mentioned among them. Evidently, the ḥalal does not belong there, because all the contacts enumerated are prohibited, while contact between an Israelitish (or even a priestly) woman and a ḥalal is not prohibited. But Babli, Ḳid. 74b, quoting this tosephta, includes also ḥalal. Another uncertain tannaitic text is M. Yeb. 9,1, which speaks of a ḥalal married to a woman as a case in which levirate marriage is impossible, because the levir who is a priest cannot marry a woman who has been the wife of a ḥalal. The mishnah reading in the Yerushalmi text has it, "a kosher priest married to a woman and having a brother, the prospective levir, who is a ḥalal."

The date of these uncertain texts falls in the second century, as is evident by the authorities cited, R. Jose and R. Simeon b. Gamaliel. Furthermore, R. Dostai b. R. Judah who maintains (Ḳid. 77a) that if a ḥalal is married to an Israelitish woman, their daughter is fit for priestly marriage, definitely defies the ruling of this beraita in respect to ḥalal, for it is impossible that the ḥalal's daughter shall be permitted and the ḥalal's wife shall be prohibited. Hence, it is evident that even at that late period this ruling of the beraita in respect to ḥalal (even if the reading be correct) was not accepted by some authorities.

[163] Rosenthal (MGWJ, 30, p. 42) is forced to the conclusion that M. 'Eduyot has two traditions; one concerning the widow is the older tradition, the other concerning the *'issah* family is the later, and belongs to what Tos. 'Eduyot 3,2, calls "the later *bet-din.*" This is unnecessary. The argument that the mishnah (of the same tradition) offers is that so long as the *'issah* can offer testimony for its purity, then it evidently is not a case of remote suspicion occurring in the time of Ezra, but of ḥalalut that needs investigation; therefore, the *'issah* widow is permitted to marry a priest. See note 161 above.

the priests. The principle, ascribed to R. Me'ir, is that the *'issah* family has the same legal character as any Hebrew family that cannot prove its pure origin by a genealogical record. Priests may look for documented aristocracy, but the law sets up no barrier between the common Israelite and the priest. The possible blemish in the *'issah* family is thus analyzed by the law: The blemish of foreign blood may be entirely ignored, both for the *'issah* widow and the *'issah* daughter, for at this stage of the halakah even a first generation proselyte married to an Israelitish woman imposes no blemish upon his wife or upon his daughter.[164] The suspicion that there may be an unbroken line of male ḥalalim in the family has no bearing upon the widow, for as yet a ḥalal's wife was not considered defiled. But it has a bearing indeed on the daughter, for the daughter of a ḥalal is a ḥalalah, according to the law of that day. The case of the daughter, then, is treated in this manner. If only the name of *'issah* clings to the family but no facts are brought to light to substantiate suspicions of ḥalalut, the *'issah* family itself can dispel those suspicions by testimony or proof of their own, and the *'issah* daughter is declared fit for priestly marriage. If the suspicions are grounded in certain facts, then a court investigation is necessary.[165]

[164] This is the ruling of R. Eliezer b. Jacob (M. Ḳid. 77a) which the priests followed since the Temple days (Ḳid. 78b). Rosenthal (ibid. p. 209, note 2) believes the view of R. Judah to be the older tradition, and to include a ruling that the widow of a proselyte or of a ḥalal is prohibited to marry a priest. As to the widow of a proselyte, he has some support from an amoraic statement (Ḳid. 78a: *Ger nami posel be-bi'ato*) which of course, is only part of an argument and is not to be taken seriously as an interpretation of the view of R. Judah. But as to the widow of a ḥalal, he has no support from any source at all.

[165] R. Me'ir's view is given in a beraita quoted in Yer. Ket. 25d and in Babli Ket. 14a. Büchler takes these two beraitot to be identical, but that is not conclusive. The beraita in Babli speaks of the *'issah* widow and seeks to interpret M. Eduyot. Therefore ḥalal is not mentioned, because ḥalal is the main problem in that mishnah. The beraita in Yerushalmi speaks of *'issah kesherah* and not of the widow, and it is a case of *issah kesherah* just because the ḥalal problem is also eliminated. The investigation that R. Me'ir proposes for the family that has a suspicious record is the examination of four generations. Apparently he holds to the old tradition of the Mishnah, which in his time was no longer valid. Possibly, he applied this measure for the elimination of ḥalalut suspicions, but agreed with the cur-

At this time the identity of the *'issah* group was breaking up and families to which the *'issah* name clung had to be judged individually. Then it was that the law distinguished between two kinds of *'issah* families. Those that had nothing against their reputation but the unwarranted slanderous name were called by the law the *'issah kesherah,* fit for priestly marriage, and those that had facts of a ḥalal strain to support their ill reputation were designated as *'issah pesulah,* disqualified for priestly marriage.

It was at the end of the tannaitic period that the term *'issah* no longer was applied to a distinct historical group, but was used as a legal concept to designate any family suspected of a ḥalal strain. Now it was no longer a question of documented aristocracy, which meant much to the priests and little to the rabbis, but of priestly marriage laws which the rabbis sought to enforce as did the priests themselves. In fact, the rabbis gave special attention to the priestly marriage laws which they considered valid in their halakah, and were more scrupulous about their enforcement than about the Israelitish marriage laws. The blemish of foreign blood was not valid in the rabbinic halakah, but that of being born of a union prohibited for priests was a serious matter to the rabbis. In this last generation of tannaim, it was taught, therefore, that the widow of a ḥalal like his daughter was unfit for priestly marriage. Rabban Simeon b. Gamaliel put it this way. Any blemish that attaches to one's daughter attaches equally to one's widow.[166] From this principle followed the conclusion that in any *'issah* case, contrary to the older view, the *'issah* widow and the *'issah* daughter are under

---

rent halakah that investigation of four generations is not necessary for the elimination of suspicion of foreign blood, because ḥalalut was treated by the rabbis more seriously than foreign descent. The ruling of Tos. Eduy. 3,2, that the *'issah* widow is no problem at all, but that the *'issah* daughter is admitted to priestly marriage on her testimony, follows the view of R. Me'ir, except perhaps that it does not subscribe to the need of investigating four generations where there is suspicion of ḥalalut.

166 See beraita quoted in Ḳid. 74b–75a; the view of R. Simeon b. Gamaliel is taken by the amoraim (Ḳid. 75a) to include a ruling that the *'issah* widow is prohibited marrying into the priesthood, like the *'issah* daughter. Perhaps this amoraic view accounts for the addition of the word ḥalal to the original statement of the beraita. See note 162 above.

the same suspicion; and if the daughter may not marry a priest, the widow, too, may not marry a priest. This ruling has been accepted by the halakah as a bit of abstraction, without the slightest reference to the historical group, and is formulated in Maimonides' code in this manner: "Any family in whose midst is intermixed a doubtful ḥalal – the widow of any one of that family may not marry a priest." [167]

We turn now to the basic biblical prohibitions in the marriage law of priests contained in the Book of Leviticus [168] and to the extension of these prohibitions in rabbinic law. Leviticus legislates that a priest may not marry a *zonah,* a ḥalalah, or a divorcee; that the high priest may not marry a non-virgin. These prohibitions are older than the date of the Book of Leviticus. In fact, they seem to be a formulation in legal detail of the general rule laid down by Ezekiel that priests should marry only virgins of the house of Israel. The *zonah,* the ḥalalah, and the divorcee are eliminated from priestly marriage because they are non-virgins. But Leviticus is more lenient than Ezekiel, in that Ezekiel makes one exception to the rule permitting priests to marry a priest's widow, while Leviticus permits priests to marry any widow, whether of a priest or of an Israelite. The sociological motive in the rules of priestly marriage can easily be understood. It is beneath the dignity of a priest to use a woman who had been formerly the sexual tool of another whether in a legitimate or illegitimate way. However, if she was the tool of another priest and was used in a legitimate way, according to Ezekiel, there is no degradation of priesthood if she be taken by a priest of equal standing. According to Leviticus, no dignity to priesthood is lost even if she was the legitimate tool of an Israelite. The high priest, however, has no equal, and it would be a degradation to him if he were to use the same woman who had been used by any man of lower social stratum.[169] The woman rejected by any man (divorced) is, of course, unacceptable to one of the dignity of priesthood.

[167] Yad, Issure Bi'ah 19,23.
[168] Lev. 21.7, 13–14.
[169] The same sentiment is expressed with reference to a king. See San. 22a.

Of the three categories prohibited to priests by levitical legislation, the third, that of the divorcee, is clear enough, but the other two, *zonah* and ḥalalah, are beclouded by uncertainties and complexities. To the biblical author *zonah* meant probably all that the term represented philologically, a woman guilty of adultery, a harlot for hire or for lust, and probably also one who was ante-nuptially unchaste. Ḥalalah probably meant the "perforated" and included the seduced maiden, the girl who, according to the custom of the time among non-Jews, was deflowered either artificially or by male contact, and the captive maiden violated by her captor. Evidently *zonah* and ḥalalah shaded into each other, and this accounts for the fact that a clear distinction between the two is lacking not only in the Bible itself but also in the literature of the Second Commonwealth.

During the Second Commonwealth a new definition of ḥalalah arose which helped to indicate clearer lines of distinction between the *zonah* and the ḥalalah. The term ḥalalah was taken as feminine of ḥalal, the latter meaning one demoted from priesthood, made profane. The ḥalalah, then, was the woman excluded from the priestly caste, who, if she were a man, would be excluded from priestly ministrations. Originally this meant a woman of non-Jewish origin, and Ezra singled out these families for demotion from priesthood. During the Hasmonean period we already find that a child born of a union prohibited for priests was demoted from the priesthood,[170] and it is logical to assume that the female of that family was then considered a ḥalalah, whether the name was applied to her technically or not. Then a suggestive distinction between *zonah* and ḥalalah came to the surface. A *zonah* is a woman profaned by her conduct; one could not be born a *zonah*. A ḥalalah is a woman born profaned; she cannot become a ḥalalah by misconduct. There appears to be no mention of the ḥalalah by Philo and Josephus in their outlines of priestly marriage laws. We must assume that when they mention the requirement that the maiden be one who is born of pure parents and grandparents, "highly distinguished for the excellence of

[170] See note 159 above.

their conduct and lineage," [171] they really give us the law of ḥalalah as understood in their time. Even in late tannaitic sources we have the tradition that the "ḥalalah is one who was *born* of a marriage prohibited (for priests)," and the amoraim admit that in the biblical sense a ḥalalah is born into her status and only by rabbinical extension is it possible for a woman to become a ḥalalah by misconduct.[172] However, just because of this rabbinic extension of the meaning of the term ḥalalah, the distinction between one born profaned and one become profaned did not any longer hold good for the later generations of tannaim; and a technical, sometimes statutory, definition of the two terms, *zonah* and ḥalalah, became necessary in order to give accurate legal form to the priestly marriage code.

Zonah to the Septuagint and Philo and Josephus and probably also to the rabbinic teachers of the Second Commonwealth was the harlot, who gave herself, for gain or for lust, to many men. R. Akiba supported this old tradition. R. Elazar went further and said that any unmarried contact between a maiden and a man gives her the status of a *zonah* and she is prohibited to marry a priest.[173] Josephus includes the innkeeper among those prohibited to marry a priest under the category of *zonah,* because her trade is one that requires loose moral conduct.[174] R. Huna declared that even a woman who has practiced lewdness with a woman companion be accounted a harlot.[175] Later halakah, however, rejected the views of R. Elazar, Josephus, R. Huna,[176] and, according to Maimonides,[177] also that of R. Akiba. But R. Moses of Coucy maintains that the decision of R. Akiba

[171] Philo, *Spec. Leg.* I,8,101. Josephus in different words, *Ant.* 3,12,2, and *Against Apion,* 1,7.

[172] Sifra, ed. Weiss, pp. 94b, 95a. This beraita is quoted in Ḳid. 77a with the addition of the words "for priests" which we enclosed in parentheses; and the amoraic comment is made that the born ḥalalah is biblical. In respect to the male ḥalal, the halakah consistently maintains to the end that he must be born into that disqualification and cannot become a ḥalal by any act of his own.

[173] Yeb. 61b.

[174] Josephus, *Ant.* 3,12,2.

[175] Yeb. 76a.

[176] Yeb. 61b; 76a.

[177] Yad, Issure Bi'ah 18,2.

remains valid in the final halakah.[178] The leading codes follow the view of Maimonides and rule that a priest may marry a Jewish harlot, if she is guilty only of unmarried contact with men, under whatever circumstances, so long as in her harlotry she has had no sex relations with gentiles, slaves, or men of incestuous kinship to her.[179] This lenient view of the later halakah, which is totally contrary to the older tradition, arises from a fine exegetical point. The Bible has two terms for the harlot, *ḳedeshah* and *zonah.* Concerning the *ḳedeshah* the law reads: "There shall be no *ḳedeshah* among the daughters of Israel." [180] The *zonah* is prohibited to priests only, according to levitical law. The prostitute, according to the rabbis, is the *ḳedeshah,* and the deuteronomic law prohibiting the *ḳedeshah* does not mean that she is excluded from marriage with Jews,[181] but that she shall not be permitted to practice her profession. Both she and her male companion, be he Israelite or priest, are punished for sex relations without marriage. Marrying the *ḳedeshah,* however, is permitted either to an Israelite or a priest. The *zonah* who is permitted in marriage to Israelites but not to priests, therefore, must be other than the prostitute.

A contemporary of R. Akiba defined the term *zonah* in the most common biblical sense as the woman who has committed adultery.[182] Later teachers broadened this definition and included all sinful unions under the term, but no one denied that the adulteress is a *zonah,* and when widowed from her husband may not be taken in marriage by a priest. But the law goes further and teaches that even where the case of adultery against the woman has not been proven, where she has been charged by her husband with adultery before the court, and ordered to be put through the ordeal of bitter waters, but has not gone through the ordeal for what-

178 *Sefer Miẓwot Gadol,* negative command 121.

179 E.H. 6,8.

180 Deut. 23.18.

181 Josephus, *Ant.* IV, 8.23, states that it is prohibited for an Israelite, even a layman, to marry a harlot. He probably interprets the deuteronomic verse to mean that a *ḳedeshah* shall not be taken in marriage.

182 Yeb. 61b, the view of R. Eliezer, probably the teacher of R. Akiba.

ever reason, she is technically a *zonah* and cannot thereafter be married to a priest.[183] Likewise, a priest who approaches his bride for the first time and finds her non-virginal, suspecting that she has violated her betrothal, even though the charge of adultery would at its worst be only doubtful, must divorce her on the basis of that suspicion.[184] The difference between a priest and a layman in respect to an adulteress is a double one. An Israelite, too, must divorce his wife if she is guilty of voluntary adultery but not if she has been violated by force. Again, an Israelite may marry a woman who has committed adultery while the wife of a former husband. A priest cannot marry or retain as wife a woman forced into involuntary adultery, whether at the time of the crime she was his wife or the wife of a former husband. Voluntary adultery makes a woman unfit for her own Israelitish husband but to no other Israelite; even involuntary adultery makes a woman unfit for any priest, her husband, or any one else.

The blemish of foreign blood in relation to priestly marriage has been sufficiently discussed in various other connections. We shall recall here only one conclusion, that to the rabbis foreign blood as such was no hindrance to marriage with Jews, and that it was a hindrance to marriage with priests only because they declared the foreign woman a statutory *zonah*.[185] We may now observe the operation of this legal principle. While contact with a gentile woman is prohibited also for an Israelite, if it is unmarried contact the prohibition is only rabbinical. But contact with a gentile woman, even unmarried contact, is biblically prohibited for a priest under the head of *zonah*.[186] The same

[183] M. Soṭah 6a; Yad, Issure Bi'ah 18,12.

[184] Ket. 9a, top; Yad, Issure Bi'ah 18,10.

[185] See note 147 above.

[186] Tem. 29b records a discussion between Abaye and Raba, the latter maintaining that a priest's contact with a gentile woman is penalized by flagellation because she is a *zonah*. The halakah agrees with this view (Yad, Issure Bi'ah, 12,3) and there is much support from other texts — see Tosafot, 'Ab. Zar. 36b, s.v. *mishum*. The view of Abaye, according to Tosafot, ibid., is not that he challenges the idea of *zonah* for a gentile but that the specific prohibition of Leviticus does not apply to the gentile woman while she is gentile and not converted, because the children born of her will not be ḥalalim but gentiles. See also Tosafot Tem. 29b s.v. *we-raba*.

is true of a female slave, who, because she is gentile, is in the eyes of the law a statutory *zonah*. A proselyte woman, who is permitted to an Israelite, is still prohibited to a priest, even though converted before the age of three, as a statutory *zonah;* and the same is true of a liberated female slave.[187] Also a female born as a Jewess whose parents were both proselytes or descendants of unmixed proselyte stock is unfit for marriage with a priest.[188] Not only is a female gentile or one of wholly gentile stock prohibited to priests, but an Israelitish woman who has had contact with a gentile begets the status of a *zonah* and may not thereafter marry into priesthood.[189] Contact with a proselyte does not make a woman a *zonah,* because a woman, even the daughter of a priest, is permitted to marry a proselyte. But certain proselytes are not permitted to marry Jewish women, the Ammonite, Moabite, Egyptian, Edomite, Samaritan, and Nathin. Hence, contact between one of these prohibited proselytes and a Jewish woman makes her a *zonah* and therefore unfit to marry a priest.[190]

Just as a woman becomes a *zonah* through involuntary adultery so she also becomes a *zonah* through forced contact with a gentile, and for that matter through any involuntary prohibited intercourse. This point of law created havoc in old time Jewish families; it raised the horrible problem of the *shebuyah,* "captive woman." By this law, if a husband who was a priest and his wife started out on a journey to-

[187] M. Yeb. 61a, and the Talmud decide (Yeb. 60b) contrary to the view of R. Simeon b. Yoḥai that the proselyte converted even before the age of three is prohibited to a priest. RABD, ad Yad, Issure Bi'ah 18,1,3, maintains that the proselyte woman is prohibited because of her non-Jewish descent, but not as *zonah*. See *Maggid* thereto.

[188] M. Ḳid. 77a; Ḳid. 78b. The blemish in this case is not *zonah,* because there is no *zonah* by birth; it is ḥalalah, and we have seen that the original ḥalalah had the blemish of foreign blood. The law rules, however, that, if the priest has married such a descendant of proselytes, no compulsion is applied upon the priest to divorce her. From this follows, of course, that the child born of such a union is not a ḥalal. See Yad, Issure Bi'ah 19,12.

[189] Yeb. 68b–69a; M. Yeb. 69b; Yad, Issure Bi'ah 18,2.

[190] Tos. Nid. 6,1. In the case of the Ammonite, Moabite, Edomite, and Egyptian, R. Johanan teaches that though the woman who had contact with them is unfit for priesthood because she is a *zonah,* the daughter born of the union is not a ḥalalah and is fit for priestly marriage. See Yeb. 77a–b; Yad, Issure Bi'ah 19,13.

gether and were held up by bandits who took them both captive, the priest could never again live with his wife because she was a captive and therefore a *zonah*. Or, in the case of war, if the enemy overpowered a city of Jews, the women in that city, married or unmarried, young or old, could not be married to priests, and the priests of the city had to divorce their wives. Neither of these two occurrences were unusual in olden times. Nor was it unusual for the government to imprison Jewish families as penalties for one offense or another or to hold Jewish families as hostages in order to enforce obedience or payment of ransom. In all these cases, so long as the woman came under control of gentiles, there was an assumption of the law, certainly justified by the morality of that day, that the woman had been forced into sex relations with her captors and was therefore unfit any longer to be the wife of a priest. We shall recall that John Hyrcanus was accused by the Pharisees that his mother had been made captive and was therefore unfit to remain his father's wife thereafter.[191] In the old time ketubah, prior to the destruction of the Temple, there was a special clause obligating the husband, if an Israelite, to pay ransom for his wife in case she was made captive and to take her back as wife. In the case of priests, the stipulation of the ketubah clause was that he pay ransom for her and cause her to return to her family, because, as a captive woman, she could not return to her priestly husband.[192] No wonder that the Mishnah and Josephus record it as a well settled law that a priest cannot marry a captive nor retain a wife after she has been made captive.[193] The matter was the more difficult because of the fact that the law, except under extraordinary circumstances, did not trust the woman herself as to her sexual innocence during captivity, and the husband was equally unreliable as to his testimony concerning his wife, even though he had been with her during the entire time she was in captivity.[194]

[191] See note 159 above.
[192] M. Ket. 51a; JMC, p. 165.
[193] Josephus, *Ant.* 3,12,2; M. Ket. 2,5–9.
[194] M. Ket. 27b.

As in the problem of *'agunah,* i.e., the wife of a missing husband whose death cannot be established by the regular legal evidences, so in the problem of the captive woman the law had to yield to the tragic human problem and permit in evidence such testimony as would otherwise not be recognized by the law. The testimony of one witness, a woman, a slave, a relative, or the testimony of a child telling his story in his innocence, unconscious of the legal problem involved, is satisfactory in clearing the woman of the charge of *zonah.*[195] Again, if the court has reason to expect testimony, it will issue permission to the woman to be the wife of a priest even before the witnesses have testified.[196] Further leniencies were granted in the case of siege and attack upon a city. In the first place, an attack for plunder does not cast doubts about the women in the city, except on those whom the attackers have carried off. Second, if there was an escape for any woman in the city or if there was a single hiding place, all the women of the city could testify on their own behalf and be freed of any suspicion of having been violated.[197]

A further widening of the category of *zonah* by the tannaim extended it to any woman who had had intercourse, voluntarily or by compulsion, with a man with whom she is prohibited to cohabit by biblical law. This includes, in addition to adultery and contact with a gentile or slave, already mentioned, contact with a mamzer or a eunuch, or a woman who in a state of ziḳah has had contact with any man other than the levir – in short, all sex contacts biblically prohibited by a negative injunction.[198] There are two exceptions to this rule, contact with a man while the woman is in a state of menstrual impurity, and remarriage between a divorced

[195] Ket. 27a–b.

[196] Ket. 23a; Yad, Issure Bi'ah 18,23.

[197] Ket. 27a; Yad, Issure Bi'ah 18,27–29.

[198] M. Yeb. 61a; beraita Yeb. 61b; Tos. Nid. 6,1; Yeb. 68b; Yad, Issure Bi'ah 18,2; E.H. 6,8. This is the view of Rashi and Maimonides, but Tosafot, Asheri, and *Sefer Miẓwot Gadol* maintain that, while for the violation of a negative biblical injunction the woman becomes unfit for priestly marriage, she does not have the status of *zonah.* See *Bet Shemuel* and Elijah Wilna, notes ad E.H. 6,8.

couple after the woman had been married to another[199] — in which cases, despite the violation of the law, the woman does not beget the status of a *zonah*. All incestuous contacts of biblical origin, exclusive, of course, of rabbinical incest, impose the blemish of *zonah* upon the woman.[200] A late beraita rules that contact between a woman and a ḥalal makes her unfit for priestly marriage,[201] and according to Maimonides, the disqualification is in the nature of *zonah*, but other authorities differ with him, admitting that she is disqualified but not as a *zonah*.[202]

All prohibited contacts which have been recorded here as the basis of making the woman a *zonah* are presupposed to be contacts between the female after she has attained her third year of age and a male of nine years. Prior to these ages the intercourse is considered to be non-sexual and having no legal effect.[203] In the same spirit the law teaches that unnatural relation with beasts, though criminal, is non-sexual in the legal sense, and the woman does not become a *zonah* through it.[204]

The tannaitic definition of ḥalalah is a woman who voluntarily or by compulsion has violated the law of priesthood through a contact prohibited for priests, or the daughter born of such a union.[205] The male born thereof is a ḥalal. Thus the son or daughter born of a union between a priest and a divorcee or *zonah* or ḥalalah or proselyte or liberated slave is a ḥalal or ḥalalah respectively.[206] They have the

[199] Yeb. 60a; 69a. That she is prohibited to marry a priest after being divorced and remarried by her former husband goes without saying, for she is a divorcee, but the status of *zonah* does not apply to her, and that is why the child born of the prohibited remarriage is fit for the priesthood. See Yeb. 44b, and Rashi ibid., s.v. *she-ken*.

[200] M. Yeb. 13b; Yeb. 44b; 68b; Yad, ibid.; E.H. ibid. That a woman does not become a *zonah* through violation of a rabbinical marriage prohibition, see Yeb. 85a, bottom; Yad. Issure Bi'ah 18,4.

[201] Yeb. 68a; Ḳid. 74b. The reading in Tos. Nid. 6,1, omits the word ḥalal. See note 162 above.

[202] Yad, Issure Bi'ah 18,3. See also Yad, Issure Bi'ah 18,1 and RABD and *Maggid* thereto.

[203] M. Yeb. 67b; Yeb. 68a; M. Nid. 44b, 45a.

[204] Yeb. 60a.

[205] Ḳid. 77a–b.

[206] Sifra, ed. Weiss, pp. 94b, 95a.

same blemish if born of the union of a high priest and a widow or of a legal marriage between a high priest and an unmarried non-virgin.[207] The mother, likewise, if not a ḥalalah before, becomes a ḥalalah as result of that contact.[208] The sharpness of the legal definition of the term ḥalalah can be illustrated by the following example. A priest has incestuous contact with a woman; the woman becomes a *zonah;* the child is a mamzer but not a ḥalal; because the contact is not a violation of priestly law but of general marriage law. Suppose there is a second contact and another child is born; the woman is now both *zonah* and ḥalalah, *zonah* for the first, ḥalalah for the second contact, which is a violation of priestly law in addition to incest; and the child born of the second union is mamzer and ḥalal, mamzer because born of incest, ḥalal because born of an intercourse which is a violation of priestly marriage law.[209]

The blemish of *zonah* cannot be conveyed from mother to daughter, since it is one that can only be acquired and cannot be inherited. But the blemish of ḥalalah is different. Ḥalalut in priestly marriage is very much like mamzerut in Israelitish marriage. Yet ḥalalut does not perpetuate itself like mamzerut. One parent mamzer makes the offspring mamzer; therefore there is no escape. But one parent ḥalal does not always make the child ḥalal or ḥalalah. If the father is ḥalal his son is ḥalal and his daughter is ḥalalah, no matter who the mother. On the male line this is endless, for the son's son is also a ḥalal, no matter who the mother. But on the female line it stops at the first generation, for the ḥalalah, if married in accordance with the law, namely to an Israelite, does not convey her blemish to either son or daughter, while if she marries a priest, she has committed a new violation of priestly law — in which case the child is a ḥalal or ḥalalah because of the new infraction, not as a result of the blemish

[207] See Yad, Issure Bi'ah 19,3. In 19,4, Maimonides remarks that in the case of a non-virgin, for the child to be a ḥalal the woman must be married to the high priest. An unmarried contact between a non-virgin and a high priest does not make the child a ḥalal. *Maggid* explains this correctly and sufficiently.

[208] Sifra, ibid. p. 95a (sec. 7); Ḳid. 77a.

[209] Ḳid. 77b bottom.

being conveyed from mother to child. It may be said, therefore, that ḥalalut perpetuates itself in the male line but not in the female.[210]

The levitical prohibition against a priest marrying a divorcee required little elaboration by the rabbis, for the concept of the divorcee is clear and definite enough. However, rabbinic law made certain extensions of this prohibition. It ruled that the divorcee is one not only divorced after nuptials but also after betrothal.[211] The priest cannot marry even the wife whom he himself has divorced. Even if the divorce was of doubtful legal validity, even if made necessary for legal discipline without legal validity, or even, as in the case of a minor orphan girl who can free herself from her husband without a divorce, if a divorce was given unnecessarily, the divorce is accounted valid enough for the purpose of prohibiting the woman from marrying a priest.[212] There was one definite rabbinical enactment in this connection. The rabbis declared that a levirate woman released from the levir by the ḥaliẓah ceremony has the status of a divorcee and may not marry a priest. This prohibition is rabbinical,[213] and the child born of a union violating this prohibition is a rabbinical ḥalal or ḥalalah.

The high priest is included in all the priestly marriage prohibitions here enumerated. But beyond these he is also prohibited to marry a widow or even a woman never married before but non-virgin.[214] Under the term widow we understand one widowed after nuptials or after betrothal.[215] Under the term non-virgin, the law prohibits the high priest to marry a girl seduced or violated by another man or by the high priest himself,[216] one deflowered artificially or by acci-

[210] M. Ḳid. 77a. R. Dostai, ibid. takes exception to this law. See Yad, Issure Bi'ah 19,14.

[211] Yeb. 59a; Yad. ibid., 17,18. So also Philo, *Spec. Leg.*, I,20,107.

[212] Yeb. 52a; M. Yeb. 92a. See E.H. 6,1, and note of Isserles thereto. For the status of the *mema'enet* see Yeb. 108a–b, from which the conclusion is drawn that if there has been no *mi'un* from a marriage following divorce, the divorce has validity sufficient to make the minor girl unfit for priestly marriage. See Yad, ibid., 17,18.

[213] Sifra, ibid, p. 94b bottom; Yeb. 24a; Ḳid. 78a.

[214] Yeb. 59a; Ket. 30a.

[215] M. Yeb. 59a.

[216] M. Yeb. ibid.; Yeb. 59b.

dent or by contact with a beast, or a girl who has attained the age of puberty, when she is no longer in her full virginity.[217] The offspring of a marriage prohibited to the high priest have the status of ḥalal, because born of violation of a priestly marriage law. An exception to this rule is the offspring of a union between a high priest and a woman non-virgin without male contact, because the violation of law in this case is less serious, even to the point of permitting husband and wife to stay married once they have braved the violation.[218]

There are two additional marriage prohibitions for high priests which are of a different category, without the implication of profaning the priesthood. They are, that the high priest shall not marry a minor girl,[219] and against the high priest marrying more than one wife.[220] It should be mentioned that, since the high priesthood is an appointment that comes to a lower priest some time during his maturer years, it is possible that by that time he already has a wife or wives prohibited for a high priest. In such a case the law permits him to retain his wife or wives. Even if only betrothed to them at the time he is raised to the high priesthood, he is permitted to celebrate the nuptials, because after betrothal they are his wives in the eyes of the law.[221] There is one exception. A priest who has betrothed a minor girl before he received his elevation to the high priesthood, and if at the time he took office she has already attained her puberty, is not allowed to celebrate nuptials with her, since the status of both has changed from the time of betrothal to the time of marriage.[222]

[217] M. Yeb. ibid.; Yad, Issure Bi'ah 17,13,14. The statement in Yad, section 14 that intercourse with a beast does not make the woman unfit for marriage with a high priest refers to *shelo kedarkah;* but in the regular sexual manner, the contact makes her unfit for such marriage. That is the evidence from Yeb. 59b. See Rashi Yeb. ibid., s.v. *me-aḥurehah.*

[218] See Yad, Issure Bi'ah 19,4 and the logical interpretation of this rule by *Maggid.*

[219] Yeb. 61b. R. Eliezer would prohibit any priest also from marrying a minor but the halakah limits the prohibition to a high priest only. See Yad, Issure Bi'ah 17,13.

[220] Yad, ibid. but RABD disagrees with the ruling. See *Maggid,* ibid. and *Oẓar,* Lewin, Yeb. p. 138 and note 2.

[221] M. Yeb. 61a.

[222] Yeb. 59a; Yad, Issure Bi'ah 17,17.

ABBREVIATIONS

AJSL	*American Journal of Semitic Languages*
Asheri	R. Asher ben Jehiel
C.H.	The Code of Hammurabi
E.H.	Eben ha-'Ezer
HHM	*The History of Human Marriage,* by E. Westermarck
JE	*Jewish Encyclopedia*
JMC	*The Jewish Marriage Contract,* by L. M. Epstein
J.Q.R.	*The Jewish Quarterly Review*
MABIT	R. Moses di Trani
Maggid	*Maggid Mishneh,* commentary on Yad
MGWJ	*Monatsschrift für die Geschichte und Wissenschaft des Judenthums*
N.S.	New Series
O.S.	Old Series
Oẓar	*Oẓar ha-Geonim,* by B. M. Lewin
RABD	R. Abraham ben David of Posquières
Rashi	R. Solomon Yiẓḥaḳi
RDBZ	R. David ben Zimra
RDḲ	R. David Ḳimḥi
REBJH	R. Eliezer ben Joel ha-Levi
R.E.J.	*Revue des Études Juives*
RIBS	R. Isaac ben Sheshet
RMA	R. Moses Isserles
RMBM	R. Moses ben Maimon
RMBN	R. Moses ben Naḥman
RN	R. Nissim Gerondi
RSBA	R. Solomon ben Adret
RSBS	R. Solomon ben Simeon Duran
RSBZ	R. Simeon ben Ẓemaḥ Duran
RSL	R. Solomon Luria
Sekte	*Eine unbekannte jüdische Sekte,* by L. Ginzberg

SMG	*Sefer Miẓwot Gadol*
ThLZ	*Theologische Literaturzeitung*
Yad	*Yad ha-Ḥazaḳah,* by Maimonides
Y.D.	Yoreh De'ah
ZDMG	*Zeitschrift der Deutschen Morgenländischen Gesellschaft*
ZVR	*Zeitschrift für die vergleichende Rechtswissenschaft*

REGISTER OF FOREIGN TERMS

'Agunah	Deserted wife
Ailonit	Man-like woman, congenitally sterile
Amah	Maidservant, slave-wife
'Am ha-areẓ	Rustic, illiterate person
Amtu (Babyl.)	Maidservant, slave-wife
Androgynus (G)	Hermaphrodite
Arusah	Betrothed bride
Ashkenazi	Of Germanic Jewish tradition
Asufi	Foundling
Ba'al	Master, owner, husband
Ba'ale ha-Heḳesh	Karaites who employ the "analogy" method
Ba'ale ha-Rikkub	Karaites who employ the "grafting" method
Ba'ale ha-Ẓe'idah	Karaites who employ the "transfer" method
Babli	The Babylonian Talmud
Bediḳah	Examination, investigation
Benin Dikrin	Ketubah provision for sons to inherit the property of their mothers
Bet Din	Court
Birekat ha-Minim	The twelfth section in the Eighteen Benedictions containing an imprecation against sectarians
Dod	Paternal uncle
Epitropos (G)	Guardian, administrator
Erusin	Betrothal
Esirtu (Assyr.)	Captive wife
Gebirah	Chief wife
Gemara	That part of the Talmud which represents the amoraic discussion of the Mishnah

Ger	Resident alien, proselyte
Gere Arayot	Lion-proselytes, converted out of fear
Gere Ẓedeḳ	True proselytes, of righteous motives
Ge'ullah	Right (or process) of redemption
Gezerah	Legal decree, restriction
Giyyoret Mikkannah	A woman proselyte born after the conversion of her parents both of whom were of the same nation
Go'el	He who has the right of redemption
Hagbarah	Method of extension of a law in the direction of severity among the Karaites
Ḥalal (*f. Ḥalalah*)	Profaned, born from a union prohibited to priests
Ḥaliẓah	Removal of shoe, release from levirate
Ḥaliẓah Kesherah	A fully valid ḥaliẓah
Ḥaliẓah Pesulah	Defective ḥaliẓah
Ḥaluẓah	Widow released from levirate duty by ḥaliẓah
Ḥazaḳah	Legal presumption
Heḳesh	Principle of analogy
Ḥerem	Ban, more specifically the ban against polygamy
Ḥuppah	Canopy, wedding ceremony
'Ir'ur	Protest, alleged evidence of disqualification
'Issah	A family of alleged impurity of stock
Issur Ḳedushah	A marriage prohibition incumbent on priests
Issur Miẓwah	A marriage forbidden by rabbinical enactment as an extension of the law of incest
Karaites	A Jewish sect that recognizes the authority of the Bible but not of the Talmud
Karet	Divine punishment through sudden or premature death

Ḳaṭlanit	A killer, a woman widowed twice or thrice
Ḳedeshah	A sacred prostitute
Ketubah	Marriage contract
Ḳeẓaẓah	Cutting off, a ceremony attending the severing of family connections
Ḳiddushin	Betrothal, betrothal ceremony
Kuti	Cuthean, Samaritan
Ma'amar	Levirate betrothal
Mamzer	Child of incestuous union or adultery
Mamzerut	The legal condition of mamzer
Manus (*L*)	The power or right of husband over his wife
Mattan	Wedding presents of groom to bride
Mesirat Moda'a	Recording a protest in advance against one's own legal action or statement
Meyuḥas	Of noble descent
Mishnah Aḥaronah	The later Mishnah
Mishnah Rishonah	The earlier Mishnah
Mi'un	A woman's protest against a marriage contracted while she was a minor
Miẓwah	Command, religious act
Mohar	Marriage price paid for the wife
Moredet	Rebellious wife
Nakri	Sojourner, foreigner
Napṭartu (*Hittite*)	Wife who was a freed captive
Noahide laws	Laws obligatory upon all mankind, in contrast to laws obligatory upon Jews
Nudunnu (*Babyl.*)	Husband's wedding gifts to wife
Paelicatus (*L*)	Concubinage, the cohabiting with a kept mistress
Pellex (*L*)	Concubine
Pilegesh	Concubine
Rosh Galuta	Exilarch, the title of the political head of the Jewish community in Babylonia

Sephardi	Of Spanish Jewish tradition
Setam Gemara	The anonymous statement or discussion of the Gemara
Shabbethaians	Followers of the pseudo-messiah, Shabbethai Zebi
Shadkan	Match maker
Shaliaḥ	Deputy, agent, messenger
Shebuyah	Captive woman
She'er Basar	Near of kin, relative by blood
Sheḥiṭah	Slaughtering according to Jewish ritual
Sheniyyot	Cases of secondary incest
Shifḥah	Female slave
Shifḥah Ḥarufah	Female slave designated as the wife of one selected by the master
Shomeret Yabam	A widow waiting for the levir to discharge his levirate duty
Shtuḳi	"Hush child," one whose father is not known
Soṭah	A wife suspected of unfaithfulness
Šugetu (*Babyl.*)	Marriage price paid for bride
Terumah	Heave-offering, may be eaten by priests and their families only
Theios (G)	Uncle, father's or mother's brother
Tosafists	French rabbinic scholars following Rashi who wrote notes on the Babylonian Talmud called "Tosafot"
Ṭumṭum	A person whose genitals are hidden or undeveloped and whose sex is therefore unknown
Wali (*Arab.*)	Maternal uncle
Yabam (*f. Yebamah*)	Levir, (f. levirate widow)
Yebamah le-shuḳ	The levirate widow marrying one not a brother to the deceased husband without release from her levirate obligation
Yerushalmi	Palestinian Talmud

Yibbum	Levirate marriage
Yi'ud	Designation, betrothal of a female slave to her master or his son
Yoḥasin	Matters or records of genealogical import
Zadokites	A Jewish sect during the first century B.C.E., also known as the Damascus sect
Zaḳen mamre	An elder ruling contrary to the decisions of the high court
Ẓarah	Rival wife
Ẓarat ha-Bat	A daughter's rival, a case where one's daughter and her co-wife are under ziḳah bond to him
Ziḳah	The bond of mutual levirate obligation existing between the widow and the levir
Zimmah	Lewdness, applied to special cases of incest
Zimmun	Summoning a group or being counted as one of a group who after a common meal offer grace in common
Zonah	Harlot, adulteress
Zuz (*pl. Zuzim*)	Standard silver coin in talmudic times

BIBLIOGRAPHY

A. SOURCES

I. PAGAN

The Code of Hammurabi, translated by D. D. Luckenbill, ed. E. Chiera, in *The Origin and History of Hebrew Law* by J. M. P. Smith, Chicago, 1931, pp. 181–222.

The Assyrian Code, translated by D. D. Luckenbill, ed. F. W. Geers, ibid., pp. 223–43.

The Hittite Code, translated by Arnold Walther, ibid., pp. 247–74.

Contract-tablets, ed. E. Chiera, *Old Babylonian Contracts,* University of Pennsylvania Publications, Babylonian section, VIII, Part II, 1922; Kohler and Ungnad, *Hammurabi's Gesetz,* Leipzig, 1909; Koschaker and Ungnad, *Hammurabi's Gesetz,* Leipzig, 1923.

Syrian-Roman Code, ed. Bruns and Sachau, *Syrisch-römisches Rechtsbuch aus den fünften Jahrhundert,* Leipzig, 1880.

II. JEWISH

a. Biblical Literature

The Bible, standard Masoretic text; English translation of the Jewish Publication Society, Philadelphia, 1917.

The Septuagint, Greek text and English translation, published by James Prott and Company (n.d.), N. Y.

Targum Onkelos of Pentateuch, ed. A. Berliner, Berlin, 1884; Targum Jonathan ben 'Uziel of Pentateuch, ed. M. Ginsburger, Berlin, 1903; Targum of Prophets and Megillot, *Miḳra'ot Gedolot,* Warsaw, 1902; Targum Yerushalmi, ibid.

b. Hellenistic Literature

Apocrypha and Pseudepigrapha of the Old Testament, ed. R. H. Charles, London, 1913.

Philo with an English Translation, by F. H. Colson and G. H. Whitaker, in the Loeb Classical Library, Cambridge, 1929.
The works of Josephus are cited according to the standard editions.

c. Talmudic Literature

Megillat Ta'anit, Warsaw, 1874; translation and critical edition by S. Zeitlin, *Megillat Ta'anit as a Source for Jewish Chronology,* Philadelphia, 1922.
Mishnah, standard texts in the Babylonian and Palestinian Talmuds, cited by treatise, folio, and side of the Babylonian text (where there is Gemara) or by treatise, chapter, and section (where there is no Gemara).
Tosephta, ed. M. Z. Zuckermandel, Pasewalk, 1881.
Meḳilta de R. Ishmael, ed. M. Friedmann, Vienna, 1870.
Meḳilta de R. Simeon, ed. D. Hoffmann, Frankfurt a. M., 1905.
Sifra, ed. I. H. Weiss, Vienna, 1862.
Sifre on Numbers and Deuteronomy, ed. M. Friedmann, Vienna, 1864.
Midrash Tannaim, ed. D. Hoffmann, Berlin, 1908–9.
Midrash Rabbah on Pentateuch, Warsaw, 1924.
Midrash on Megillot, Warsaw, 1924.
Pesiḳta Rabbati, ed. M. Friedmann, Vienna, 1885.
Pesiḳta de R. Kahana, ed. S. Buber, Lyck, 1868.
Midrash Shemuel, ed. S. Buber, Cracow, 1893.
Midrash Tehillim, ed. S. Buber, Wilna, 1891.
Yalḳut Shime'oni, Warsaw, 1876.
Pirḳe de R. Eliezer, Warsaw, 1879.
Babylonian Talmud, standard edition, cited by treatise, folio, and side.
Palestinian Talmud, Venice, 1523, cited by treatise, folio, and column.
The Minor Treatises, in the standard edition of the Babylonian Talmud, cited by treatise and chapter.

d. Post-talmudic Sources

Abraham b. David (RABD), marginal notes to Yad, in standard edition of the *Yad ha-Ḥazaḳah.*

Aderet Eliyahu, by Elijah Bashyazi (Karaite), Odessa, 1870.
Adret; see Solomon ben Adret.
Alfasi; see Isaac Alfasi.
'Anan, founder of Karaism, Sefer ha-Miẓwot, ed. A. Harkavy, in *Studien und Mittheilungen,* Vol. VIII, St. Petersburg, 1903.
'Aruk ha-Shulḥan, code, by Jehiel Michal Epstein, Wilna, 1924.
Asher b. Jehiel (Asheri), abstract of talmudic law (Halakot), in the standard edition of the Babylonian Talmud.
——— responsa, Venice, 1607.
'Aẓmot Yosef, by Joseph Ibn Ezra, talmudic novelae, Fürth, 1767.

Benjamin Ze'eb, responsa, Venice, 1538.
Bet Ḥadash, by Joel Sirkes, commentary on *Ṭur,* in standard edition of *Ṭur.*
Bet Yosef; see Joseph Karo.
Bet Shemu'el, Samuel b. Uri Shraga Phoebus, commentary on *Shulḥan 'Aruk,* Eben ha-'Ezer, in the standard edition of Eben ha-'Ezer.

Coronel, N. Teshubot ha-Geonim, Vienna, 1871.

David b. Zimra (RDBZ), responsa, I and II, Venice, 1773; III, Fürth, 1781; IV, Livorno, 1652; V, Livorno, 1818.
David Ḳimḥi (RDḲ), Bible commentary, in *Miḳra'ot Gedolot,* Warsaw, 1902.
Dine de-Ḥayye, by Ḥayyim Benvenisti, commentary on *Sefer Miẓwot Gadol,* Constantinople, 1742.

Eben ha-'Ezer; unless otherwise specified, refers to *Shulḥan 'Aruk,* Eben ha-'Ezer; See Joseph Karo.
Eliezer b. R. Joel ha-Levi (REBJH), codification of talmudic law under the name of REBJH, ed. V. Aptowitzer, Berlin, 1912–36.
Elijah Mizraḥi, responsa, "Darom" edition, Jerusalem, 1938.
Elijah Wilna, notes on *Shulḥan 'Aruk,* in standard edition of *Shulḥan 'Aruk.*
Eshkol ha-Kofer, by Judah Hadassi, karaitic code, Gozlowa, 1836.

Gan 'Eden, by Aaron b. Elijah of Nicomedia, karaitic code, Gozlowa, 1866.
Geonica; see Ginzberg, L.
Geonic responsa; see Coronel, N., Sha'are Ẓedeḳ, Toratan shel Rishonim.
Ginzberg, L., Geonica, New York, 1909.
——— Ginze Schechter, New York, 1928.
Ginze Ḳedem; see Lewin, B. M.
Ginze Schechter; see Ginzberg, L.
Gulak, A., Oẓar ha-Sheṭarot, Jerusalem, 1926.

Hagahot Maimuniyyot, by Me'ir ha-Kohen, notes on Yad, in standard edition of the *Yad ha-Ḥazaḳah.*
Halakot Gedolot, geonic code, ed. J. Hildesheimer, Berlin, 1890.
Halakot Pesuḳot, geonic code, ed. L. Slossberg, Versailles, 1886.
Harkavy, A., Studien und Mittheillungen, St. Petersburg, 1903; See 'Anan.
Ḥatam Sofer, by Moses Sofer, responsa, Vienna, 1880.
Ḥelḳat Meḥoḳeḳ, by Moses Lima, notes on *Shulḥan 'Aruk,* Eben ha-'Ezer, in standard edition of Eben ha-'Ezer.
Ḥilluf Minhagim, by Joel Miller, Vienna, 1878.

Ibn Ezra, Abraham, biblical commentary, in *Miḳra'ot Gedolot,* Warsaw, 1902.
Iggerot ha-Rambam; see Maimonides.
Isaac Alfasi, abstract of talmudic law (Halakot), in standard edition of the Babylonian Talmud.
Isaac b. Sheshet (RIBS), responsa, Constantinople, 1547.
Isaac de Latas, responsa, ed. M. H. Friedlaender, Vienna, 1860.
Isserles, Moses (RMA), notes on *Shulḥan 'Aruk,* in standard edition of *Shulḥan 'Aruk.*
Isserlein, Israel, Terumat ha-Deshen, responsa, Venice, 1519.

Jacob Emden, She'elat Ya'abeẓ, Lemberg, 1884.
——— Torat ha-Ḳena'ot, Amsterdam, 1752.
Joseph Colon, responsa, Venice, 1519.

Joseph Karo, Bet Yosef, notes on *Ṭur,* in standard edition of *Ṭur.*
——— Kesef Mishneh, notes on Yad, in standard edition of *Yad ha-Ḥazaḳah.*
——— Shulḥan 'Aruk, code, standard edition.
Joseph di Trani, responsa, Fürth, 1765–7.
Joshua b. Judah, the Karaite, Sefer ha-Yashar, ed. I. Markon, St. Petersburg, 1908.
Judah b. Barzilai, Sefer ha-Sheṭarot, ed. S. J. Halberstam, Berlin, 1898.
Judah he-Ḥasid, Sefer Ḥasidim, ed. J. Wistinetzki, Frankfurt am Main, 1924.
——— Testament, printed in most editions of *Sefer Ḥasidim.*
Judah Minz, responsa, Cracow, 1882.

Kaftor wa-Feraḥ, Estori ha-Parḥi, ed. A. M. Luncz, Jerusalem, 1897.
Karo; see Joseph Karo.
Kesef Mishneh; see Joseph Karo.
Keter Torah, by Aaron b. Elijah of Nicomedia, karaitic commentary on the Pentateuch, Gozlowa, 1866.
Ḳimḥi; see David Ḳimḥi.

Leon de Modena, Historia dei Riti Ebraici, translated into Hebrew by Solomon Rubin under the title of "Shulḥan 'Aruk," Vienna, 1867.
Levi b. Ḥabib, responsa, Lemberg, 1865.
Lewin, B. M., Ginze Ḳedem, Haifa, 1922–Jerusalem, 1934.
——— Oẓar ha-Geonim (*Oẓar*), Haifa, 1928–Jerusalem, 1940.

MABIT; see Moses di Trani.
Maggid Mishneh (*Maggid*), by Vidal of Tolosa, notes on Yad, in standard edition of *Yad ha-Ḥazaḳah.*
Maimonides; see Moses ben Maimon.
Malmad ha-Talmidim, by Jacob Anatoli, Lyck, 1866.
Me'ir of Padua, responsa, Cracow, 1882.
Me'ir of Rothenburg, responsa, Prague, 1608; Budapest, 1885; Berlin, 1891.
Modena; see Leon de Modena.

Mordecai, abstract of talmudic law (Halakot), by Mordecai b. R. Hillel Ashkenazi, in standard edition of the Babylonian Talmud.

Moses Isserles (RMA), see Isserles, Moses.

Moses b. Maimon (RMBM), Mishnah commentary, in standard edition of Babylonian Talmud.

——— responsa, ed. A. Freimann, Jerusalem, 1934.

——— responsa and correspondences under the title of Iggerot u-She'elot u-Teshubot ha-RMBM, Brünn, 1797.

——— Yad ha-Ḥazaḳah or Mishneh Torah, code, standard edition.

Moses b. Naḥman (RMBN), commentary on Pentateuch, in *Miḳra'ot Gedolot.*

——— novellae on Talmud, Jerusalem, 1928–29.

Moses di Trani (MABIT), responsa, Venice, 1719.

Naḥalat Shib'ah, by Samuel b. David ha-Levi, Königsberg, 1869.

Naḥmanides; see Moses b. Naḥman.

Neubauer, A., Geschichte des Karäerthums, karaitic texts, Leipzig, 1866.

Nimmuḳe Yosef, commentary on *Alfasi,* by Joseph Ibn Ḥabib, in standard edition of *Alfasi.*

Nissim b. Reuben Gerondi (RN), commentary on *Alfasi,* in standard edition of *Alfasi.*

——— responsa, Cremona, 1686.

Noda' bi-Yehudah, responsa, by Ezekiel Landau, Warsaw, 1880–82.

Ohale Ya'aḳob, responsa, by Jacob Castro, Livorno, 1783.

Or Zaru'a, code, by Isaac of Vienna, Zhitomir, 1862.

Oẓar ha-Geonim (*Oẓar*); see Lewin, B. M.

Oẓar ha-Sheṭarot; see Gulak, A.

Pitḥe Teshubah, by Abraham Hirsh Eisenstadt, index to responsa arranged according to the order of the code of the *Shulḥan 'Aruk* and printed in most editions of the *Shulḥan 'Aruk.*

Protokole der ersten Rabbinervesammlung abgehalten in Braunschweig, Braunschweig, 1844.

Rashi; see Solomon Yiẓḥaḳi.

Responsa collections that have titles are recorded in the bibliography under the title; those that are known by the name of the author are recorded under the author's name.

Sefer Ḥasidim; see Judah he-Ḥasid.

Sefer ha-Miẓwot; see ʻAnan.

Sefer Miẓwot Gadol (SMG) by Moses of Coucy, code, Munkacs, 1905.

Sefer ha-Sheṭarot; see Judah b. Barzilai.

Sefer ha-Terumah, code, by Baruch b. Isaac, Warsaw, 1897.

Sefer ha-Yashar; see Joshua b. Judah.

Sefer Yere'im, code, by Eleazar b. Samuel of Metz, Zalkowa, 1804.

Shaʻare Ẓedeḳ, geonic responsa, ed. Joseph ha-Kohen Ardit, Saloniki, 1792.

Shaʻar ha-Melek, novellae based on Yad, by Isaac Bilmonti, Lemberg, 1859.

Shaʻar Yehudah, treatise on karaitic law of incest, by Judah Poki Tchelebi, Constantinople, 1686.

She'elat Yaʻabeẓ; see Jacob Emden.

Shilṭe ha-Gibborim, by Joshua Boaz Baruch, notes on *Alfasi*, in standard edition of *Alfasi*.

Shulḥan ʻAruk; see Joseph Karo.

Simeon b. Ẓemah (RSBZ), responsa, Amsterdam, 1738.

Solomon ben Adret (RSBA), responsa, I, Bologna, 1539; II, Livorno, 1657; III, Livorno, 1778; IV, Petrokow, 1883; V, Livorno, 1825; VI–VII, Warsaw, 1868; VIII (ascribed to Naḥmanides), Warsaw, 1883.

——— Torat ha-Bayit, code, Vienna, 1811.

Solomon Luria (RSL), responsa, Lublin, 1575.

——— Yam shel Shelomoh, novellae on Babylonian Talmud, Stetin, 1861.

Solomon b. Simeon (RSBS), responsa, Livorno, 1742.

Solomon Yiẓḥaḳi (Rashi), Bible commentary, in standard edition of Bible.

——— Talmud commentary, in standard edition of Babylonian Talmud.

Tama, D., Transactions of the Parisian Sanhedrin, translated from the French by F. D. Kirwan, London, 1807.

Terumat ha-Deshen; see Isserlein, Israel.
Teshubah me-Ahabah, by Eliezer Fleckeles, Prague, 1804.
Testament; see Judah he-Ḥasid.
Tiḳḳun Soferim, Samuel Jaffe, Livorno, 1789.
Toratan shel Rishonim, geonic responsa, ed. C. M. Horowitz, Frankfurt a. M., 1881.
Torat ha-Bayit; see Solomon ben Adret.
Torat ha-Ḳena'ot; see Jacob Emden.
Tosafot, marginal notes on the Babylonian Talmud, in standard edition of the Babylonian Talmud.
Trier, S. A., Rabbinische Gutachten, Frankfurt a. M., 1844.
Ṭur, code, by Jacob b. Asher, standard edition.

Yad ha-Ḥazaḳah (Yad); see Moses b. Maimon.
Yam shel Shelomoh; see Solomon Luria.

Ẓedah la-Derek, code, by Menaḥem b. Zeraḥ, Ferrara, 1554.
Ẓemaḥ Ẓedeḳ, responsa, by Menaḥem Nickelsburg, Amsterdam, 1766.
Ẓemaḥ Ẓedeḳ, responsa, by Menaḥem Mendel Schneersohn of Lyubavich, Wilna, 1871–84.

III. CHRISTIAN

New Testament, revised version, standard edition.
Justin Martyr, Cum Tryphone Judaeo Dialogus, translated by G. S. Davie, Oxford, 1861.
Eusebius, Historia Ecclesiastica, translated by Lawler and Dulton, London, 1927–8.
Corpus Juris Canonici, German translation by Bruno Schilling, Leipzig, 1834.

IV. MOHAMMEDAN

Koran, translated by Maulvi Muhammad Ali, second edition, London, 1920.

B. LITERATURE

Abrahams, I., Jewish Life in the Middle Ages, Philadelphia, 1896.
Albeck, Ch., Das Buch der Judäen und die Halacha, Berlin, 1930.

Aptowitzer, V., "Spuren des Matriarchats im jüdischen Schrifttum," *Hebrew Union College Annual,* IV (1927), pp. 207–40.

Ayrinhac, H. A., Marriage Legislation in the New Code of Canon Law, New York, 1919.

Bamberger, B. J., Proselytism in the Talmudic Period, Cincinnati, 1939.

Belkin, S., Philo and the Oral Law, Cambridge, 1940.

Benzinger, I., Hebräische Archäologie, Tubingen, 1907.

Bertholet, A., Die Stellung der Israeliten und Juden zu den Fremden, Leipzig, 1896.

Bewer, J. A., "Die Leviratsehe im Buche Ruth," *Theologische Studien und Kritiken,* LXXVI (1903), pp. 328–32.

——— "The Ge'ullah in the Book of Ruth," AJSL, XIX (1903), pp. 143–8.

Bialoblocki, S., Materialien zum islamischen und jüdischen Eherecht, Giesen, 1928.

Bokser, B., Pharisaic Judaism in Transition, New York, 1935.

Büchler, A., "Familienreinheit und Familienmakel in Jerusalem," *Schwartz Festschrift,* Berlin, 1917, pp. 133–162.

——— Die Priester u. d. Cultus in letzten Yahrzent d. jerus. Tempels, Vienna, 1895.

——— "The Levitical Impurity of the Gentiles," J.Q.R., N.S., XVII (1926), pp. 1–81.

——— Review of Schechter's *Sectaries,* J.Q.R., N.S., III (1912–13), pp. 429–85.

Cook, S. A., The Laws of Moses and the Code of Hammurabi, London, 1903.

Cross, E. B., The Hebrew Family, Chicago, 1927.

Cruveilhier, P., "Le Levirat chez les Hébreux et les Assyriens," *Revue Biblique,* XXXIV (1925), pp. 524–46.

Drachsler, J., Democracy and Assimilation, New York, 1920.

Eberharter, A., Alttestamentliche Abhandlungen, Das Ehe- und Familienrecht d. Hebräer, München, 1914.

Elbogen, I., Der jüdische Gottesdienst, Leipzig, 1913.

Epstein, I., The Responsa of R. Simon Duran, London, 1930.

Epstein, L. M., The Jewish Marriage Contract (JMC), New York, 1927.

——— "The Institution of Concubinage among the Jews," *Proceedings of the American Academy of Jewish Research,* VI (1935), pp. 153–88.

Ewald, H., Die Alterthümer des Volkes Israels, Göttingen, 1866.

Feigin, S., "The Captives in Cuneiform Inscriptions," AJSL, 50 (1934), pp. 217–45; 51 (1934), pp. 22–29.

Finkelstein, L., Jewish Self-Government in the Middle Ages, New York, 1924.

Frankel, Z., Darke ha-Mishnah, Leipzig, 1859.

Freund, L., "Über Genealogien- und Familienreinheit in biblischer und talmudischer Zeit," *Schwartz Festschrift,* Berlin, 1917, pp. 163–92.

Geiger, A., "Die Leviratsehe," *Jüdische Zeitschrift für Wissenschaft und Leben,* I (1862), pp. 19–39.

——— Ḳebuẓat Ma'amarim, Berlin, 1877 (later edition by Poznanski, Warsaw, 1910).

——— Urschrift, Breslau, 1857.

Gesenius, W., Hebrew and Chaldee Lexicon, London–New York, 1890.

Ginzberg, L., Eine unbekannte jüdische Sekte (*Sekte*), New York, 1922.

——— Notes to Geiger's *Ḳebuẓat Ma'amarim,* Poznanski's edition, Warsaw, 1910.

Graetz, H., History of the Jews, Philadelphia, 1891–98.

Granquist, H., Marriage Conditions in a Palestine Village, Helsingfors, 1931–35.

Güdemann, M., Geschichte d. Erziehungswesen und der Cultur der Juden in Deutschland, Vienna, 1888.

Guttman, M., "Über die Leviratsehe," *Zeitschrift für jüdische Theologie,* IV (1839), pp. 61–87.

Harper's Dictionary of Classical Literature and Antiquities, New York, 1897.

Holdheim, S., Gemischte Ehen zwischen Juden und Christen, Berlin, 1850.

Jacobs, J., The Jews in Spain, London, 1894.
Jeremias, J., Review of Rengstorf's *Die Mishna Jebamot, Theologische Literaturzeitung,* LIV (1929), sp. 583.

Karl, Z., "Ha-Yibbum we-ha-Ḥaliẓah," in *Ha-Mishpaṭ,* ed. S. Eisenstadt, I, Jerusalem, 1927, pp. 266–279.
Kaufmann, E., Toledot ha-Emunah ha-Yisra'elit, Tel Aviv, 1937–8.
Kayserling, M., Geschichte der Juden in Spanien und Portugal, Leipzig, 1861–7.
Kennet, R. H., Ancient Hebrew Social Life and Custom, London, 1933.
Kohler, J., "Zur Urgeschichte der Ehe," ZVR, XII (1897), pp. 187–353.
Koschaker, P., "Quellenkritische Untersuchungen zu den altassyrischen Gesetzen," *Mittheilungen der vorderasiatisch-ägyptischen Gesellschaft,* XXVI (1921.3), pp. 1–84.
——— "Zum Levirat nach hethitischem Recht," *Revue Hittite et Asiatique,* III (1933), pp. 77–89.
Krauss, S., "Die Ehe zwischen Onkel und Nichte," *Studies in Jewish Literature in Honor of Kaufmann Kohler,* Berlin, 1913, pp. 165–75.
Krochmal, N., Moreh Nebuke ha-Zeman, Lemberg, 1865.

Loew, L., Gesammelte Schriften, III, Szegedin, 1893.

Mattuck, I. I., "The Levirate Marriage in Jewish Law," *Studies in Jewish Literature in Honor of Kaufmann Kohler,* Berlin, 1913, pp. 210–22.
McLennan, J. F., "Levirate and Polyandry," *Fortnightly Review,* N.S., XXI (1877), pp. 694–707.
Menes, A., Die vorexilischen Gesetze Israels, Giesen, 1928.
Meyer, P., Das römisches Koncubinat, Leipzig, 1895.
Michaelis, J. D., Mosaisches Recht, Frankfurt a. M., 1774.
Mielziner, M., The Jewish Law of Marriage and Divorce, Cincinnati, 1901.
Mittelmann, J., Der altisraelitische Levirat, Leiden, 1934.
Moore, G. F., Judaism in the First Centuries of the Christian Era, Cambridge, 1932.
Morgenstern, J., "Beena Marriage in Ancient Israel," ZAW, N.S., VI (1929), pp. 91–110.

Nacht, J., "The Symbolism of the Shoe," J.Q.R., N.S., VI (1915), pp. 1–22.
Nowack, W., Lehrbuch der hebräischen Archäologie, Leipzig, 1894.

Obermeyer, J., Die Landschaft Babyloniens, Frankfurt a. M., 1929.

Pinsker, S. Liḳḳuṭe Ḳadmoniyyot, Vienna, 1860.

Rauh, S., Hebräische Familienrecht in vorprophetische Zeit, Berlin, 1907.
Rengstorf, K. H., Die Mishna Jebamot, Giesen, 1929.
Rosenthal, F., "Über 'Issah," MGWJ, XXX (1881), pp. 38–48; 113–23; 162–71; 207–17.

Scheftelowitz, J., "Leviratsehe," *Archiv für Religionswissenschaft,* XVIII (1915), pp. 250–6.
Seymour, T. D., Life in the Homeric Age, London, 1907.
Shelden, J., Uxor Hebraica, Frankfurt am Oder, 1673.
Slouschz, N., Travels in North Africa, Philadelphia, 1927.
Smith, Mayte and Merindin, Dictionary of Greek and Roman Antiquities, London, 1890.
Smith, W. R., Kinship and Marriage in Early Arabia, London, 1903.
Steinschneider, M., Polemische Literatur, Leipzig, 1877.

Wechsler, B., "Die Leviratsehe," *Jüdische Zeitschrift für Wissenschaft und Leben,* I (1862), pp. 253–63.
Weiss, I. H., Dor Dor we-Dorshav, Wilna, 1910–11.
Westermarck, E., The History of Human Marriage (HHM), New York, 1922.
Wilkinson, J. G., The Ancient Egyptians, London, 1878.
Wolf, A., Das jüdische Erbrecht, Berlin, 1888.
Wolfenson, L. B., "The Character, Contents and Date of Ruth," AJSL, XXVII (1910–11), pp. 285–300.

Zeitlin, S., "Les Dix huit Mesures," R.E.J., LXVIII (1914), pp. 22–36.
——— "Studies in the Beginnings of Christianity," J.Q.R., N.S., XIV (1923), pp. 111–29.
Zunz, L., Gesammelte Schriften, Berlin, 1875–6.

INDEX

INDEX OF SUBJECTS AND NAMES

Citations and references from the Old Testament and rabbinic literature are not recorded in the Index, except such as represent basic subjects discussed in the book.

marriage law or one born of such a union, 329f; prohibited to a priest, 321f

Ḥalalut, a perpetual stain on the male line, 330

Halberstamm, S. J., 120

Ḥaliẓah, 122f; ceremonial, 127–9; inducements offered to obtain, 137–8; instrument of, 129–30; judicial formalities required, 127; performed by oldest brother, 126; preferred to levirate marriage, 21, 26, 27, 121, 122, 123–4; promised by pledge and special instrument in advance of the marriage, 138; ḥaliẓah-kinship and ḥaliẓah-incest, 277f; hindrances to the performance of, 126, 127; the spirit of, changes, 122; superstitions connected with, 128–9; where ḥaliẓah alone is possible and where it is impossible, 125–7. *See* Levirate, Ziḳah

Ḥaluẓah, prohibited in marriage to priests, 331

Hammurabi. *See* Code Hammurabi

Harem, 9, *et passim;* in Canaan, 10; in Egypt, 9, 10; size of king's, 11, 12

Hasmonean, laws to prevent intermarriage, 169; attitude to racialism, 170–71; prohibition against contact with gentiles, 70; reformation, 169

Heḳesh. *See* "Analogy"

Ḥerem of R. Gershom, 24–33; its acceptance in mediaeval Jewish communities, 30–33; its suspension by decree of a hundred rabbis, 28, 29; its expiration at the end of the fifth millennium, 26; its operation in a levirate situation, 26, 27; or where the wife is barren, 27; or converted, 27, 28, 29; or insane, 28, 29; or unfaithful, 28, 29. *See* Polygamy

Ḥerem of R. Samson, against marriage with Karaites, 216

Hermaphrodite, marriage laws for, 291–2

Herod, burned the archives, 189

Hezekiah, reformation of, 154

High priest, marriage laws of, 331–2

Hillel, on mamzer, 280

Hillelites and Shammaites, 103, *et passim*

Ḥirtu, 35

Hittite code, 47, 224, 239

Holdheim, S., 181

Ḥuppah, 72, 117

Hush-child, 286f; doubtful mamzer, 287; how paternity may be established, 287–8

Incest, ch. 5; brother's wife, 229, 232; daughter, 223, 224, 228, 230, 239, 240; daughter by a gentile mother, 239; by a metronymic mother, 234; natural daughter, 93, 239; step-daughter, 229, 231, 234; daughter-in-law, 224, 225, 229, 230, 232; father's brother's wife, 232, 236, 241; father's secondary wife, 226, 228; father's sister, 227, 232, 234, 241; granddaughter, 231, 236, 239; step-granddaughter, 232, 236; grandmother, 232, 236, 254; step-grandmother, 229, 254; mother, 222, 223, 230, 238; mother's brother's wife, 232, 236, 241; mother's sister, 234, 241; mother-in-law, 228, 230, 234; step-mother, 225, 226, 228, 229, 230, 232; niece, 250f; sister, 240; sister born out of wedlock, 93, 240; from gentile mother, 240; from metronymic mother, 234, 240; maternal half-sister, 222, 223–4, 230, 233; paternal half-sister, 227, 228, 229–30; wife's grandmother, 229, 232, 236, 256f; wife's sister, 22, 227, 229, 234; wife's sister after wife's death, 22, 254; betrothal establishes incestuous kinship, 242f; incestuous marriage not valid, 246–7; penalties, 238, 239, 240, 241, 246, 256; prohibition continues in all cases of incest based on affinity after dissolution of marriage, 244–5. *See* Secondary incest

Incest, law of, divided into five stages,

220; pre-deuteronomic, 221; deuteronomic, 227–9; in Ezekiel, 225, 226, 229–30; levitical, 230f; levitical law characterized, 235–7; summarized (1–15), 234–5; rabbinic interpretation, 237f; penalties, 238f; supersedes levirate, 101–2; ḥaliẓah-incest, 277f; ziḳah-incest, 275f; for gentiles, 247f; for proselytes, 248–9; for slaves, 249
Incest, law of, in the Assyrian code, 226, 227; in the Hittite code, 239; of the Karaites, 263f; of the Reformists, 273–4; of the Samaritans, 91–92; of the Zadokites, 250f
Intermarriage, ch. 4; attitude to, pre-deuteronomic, 149, 150–51; deuteronomic, 153f; in Book of Ruth, 151, 152; of Ezra, 166–7; in exilic and post-exilic records, 161–2, 165–6; in pre-Hasmonean time, 167–8; under the early tannaim, 172f; of the rabbis, 175f; of East European Jewry, 182–3; change of attitude resulting from Jewish emancipation, 177–8; statistics on, 182–3
Intermarriage, prohibition based upon five motives, 145f; rooted in endogamy, 149–50; prohibited biblically or rabbinically, 175–6; for male and female, 160–61; has no legal validity, 160, 174
Intermarriage, with Amalekites, 159; with Ammonites and Moabites, 159, 206–7; with Christians and Mohammedans, 176–7; with Egyptians and Edomites, 160; with Karaites, 216f; with mamzer, 159; with Nethinim, 204; with sectarians, 215; with the "seven nations," 156f; with Zidonites, Midianites, Ashdodites, 160
"Inversion," 267
Isarti, 35, 41
'Issah, 313f; the original, in Ezra's time, 314–5; rabbinic attitude to the original, 316–7; synonymous with original ḥalal, 315f; new rabbinic definition, 313–4; *'issah*-widow and *'issah*-daughter, 313f, 320; *'issah kesherah* and *'issah pesulah*, 320; investigation, 319
Italy, 30

Jacobs, J., 31
Jeremias, J., 82
Jerome, St., 16
Jerusalem, 18, *et passim*
John the Baptist, 252
Jose, R., on *yi'ud*, 66
Josephus, 12, 17, 18, 36, 64, 67, 151, 169, 316, 327; on foreign blood, 193; on genealogical records, 186; on ḥalalah and *zonah*, 323; on levirate, 90, 96, 98; on mamzer, 279; on polygamy, 18; on Samaritans, 211
Josiah, reformation of, 155–6
Jubilee year, 39, 58, 59, 65
Jubilees, Book of, on incest, 92, 225, 239, 242, 244, 246; on intermarriage, 169, 170, 195; on endogamy, 148
Judah he-Ḥasid, 254
Judah, R., on concubinage, 62
Justin Martyr, 17, 18

Karaites, intermarriage with, 216f; when converted to Rabbanism, 217–8. *See* Ḥerem of R. Samson, Intermarriage
Karaites, law of incest of, 263f; analyzed into categories, 270–73; characterized, 264–5; compared with that of Rabbanites, 264f; prohibit marriage of niece, 251; prohibit wife's sister after wife's death, 22; law of levirate of, 143f; law of polygamy of, 22–4; influenced by Rabbanites and Zadokites, 22; permit polygamy when wife is childless, 23; when wife is converted, 29; when wife is not "vexed," 23
Karet, 238, *et passim*
Ḳaṭlanit, 296
Kaufmann, E., on Nethinim, 203
Kayseling, M., 31
Ḳedeshah and *zonah*, 70, 71, 324
Kennet, R. H., 154
Ketubah, 18, *et passim;* clause provid-

ing for maintenance of the widow, 107; clause providing ransom in case of the wife's becoming captive, 327; clause guaranteeing monogamy, 24–5, 31, 32; in levirate marriage, 119–21

Ḳeẓaẓah, 189, 311

Ḳiddushin, 117, 179

King, may not multiply wives, 11–12, 13; in levirate situation, 125–6; permission of, required in Spain for polygamy, 31

Kinship, by affinity, 222, 228; established by betrothal, 242f; "direction" of, 235–6; reckoned from the woman as from the man, 250; "flesh kinship," 231, 233, 234; in Deuteronomy, 227–8; in the levitical law, 230f; of half-brother or half-sister, 245–6; maternal versus paternal, 221, 236; step-kinship, 265; ḥaliẓah-kinship, 276f; ziḳah-kinship, 275f; kinship derived from the marriage of a minor, 278; of relatives by marriage, continues after the dissolution of the marriage, 245; original concept of, tribal and based on ownership, 223, 227

Kohler, J., 41, 44, 79

Koran, 23

Koschaker, P., 41, 89, 224

Krauss, S., 18, 251, 253; on marriage of niece, 253

Krochmal, N., 257

Landsberger, B., 43

"Legal" monogamy, 3

Leo I, 16

Leon de Modena, 30

Levi b. Ḥabib, on polygamy, 32

Levirate, ch. 3; three motives for primitive, 78–80; changes during biblical period, 80–81; contradictions in the biblical law of, 81–2; rabbinic adjustment, 93; sociological background of, 82–8; its relation, if any, to polyandry, 79; based upon patriarchal family structure, 86f; and disappears with the break-down of the same, 88–9; contrasted with *ge'ullah* and succession, 82–8

Levirate, law of, according to Samaritans, Sadducees, Hellenists, 89–90; according to Karaites, 142f; as reflected in the Judah-Tamar story, 80; in Deuteronomy, 81; in the Book of Ruth, 81, 85; in Leviticus and Numbers, 81; the rabbinic, 93f; for betrothed and wedded, 92, 93; duty on oldest brother, 121; manner of enforcement, 134f; disposition of the estate of the deceased, 139f; the position of the levirate child, 87–8; the position of the levirate widow, 108–9

Levirate marriage, ceremonies, 117, 119; cohabitation essential, 116, 119; consent of widow whether required, 122; ketubah in, 119–21; three months' waiting required from the death of the husband, 119; whether preferred to ḥaliẓah, 123–4; where marriage and no ḥaliẓah is legally possible, 124–5. *See* Ḥaliẓah, Ziḳah, *Ma'amar*

Levirate situation, defined, 94; exists only where brother survives, 99f; where no issue male or female remains behind, 96–9; where marriage to the deceased was legally valid, 94–5; and capable of begetting issue, 101; where marriage to the levir is legally possible, 101f; and capable of being productive, 95–6; effect of the, in cases of polygamy, 102; where co-widow is incestuously prohibited to the levir, 102, 103, 104; in case of converted levir, 100–101; where the surviving child is by a gentile mother, 99; or where the surviving brother is by a gentile mother, 100; in prohibited marriages, 95; in royal family, 125–6; where the deceased was a eunuch or hemaphrodite, 96; restrictions against sale of the estate of the deceased in a, 120, 121; wife's childlessness irrelevant

Printed in the United States
By Bookmasters